DATE DUE

Growth and Development of

the Nigerian Economy

Growth and Development

of the

Nigerian Economy

EDITED BY

CARL K. EICHER *and* CARL LIEDHOLM

MICHIGAN STATE UNIVERSITY PRESS

1970

Contents

v

Preface

The purpose of this volume is to analyze the long-term growth process of the Nigerian economy from 1900 to Independence in 1960, to review the performance of the economy in the 1960's and to focus on the leading economic policy issues of the 1970's.

In the mid-1960's, a number of important books were published on the Nigerian economy such as O. Aboyade's, *Foundations of an African Economy*, C. V. Brown's, *The Nigerian Banking System*, G. Helleiner's, *Peasant Agriculture, Government, and Economic Growth in Nigeria*, W. A. Lewis', *Reflections on Nigeria's Economic Growth*, P. Okigbo's, *Nigerian Public Finance*, H. Oluwasanmi's, *Agriculture and Nigerian Economic Development*, and W. Stolper's, *Planning Without Facts: Lessons in Resource Allocation from Nigeria's Development*. Since these books are readily available in Africa and overseas, the present volume is designed not to duplicate, but rather to supplement and up-date these contributions. A number of important events, for example, have occurred since these books were published, such as the petroleum boom, the Nigerian-Biafran Civil War and the division of four regions into twelve states. Moreover, a number of research studies have recently been completed which provide additional insights into the dynamics of Nigeria's economic development.

The present volume contains 21 chapters of which 13 are original contributions. It is our belief that the 13 original contributions will help clarify, supplement and up-date the above mentioned standard books on Nigerian economic development as well as add important insights into the development problems of the 1970's. Eight chapters are reprints of important government documents or journal articles that are not readily available in libraries outside of Nigeria.

The volume also contains an extensive bibliography on Nigerian economic development for the 1966–69 period. This bibliography is designed to supplement the excellent bibliography contained in Gerald Helleiner's *Peasant Agriculture, Government and Economic Growth in Nigeria*, which covers the literature through 1965.

Although several chapters focus on general political and social factors, such as the politics of marketing boards and the social factors in economic planning, this book is primarily concerned with economic problems. Also this volume has not focused on the tragic Nigerian-Biafran Civil War even though several chapters, such as the politics of marketing boards, petroleum, and policy for agricultural development in the 1970's, should provide insights into some of the causes of the war and the implications of the war for planning in the 1970's.

Several chapters in this volume are revisions of papers which were presented at a workshop on "Economic Growth and Political Instability in West Africa: The Nigerian Case," which was held at Michigan State University in the summer of 1968 and was sponsored by MUCIA— The Midwest Universities Consortium for International Activities. (MUCIA is composed of the Universities of Illinois, Wisconsin and Minnesota as well as Indiana University and Michigan State University.) The financial aid of MUCIA in supporting the workshop is appreciated.

The Nigerian workshop was one of a series of inter-disciplinary workshops on economic development held at Michigan State University over the 1968–70 period. We should like to acknowledge the role played by Robert Solo of Michigan State University in organizing this series of workshops.

We also have a pleasant task of acknowledging the aid of many scholars and government officers who have shared their insights and knowledge of Nigeria. In addition to the contributors to this volume, we especially wish to thank: Ojetunji Aboyade, Sam Aluko, Peter Bauer, Archibald Callaway, Anson Chong, Edwin Dean, George Dike, Arthur Hazlewood, Peter Kilby, W. Arthur Lewis, David Norman, Godwin Okurume, Dupe Olatunbosun, and Sylvester Ugoh.

PART ONE: *The Colonial Period*

The stereotype of a tropical Africa inhabited by stagnant, subsistence farmers with little or no contact with other continents is rapidly being modified by research which indicates that extensive trading patterns were developed 300 and 400 years ago. In fact, there are references to trans-Saharan trade, with Kano as the chief entrepot, by the end of the 15th century. Also, the Kano market in Northern Nigeria was the largest market in West Africa in the 19th century. For these reasons any analysis of Nigerian development during the Colonial period (1900-1960) must take this pre-colonial period into account. Likewise, any analysis of Nigerian development since 1960 also must consider how British colonial policy shaped legal, educational and political institutions, as well as international trading links which are not easily modified. In other words, Nigeria's problems in the 1970's can only be understood in historical perspective.

Fortunately, a number of pioneering studies of Nigeria's economic history during the Colonial period have been recently completed by Helleiner,[1] Oluwasanmi[2] and others. These studies have helped improve our understanding of the development process—especially around the turn of the 20th century when an explosion of agricultural exports coincided with the Nigeria's emergence as a British colony. The export boom in Nigerian oil palm, groundnuts, and cocoa which occurred between 1900-1930 has frequently been analyzed as responses to the various external forces introduced by the colonial administration. However, new evidence indicates that substantial internal changes were also made by small indigenous farmers around the turn of the century *and* that the key features of this expansion process—effective demand, smallholder farming, and incentives—play a central role in shaping Nigerian agricultural policy in the 1970's.

There are two important background issues in a discussion of the economics of the development process in Nigeria during its Colonial period. First, the surplus labor model of development—often called the Indian model of development,—has tended to dominate our thinking about the development process in less developed countries (LDCs) in general. This tendency to generalize from India's development to other LDCs is only natural in light of the fact that India's population in 1970 exceeds the *combined* populations of Africa and South America. Also, India has traditionally been the largest single recipient of foreign aid for many years. A number of scholars such as Hla Myint of the London School of Economics, however, have demolished the simplistic notion that a

1

single model of development is appropriate for numerous LDCs.[3] In fact, Myint urges scholars to search for theoretical insights into the development process with the expectation that alternative models are necessary for different types of LDCs and for different stages in their development. Therefore, in analyzing the Nigerian development process, one should be extremely cautious about borrowing growth models from other nations.

The theoretical analysis of development in tropical African nations has focused on models of development whereby the economy is led by an enclave of foreign investors in plantations and in the mining industries. Robert Baldwin's penetrating analysis has served as a point of departure for an analysis of dualism and the enclave economies.[4] Baldwin analyzes the choice of technology in the leading sector—copper in Northern Rhodesia—and shows how this affected subsequent development of other sectors of the Rhodesian economy.[5] Essentially Baldwin asks how growth by a foreign-financed and foreign-directed industry such as copper in Rhodesia, petroleum in Libya, plantations or timber in Liberia affects economic development of the future. A study of the economic development process in Liberia by a team of Northwestern University economists concludes that the foreign-financed and foreign-directed iron ore, timber and rubber industries generated impressive growth rates of 9-10 per cent per year in Liberia but this growth did not lay the foundation for social and economic change for the rank and file Liberian.[6] Elliott Berg of the University of Michigan refutes these conclusions and contends that the growth process has indeed laid a foundation for development which will benefit Liberians.[7] Moreover, Berg concludes that "Given all of the problems in making a meaningful distinction between growth and development, there is much to be said for simply dropping the whole idea."[8]

Although the enclave model of development provides useful insights into the development process in some African countries, the model, of course, is not applicable in countries such as Nigeria where indigenous producers dominate the economic landscape. For this reason, Myint's vent-for-surplus model[9] is particularly applicable to a number of African countries including Nigeria. Myint contends that effective demand was the major constraint on West African economies which had a sparse population in relation to natural resources in the early part of this century. Since farmers were able to provide a subsistence diet and still have surplus land and underemployed labor, they were able to add export crops to their normal staple food production with little risk involved. Colonial policy provided internal transport and international trading firms provided the "effective demand" or what Myint calls the "vent" for this surplus productive capacity.

Part One of this volume supplements our meagre knowledge about Nigeria's development during the Colonial period when Nigeria emerged as one of the leading world exporters of groundnuts, oil palm and cocoa and tin. In Chapter 1, Eicher analyzes the dynamics of long-term agricultural development from 1900 to 1960. He places considerable emphasis on how three key British policies affected Nigerian development. First, the colonial land policies of Nigeria of 1910 and 1917 effectively reserved agricultural production for Nigerians in contrast to East African countries where white settlers were encouraged to settle on the land. Second, the biological research policy for export crops demonstrated impressive foresight by the British in developing *local* agricultural technology which has paid handsome returns in the 1950's and 1960's in the form of hybrid oil palm varieties, hybrid cocoa trees, insecticides and fungicides for controlling cocoa diseases, and improved groundnut and cotton varieties. Third, the British replaced foreign private trading firms with government marketing boards in the late 1930's.

In Chapter 2, Sara Berry reports on her recent field work on the origin of cocoa production in Western Nigeria. Since Nigerian cocoa exports grew from 202 tons in 1900 to 9,105 tons in 1915 and 52,331 tons in 1930, Berry is seeking to clarify how Nigeria suddenly became a major cocoa exporter—long before the days of formal development plans. She uses Myint's vent-for-surplus model of development as a point of departure. After intensive research in the archives in London, and Nigeria, and through interviews in Nigeria she concludes that Myint's vent-for-surplus model which focuses on two factors—land and labor—in the expansion process is an oversimplification in the case of cocoa production. Berry notes that cocoa expansion took place not only through employment of hitherto idle land and labor but also through a process of reallocating and recombining available resources. Examples of organizational changes which occurred are: new methods were devised for acquiring rights to land, for obtaining credit and for mobilizing and employing labor services. Berry concludes that any model of early stage development which is relevant to West African conditions should go beyond an analysis of mobilizing idle land and consider the organizational changes which influence the use of resources.

Since Nigeria is now the world's largest groundnut exporter and since there has been a paucity of economic research on Northern Nigeria relative to Southern Nigeria, Jan Hogendorn's recent research, reported in Chapter 3, into the origin of groundnut production in Northern Nigeria is significant. Hogendorn also uses Myint's vent-for-surplus model of development as a point of departure. Hogendorn asks why Hausa farmers went overboard in producing groundnuts following the 1912 opening of the Ibadan-Kano railroad rather than producing cotton as anticipated.

In fact, Winston S. Churchill, under-secretary for the colonies, repeatedly suggested in speeches in the Commons that a railroad would open up Northern Nigeria as a major cotton producing area for British textile mills. Hogendorn reports that Hausa farmers in Northern Nigeria switched from cotton to groundnuts in response to the greater *profitability* of producing groundnuts, thus helping shatter the myth that Hausa farmers were unresponsive to economic incentives.

Liedholm, in Chapter 4, examines the influence of colonial policy on the growth and development of Nigeria's industrial sector from 1900 to 1940. He focuses on mining and the modern manufacturing components of Nigeria's industrial sector. Although minerals were not a mainspring of Nigerian growth during the Colonial period, Liedholm points out that colonial policies aided foreign rather than Nigerian investors in the expansion of Nigeria's tin industry. He also reports new evidence indicating that certain colonial policies held back the growth of Nigeria's industrial sector until the 1954 constitution which permitted regions to promote industrial development.

Any discussion of economic development during the Colonial period naturally should devote considerable emphasis to the foreign trading companies such as the United Africa Company. The colonial government maintained a laissez-faire position on trading and encouraged foreign investment in trading activities. However, a chapter on trading was not included because both W. K. Hancock's[10] and P. T. Bauer's[11] books have recently been reprinted and are readily available. Also, the role of trading firms in lubricating the expansion of the groundnut trade forms a central part of Chapter 3 by Jan Hogendorn, a former student of Professor P. T. Bauer.

NOTES

1. Gerald Helleiner, *Peasant Agriculture, Government and Economic Growth*, Homewood, Illinois: Richard T. Irwin, 1966.
2. H. A. Oluwasanmi, *Agriculture and Nigerian Economic Growth*, Ibadan: Oxford University Press, 1966.
3. Hla Myint, *The Economics of Developing Countries*, London: Hutchinson and Co., 1964, Chapter 1.
4. Robert E. Baldwin, "Patterns of Development in Newly Settled Regions," *The Manchester School of Economic and Social Studies*, vol. 24, May, 1956. Reprinted in *Agriculture in Economic Development*, edited by C. K. Eicher and L. Witt, New York: McGraw-Hill Book Co., 1964.

5. ——————, *Economic Development and Export Growth: A Study of Northern Rhodesia, 1920-1960*, Berkeley: University of California Press, 1966.

6. R. W. Clower, G. Dalton, M. Harwitz, and A. A. Walter, *Growth Without Development: An Economic Survey of Liberia*, Evanston: Northwestern University Press, 1966.

7. Elliot J. Berg, "Growth, Development and All That: Thoughts on the Liberian Experience," Draft paper, Center for Research on Economic Development, University of Michigan, March, 1969.

8. Berg, *op. cit.*

9. H. Myint, "The 'Classical Theory' of International Trade and the Underdeveloped Countries," *Economic Journal*, vol. 68 (June, 1958), pp. 317-337.

10. W. K. Hancock, *Survey of British Commonwealth Affairs*, Vol. 2, London: Oxford University Press, 1940. (Reprinted in 1964.) See Chapter 2 "Evolution of the Traders' Frontier, West Africa."

11. P. T. Bauer, *West African Trade: A Study of Competition, Oligopoly and Monopoly in a Changing Economy*, London: Cambridge University Press, 1954; reissued with a new preface by Routledge and Kegan Paul, Ltd., 1963.

1. The Dynamics of Long-Term Agricultural Development in Nigeria*

CARL K. EICHER

STATUS OF THEORETICAL ANALYSIS OF AFRICAN ECONOMIC DEVELOPMENT

Until recently the literature on the economic development of less developed countries has been dominated by surplus labor models of development.[1] However, the theoretical analysis of development in tropical African nations has primarily focused on development by an enclave of foreign investors in plantations and in the mining industries. Baldwin's analysis of how the technological nature of the production function of export commodities affects subsequent development of the other sectors of the economy has provided a point of departure for these studies in Africa.[2] Baldwin's study of the development of Northern Rhodesia from 1920 to 1960[3] through the introduction of foreign-financed and foreign-directed copper industry, and a Liberian study entitled *Growth Without Development*,[4] are examples of this type of analysis. However, the development of African nations by indigenous farmers has only recently received attention by researchers such as Helleiner,[5] Polly Hill,[6] Oluwasanmi[7] and Myint.[8]

Myint formulated a "surplus land and labor" model of indigenous-led development by applying Adam Smith's "vent-for-surplus" theory of international trade to less-developed economies such as Thailand, Burma, and West African nations. In the vent-for-surplus model of development, international trade provides a vent for the surplus productive capacity of a nation with sparse population in relation to natural resources. The essential aspects of the vent-for-surplus model are as follows:

1. A previously isolated country entering international trade possesses a potential surplus productive capacity (land and labor).

---

* From *Journal of Farm Economics*, Volume 49, Number 5 (December, 1967), pp. 1158-1170, with minor modifications. Reprinted by permission of the American Agricultural Economics Association.

2. Population density is a major determinant of export capacity.

3. The function of trade is not so much to reallocate the given resources but to provide the new effective demand for the output of the surplus resources.

4. Improvement in transport and communication can accelerate the expansion process.

5. Surplus productive capacity enables a farmer to produce export crops in addition to subsistence crops and hence enables export production to be expanded with virtually little risk.[9]

Thus, the vent-for-surplus model which stresses the key role of effective demand in the development process is very useful in analyzing this process in African countries which are dominated by African farmers operating with unlimited supplies of land.

Szereszewski uses Myint's vent-for-surplus model to analyze the early-stage development process in Ghana focusing on the 1891-1911 cocoa boom.[10] Helleiner uses the same model as his analytical framework of analysis of the overall development process in Nigeria from 1900 on.[11] Berry suggests how the vent-for-surplus model should be modified in light of her research into the origins of cocoa production in Western Nigeria in this century.[12] (See Chapter 2.) Finally, Hogendorn analyzes the emergence of the groundnut industry in Northern Nigeria in the early 1900's, through a vent-for-surplus model of development.[13] (See Chapter 3.)

COLONIAL POLICY

Land, Trade and Infrastructure Policies: 1900-1940

The expansion of trade was the primary British instrument for carrying out their "Dual Mandate" doctrine in Nigeria, which meant that the resources of a colony were to be developed to help the native population as well as the other nations in the world.[14] To this end major emphasis was placed on the development of transport, communication and the maintenance of law and order. The British relied largely on the railroad to open up the country and railroad construction proceeded well ahead of demand.[15]

Colonial land policy played a central role in the organization of agricultural production. The Land and Native Rights ordinances of 1910 and 1917 prevented an enclave of foreign investors in agricultural production.[16] Foreign firms invested, instead, in trading activities. Therefore, the development literature which is preoccupied with "enclave economies" is of little relevance for understanding early-stage Nigerian agriculture development.

In summary, the colonial development policy from 1900 to 1940 was law and order, laissez-faire and foreign-trade-oriented. However, the colonial policy of preserving land for Nigerian farmers has played a dominant role in the organization of agricultural production to date. Nigeria's agriculture in the early 1970's is essentially composed of six million small farmers who simultaneously produce both food and export crops on scattered plots of land totaling from four to eight acres per farm.

Emergence of Colonial Economic Planning: 1940-1960

Between 1940 and 1960 colonial policy instituted three important institutions which influenced agricultural development in this period: (1) government marketing boards were established in 1939-40, (2) a biological research system for sustained research into export crops was inaugurated in 1940, and (3) deliberate government development planning was started in 1946.

Although the marketing boards were designed to stabilize prices of all major export crops except rubber, they slowly assumed the function of taxing agriculture. In fact, marketing boards have been used as a central instrument of financing infrastructure, state plantations and farm settlements, as approximately twenty-one to thirty-two per cent of the potential gross income of farmers producing export crops was withdrawn by the marketing boards from 1947 to 1961. (See Chapter 7.) Although marketing board pricing policies have been criticized by many scholars for their discentive effect on export crop farmers, the marketing board performed an important fiscal role in capturing the agricultural surplus to finance overall national development until alternative sources of revenue such as taxes on petroleum became available in the mid-1960's.

The second institution—biological research stations for export crops— has generally been underplayed in the analysis of Nigerian agricultural development. The Colonial Development and Welfare Act of 1940 provided for sustained British personnel and financing to expand the Cocoa Research Institute in Ghana, which was started in 1938, and the Oil Palm Research Station, which was launched in 1939 in Nigeria. Later, in 1951, these commodity research stations were expanded from national to West African institutes, and the West African Cocoa Research Institute (Ghana), West African Rice Research Institute (Sierra Leone), West African Oil Palm Research Institute (Nigeria), West African Maize Research Unit (Nigeria), as well as six other West African Research institutes were established. As West African nations gained independence, starting with Ghana in 1957, problems emerged which led to the break-up of West African institutes, beginning in 1961, and the return to national research institutes. Although these biological research stations were set up following major disease problems of cocoa and maize, the productivity gains in export agriculture since 1940, and especially since 1950, can be closely linked to a sustained period of biological research starting with the formation of the Cocoa Research Institute in Ghana in 1938.[17]

The third major institution—government development planning—was started in 1946 following the passage of the 1945 Colonial Development and Welfare Act, which required that each British colony prepare a ten-year development plan. Planning during this period is discussed by Berry and Liedholm. (See Chapter 5.)

In brief, the colonial laissez-faire-oriented development policy from 1900 to 1940 was replaced in the 1940's by deliberate government development planning, sweeping reorganization of the market structure by the introduction of marketing boards to control the foreign sale of all major export crops except rubber, and the inauguration of sustained government biological research for all of the major export crops and a few of the foods crops, such as maize.

THE DYNAMICS OF AGRICULTURAL DEVELOPMENT:
1900-1960

At the beginning of the twentieth century, Nigeria's population was sparse in relation to its natural resources. The principal Nigerian exports in 1900 were "naturally occurring products"[18] extracted from the Southern rain forest belt—wild palm oil and palm kernels and wild rubber—which accounted for roughly 90 per cent of the value of all exports. Virtually all production and transportation were handled by Nigerians, who headloaded the products or moved them by canoe to European trading stations on the coast. The European coastal traders handled the export trade and offered textiles, spirits, and tobacco as incentives to the farmers. In fact, textiles, spirits, and tobacco accounted for over fifty per cent of the value of all imports in 1900.

The 1900-1940 Period

Unlike the "enclave economies" of African nations such as Liberia, the Congo, Rhodesia, and Zambia, the production of Nigerian agricultural exports increased rapidly from 1900 to 1940 with very little foreign participation. The colonial policy of placing high priority on developing a transportation and communication system greatly facilitated the tapping of the surplus productive capacity of indigenous farmers. For example, when the railroad from Lagos to Kano was completed in 1914, groundnuts became a major new export crop in Northern Nigeria. Also, cocoa production expanded rapidly as feeder roads were developed in Western Nigeria following World War I. Next, foreign trading firms played an important role in the expansion process as they served as a link between the Nigerian farmers and the world market and stimulated new farmer demands for consumer goods. On the resource supply side, the new land was not brought into production by imported labor or capital, but by the small farmers who sacrificed leisure and redirected their efforts to meet the effective demand which had been created by linking the world market with the output of small farmers.

Szereszewski reports in detail how two new exports—cocoa and gold—radically changed the structure of the Gold Coast (Ghana) economy from 1891 to 1911 and increased the GDP by 43 per cent in the 20-year period. Szereszewski describes the vent-for-surplus process in Ghana in the late 1890's as follows: "The phenomenal spread of cocoa over the period (1891-1911) is the main prima-facie evidence of a disruption of some initial . . . equilibrium." He adds that the "pattern of developments of the Gold Coast economy over the two decades was very labor-absorptive", and the formation of the cocoa capital was simply the capitalization of current local labor. The labor intake of the cocoa industry increased from 100,000 labor days in 1891 to 37 million in 1911.[19] The structure of the Ghanaian economy was radically changed from the production of wild palm produce in the 1890's to cocoa and gold by 1911.

In Nigeria, the principal expansion of export crops from 1900 to 1940 came about almost exclusively as a result of bringing more land into production. As the transport network expanded rapidly from 1900 to 1930, the principal nineteenth century exports—palm and cotton—were supplemented by new export crops—cocoa, groundnuts, and cultivated rubber—and regional specialization of production emerged. In fact, the present ecological specialization of production was largely determined in the 1910-1930 period, when Northern Nigeria emerged as an important groundnut and cotton producer. Also, cocoa and rubber replaced palm products and cotton in Western Nigeria, and Western Nigeria became a major world producer of cocoa. The vast range of ecological zones in Nigeria—from 10 inches of rainfall in Northern Nigeria to 220 inches in Southern Nigeria—plus the extensive railroad and road network enabled Nigeria to develop a diversified export agriculture within thirty years (1900-1930), while the Ghanaian economy remained tied to cocoa and gold for fifty years (1911-1960).[20]

During the 1900-1940 period, the source of increase in Nigerian agricultural output came from small farmers who expanded export crops primarily through additional labor and land inputs. Small farmers (3-6 acres) usually produced at one and the same time (1) export crops, (2) food crops for both home consumption and trade, and (3) products for internal trade such as cattle, kola nuts, and palm oil. The expansion in export crop trade is reported by Ugoh[21] and shown in Table 1. Berry

TABLE 1. *Principal Exports from Nigeria*

Year	Cocoa (Long tons)	£ 000	Palm Kernels (Long tons)	£ 000	Palm Oil (Long tons)	£ 000	Peanuts (Long tons)	£ 000
1900	202	9	85,624	834	45,508	681	599	4
1905	470	17	108,822	1,090	50,562	858	790	7
1910	2,932	101	172,907	2,451	76,851	1,742	995	9
1915	9,105	314	153,319	1,693	72,994	1,462	8,910	72
1920	17,155	1,238	207,010	5,718	84,856	4,677	45,409	1,120
1925	44,705	1,484	272,925	4,937	128,113	4,166	127,226	2,394
1930	52,331	1,756	260,022	3,679	135,801	3,250	146,371	2,196
1935	88,143	1,584	312,746	2,245	142,628	1,656	183,993	2,093
1940	89,737	1,583	235,521	1,500	132,723	1,099	169,480	1,476
1945	77,004	2,150	292,588	3,496	114,199	1,894	176,242	2,696
1950	99,949	18,984	415,906	16,694	173,010	12,072	311,221	15,237
1955	88,413	26,187	433,234	19,196	182,143	13,151	396,904	23,134
1960	154,176	36,772	418,176	26,062	183,360	13,982	332,916	22,878

SOURCE: Nigeria, *Trade Reports.*

11

and Hogendorn have documented the origins of cocoa and groundnut production in Nigeria in the early part of this century. (See Chapters 2 and 3.)

The 1940-1960 Period

The period from 1940 to 1960 is marked by a rapid increase in export crop production as shown in Table 1. The annual rate of growth of population increased from about 0.6 per cent in 1940 to approximately 2.3 per cent by 1960. Food crop output appears to have expanded about as rapidly as population growth, while food imports remained at a low level. Exports of palm products, cocoa, and groundnuts roughly doubled from 1940 to 1960, while cotton exports increased 300 per cent and rubber increased twentyfold. Although the primary expansion of export crops came about during this period from bringing more land under cultivation, important productivity gains in cocoa and groundnuts can be attributed to the biological research process which was started at the beginning of this period—1940. For example, after researchers had isolated the causes of blackpod and capsid diseases of cocoa, a campaign was started in the 1950's with emphasis being directed to farmers using their own equipment, mainly hand-operated pneumatic sprayers. "It has been estimated that the heavy spraying campaign of 1958-59 in Nigeria and Ghana may have contributed as much as 75 per cent to the 100,000 ton increase of total African production in 1959/60, and perhaps as much as 40-50 per cent to the 200,000 ton jump in 1960/61."[22] During the period 1940-1960, Nigeria emerged as the largest groundnut exporter in the world, with exports increasing from 169,480 tons in 1940 to 332,916 tons in 1960. The Institute for Agricultural Research, Samaru, Northern Nigeria, now has one of the largest groundnut gene pools in Africa, and new groundnut varieties producing up to 2,000 pounds of nuts per acre are now available, as compared with yields of 600-700 pounds by farmers. Also, fertilizer research on groundnuts started in the early 1950's, and now farmers can increase yields by early planting, the application of ammonium sulfate and using improved varieties. Fertilizer consumption in Northern Nigeria increased from 3,000 tons in 1960 to 50,000 tons in 1966.

Hybrid oil palms were developed in the Belgian Congo in the 1940's and then adapted for Nigerian conditions by the Nigerian (formerly West African) Institute for Oil Palm Research over the 1950-1960 period; these varieties can increase average farm yields 300 per cent over the wild variety.[23] Although low marketing board prices of palm products to farmers have acted as an obstacle to the widespread adoption of the hybrid palms, a scheme offering a modest subsidy to smallholders resulted in 50,000 acres of hybrid palms being planted in Eastern Nigeria during the first five years of the 1962-68 Development Plan. (See Chapter 15.) The sustained biological research in oil palms in the Congo and Nigeria in the early 1940's has facilitated a major expansion in oil palm plantings in Nigeria in the 1960's, even though farmers received only 50-60 per cent of the world price for oil palm—the remainder being skimmed off as marketing board surpluses (profits).

Virtually token effort has been devoted to research on domestic food crops. However, on close examination such token effort can be justified in light of the fact that (a) food production has expanded almost automatically in line with population growth rates, (b) Nigeria is virtually self-sufficient in staple food production, (c) prices have been relatively stable in Nigeria in the past twenty years and (d) a lack of effective demand (lack of purchasing power) is a major constraint when food production growth rates greatly exceed population growth rates. Also, protein deficiencies are to a large part attributed to a lack of effective demand (purchasing power) and consumer knowledge about nutritionally "superior" foods such as protein. Therefore, research and development strategy to date has rightly focused on expanding export rather than on food crop production. However, the population explosion which will boost Nigeria's population from roughly 65 million in 1970 to 90-100 million by 1985 calls for a crash research and development program on food crops. (See Chapter 19).

The long-term growth process of Nigeria has been aided by the complementarity between government infrastructure development (roads, agricultural research and disease control) and private investment by millions of small Nigerian bush farmers. The colonial government acted with impressive foresight in developing both a land and a biological research policy, which have induced investment by small farmers. As a result, agriculture has not acted as a brake on the economy but served as the leading sector of the economy.

NOTES

1. For a discussion of this point see H. Myint, "Economic Theory and Underdeveloped Countries," *Journal of Political Economy*, vol. 74 (October 1965).

2. Robert E. Baldwin, "Patterns of Development in Newly Settled Regions," *The Manchester School of Economic and Social Studies*, vol. 24, May, 1956. Reprinted in *Agriculture in Economic Development*, Edited by C. Eicher and L. Witt, New York, McGraw-Hill Book Company, 1964.

3. _____, *Economic Development and Export Growth: A Study of Northern Rhodesia, 1920-1960*, Berkeley, University of California Press, 1966.

4. R. W. Clower, G. Dalton, M. Harwitz, and A. A. Walter, *Growth Without Development: An Economic Survey of Liberia*, Evanston, Northwestern University Press, 1966.

5. Gerald Helleiner, *Peasant Agriculture, Government and Economic Growth in Nigeria*, Homewood, Illinois, Richard D. Irwin, Inc., 1966.

6. Polly Hill, *The Migrant Cocoa Farmers of Southern Ghana: A Study in Rural Capitalism*, Cambridge, England, Cambridge University Press, 1963.

7. H. A. Oluwasanmi, *Agriculture and Nigerian Economic Development*, Ibadan, Oxford University Press, 1966.

8. H. Myint, "The 'Classical Theory' of International Trade and the Underdeveloped Countries," *Economic Journal*, vol. 68 (June, 1958), pp. 317-37.

9. *Ibid.*

10. R. Szereszewski, *Structural Changes in the Economy of Ghana: 1891-1911*, London, Weidenfeld and Nicolson, 1965.

11. Helleiner, *op. cit.*

12. Sara Berry, "Cocoa in Western Nigeria, 1890-1940: A Study of an Innovation in a Developing Country," unpublished Ph.D. thesis, University of Michigan, 1967.

13. Jan Hogendorn, "The Origins of the Groundnut Trade in Northern Nigeria," unpublished Ph.D. dissertation, University of London, 1966.

14. Standard references are: W. K. Hancock, *Survey of British Commonwealth Affairs*, vol. 2, London, Oxford University Press, 1940 and Allan McPhee, *The Economic Revolution in British West Africa*, Aberdeen, Routledge and Sons, 1926.

15. S. Herbert Frankel, *Capital Investment in Africa*, London, Oxford University Press, 1938, p. 390.

16. Oluwasanmi, *op. cit.*

17. For a good review of colonial research policy see Sir Charles Jeffries, ed., *A Review of Colonial Research 1940-1960*, London, H.M.S.O., 1964.

18. A phrase borrowed from Szereszewski, *op. cit.*

19. *Ibid.*, pp. 74, 75, 82.

20. *Ibid.*, p. 95. The combined weight of cocoa and mining exports in Ghana has remained practically unchanged, with 74 per cent of the export earnings in 1911 and 77 per cent in 1960 originating from these two exports.

21. S. Ugoh, "Nigerian International Trade: 1911-1960," unpublished Ph.D. thesis, Harvard University, 1964.

22. United Nations, FAO, *Agricultural Development in Nigeria: 1965-1980*, Rome, 1966.

23. The definitive book on the oil palm is C. W. S. Hartley, *The Oil Palm*, London, Longmans, 1967. Also see C. W. S. Hartley, "Advances in Oil Palm Research in Nigeria in the Last Twenty-Five Years," *Empire Journal of Experimental Agriculture*, vol. XXVI, No. 102 (April, 1958), pp. 136-51.

2. Cocoa and Economic Development in Western Nigeria

SARA S. BERRY

A central problem in the study of West African economic history in the twentieth century is to explain the rapid increase in exports which began around the turn of the century and in many areas continues today. In Nigeria, for example, the volume of palm oil and kernels exported rose almost fivefold from 1900 to 1960, and exports of cocoa, peanuts and cotton grew enormously from almost negligible initial levels. (See Table 1 in Chapter 1.) To many Western observers, the production of primary products for export has appeared the most dynamic feature of economic life in Nigeria, apparently responsible for most of the growth in per capita income during this period. Since this development coincided in time with the advent of colonial rule, it has commonly been analyzed as a response to the various outside contacts introduced into Nigerian society by the colonial regime.

The model which is usually employed to explain the growth of export production in Nigeria is Hla Myint's analysis of the effect of exposing a traditional peasant society to international trade.[1] Myint argues that the opening up of trade provides an opportunity for the profitable employment of hitherto idle resources—a "vent" for the economy's potential surplus production. If, before trade is opened up, the level of effective demand within the domestic economy was too low to absorb the potential output of available resources, some of these resources would not be employed. When the economy is suddenly exposed to the international market, the effective demand for its products is greatly increased and, at the same time, the inhabitants are offered the opportunity to acquire a whole range of new commodities from abroad. Assuming that the demonstration effect of the new import goods is positive, the economy will attempt to produce additional output to exchange for imports. As long as there are available reserves of idle resources, output can expand very rapidly, without any change in traditional modes or techniques of production. Myint suggests that this is approximately what happened in West Africa and Southeast Asia during the early decades of the twentieth century.

The physical output of peasant exports grew most rapidly, well above any possible rate of natural increase in working population, in the early phase of expansion when most of the labor requirement must have been supplied from within the peasant families. This suggests that initially there must have been a considerable amount of under-employed or surplus labor in these families.[2]

Other writers have reaffirmed the relevance of Myint's hypothesis for Nigeria. According to Gerald Helleiner, "When world trade first made its influence strongly felt in Nigeria in this century it did so by reaching into the very midst of the peasant economy, offering rewards directly to the peasant producer."[3] The expansion of Nigerian cocoa exports, for example, "was achieved principally through the steady bringing of more land under cultivation and the abandonment of former leisure activities in response to the higher returns earnable from cocoa."[4] Carl Eicher has emphasized the availability of unused land in Nigeria, which was cultivated after the turn of the century by Nigerian farmers (See Chapter 1).[5]

Both Myint and writers who have applied his model to Nigeria assume, either implicitly or explicitly, that the expansion of production for export involved only two factors of production—land and labor. By implication, neither capital nor entrepreneurship was required to effect higher levels of output. Nor did the growth of exports involve any significant reorganization of established methods of mobilizing or combining land and labor: in Nigeria, "the staple items of export trade" were "all, even when they involved the introduction of new crops, capable of being produced with very little alteration of existing technologies and traditions."[6] The whole process seems to have been one of growth without development—the traditional economy expanded, soaking up idle resources to take advantage of a wider market, but it was not transformed.

In studying the development of cocoa farming in parts of Western Nigeria,[7] I encountered various pieces of evidence which do not correspond to the Myint hypothesis. For one thing, it is historically inaccurate to suppose that trade between Africa and the rest of the world was "opened up" by the partition of Africa into spheres of influence of various European powers in the late nineteenth century and the subsequent establishment of formal colonies and protectorates there. Second, in the case of cocoa, the expansion of export production involved both capital formation (and sufficient entrepreneurial skill to carry that out) and a number of changes in the organization of productive activity which are not economically uninteresting just because they do not correspond to the patterns of institutional change which accompanied the rapid growth of output in Europe and North America.

Maritime trade between Europe and the coast of West Africa was opened up 500 years ago—not seventy. Portuguese sailors and merchants began to establish contacts along the coast in the fifteenth century; in the sixteenth century, England, France and Holland followed suit.[8] During the seventeenth and eighteenth centuries, the major commodity exported from West Africa was human beings and the traffic in this commodity was substantial. It has been estimated that in the early eighteenth century, 14,500 slaves were exported annually from the port of Whydah alone; at least part of these slaves were supplied by the Yoruba state of Oyo.[9] Later, in the early nineteenth century, Lagos became an important slave port, despite early British efforts to stem the trade.[10]

What happened in the nineteenth century was not, therefore, an "opening up" of trade but a change in the composition of European demand which was met, ultimately, by corresponding changes in the composition of West African supply. Both transitions were gradual; British attempts to negotiate and enforce an end to the slave trade were not very effective until the middle of the century and both European and African merchants continued to profit from it for at least that long. In the latter half of the century, however, it was becoming increasingly difficult to sustain the illegal trade, and West African traders began searching for other goods to export. During the latter half of the nineteenth century, they experimented with a number of commodities, including cotton, rubber, coffee, cocoa and groundnuts.[11] In terms of its long-run contribution to Nigerian foreign exchange earnings, cocoa was one of the most successful experiments.

Cocoa is not indigenous to West Africa but was brought there from Brazil, by way of the Spanish and Portuguese islands of San Thome, Principe and Fernando Po, in the latter half of the nineteenth century. In Nigeria, it has been grown primarily in the rain forest areas of the Western Region which are occupied almost entirely by Yoruba speaking peoples. The field work on which this essay is based was carried out in two Yoruba kingdoms or city-states—Ibadan and Ondo. (See Map I.) Cocoa seeds were introduced to both Ibadan and Ondo in the 1890's but farmers adopted the crop more quickly in Ibadan. Available data suggests that the acreage planted in cocoa each year rose steadily in Ibadan from about 1905 through the 1920's, whereas in Ondo the period of expansion began in the early 1920's and continued into the mid-1940's.[12]

It is undoubtedly true, as Myint's hypothesis would suggest, that the spread of cocoa growing in Western Nigeria involved the permanent (or at least long term) cultivation of much land which had been previously unused. In both Ibadan and Ondo, I found that during the period of expansion, many new villages were established in uninhabited or sparsely populated parts of the states' territories by farmers seeking more and better land for planting cocoa than they could obtain on their old farms or family lands. However, in other respects, the Myint model is not so applicable to the expansion of cocoa growing. For one thing, it is impossible to tell to what extent the labor employed in producing cocoa had previously been idle and to what extent cocoa growing was substituted for other income earning activities. Moreover, the planting of cocoa trees is in itself an act of capital formation. During the first six or seven years, resources must be employed to clear land—a major task in the rain forest, even though the clearing was only partial—and to plant and maintain the trees so that they will yield output and income in the future. In other words, cocoa farmers had at the outset to mobilize and finance productive services well in advance of any increase in their earnings.

In addition, as more and more people became engaged in growing cocoa, various organizational problems arose which had to be solved by altering established systems of economic activity. Old methods of acquiring land and labor services changed considerably and traditional forms of credit were adapted to permit farmers to convert their fixed capital (cocoa trees) to more liquid assets, should they wish to do so. Finally, the spread of cocoa farming appears to have induced investment in several related activities, much as Hirschman suggests will happen in a successfully developing economy.[13] Let me elaborate these points in turn.

Investment in Cocoa Trees

Most farmers solved the problem of supplying working capital during the years before their first cocoa trees began to bear by starting to grow cocoa on a very small scale. Usually a farmer planted cocoa seeds close together on a plot small enough to be cultivated by him and his children. During the first two or three years he could plant enough food crops between the young cocoa trees, which require shade, and thus produce his own food, and weed and protect the cocoa trees at the same time. After that, he would have to establish a separate food plot and weed the cocoa in addition, so the initial cocoa plot had to be small enough to permit this. According to my informants, many people began with cocoa plots of less than one acre. Once the first cocoa plot began to yield, the farmer could use the proceeds either to purchase food while he planted additional cocoa plots, or to hire labor to assist with growing cocoa and food. In practice, farmers usually combined these alternatives. Thus I rarely encountered anyone who had entirely given up growing food crops even today, although most of the farmers I talked to said they did not grow enough for their own subsistence.

Since there are no economies of scale involved in growing cocoa, farmers suffered no disadvantages from beginning with small plots and financ-

MAP I   COCOA BELT OF WESTERN NIGERIA

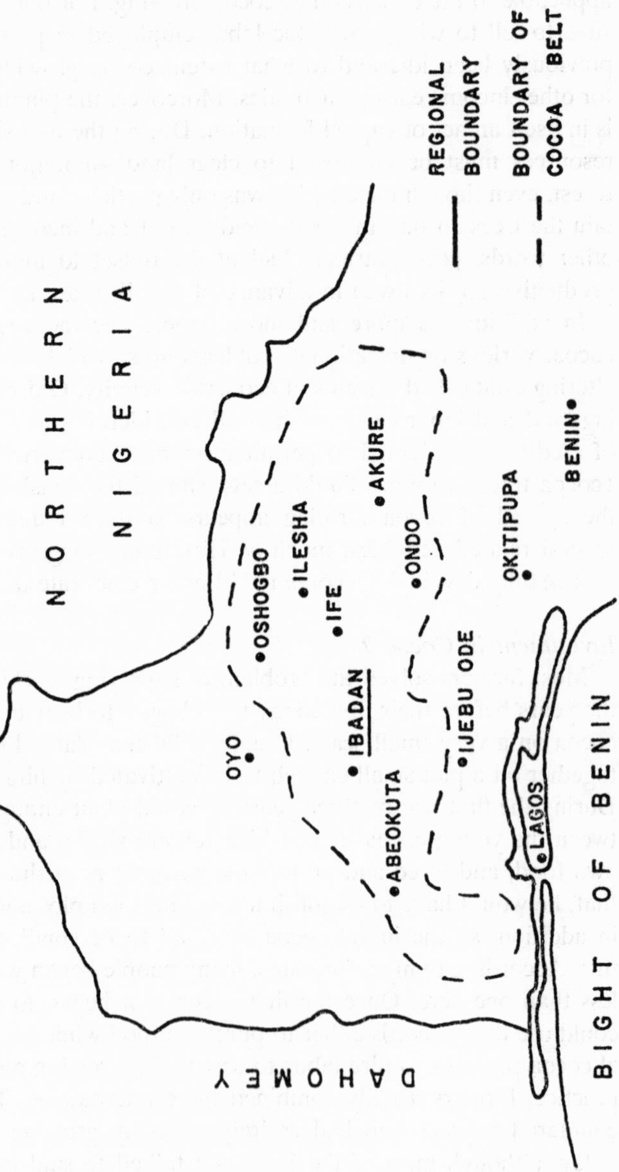

NORTHERN NIGERIA

DAHOMEY

OYO
•ABEOKUTA
•OSHOGBO
•ILESHA
•IFE
•IBADAN
•AKURE
•ONDO
•IJEBU ODE
OKITIPUPA•
BENIN•
•LAGOS

REGIONAL BOUNDARY
BOUNDARY OF COCOA BELT

BIGHT OF BENIN

ing additional plots by ploughing back proceeds from earlier ones. The main operations—clearing land, planting seeds or seedlings, weeding, harvesting the pods, breaking them open and fermenting the beans—can be performed most economically by hand. Clearing and weeding should be partial, since cocoa needs shade and some ground cover helps to preserve moisture in the soil and to prevent erosion.[14] Machinery is of little use in achieving this end. Similarly, harvesting and breaking open the pods are delicate tasks, best performed by hand, and the traditional method of fermenting cocoa by placing it in a heap covered with banana leaves, is still the cheapest technique known. In short, there is no reason why a large number of laborers working a big tract of land can produce cocoa more efficiently than a single worker on a small plot.

Methods of Acquiring Land

Although there was plenty of unused land available in both Ibadan and Ondo for planting cocoa, the land was not unowned. In Ibadan, rural land was and is held by patrilineages; in Ondo, by the whole community, represented by the king or Oshemawe.[15] As farmers began to seek more and better land to grow cocoa, they had in theory at least to approach the "owner" of the land for permission to use it. In Ibadan, this meant asking the head of a family for a piece of its land; in Ondo, since all land belongs to all the Ondos, an individual could farm any unused piece of land that he liked, without asking anyone's permission.

In both communities, however, individual farmers could acquire only the right to use land, and not the ownership of it which continued to be vested in the group (family or community). In Ibadan, it was customary for a farmer to give a present of food or drink to the family who "showed" him land for farming. As the demand for good cocoa land increased, the value of these "presents" began to rise. The process was described to the West African Lands Committee in 1913 by an Egba witness, as follows:

> It has come about naturally by process of development. Anciently you would almost beg people to come and live with you. A man settles in a forest, say with his children; it is to his interest to try to get as many as possible to stay with him. Later on the community has grown and others have come. They do not give up land for nothing. They say 'You bring a bottle of gin or some little present.' After that the community becomes very important. Good roads are made, trading is flourishing, and people begin to think 'You cannot have it free; you must pay something.' . . . where there are good roads or where the soil is very fertile and there is a stream near it you cannot expect to get it for nothing.[16]

In Ibadan, most of the farmers I interviewed said that around the turn of the century, their fathers had given "a bottle or two of gin" for land on which to plant cocoa, but that later they made presents of cash. In 1930, a district officer reported that one Ibadan family had received presents of anywhere from £5 to £50 from farmers to whom they had granted land.[17] However, even a payment of £50 did not constitute a purchase in the usual sense; the "grantee" acquired only the right to use the land as long as he liked. Thus the spread of cocoa growing in Ibadan led to the development of a market not for land as a commodity or factor of production, but for the productive services rendered by land—much as, historically, some European economies developed markets for labor services rather than for human beings.

Cocoa Trees as Marketable Capital Goods

Although land itself rarely became individual property in Ibadan and Ondo, man-made improvements on the land have always been treated as the property of the individual who made them. In Ondo, farmers have been able to realize their investments in cocoa trees by selling them to other Ondos; since the land on which they stand belonged to the whole community, it didn't matter which member of the community happened to be using a particular piece of it.[18] In Ibadan, however, families have not been willing to risk losing control of their lands by permitting trees to be bought and sold. Instead, the Ibadans have adapted an old system of putting up fixed productive assets as collateral for cash loans to fit the needs of the cocoa economy.

In the nineteenth century, a man who wished to borrow money could "pawn" himself or one of his children to the creditor until he could repay the loan.[19] The "pawn" (iwofa) performed certain services—usually farm work—for the creditor which constituted interest on the loan, but did not count toward repayment of the principal. As cultivation of cocoa and other tree crops spread in Western Nigeria, farmers began to pawn their trees instead of themselves.[20] The creditor had the right to harvest the cocoa and keep the proceeds for himself until the borrower repaid the loan, but he acquired no claim to the land on which the trees were planted. The borrower might never repay the loan, in which case the transaction was in effect a sale, although the borrowers' descendants could, theoretically, redeem the trees if they could produce evidence of the original loan. However, the transaction was not called a sale, so that the creditor could not use it to claim ownership of the land, which continued to belong to the debtor's family or to the family who originally granted him use of the land.

Systems of Labor Employment

The spread of cocoa growing in Western Nigeria was accompanied by changes in methods of employing labor services as well as by the "commercialization" of land transactions. During the nineteenth century Yoruba farmers relied mostly on slaves for labor services beyond what they and their children could supply. In Ibadan, where the army's military successes ensured a substantial supply of captives,

> The chiefs had large farms and farm houses containing from a hundred to over a thousand souls. . . . These extensive plantations not only support their huge establishments but also supply the markets, so that a military state though Ibadan was, food was actually cheaper there than in many other towns.[21]

A man who had no slaves had to use *iwofas* or, for special projects such as building a house or clearing a piece of land, to call on his friends and neighbors for assistance, with the understanding that he was ready to do the same for them when the need arose. Such mutual assistance schemes could not, obviously, be used to supply regular labor throughout the rainy season. Consequently, when the British colonial administration abolished domestic slavery in Southern Nigeria around the turn of the century, a farmer with more land and crops than he and his sons could handle, had only the *iwofa* system to fall back on. The *iwofa* system has, however, the major disadvantage that one must be able to make the *iwofa* a cash loan at the time one engages his services. For many farmers, this is difficult to do in the spring, five or six months after the cocoa harvest. Hence, it was necessary for Yoruba farmers to devise new ways of employing laborers if they wished to plant more cocoa than they and their families could cultivate.

The farmers whom I interviewed in Ibadan and Ondo described two methods of hiring labor—which I shall refer to as "casual" and "seasonal" employment—that they and their fathers had used on their cocoa farms. Since I returned from Nigeria, I have encountered references to a Nigerian variation of the *abusa* system which is common in Ghana and the Ivory Coast;[22] unfortunately, I can offer no first hand evidence on how widely it is used in Western Nigeria.

In both Ibadan and Ondo, farmers sometimes employed laborers to perform a specific task, such as weeding or harvesting a plot of cocoa, and paid them in cash as soon as the job was done. Since such casual laborers were hired only for a few days at a time, they were usually residents of the community in which they worked. During peak season, local labor was likely to have been in short supply. Also, hiring casual laborers required that the farmer have the financial resources to pay their wages which was often not the case except at harvest time. Consequently, many farmers employed laborers for the whole growing season and paid them after the cocoa had been harvested and sold, in late November or December.

Since practically anyone in Ibadan or Ondo who wished to grow cocoa could do so for himself, most seasonal laborers were migrants from other communities. At first, laborers came from other Yoruba states, particularly the Ekiti kingdoms in the northeastern part of Yorubaland. In Ibadan, some of my informants said their fathers had begun to hire Ekiti laborers around the turn of the century; in Ondo, people were migrating in search of employment themselves at this time—chiefly to Lagos, where some found employment on cocoa farms at Agege. In 1926, when cocoa was beginning to be widely planted in Ondo, a district officer complained that the cocoa farmers were beginning to compete with the government for local labor and predicted that the farmers would soon have to employ workers from Ekiti.[23] However, before long, the Ekitis also began to grow cocoa for themselves and farmers in Ibadan and Ondo had to draw laborers from Northern Nigeria or the central and eastern provinces of Southern Nigeria. By the late 1920's, the annual flow of laborers into some of the older parts of the cocoa belt, such as Ibadan, was apparent to foreign officials and observers.[24] In the early 1950's, when cocoa prices were exceptionally high, the Public Works Department discovered that it could not hold on to laborers recruited to work on the roads in Western Nigeria. The workers, "as they could earn very much more on the cocoa farms, merely took advantage of the transport arranged for them and as soon as possible departed to a farming settlement."[25]

Migrant laborers in Ibadan and Ondo were employed primarily by cocoa farmers, but they worked on their employers' food farms as well as on their cocoa plots. If a farmer had planted all his cocoa in one area; he and his laborers lived and worked together. If his plots were scattered at some distance from each other, in different villages, he might assign a few laborers to each, sending one of his own relatives to live with them, and visiting each farm periodically himself to supervise the work. Usually the farmer paid his laborers something in advance to cover the cost of their subsistence or fed them out of his own supply of foodstuffs (which they helped to raise) while they worked for him. After the cocoa was harvested and sold, he paid the balance of their wage in cash. So far as I know, the laborer's wage was a cash sum agreed upon in advance by the laborer and the farmer, rather than the value of a certain portion of the crop, as is the case under the *abusa* system. Thus, in 1966, when I interviewed them, farmers were complaining that they could not afford laborers that year because of the low cocoa prices. However, the payment of a money wage may be a fairly recent development which has displaced the practice of giving out a plot of cocoa to a laborer who would harvest it in return for a third of the crop.

In any case, the spread of cocoa growing in both Ibadan and Ondo

involved considerable changes in pre-existing patterns of labor employment. Not only did cocoa farmers work out new ways of employing and
remunerating workers which were geared to the seasonal needs of the
new crop, but also the growing demand for labor in the cocoa belt apparently contributed to the development of new patterns of labor migration in Nigeria.

Induced Investment

In addition to modifying the mobilization and organization of productive services in agriculture, some cocoa farmers became interested in
other, related productive activities. On the one hand, prosperous cocoa
farmers and traders began to invest their own savings in income-earning
assets such as lorries or buildings in town. On the other, farmers put
pressure on the government to invest in social overhead facilities, particularly roads, which would facilitate the spread of cocoa farming. Both
represent examples of investments induced by what Hirschman has
called the "complementarities" of the increased production of one commodity—in this case cocoa. Such complementarities may involve either
pecuniary incentives to undertake a new activity—as in the case of
lorries which private entrepreneurs purchased to transport cocoa from
farms or villages to the towns—or political pressures on the government
to provide necessary public services—such as roads for the lorries to
travel on.[26]

In Ibadan, private investment in buildings and motor vehicles was
much in evidence by the early 1920's. The Resident of Oyo Province
remarked in 1922 that

> In the big cocoa and kernel centers such as Ibadan, Ede, Os-
> hogbo, Ilesha and Ife there has been a remarkable increase in
> the number of new and well built stores and houses with cor-
> rugated iron roofs.[27]

One trader in Ibadan was described as owning a "fleet" of lorries and a
repair garage, and the Resident noted with scant enthusiasm that "an
illiterate trader at Iseyin" with three Reo lorries was competing with the
government operated transport service to Ibadan.[28] The rapid expansion
of cocoa growing in Ondo was closely associated with similar types of
investment. One of my informants who had left Ondo in 1910 and
worked for many years as a tailor in Ilesha and Ibadan, said that when
he left, all the houses in Ondo had thatched roofs. When he returned, in
1926, many houses had iron roofs and people told him that the money
to buy such roofs came from cocoa. On hearing this the man decided to
settle down in Ondo and grow cocoa.

Cocoa farmers were also active in promoting public investment in transportation facilities. Both Ibadan and Ondo boasted agricultural societies, originally organized by progressive farmers in order to spread information about new crops and improved techniques within their respective communities. The Ibadan Agricultural Society established an experimental farm in 1903 where they planted various commercial crops such as cotton, coffee and cocoa. The British administration supported the farm financially for a while, but grew alarmed at the extent of their commitment when it reached the grand total of £200 and ordered the Society immediately to "sell the cotton and cocoa grown thereon, and thus to reimburse to such an extent as might be possible the Provincial Funds."[29]

In spite of this set-back, the Society continued to exist and, in 1917, began to exert pressure on the government to build more roads into Ibadan's main cocoa growing areas.[30] By 1921, their pleas had evidently reached a wide audience; the district officer admitted that "the people in all parts of the Province are clamoring for more motor roads but it is useless to attempt anything further until the engineer arrives."[31] Finally, in the mid-twenties, the government did begin to construct motorable roads into the major cocoa areas south and east of town. Some enterprising villages built spurs of their own to connect their farms and markets with the government roads. In Ondo, too, farmers and traders urged the construction of a road to link Ondo with the network of creeks and lagoons along which they could ship produce to Lagos, and the government finally did so, opening a road to Agbabu in 1927.[32] Since Ondo had not previously enjoyed the services of a railway, the opening of the Agbabu road ushered in an era of cheap transport and rapid expansion of cocoa plantings.

The evidence I have presented suggests that the spread of cocoa growing in Western Nigeria effected a number of changes in the organization of productive activities there. Methods of acquiring rights to land, of obtaining credit, and of mobilizing and employing labor services have all been modified in accordance with cocoa farmers' needs. The growth of income from cocoa exports has been reflected in increases in both consumption and investment expenditures by cocoa farmers. Farmers also put pressure on the colonial administration to provide capital goods and services beneficial to the cocoa economy. In view of these developments, I would argue that the rapid expansion of cocoa exports involved not only the employment of hitherto idle land and labor, as Myint and others have suggested, but also reallocations and recombinations of available resources which, over time, have altered the organization and structure as well as the volume of productive activity in Western Nigeria.

NOTES

1. Hla Myint, *The Economics of the Developing Countries* (London: Hutchinson and Co., 1964), chapter 3. Cf. "The Classical Theory of International Trade and the Underdeveloped Countries," *Economic Journal*, LXVIII, 270 (June, 1958).

2. *Ibid.*, pp. 42-43.

3. Gerald K. Helleiner, *Peasant Agriculture, Government and Economic Growth in Nigeria* (Homewood, Illinois: Richard D. Irwin, Inc., 1966), p. 48.

4. *Ibid.*, p. 49.

5. A somewhat different view of the historical development of export production in Nigeria is suggested by H. A. Oluwasanmi, *Agriculture and Nigerian Economic Development* (Ibadan: Oxford University Press, 1966), who points out, for example, that "commercial agricultural production . . . created the cash basis for the growth of modern commerce and the building by governments of the social overhead capital essential to the development of the non-agricultural sectors of the economy" (p. 118). Oluwasanmi says little, however, about developments within the agricultural sector which accompanied the expansion of exports.

6. Helleiner, *op. cit.*, p. 49.

7. The evidence presented in this essay is based on my unpublished Ph.D. dissertation, *Cocoa in Western Nigeria, 1890-1940: A Study of an Innovation in a Developing Economy* (University of Michigan, 1967). I spent eight months in Nigeria in 1966, collecting material from archives and through interviews, on the historical development of cocoa growing in two Yoruba states (Ibadan and Ondo) in Western Nigeria.

8. See, for example, K. O. Dike, *Trade and Politics in the Niger Delta, 1830-1885* (Oxford: Clarendon Press, 1956), pp. 1-4.

9. C. W. Newbury, *The Western Slave Coast and Its Rulers* (Oxford: Clarendon Press, 1961), p. 22; P. Morton-Williams, "The Oyo Yoruba and the Atlantic Trade, 1670-1830," *Journal of the Historical Society of Nigeria*, III, 1 (1964), p. 25.

10. *Ibid.*, pp. 36, 38.

11. In Kano, for example, the cultivation of groundnuts for export was organized entirely by Hausa traders and farmers, *despite* the efforts of the colonial administration to encourage farmers to grow cotton for export. Groundnuts were more profitable. See J. S. Hogendorn, *The Origins of the Groundnut Trade in Northern Nigeria*, unpublished Ph.D. dissertation (University of London, 1966). For brief discussions of early experiments with cotton and the spectacular rubber

boom of the mid-1890's, when Nigerian exports of wild rubber increased from 5,000 to 5,000,000 pounds in one year, see my dissertation cited above. Similar developments were also taking place in other areas, Polly Hill, *Migrant Cocoa Farmers of Southern Ghana* (Cambridge: Cambridge University Press, 1963) and Marguerite Dupire, "Planteurs Autochtones et etrangers en Basse-Cote d'Ivoire Orientale," *Etudes Eburneennes*, VIII (1960) are especially valuable.

12. Information on the time pattern of cocoa plantings in Western Nigeria was collected by the Nigerian Department of Agriculture in the late 1940s and early 1950s. For a summary of the results see Western Nigeria, Ministry of Agriculture and Natural Resources, *Tree Crop Planting Projects* (Ibadan: Government Printer, n. d.), p. 16.

13. Albert O. Hirschman, *The Strategy of Economic Development* (New Haven: Yale University Press, 1958), especially pp. 68-72.

14. D. Urquhart, *Cocoa* (London: Longmans, Green and Co., 1955), pp. 102-03.

15. Cf. Peter C. Lloyd, *Yoruba Land Law* (London: Oxford University Press, 1962), pp. 125-35; H. L. Ward Price, *Land Tenure in the Yoruba Provinces* (Lagos: The Government Printer, 1939); and West African Lands Committee, *Minutes of Evidence and Papers and Correspondence* (Printed for the use of the Colonial Office, 1916).

16. West African Lands Committee, *Minutes of Evidence*, Q13126.

17. Memorandum by the Assistant District Officer, Ibadan, October 14, 1930 (Nigerian National Archives, OYOPROF 3/1181, Vol. 7).

18. Cf. Lloyd, *op. cit.*, p. 128.

19. On the iwofa system, see Samuel Johnson, *History of the Yorubas* (Lagos: C.M.S. Bookshops [Nigeria] Ltd., 1921), pp. 126-30; Lloyd, *op. cit.*, pp. 310; W.A.L.C., *Minutes of Evidence*, Q7538-7563; Oni of Ife, "Iwofa," *Odu: Journal of Yoruba and Related Studies*, 3, pp. 16-18.

20. Cf. Lloyd, *op. cit.*, pp. 309-21.

21. Johnson, *op. cit.*, p. 325.

22. Lloyd, *op. cit.*, p. 308. Cf. Hill, *The Gold Coast Cocoa Farmer* (London: Oxford University Press, 1956); and *Migrant Cocoa Farmers of Southern Ghana*; Dupire, *op. cit.*; and A. J. F. Kobben, "Le Planteur Noir," *Etudes Eburneennes*, V, 1956.

23. Ondo Province, *Annual Report, 1926* (Nigerian National Archives, CSO 26/11874, Vol. V).

24. Oyo Province, *Annual Report, 1927* (Nigerian National Archives, CSO 26/12723, Vol. V); Lloyd, *op. cit.*, pp. 88, 329; R. M. Prothero, "Migratory Labour from Northwestern Nigeria," *Africa*, XXVII, 3 (July, 1957).

25. R. Galletti, *et al.*, *Nigerian Cocoa Farmers* (London: Oxford University Press, 1956), p. 211, n. 1.

26. Hirschman, *op. cit.*, pp. 68-69.

27. Oyo Province, *Annual Report, 1922* (Nigerian National Archives, CSO 26/09723).

28. *Idem.*

29. Ibadan Town Council Minutes, October 22, 1904 (Mapo Hall, Ibadan).

30. Ibadan Division, *Annual Report, 1917* (Nigerian National Archives, OYOPROF 4/6, 355/1917).

31. Oyo Province, *Annual Report, 1921* (Nigerian National Archives, CSO 26/06027).

32. Ondo Province, *Annual Reports, 1924-1927* (Nigerian National Archives, CSO 26/11874, Vols. IV-VII).

3. The Origins of the Groundnut Trade in Northern Nigeria

J. S. HOGENDORN

The discovery of unsuspected entrepreneurial ability in relatively primitive societies, when these societies have undergone their first extensive contact with developed areas, has resulted in a growing body of literature in recent years.[1] Surprisingly, a most interesting and widespread manifestation of economic initiative and adaptability among peasant farmers and traders newly in contact with the developed world has passed practically unnoticed. This was the sudden, unexpected genesis of the Northern Nigerian groundnut (peanut) industry late in the year 1912.

At present it is customary, even among some professional economists, to denigrate the economic initiative of the Hausa people of Northern Nigeria; such arguments have even achieved political status during the recent Nigerian Civil War. Yet the events of 1912 show that, historically, no infusion of western business ethic was needed to promote a new trade which significantly altered cropping patterns, lines of commerce, and standards of living for a population group which is one of the largest in sub-Saharan Africa.

THE COTTON SCHEME

After centuries of slave-raiding and strife among the semi-independent Hausa emirates of Northern Nigeria, peace was achieved during the period 1900-1906 under Governor F. D. Lugard. With this imposition of British suzerainty came great hopes that the agricultural area of Hausaland, centered around the market city of Kano, would provide an important source of raw materials for industry in the United Kingdom. The raw material which was in mind was not, however, groundnuts. It was cotton to supply the looms of Britain's largest manufacturing enterprise, textiles. The influential British Cotton Growing Association, Manchester-based and agent of the cotton millers, was attempting after 1902 to find a substitute for Britain's main source of supply, the Cotton Belt

30

of the U.S.A. This area, hard hit by the infamous boll weevil plague, was also shipping ever more raw fibre to American mills, lending urgency to Lancashire's efforts to find a new source of supply.

Cotton had been grown and even exported from Southern Nigeria as early as the 1860's,[2] but the B.C.G.A.'s hopes were focused on the North where its agents reported that "there are unlimited lands, suitable for cotton growing, and that labour is available. The soil in some districts is reported to be 'the finest cotton soil in the world.' " Reports received in London estimated that in Northern Nigeria "almost sufficient cotton can be grown to supply the wants of Lancashire."[3]

Kano and Zaria were supposed to be the dual centres of this immense development.[4] Particular attention was paid to the Kano area, with its relatively high degree of indigenous agricultural sophistication and large farming population. Kano also had the advantages of a large local hand-loom weaving industry, already attracting supplies of home-grown cotton. In addition it was the home of some very capable Hausa merchants trading on a large scale, and had a system of local taxation and land tenure which did not, on the whole, impede agricultural development.[5]

During subsequent years, even more sanguine predictions for cotton became commonplace. A campaign to acquire parliamentary support was launched and the B.C.G.A. centered its activities on the promotion of a new railway line, to be extended northward from the Lagos area, its destination Kano. Concurrently, a branch line was to be built to Baro on the River Niger so that cargo from the newly-opened territory could be carried by shallow-draught steamer during the annual period of high water.

By the time officials of the B.C.G.A. met Prime-Minister Campbell-Bannerman and Chancellor of the Exchequer Herbert Asquith in May, 1906, the campaign for a railway to tap the cotton areas of Northern Nigeria had gathered considerable public support. It was widely noted in the press that among the large delegation accompanying the Association's spokesmen were over sixty M.P.s and thirty mayors.[6] Some prominent politicians at the meeting had already been enrolled on the B.C.G.A.'s staff: Sir Ralph Moor, a former High Commissioner of Southern Nigeria, and Lord Marlborough, Under-Secretary for the Colonies until just six months before. The group made it clear that it was not attempting to gain transport in every prospective cotton area, but was concentrating its attention "on this one point. We say that Northern Nigeria offers the best hopes for Lancashire."[7]

The part taken in behalf of the railway by the new Under-Secretary for the Colonies, Winston S. Churchill, enhanced his reputation as the B.C.G.A.'s principal parliamentary supporter.[8] In several speeches at

London and Manchester, as well as in the Commons, Churchill emphasized the importance of cotton to British prosperity. He argued that a railway to Northern Nigeria was vital, as that area formed "the best cotton-growing region . . . discovered in the wide reconnaissances of the B.C.G.A."[9]

There were certainly several other reasons for a railway from the coast to Kano. The Colonial Office felt that defense would be simplified and the rapid concentration of troops made possible. However, the fact that the railway was not built nearer the eastern border with the German Kamerun Colony, the only frontier where serious military difficulties were likely to arise, suggests that the strategy argument was not paramount. A Calabar-Lake Chad line along the eastern line of demarcation was indeed advocated for a time, but was ultimately forgotten.[10]

The only other case put forward seriously was for the exploitation of the tin deposits in the Plateau area, near Jos. The Niger Company, largest of the trading firms operating in the north, spent much effort developing these mines. By 1910 when the railway was far advanced toward Kano, the Company argued that it should be swung in an easterly direction to the tin areas, but work was too near to completion and the mines had to settle for a narrow gauge branch connecting with the main line, not completed until 1912-1914.[11] As for other commercial possibilities advanced in connection with the railway, there were only some scattered suggestions to the effect that an export trade might develop in hides and skins, shea nuts, shea butter, groundnuts, peppers, maize, gum, etc.[12]

On the evidence, then, it seems quite fair to say that the primary motivation for the railway was—as stated in a 1909 Parliamentary Command Paper—"the prospect which the construction of a railway opens up of a great development in the cultivation and export of cotton."[13] Construction was begun in August, 1907, and the line reached Kano during 1911, its entire length being opened for general traffic on April 1, 1912.

It is a well-known fact that groundnuts and not cotton became the great cash crop of Northern Nigeria, particularly above the 12th parallel of latitude and in Kano Province, with cotton on the whole squeezed into the smaller and less densely populated area to the south. In view of this, it is necessary to ask whether there was ever any chance whatsoever that cotton would hold sway in accord with the expectations of the B.C.G.A. and His Majesty's Government. Can cotton be grown successfully in the region around Kano city or indeed anywhere north of latitude 12°N? The answer is an unequivocal yes. It was seen growing in "an abundance" by Leo Africanus as early as the sixteenth century and, even far to the north of the city, Dr. Barth found cotton fields "the greatest and most permanent ornament of any landscape in these regions.[14] Folk wisdom among the Hausa farmers had resulted, before the advent of the British, in the employment of four varieties with different degrees of appropriateness for local conditions of soil and rainfall.[15]

During the first decade of British administration it was noted that "a small plot of cotton" occupied "a part of nearly every holding."[16] Soon estimates of annual production for local weaving began to flow back to Britain from the District Officers. They were thought to be very rough, even at the time, but for our purposes they make clear why Kano received such excited attention in comparison with Zaria and southern Katsina, which are today the main producing areas. The total annual output of Kano was eventually put at 3,500 tons, with Zaria and Katsina at about 1,000 tons each.[17]

Modern research at the Kano Experimental Farm, covering a period of about 40 years, shows cotton yields comparing quite favorably with results obtained further south in the area of Zaria.[18] Because rainfall is less abundant, due to a greater distance from the Gulf of Guinea whence comes the annual rains, there is somewhat greater risk of crop failure in years of deficient rainfall. Also, in areas north of Kano soil conditions become sandier, allowing rapid run-off and making cotton ever less suitable. The fact remains that it can be grown and will, under the standards of peasant agriculture, give reasonable yields. In short, neither the B.C.G.A. nor His Majesty's Government were far off the mark in claiming that Kano *could* be, in a phrase used commonly at the time, the "Mecca of Lancashire."

British interests moved rapidly to promote universal cotton growing after approval of the railway extension in 1907. Within the year three large ginneries were constructed by the B.C.G.A. under government subsidy (one named the "Churchill") and plans were made for ginning and buying stations to be set up at Zaria and Kano when the railway arrived.[19] B.C.G.A. agents, who "explain to the natives the value of growing cotton for export," toured the area and enlisted the support of village heads. Free cotton seed was made available, buying stations established, and a fixed price adopted of ld. per lb.[20]

The government itself was actively involved in the promotion of cotton-growing. The railway charged special low rates for shipments of ginned cotton, and local authorities appropriated grants of several hundred pounds to encourage planting in the Kano area.[21] This latter move was without question due to the influence of the British District Officers, or "Residents," on the spot.

By 1910-1911, Governor H. Hesketh Bell of Northern Nigeria was enthusiastically using administrative staff as propagandists for cotton. "Strenuous efforts are being made to encourage the natives to grow cotton on a large scale" he wrote in the annual *Colonial Report*. And, in a dispatch to the Colonial Office, "My officers will do all they can to open the eyes of the chiefs and people as to the advantages and probably profits of growing cotton, and I believe attention will be paid to their advice."[22]

There are a good many references to the inculcation carried on in Nigeria during the final year of railway construction. "Officers of the Political or Administrative staff," says the *Northern Nigeria Gazette*, have been used "generally to encourage the natives to take up the industry."[23] This, according to an official of the Department of Agriculture, "has a moral effect by creating an impression that Government 'expects' cotton to be grown for export in preference to other crops."[24]

Records surviving in the National Archives, Kaduna, show that at least one emir (Katsina) issued instructions to district chiefs designed to ensure that every adult male would plant at least one acre of cotton. Says the *Kano Province Report* for 1911, "No compulsion will of course be used but short of that, the District Headmen have been told to do their utmost to make the scheme a success."[25]

The British Resident at Kano voiced strong doubts concerning this policy in early 1912. "In my experience the farmers of this Province are keen businessmen. They grow what it pays them to grow." For cotton or any other cash crop "the farmer is the best judge of whether it would pay."[26] The Governor's succinct comment on this is clipped to the back of the report: "I concur—the cultivation of cotton excepted."

In summary, the need for cotton led to the hope that the Zaria-Kano area of Northern Nigeria would supply it; this was the most important reason for the construction of the Kano railway, the success of which was to be dependent on cotton exports; and the government labored actively to promote these exports. In Churchill's words, "There is no part of the British Empire in which cotton-growing is being more powerfully pushed forward than in Nigeria."[27] With the opening of the railway in 1912, the stage was set for the long-sought and eagerly-awaited flood of cotton.

For at least five years there had been a few sceptics. In particular the editor of the *African Mail*, E.D. Morel, deprecated the raising of inflated expectations and accusing Churchill, though not naming him, for "flights of rhetoric."[28] [Morel was a perennial gadfly for Churchill, defeating him "spectacularly" ten years later for the seat at Dundee in the parliamentary elections of 1922.][29] The main point of contention involved the fixed ld. per lb. B.C.G.A. buying price for cotton. Morel, correspondents of his newspaper, and even some government officials argued that this was very close to the prevailing price already being paid for cotton by the local weaving industry at Kano. Why expect an enormous extension of acreage with so little in the way of incentives for the farmer? Even Governor Bell had some doubts on this issue.[30]

The sceptics did not in fact attract much attention. The B.C.G.A. and the government officials concerned apparently felt that imports of Manchester textiles to Nigeria would make significant inroads into the market for locally-produced Kano cloth, thus lowering the home demand for cotton.[31] It had also been established that the fibre could be purchased at below ld. per lb. in outlying areas away from Kano and Zaria, and the expectation was that European buyers would simply travel to the smaller village markets and outbid the Hausa traders. Lastly, too much reliance seems to have been placed on the propaganda and influence being employed in Northern Nigeria—an error which was shortly to be made patently clear. Interestingly, one argument *not* made by the pre-1912 sceptics was that cultivation of the groundnut might in some way interfere with the plans for cotton.

THE NEW DEMAND FOR GROUNDNUTS

Groundnuts, native to the Western Hemisphere, were introduced to West Africa during the slave trade; it is said that their purpose was to supplement the meagre diet of slaves being shipped to the Americas.[32] The plant spread rapidly, and by the 1850's Dr. Barth found it widely used for food and oil.[33]

In the 1830's the nuts were being crushed commercially in France for their oil which was used as an ingredient in soap and for table or cooking purposes as a substitute for higher-priced olive oil. The Gambia began exporting nuts in 1830, with Senegalese shipments initiated in 1840.[34] In Britain, on the other hand, groundnut oil was little used and the sole attempt to operate a crushing plant for the nuts, in London, 1835, was apparently a failure.[35]

What we may term the "new demand" for groundnuts, which arose between 1906 and 1914 with profound effect on Northern Nigeria, came as the result of the manufacture of an entirely novel product—margarine. By the turn of the century two Dutch companies, Anton Jurgens and Van den Bergh (today merged in the giant Unilever combine) had captured most of the margarine market in Germany, the Low Countries, and Britain.[36] The trade was dependent for a long while on oleo, an extract of animal fat. Due to higher personal incomes and increasing public acceptance, consumption of margarine rose rapidly, more than doubling in Britain from 1906 to 1913, and up by two and one-half times in Germany from 1906 to 1914. An effect of this was that oleo prices rose dramatically (£18 per ton at Rotterdam in 1906, £62 in 1912).[37] The prices of several other fats and oils rose comparably during the period, focusing attention on the groundnut. At £11 per ton c.i.f. in 1906 and still only about £13 in 1912, the nuts were strongly competitive.[38] The fact that groundnut oil is a liquid at room temperature, with the solidifying process called hydrogenation not to be perfected until the mid-1920s, kept demand limited. Even so, margarine could include up to 20 or 30% groundnut oil, resulting in a boom for this article. Most of the new demand came initially from Germany, where crushing plants in the Hamburg-Bremen area supplied margarine factories in that country, the Netherlands, and Britain.

Unhappily for the proponents of cotton, the Kano area of Northern Nigeria was suited to grow the groundnut on an enormous scale. Light, sandy soils are a great advantage since harvesting involves lifting the entire plant out of the earth by hand. Such soils are present in much of Kano Province. The groundnut also needs at least 22 to 24 inches of rain during the growing season, and this too is almost always achieved in the region of Kano.[39]

With the completion of the railway, European trading firms began to set up agencies in Kano, the most important being the ancestor of today's United Africa Company, the Niger Co., Ltd. These firms brought with them the trade goods heretofore absent from the market or very high in price, which were in great demand among the Hausa population. Paramount were refined salt to replace the scarce and poor quality product obtained from Saharan oases, and cheap European cotton cloth.

There was absolutely no initial excitement over the groundnut—just a few passing references stating that they might be exported in the future.[40] Occasionally an author would refer to a list of potentially valuable products; we find ordinarily long pages or paragraphs on cotton, shorter references to hides and minerals, then perhaps groundnuts, sandwiched between ostrich feathers, acacia gum, shea nuts, and beeswax.[41] The Niger Company was far off the mark as far as oilseeds were concerned, concentrating on shea nuts and exporting nearly 9,000 tons in 1912.[42] As late as October, 1912, the suggestion was made for the first time in the Niger Company papers that a study be made of "the prospects of the groundnut industry" in the North.[43]

How was it that groundnuts were so long neglected? Five reasons stand out.

(1) The propaganda campaign for cotton of the B.C.G.A. and the Colonial Government had certainly played a role in distracting official attention from other crops.

(2) The largest and most influential trading firm in the North was deeply involved in its own pet project, the export of shea nuts.

(3) There was no groundnut crushing in Britain before the First World War. The processing mills and chief markets for the nuts were on the Continent, particularly in Germany, France, and the Netherlands. Thus neither British consumers nor millers tried to develop the trade.

Complicating matters, shipping to Europe from Nigeria was under the control of the "Ring" (Elder Dempster Lines and Woermann Linie) with practically all ships running to Liverpool or Hamburg.[44] Germany would therefore stand to be the chief beneficiary of a Nigerian groundnut boom, and with deteriorating political conditions, there was little here to excite the enthusiasm of Imperial patriots. Those members of Parliament and the government who were quick to support schemes for developing cash crop output when this was used as raw material in British industry (e.g. cotton) felt no sympathy for the idea of colonial groundnuts going to Germany.

(4) The table below shows that a rational argument, though disproved in the event, could be made to show that groundnuts would for the peasant farmer be an inferior income source as compared to cotton. These data on relative prices and yields were sketchy and often inaccurate, and their effect was, temporarily, to conceal the true relative position.[45] [The table assumes the sale for export of all output and ignores factor costs and local transport charges.]

Comparison between Cotton and Groundnuts Based on Estimates Prevailing before 1912

	Cotton	Groundnuts
Estimated yield per acre	300-350 lbs.	550-600 lbs. (shelled)
Price	ld. per lb. (B.C.G.A. official buying price).	Maximum £4.9.2 estimated (on basis of 1912 average European price of £13.0.4½ minus all costs of transport and trading margin).
Approximate gross return per acre	£1.5.0 to £1.9.2	Maximum £1.1.10 to £1.3.11

(5) The final reason for the neglect of the groundnut was lack of accurate information and foresight. In our table above, the contemporary estimates for cotton yields were over-sanguine, and we know that long-term average yields with traditional methods are about 250 lbs. per acre. Gross returns for cotton would have been perhaps £1.0.10, slightly less than the return received by groundnut farmers. Much more important was the failure to anticipate that, in the nexus of Nigerian traditional agriculture, cotton required more labor time and effort. Though even today there is little data available on this question, it should have been

foreseen that in the Kano area cotton needs deeper cultivation, more intensive weeding, and several more pickings compared to the ground-nut.[46]

In addition, there was failure to realize fully the risk element in cotton production. The Kano area is subject to periodic drought, with partial shortfall in the cotton crop to be expected about one year in every five. Groundnuts are less sensitive to reduced rainfall, and could be consumed in lieu of export should the output of other food crops be deficient.

THE START OF THE GROUNDNUT TRADE

The stereotype of sub-Saharan Africa as a land of subsistence agriculture at the most primitive level was perhaps never strictly accurate, but it is quite mistaken when applied to Kano Province. Long distance commerce and market trade had been important ingredients of Kano's relatively prosperous economy for at least 400 years before 1912. There are references to both the trans-Saharan trade, of which Kano was the southern entrepot, and to overland shipments of the kola nut, a widely-used stimulant, by the end of the fifteenth century. In the nineteenth century Kano market was one of West Africa's greatest, and the area had become well-known for its industrious farmers and enterprising traders, dealing mostly in dyed cotton cloth, kola, salt, cattle, and, until 1903, slaves.[47]

Agriculture and the marketing of food were sufficiently well-organized to provide for a population of probably 1½-2 million, including an urban segment relatively large for the era.[48] In some parts of the province permanent cropping with animal and green manure had replaced shifting cultivation, the technique of interplanting was firmly established, irrigation was used as were metal farm implements made by Kano iron-smiths.[49] In all, indigenous farmers were sufficiently skillful so that should potential sources of new income offer themselves, a reservoir of agricultural experience lay ready to be tapped.

It was the Hausa traders of Kano, however, whose quick appreciation of profit opportunities would perhaps have most to do with the establishment of the groundnut industry. Financial success was traditionally very highly regarded in Hausa society, and a large proportion of the population received childhood training in trade. Highly developed commercial relations long antedated the British hegemony. To overcome the economic problems of (a) the very long distances over which Northern Nigerian trade was conducted, and (b) the low level of working capital available to individual traders, a system of clientage was adopted.

Clientage usually meant a rich Hausa merchant at the head of a group of less well-to-do traders.[50] The latter would act as buyers or sellers on account, having been provided with a stock of merchandise or a supply of cash by the head of the clientage. The system was ubiquitous throughout Northern Nigeria.

The actual start of the export trade in groundnuts caused scarcely a ripple of comment, in contrast to the "frenzy" which swept Kano city only a few months later.[51] The first indication of a firm attempting to ascertain whether groundnut buying might be a profitable undertaking was recorded by the city's Resident in early 1912.[52] The initial decision of the firms to buy nuts is remembered by participants as quite routine. A price was established and the word was passed in the city market by interpreters. The next step was highly significant. Though details are fragmentary, it appears that several of the most well-known and prosperous Hausa merchants, each head of a separate large-scale clientage network, were sought out, particularly by the Niger Company.

In turn three or four Hausa merchants, entirely on their own initiative insofar as can be discovered, employed several measures to ensure that they would secure a suitably large proportion of the crop. These methods, which seem to have had the added effect of raising acreage to some extent, are especially interesting in that they show the importance of pecuniary values in Hausa society, and display the economic acumen of the Kano middlemen. Some of these practices of 1912 have survived, often in the face of opposition by the government and Marketing Board, and are a feature of the groundnut trade today.

The simplest tactic was propaganda. The merchants sent their clientage agents into the countryside with instructions to spread the news directly via village headmen and traders in village and hamlet markets. Generally, the agents argued that more cash could be obtained by selling nuts than by marketing cotton or staple foodstuffs such as millet or guinea corn. They went on to paint a rosy picture of the cloth, salt, and kola that could be purchased with the new cash income. A second method was to recruit the services of the village head via money gifts. The headman was then expected to popularize a particular clientage network at harvest time.

A third technique, often applied in combination with the two described above, was most efficacious. Agent-buyers were sent into outlying areas with donkey loads of imported salt and cloth. From the village head, given presents for the purpose, the names of a number of farmers thought to be hardworking and honest would be obtained. The agent would take his trade goods to the farm compound, where the farmer would be asked to grow more groundnuts in the coming season, to take them to Kano city or to a town market close at hand after harvest, for sale to the agent's patron. Meanwhile, gifts of merchandise would be handed over. (A system closely resembling the modern practice, officially frowned upon, of cash advances to farmers). Although in later years the trade goods and cash used for advances of this type were supplied to the Hausa merchants on credit by the European and Levantine firms, it appears that most if not all of the cloth and salt handed over to farmers in 1912 was purchased outright by the well-to-do heads of clientage networks. The tying up of limited capital in this venture speaks well for Hausa entrepreneurship, which, as we shall see, was soon to be rewarded.

Some Europeans were aware of this activity, others were not. A Niger Company report during the 1912 growing season states that "the cultivation of the groundnut continues to increase. . . ."[53] But the Resident, Kano, wrote in his 1912 report, "I do not think that any efforts were made . . . to extend the cultivation of [groundnuts] in anticipation of the increased demand."[54] This well illustrates the hazy idea on the part of the small European colony at Kano as to what the Hausas were doing.

Soon after the harvest, the Kano price for nuts was up to £6.0.0. This appears to have made it profitable for farmers to sell for export within a radius of about 90 or 100 miles from the railhead at Kano. In the last two months of 1912, the enthusiasm felt by farmers, middlemen, and trading firms alike reached a frantic pitch remembered today by everyone who came into contact with it. Competition among Hausa buyers was so fevered that demands were made to exclude them from Kano market.

The enormously successful efforts of the Hausa middlemen in securing large quantities of groundnuts led to a transport problem of near-crisis proportions just before Christmas, 1912. Nothing like this had been foreseen and, as J. E. Trigge of the Niger Company wrote, the merchants "were all surprised . . . to find the station literally buried in groundnuts; they poured them in. . . ."[55] The railway was not organized to handle traffic of this magnitude. Only one train a week running south had been thought sufficient, and this was now seen to be an almost ridiculous underestimate.[56] With bags of nuts accumulating on the streets of the European trading quarter at 100 tons per day and more,[57] choking the approaches to the stores and railway station, the authorities were forced to admit that "notwithstanding that there are frequently three and sometimes four trains each way daily, there is more freight being offered at Kano than the traffic department of the railway can cope with."[58]

E. D. Morel's newspaper, the *African Mail*, wrote that "A really quite extraordinary rush of traffic has taken the railway by surprise at Kano, as although it was fully expected that Kano trade would develop yet it was hardly anticipated that during what is practically the first full season of the line being really open for traffic, a trade in groundnuts alone would have sprung up which will undoubtedly severely tax the resources of the railway."[59]

By the last week of December, 1912, there were 3,000 tons of groundnuts at Kano awaiting shipment, with special trains being run south every
day.[60] Old photographs show bagged nuts stacked in the streets, ancestors
of the larger pyramids of today which form a notable feature of the
Kano landscape.

By January 1, 1913, only 674 tons had been railed south, and still
they poured into Kano.[61] Now the nuts were being referred to as an
"embarrassment,"[62] particularly since none of today's storage innovations relating to drainage, beetle-repellant sprays, or weather-and-vulture
proof tarpaulins were in use. According to A. S. Cooper, Managing
Director of the Railway, warnings were issued to buyers that no guarantee could be given as to when their stocks would be moved.[63] As this
occurred in February or March, 1913, and since at the current rate
evacuation would not be complete until well into the next rainy season,
the companies discontinued their purchases entirely.[64]

Thus ended the first stage of the groundnut boom. In all, before the
cessation of the trade about 6,000 tons had been purchased, almost
certainly representing the whole of whatever new acreage had been
planted at the urging of the Hausa agents and a portion of the crop intended originally for use as food. It is unfortunately quite impossible to
be certain of the tonnage produced for subsistence before the export
trade. [Even now, estimates of local use are very rough]. Therefore the
interesting question of whether the new acreage planted in anticipation
of increased demand was significantly large or not must be left unanswered.

1913: BUYING RESUMES AND PRICES RISE

When stocks had been largely cleared from Kano, probably about the
end of April, 1913, buying began again at the European stores.[65] But the
conditions were changing; whereas the c.i.f. price in Europe had been in
the £12-13 range during 1912, steadily increasing demand for oilseeds
and the favorable competitive position of groundnuts referred to earlier
caused an upward price trend from January on. By mid-year most Nigerian nuts were being sold for £17 in Europe, with a maximum of
about £18 reached at the end of the year.[66]

The effects of commercial rivalry soon caused this increase to be
passed on to Nigerian producers, and the Kano purchase price rose to
the level of about £10 per ton.[67] This great increase caused a second
flurry of excitement in the province. There was still some time before the
dry season ended and quantities of nuts were regularly brought in from
as far as Zinder in French Niger.

Some idea of the new effective radius of the trade can be gathered by
determining what the price was of groundnuts used for food just before

the trade began. Figures in the *African Mail* and the *Kano Province Report* make it fairly certain that it did not exceed £1.0.0 per ton.[68] With transport costs by hired donkey of not more than 1/- per ton mile, there was the possibility of attracting supplies to Kano from a distance of up to about 170 miles.

The new price of £10 was high enough to persuade most families to part with some of the remaining stocks of food groundnuts. When interviewed by the author, contemporary participants agreed unanimously that few nuts were eaten in 1913 following the price rise. A more accurate measure of this contention is impossible, but we know that even after the railway's backlog had been cleared, purchases and railings southward continued up to an additional 4,300 tons in all.[69]

A most significant manifestation of the Hausa farmer's economic foresight made itself apparent during this period of rapidly rising income, and concerns retention of seed. About 6 or 7% of the preceding crop must be retained for seed if the previous level of output is to be maintained.[70] In mid-1913, there must have been enormous economic pressure to sell all remaining stocks of nuts for cash, and the restraint necessary for husbanding seed must have been very great indeed. Surely it is remarkable that there is no indication whatsoever of any diminution of the next year's supply of seed. Quite the opposite, all available evidence points to a large increase in seed reserved and planted for the 1913-14 season, as we shall see below. The results of that season make it apparent that the Hausa peasant's ability to plan for the future was at a far higher level than commonly believed then or now. This lesson has continued to apply in Northern Nigeria, with increases in acreage caused by higher prices always necessitating prior large-scale seed retention and restriction of current income in the expectation of future returns.

THE NEW SEASON: 1913-1914

The time had now arrived for the hoeing and planting of the second export season. The large mass of farmers who had not put in an increased crop in 1912 had by now learned their lesson. Extra incentives were again provided by the agents out in greater force just before planting and during the subsequent rains.

By March of 1913, Resident Gill of Kano was already concerned that the forthcoming planting would be to the detriment of other crops.[71] The first rains of the new season fell in May (a normal amount, causing no fear for the future) and as is traditional farmers began their hoeing. Almost immediately it became clear that the Hausas of Kano had taken to the groundnut en masse, and on June 20 Gill telegraphed that "AN ENORMOUS INCREASE IN CULTIVATION OF GROUNDNUTS IS APPARENT AND EVERY POSSIBLE PRODUCER . . . IS

STRAINING EVERY EFFORT TO HAVE A SHARE IN THE BIG PROFITS ANTICIPATED."[72] Shortly thereafter he wrote, "From all Divisions a very large increase of groundnut cultivation is reported."[73]

This information is corroborated elsewhere. Resident W. F. Govers, who succeeded Gill in November, wrote that total groundnut acreage was a great deal more than in 1912,[74] while the B.C.G.A. noted apprehensively that "the natives have . . . taken up the cultivation of groundnuts on a large scale, and there is some danger of this competing with cotton."[75] In short, as stated in the *Bulletin of the Imperial Institute,* "the arrival of the railway at Kano has within eighteen months given tremendous stimulus to groundnut cultivation in the neighborhood. . . . Every available piece of land is being planted with groundnuts. . . ."[76]

No attempt was made to measure the magnitude of the new acreage, but the increase was probably limited by (a) the supply of labor (subsistence food production had still to be maintained by farm families, especially since widespread marketing of food in the wet season was not possible due to poor transport), and (b) the quantity of seed available. Land is not included as a factor restraint because, even close to Kano city where permanent cropping was commonplace, there would be little difficulty in expanding production via interplanting. The groundnut with its shallow roots draws on soil nutrients at a different level than guinea corn and millet; planted between them (and adding nitrogen to their benefit) a harvest of nuts could be obtained with little sacrifice of foodstuffs. Outside the close-settled zone around Kano, land utilization was less intensive and land was even less a restraining factor.

The release of labor which allowed an increase in groundnut acreage came probably from three sources: (1) some decline in leisure time, though it is not likely that this was very important. (2) A reduction in that part of millet and guinea corn output which had been grown to pay taxes. The sale of groundnuts immediately became the accepted way to meet tax levies, and before the end of the year Kano merchants were forced to buy grain from nontraditional source areas, prices doubling between 1912 and 1913.[77] (3) A collapse in cotton output. This latter point is explored below.

COTTON AGAIN, 1912-1913

With the railway permanently open, cotton buying was expected to come into its own. Free seed distribution was carried out on a large scale,[78] and at the 1d. per lb. fixed buying price some success was achieved in the Zaria-Katsina area, where about 3 million lbs. of seed cotton were purchased at the B.C.G.A. buying stations in 1912 (crop planted in the wet season of 1911).[79]

At Kano itself, however, the Association's high hopes were not being realized. A buying station had been opened when the railway arrived, but the fixed price was far too low and only 6 tons were shipped from the city during 1912.[80] The thousands of tons grown in the emirate and the additional tonnage imported from the Katsina region were, as the sceptics had warned, still being used to feed the looms of the indigenous weaving industry. Yet there was still no cause for alarm, according to contemporary publications. Supporters of cotton felt it only a matter of a short time before imports of Midlands cotton goods would erode the native industry, allowing the B.C.G.A. to capture the whole of the Kano area's output and its imports from other districts as well.

The unexpected popularity of the groundnut trade in 1912-13 dealt cotton what must be termed a shattering double blow. Higher personal incomes increased the demand for locally-woven cotton goods. Hence seed cotton prices rose considerably at Kano, making it possible for Hausa traders to outbid the B.C.G.A. in southern Katsina and Zaria, where conditions were not favorable for groundnuts. More importantly, farmers largely abandoned cotton on all but river bottom land and heavy soil within the area where groundnuts had become the most profitable export crop.

In quantitative terms, seed cotton purchases in the B.C.G.A.'s northern ginning area fell from the 3 million lbs. of 1912 mentioned earlier to 1½ million lbs. in 1913.[81] The B.C.G.A. was especially irritated that its free seed and propaganda had more or less gone to waste, and tried without success to enlist the government's services in obtaining the crop at below market rates.[82]

It was widely understood that Hausa traders were outbidding the Europeans for cotton. In a revealing letter of July, 1913, P.H. Lamb, Director of Northern Nigeria's recently established Department of Agriculture, wrote as follows: "I understand from the General Manager of the B.C.G.A. that their purchases . . . have fallen far short of his expectations, amounting to little more than one-half of the total bought in the corresponding period last year, in spite of the fact that the distribution of seed was on a far larger scale than was the case in the previous year." The Manager "ascribes the falling off very largely to the keen competition experienced through native buyers . . . paying a slightly higher price than the 1d. per lb. standard of the Association." Lamb continues, "Indeed the Resident, Kano, recently informed me that the great local prosperity occasioned by the sale of groundnuts was causing the native population to revert to hand-woven material in preference to the cheaper but less durable Lancashire cloth—a most interesting example of how one trade may react upon another."[83]

The retail price of seed cotton reached 2½d. per lb. at Kano,[84] and the B.C.G.A. found it impossible to match this.

Several months later, during the planting of 1913, it became clear that farmers were deserting cotton all over Kano Province. P.H. Lamb wrote in July that because "of the extraordinary development of the groundnut trade in the north during the past six months" and "the handsome returns which the ... crop yields, I fear we cannot look for any appreciable output of cotton from these parts." He added, prophetically, "The groundnut is destined to be a far more serious competitor of the British Cotton Growing Association than the Hausa trader."[85]

The Agricultural Department went on to announce that "so far as could be judged in 1913 the popularity of cotton cultivation was on the wane in the majority of districts." In its place could be found only groundnuts and grain, as these "in the majority of instances proved much more paying crops."[86] In the interviews conducted by the author in and around Kano, several Hausas remembered a substantial contraction in cotton planted that year.

The B.C.G.A.'s attempt to buy cotton at Kano thus became a complete failure, only 18 tons being railed south in all of 1913.[87] The buying station was closed down and the plan to construct a ginnery in the city was put in abeyance. For the Association, the *hajj* to the "Mecca of Lancashire" had been distinctly unprofitable.

By June of 1914, the Department of Agriculture was aware that the disappearance of cotton in the areas suited to the groundnut was having an even further effect on the demand for the fibre in Zaria and southern Katsina. The Director, P.H. Lamb, after noting that cotton had until recently been grown on "nearly every holding," adds, "I understand, however, that owing to the high prices now obtainable for groundnuts in Kano and the very favourable conditions for producing them, this state of things has been greatly modified."

"It is found now to be more profitable to grow groundnuts locally and to buy the required cotton further south."

"This creates a demand for Zaria cotton to feed the weaving industry of the north and is likely to have the effect of reducing the surplus available for export."[88]

In short, the B.C.G.A. found itself at a double disadvantage. It had taken just one year for the Hausa farmer to switch from cotton to groundnuts, meaning reduced supplies and higher prices for the former which had now to be acquired from those areas to the south where groundnuts did not thrive.

The reaction of the *African Mail's* correspondent to this alteration in the economy of Kano expresses the universal surprise, and will serve as a summary as well. "For years those of us interested in, or concerned with, this great country have been wondering whether it would prove itself an exporting country to any extent. We have looked upon cotton as the only possible export of any importance and we have been puzzled and anxious to know how the demand of the internal trade would square with the demand of the external trade. And all the time the country's riches lay at our very feet, in the blessed groundnut . . ."[89]

1913-1914: THE TRADE IN JEOPARDY

Perhaps the main reason why the initial impact of the groundnut trade has never been fully appreciated is that the season of 1913-14 was not, in spite of all the efforts of the Hausa farmers and middlemen, to be a successful one. Northern Nigeria was during this period to be hit by the most serious drought in modern history.

The groundnut needs a minimum of 22 to 24" of rain at the peak of the growing season, July to September. As we have seen earlier, the first rains of May, 1913, signalled a normal year, but several weeks later they failed. Only 13.48" was received at Kano as compared to 25.9" on average.[90] Not only was rainfall thus 48% below normal for the main growing season, it was 18% under the second worst year on record, 1949. The result was famine of unprecedented severity for Northern Nigeria in the twentieth century, with the estimate of deaths put at 30,000 for the province as a whole.[91]

Groundnut exports were naturally much diminished. Output was cut, and a large proportion of the harvest that was obtained was eaten instead of being sold to the European firms. Some nuts on the way south to the ports were halted and returned to Kano for sale.[92]

Thus the actual figure for exports in the second season of the trade, 11,915 tons on 16% more than Kano's shipments in the initial year, provides excellent evidence for the contention that a widespread shift to groundnuts took place during the planting of 1913.[93]

How much larger the level of exports would have been in a normal year is an interesting matter for speculation. In 1949-50, when rainfall in the growing season was 26% under the commonly accepted minimum for reasonable groundnut cultivation, the crop in the Kano area was 44% below the 1948-49 figure (the statutory export price had risen between the two seasons).[94] But with the situation much less favorable in 1913, the adverse effect on yields must have been far greater than it was to be in 1949.

For a decade after 1913 the Kano area exported on average about 40,000 tons of nuts per year.[95] Barring the drought and famine, it is quite likely that this figure would have been attained in 1913 as well.

NOTES

1. Among several noteworthy examples in the West African context see Polly Hill's *The Migrant Cocoa Farmers of Southern Ghana: A Study in Rural Capitalism* (Cambridge, 1963) and the late R. Szereszewski's *Structural Changes in the Economy of Ghana, 1891-1911* (London, 1965).

2. E. D. Morel, *Nigeria: Its Peoples and Problems* (London, 2d ed., 1912), p. 225.

3. John C. Atkins, *The Story of the British Cotton Growing Association* (Manchester, 1906), p. 13.

4. See, for instance, *Further Correspondence, 1909-1911* (African no. 953, C.O. 879/105, no. 15), p. 16.

5. Particularly informative on both taxation and land tenure in the Kano area of 60 years ago is the *Report of the Northern Nigeria Lands Committee* (1910 Cd. 5102) and its associated *Minutes of Evidence and Appendix* (1910 Cd. 5103).

6. The campaign is fully described in British Cotton Growing Association (hereafter cited as B.C.G.A.), *Improved Transport Facilities in Northern Nigeria*—Deputation to the Prime Minister, May 17, 1906 (Manchester, 1906?) *passim*.

7. B.C.G.A., *Improved Transport, op. cit.*, p. 39.

8. E. D. Morel, *Affairs of West Africa* (London, 1902), p. 190, shows that as early as 1902 Churchill headed the list of M.P.S. supporting the B.C.G.A.

9. *The Times of London* (hereafter cited as *Times*), August 24, 1907.

10. C. W. J. Orr, *The Making of Northern Nigeria* (London, 1911), p. 183.

11. Orr, *op. cit.*, p. 187; *Royal Niger Company Papers, 1888-1914*, I, p. 189.

12. See *Times*, April 20, 1909, and *Correspondence Relating to Railway Construction in Nigeria* (1905 Cd. 2787), p. 178.

13. *Further Correspondence Relating to Railway Construction in Nigeria* (1909 Cd. 4523), p. 24.

14. Leo Africanus, *The History and Description of Africa*, edited by Robert Brown, III (London, 1896), p. 829, and Henry Barth, *Travels and Discoveries in North and Central Africa, 1849-1855*, II (London, 1858), p. 10.

15. Morel, *op. cit., Nigeria*, pp. 234-38.

16. *Further Correspondence Relating to Botanical and Forestry Matters in British Tropical Colonies and Protectorates in West Africa 1914-1915* (African no. 1018, C.O. 879/115, no. 154), p. 69.

17. *Kano Report, 1911*, par. 109, and Morel, *Nigeria, op. cit.*, p. 239.

18. From an examination of crop yield statistics at the Kano Experimental Farm.

19. *BCGA Report*, 1909, p. 8.

20. Cd. 5103, *op. cit.*, pp. 104-05.

21. For the grants see *Kano Province Report for the Half-Year Ending 30th June 1911*, par. 202.

22. *Northern Nigeria Report, 1910-1911*, p. 8, and *Further Correspondence, op. cit., 1909-1911* (African No. 953, C.O. 879/105), p. 80.

23. *Northern Nigeria Gazette*, September 30, 1910, p. 220.

24. *Further Correspondence, op. cit., 1914-1915* (African No. 1018, C.O. 879/115), p. 68.

25. *Kano Province Report for the Half-Year Ending 30th June, 1911*, par. 200.

26. *Kano Report 1911*, par. 93.

27. *Lagos Standard*, April 29, 1908.

28. Morel, *op. cit., Nigeria*, p. 222.

29. *Encyclopedia of the Social Sciences*, XI (London, 1933), p. 10.

30. *Lagos Standard*, September 13, 1911.

31. *Times*, September 12, 1911.

32. Lord Hailey, *An African Survey* (London, 1957), p. 822, and C. K. Meek, W. M. Macmillan, E. R. J. Hussey, *Europe and West Africa* (London, 1940), p. 17.

33. Barth, *op. cit.*, II, pp. 432-33 and III, p. 334.

34. A. McPhee, *The Economic Revolution in West Africa* (London, 1926), pp. 36-37, and R. J. Harrison-Church, *West Africa* (London, 1957), p. 124.

35. McPhee, *op. cit.*, p. 37.

36. Charles Wilson, *The History of Unilever*, II (London, 1954), pp. 122, 131, appendices 2, 3, and 5.

37. *Ibid.*, appendices 8 and 9.

38. *Ibid.*, appendix 8.

39. The attributes of the groundnut are discussed in non-technical fashion in R. J. Harrison-Church, *op. cit.*, pp. 87, 122-24; K. M. Buchanan and J. C. Pugh, *Land and People in Nigeria* (London, 1955), pp. 130-39; and "Produce Goes to Market Nigeria: Groundnuts" in United Africa Company *Statistical and Economic Review*, September, 1949, pp. 4-5.

40. As for instance in the *Northern Nigeria Report, 1905-1906*, pp. 64-70, where Lord Lugard gives his opinion that Kano will be a major centre of cotton growing for export.

41. See Orr, *op. cit.*, p. 212.

42. *Royal Niger Company Papers*, I, p. 336.

43. *Ibid.*, XIV, p. 430.

44. For details of the "Ring," see Charlotte Leubuscher, *The West African Shipping Trade*, 1909-1959 (Leyden, 1963).

45. For cotton yield, see C. A. Birtwistle, *Cotton Growing in Nigeria* (Manchester, 1908), p. 18, and *Northern Nigeria Gazette*, April 29, 1911, pp. 95-96 (The figure given by Birtwistle is for cotton lint; a ratio of lint to seed cotton of 1:3 is employed).

   Groundnut yields are a more modern figure under traditional farming methods. There is no evidence that any observer thought these figures an underestimate. See U.A.C., *Statistical and Economic Review, op. cit.*, September, 1949, p. 11.

   In the absence of reliable information, the trading margin for GNS has been assumed to be the same as that published for cotton (12-½ per cent). See *B.C.G.A. Report, 1914*, p. 19. There is no reason to expect the GN margin to have been lower.

46. From information obtained at the Kano Experimental Farm and the Institute for Agricultural Research, Samaru.

47. See the translation of the *Kano Chronicle* in H. R. Palmer, *Sudanese Memoirs* (Lagos, 1928), pp. 109, 111, and E. W. Bovill, *The Golden Trade of the Moors* (London, 1958), p. 106.

48. The difficult question of census data for Northern Nigeria is covered by R. R. Kuczynski, *Demographic Survey of the British Colonial Empire*, I (London, 1948), pp. 561-70, 587 ff. For estimates of the population of Kano city and province, see *Kano Report 1907*, and *Ibid.*, for 1913.

49. Morel, *op. cit., Nigeria*, pp. 115, 234.

50. See M. G. Smith, *The Economy of Hausa Communities of Zaria* (London, 1955), p. 163 and elsewhere.

51. "The almost frenzied development of the groundnut trade" is the phrase used by Margery Perham, *Native Administration* (London, 1937), p. 101.

52. *Kano Report, 1911*, par. 92. The firm was Lagos Stores.

53. *Royal Niger Co. Papers*, I, p. 235.

54. *Kano Report, 1912*, par. 81.

55. *Report of the Committee on Edible and Oil-Producing Nuts and Seeds, Minutes of Evidence* (1916 Cd. 8248), p. 60.

56. *Northern Nigeria Report, 1912*, p. 28.

57. *Nigerian Customs and Trade Journal*, March 17, 1913, p. 168.

58. *Northern Nigeria Report, 1912*, p. 28.

59. *African Mail*, March 14, 1913, p. 238.

60. *Ibid.*, April 25, 1913, p. 300.

61. *Kano Province Report for the Quarter Ending 31st March, 1913*, par. 70a.

62. *African Mail*, August 1, 1913, p. 444.

63. *African Mail*, January, 1914, p. 136.

64. *Kano Province Report for the Quarter Ending 31st March, 1913*, par. 30.

65. *Ibid.*, . . . *Ending 31st June, 1913*, par. 55.

66. See the issues of the *African Mail* for January-December, 1913.

67. *Kano Province Report for the Quarter Ending 30th September, 1913*, par. 40.

68. *African Mail*, April 26, 1912, p. 294, and *Kano Province Report for the Quarter Ending 31st March, 1913*, par. 30.

69. *Kano Report*, 1913, insert, "tonnage railed from Kano."

70. *U.A.C. Statistical and Economic Review, op. cit.*, September, 1949, p. 11.

71. *Kano Province Report for the Quarter Ending 31st March, 1913*, par. 28.

72. "Kano Township," File 204 m/1913, Kaduna Archives.

73. *Kano Province Report for the Quarter Ending 30th September, 1913*, par. 43.

74. *Kano Report, 1913*, par. 80.

75. *African Mail*, January 16, 1914, p. 160.

76. P. H. Lamb, "Agriculture in Hausaland, Northern Nigeria," in *Bulletin of the Imperial Institute*, XI, 1913, pp. 633-34.

77. *Kano Report, 1913*, par 81.

78. *Further Correspondence, op. cit., 1912-1913* (African No. 993, C.O. 879/111), p. 155.

79. *Ibid.*, pp. 156-57.

80. *Kano Report, 1911*, par. 109, and *Nigerian Railway Report, 1912*, p. 114.

81. *Further Correspondence, op. cit.* (African No. 1018, C.O. 879/115), p. 68.

82. *BCGA Report, 1913*, p. 22; *Kano Province Report for the Quarter Ending 31st March, 1913*, par. 27; and *Kano Report, 1913*, par. 75.

83. *Further Correspondence, op. cit., 1912-1913* (African No. 993, C.O. 879/111), pp. 223-24.

84. *Kano Report, 1913*, par. 75.

85. *Further Correspondence, op. cit., 1912-1913* (African No. 993, C.O. 879/111), pp. 223-24.

86. *African Mail*, September 24, 1915, p. 514.

87. *Nigerian Railway Appendices to Annual Report, 1913* (Ebute Metta, 1914), p. 14.

88. *Further Correspondence, op. cit., 1914-1915* (African No. 1018, C.O. 879/115), p. 69.

89. *African Mail*, March 6, 1914, p. 226.

90. For the 1913 rainfall data, see the monthly issues of the *Northern Nigeria Gazette* for that year.

91. *African Mail*, May 14, 1915, p. 322.

92. *Kano Province Report for the Half-Year Ending 30th June, 1914*, par. 60.

93. *Kano Report, 1913*, insert "tonnage railed from Kano," and *Report on Kano Township for the Year Ending 31st December 1915*, par. 11.

94. See the *First Annual Report of the Groundnut Marketing Board 1949-50*, pp. 18-19.

95. See the annual reports of the Nigerian Railway for data.

4. The Influence of Colonial Policy on The Growth and Development of Nigeria's Industrial Sector

CARL LIEDHOLM

This study will examine the influence of British colonial policy on the growth and development of Nigeria's industrial sector during the period from 1900 to 1940. Since data on "construction" and "traditional" manufacturing activities are lacking, this study will focus primarily on the policies relating to the mining and "modern" manufacturing components of Nigeria's industrial sector. Before examining the impact of British colonial policy on this sector, however, it will first be necessary to describe briefly the mining and manufacturing activities in Nigeria during this period. This discussion is primarily designed to place the subsequent analysis in a proper perspective. The description of Nigeria's manufacturing activity is of particular importance, however, because the manufacturing component has been virtually ignored in previous studies covering the 1900-1940 period.

Mining

The Nigerian economy, unlike the economies of many of its African neighbors, was not built upon a mineral base. Although the fourth largest mineral exporter among Britain's African colonies prior to World War II,[1] Nigeria's economy was so well diversified that it was not dependent upon its mineral sector. Indeed, minerals accounted for only 16 percent of Nigeria's export earnings in 1935, while in Northern Rhodesia, Southern Rhodesia, the Belgian Congo, and the Gold Coast, mineral exports in 1935 amounted to 95, 80, 62 and 41 per cent of their respective export earnings.[2]

The Nigerian minerals of commercial significance prior to World War II were tin, coal, gold, columbite, silver, and wolfram. Tin was by far the most important mineral, followed by coal and gold, a fact clearly demonstrated by the following table:

TABLE 1. *Value of Mineral Production in Nigeria, 1936.*

	Value	Per Cent
Tin	£1,880,465	76.5
Coal	269,880	11.0
Gold	233,825	9.5
Columbite	49,531	2.0
Silver	25,499	1.0
Wolfram	636	—
	£2,459,786	100.0

CALCULATED FROM: P. Bower, *op. cit.*, p. 4.

In view of the relative importance of tin, coal, and gold, each of these minerals will be briefly examined.

Tin mining in Nigeria is of an ancient date. In 1884, the Niger Co. discovered that the tin used by Hausa for tinning their brassware was not being brought across the Sahara, but was being mined by Nigerians on the Bauchi Plateau of Northern Nigeria.[3] The exploitation of these newly discovered fields by non-Nigerian mining firms was begun on an extensive scale in 1910, due importantly to the promotional efforts of both the Colonial Government and the Champion Tin Fields Company.[4] By 1913, over fifty non-Nigerian individuals and companies had invested over £4,000,000 in the Nigerian tin fields.[5] The tin boom was assisted by the extension of the railway to the Bauchi Plateau in 1914.[6]

This expansion of the Nigerian tin mines, however, was undertaken exclusively by foreign-owned enterprises; indeed, by 1923, the indigenous Nigerian tin industry had completely disappeared.[7]

The Nigerian tin mining industry reached its pre-World War II peak in 1929. At that time, Nigeria, with an output of 15,335 tons, was the fourth largest tin producing nation in the world.[8] In 1931, however, Nigeria began to participate in the International Tin Control Scheme and output remained below the 1929 level until the outbreak of World War II.

The second important mineral of Nigeria during the period from 1900 to 1940 was coal. Coal was discovered in Enugu, Eastern Nigeria, in 1909 and West Africa's only colliery was opened in that city in 1915.[9] The colliery was owned and operated by the Government, and most of the output was sold to the Nigerian railway or to other government departments. During this period, the Enugu coal mines were capable of producing 400,000 tons per year. Since the supply generally exceeded the local demand, further prospecting for coal was prohibited by the Government.[10]

The final important Nigerian mineral commercially exploited during this period was gold. When compared with the gold-mining industry in the Gold Coast, the Nigerian gold industry was always in a "primitive stage" of development, primarily because the deposits were sparse and scattered.[11] Although the Nigerian gold-mining industry did experience some growth in the thirties, there was little capital attracted to the industry, and development was confined to a few small foreign-owned operators or enterprises.

Manufacturing

The modern manufacturing component of the Nigerian economy was extremely small during the period from 1900 to 1940. Several manufacturing establishments connected with the processing of agricultural products, however, were established at the beginning of the twentieth century. Three cotton ginneries, for example, were erected by the British Cotton Growing Association in 1907.[12] Three years later, mechanical palm kernel crushing mills were established at Apapa and Opobo.[13] The palm kernel mills were abandoned a few years later, however, and very few additional modern manufacturing establishments were subsequently established in Nigeria before World War II.

Even by 1950, the first year national income data became available for Nigeria, manufacturing still amounted to only 0.45 per cent of Nigeria's Gross Domestic Product.[14] In that year, the share of manufacturing in Nigeria's Gross Domestic Product was lower than that of any country publishing national account statistics.[15]

Although the data on the manufacturing sector are sketchy prior to World War II, a few statistics relating to the foreign firms operating in Nigeria are available. One of the few sources of available information is J. Mars' paper, "Extra-Territorial Enterprises,"[16] which examines the foreign non-mining firms operating in Nigeria prior to World War II. Mars' study indirectly reveals the paucity of manufacturing activity during this period. According to his analysis, only seven of the 102 foreign non-mining firms operating in Nigeria in 1921 were engaged in some form of manufacturing activity.[17] By 1936, the number of such firms had only increased to 11.

The results of Mars' study, however, must be interpreted with some degree of caution. His statistics on the foreign firms were obtained from the lists of companies in Nigeria included in various issues of the *Nigeria Handbook*, a source of limited accuracy as Mars himself admits.[18] The 1933 *Nigeria Handbook* notes, for example, that "there are no manufacturers in Nigeria on a commercial scale." However a large, commercially viable soap factory had been established in Lagos in 1924 and was still operating.[19] Moreover, one might question Mars' definition of "manufacturing" activity. He classified "motor repairs," and "building" as "manufacturing" activities. The United Nations, however, recommends that these activities be classified outside the manufacturing sector.[20]

Despite these limitations in Mars' study, the basic point remains that manufacturing activity was extremely small during this period. Even if one reclassifies the data according to the U.N.'s strict definition of manufacturing,[21] and includes several important enterprises omitted from the Mars list of eleven industries, there did not appear to be more than fifteen modern manufacturing firms in Nigeria in 1936.[22]

With this background, it is now possible to examine the Colonial Government's industrial policies and their impact on the development of Nigeria's industrial sector.

Government and Mining

During the period from 1900 to 1940 the Colonial Government owned all of Nigeria's mineral rights and possessed the authority to regulate and administer almost all of Nigeria's land. Most of these rights were obtained from the Royal Niger Co. in 1899 when its charter was revoked.[23] The Colonial Government thus gained at an early stage, not only the right to collect rents and royalties, but also the legal power to control the development of the Nigerian mineral industry.

The authority of the Colonial Government was formalized in various legislative ordinances. Through a series of Land Ordinances and Land Proclamations in both Southern and Northern Nigeria, for example, the Government clearly established the principle that land was not saleable to non-Nigerians without the Governor's consent.[24] Moreover, in a series of Mineral Ordinances, the first of which was introduced in 1902, the Government set forth the regulations concerning the disposal of prospecting and mining concessions in Nigeria. These laws and regulations have been summarized elsewhere and will not be detailed here.[25] By manipulating these laws and regulations, however, the Colonial Government was able to implement its policies with respect to the development of Nigeria's mineral resources.

The Colonial Government's mineral policy differed sharply from its agricultural policy. The Colonial Government used its control over the alienation of land to prevent the development of an extensive foreign-owned plantation system and thus preserve the land for the Nigerian farmer.[26] In the mining sector, on the other hand, the Government was quite willing to permit foreign investors to develop Nigeria's mineral resources. By 1929, for example, there were 144 foreign operators or firms mining for tin in Nigeria.[27]

The Colonial Government evidently believed that this policy was consistent with its doctrine of the "Dual Mandate."[28] Lord Lugard, Nigeria's first Governor-General, felt, for example, that such a mineral policy would not "deprive the natives of any customary rights or profits."[29] As Lugard stated, "Their discovery is generally due to the technical knowledge of alien prospectors, and the possibility of their exploitation usually depends on the scientific methods, and the use of machinery imported by Europeans."[30]

An examination of Nigeria's mineral legislation would indicate, however, that these regulations did discriminate against the Nigerian participation in the mineral industry. For example, the mining legislation stipulated that an applicant for a mining lease should have sufficient working capital "to ensure the proper development and working of the mines" and might be required to supply the Governor with "reports on the matter made by competent engineers."[31] Moreover, the regulations specified that if the owner of the mining lease were absent from Nigeria, the agent and engineer left in charge should be European.[32] Although the mining ordinances may not have been intentionally framed to discriminate against Nigerians, the fact remains that by 1923 there were no Nigerian entrepreneurs left in the mining industry.

The Colonial Government, however, did not permit all of Nigeria's minerals to be developed by foreign investors. Coal mining, in particular, was considered to be a government monopoly in Nigeria.

The differing policy with respect to coal could be traced both to the nature of the product and to the timing of its discovery in Nigeria. Coal, unlike tin, was to be used within Nigeria and the Government was to be the chief consumer. In addition, the Nigerian coal mining industry was developed during the First World War, a time when Government exploitation of coal resources was felt to be essential for strategic reasons.[33] The policies of the Colonial Government thus ensured that the Nigerian mining industry would be developed, not by Nigerians as was the case with agriculture, but by either foreign capital or the Government.

Government and Manufacturing

The official policy of the Colonial Government with respect to the manufacturing sector, on the other hand, is more difficult to ascertain. There appeared to be few legislative restrictions on the firms engaged in manufacturing. The commercial law of Nigeria, which was contained in the Companies Ordinance of 1922, did not even require companies to be registered in Nigeria before doing business there.[34] Moreover, no company income tax existed until 1939.

Although there appeared to be few legislative restrictions on these firms, the Colonial Government could still indirectly regulate them. For most of Nigeria, for example, the Governor had the power to regulate the disposition of sites for trading and manufacturing firms.[35] Moreover, by manipulating the structure of import and export duties, the Government could affect the viability of the firms and thus exercise a measure of control over them.

Although the policy was never made explicit, there is some evidence to indicate that certain types of manufacturing activities were actively discouraged by the Colonial Government. Indeed, this might partially explain why there were so few modern manufacturing enterprises in Nigeria.[36]

One of the domestic manufacturing industries that appeared to be actively discouraged by the Colonial Government was cotton textiles. In the 1930's, for example, the United Africa Company was "dissuaded by the government" from starting a spinning and weaving mill near the cotton area in Nigeria and a garment factory near Lagos.[37] Moreover, in the early 1950's, the World Bank Mission was compelled to recommend with respect to the numerous requests for permission to establish domestic textile mills in Nigeria that "proposals of this type warrant active consideration by the authorities concerned rather than the cool and overcautious reception which they appear to have received."[38]

The palm kernel oil processing industry also did not appear to be favored by the Colonial Government. Such a conclusion may be derived from an examination of Nigeria's export duty structure. During the 1930's, the export duty on palm kernel oil was £2 per ton, while that on palm kernels, the primary raw material for the palm kernel oil industry, was only 10s 6d per ton.[39] Moreover, on the basis of the average price for these products between 1935 and 1939, even the "ad valorem" duty for palm kernel oil amounted to 6.7 per cent while that for palm kernels amounted to only 4.6 per cent.[40] Thus, since the export duty was higher on the finished processed product than on the basic required raw material, there was a positive disincentive to establish a domestic palm kernel oil mill. The export duty structure explains at least partially, why, as Helleiner states, "large scale palm kernel oil extraction facilities were not successfully introduced into Nigeria, as they were in the Congo."[41]

One might speculate that the Colonial Government's actions with respect to manufacturing were traceable, at least in part, to an important keystone of British colonial policy, the desire to secure and preserve markets for British-made goods. As Joseph Chamberlain, Great Britain's Prime Minister in the early part of the twentieth century, noted, "The Foreign Office and the Colonial Office are chiefly engaged in finding new markets and defending old ones."[42] It was alleged that many individuals in the Colonial Office believed that the establishment of manufacturing firms in the colonies should thus be retarded, because these competing firms would reduce the market for British-made goods.[43]

It should be noted, however, that Lord Lugard did not feel that the development of manufacturing in Africa would reduce the Africans' demand for British-made goods. Indeed, he held the rather sophisticated view that it would "merely change the nature of their demands."[44] Nevertheless, Lugard also felt that "a Government would not be wise to hasten the advent of the factory in Africa."[45] Lugard's position was derived from his concern for the disruptive social effects that would accompany attempts to industrialize economies whose population was almost entirely agricultural. Lugard stated, for example, that "when trade is slack, with consequent unemployment, discontent will be rife, and there will be no lack of labour leaders eager to organize agitation on the worst models of the West."[46] The instability accompanying industrial development was thus felt to interfere with the Colonial Government's aim of maintaining law and order. For this reason, Lugard and his successors may have been rather cautious in permitting the establishment of manufacturing firms in Nigeria.

NOTES

1. "Mineral exports from Northern Rhodesia, Southern Rhodesia and the Gold Coast were larger. In 1935 for example, Northern Rhodesia exported minerals worth £5,094,000; Southern Rhodesia, £4,422,000; Gold Coast, £4,248,000; and Nigeria £2,124,213." Source: P. Bower, "The Mining Industry," in M. Perham (ed.), *Mining, Commerce, and Finance in Nigeria* (Faber and Faber, 1947), p. 1. Bower's chapter provides most of the basic data on the Nigerian mining industry prior to World War II.

2. S. H. Frankel, *Capital Investment in Africa* (London: Oxford University Press, 1938), pp. 231, 253, 293, 307, 321.

3. A. F. Calvert, *Nigeria and Its Tin Fields* (London: Edward Stanford, 1910), p. 13.

4. Allan McPhee, *The Economic Revolution in British West Africa* (London: Routledge, 1926), p. 57.

5. *Ibid.*

6. See Bower, *op. cit.*, p. 16.

7. *Ibid.*, p. 4.

8. Lord Hailey, *An African Survey* (London: Oxford University Press, 1938), p. 1501.

9. I.B.R.D., *The Economic Development of Nigeria* (Baltimore: Johns Hopkins Press, 1955), p. 411.

10. Hailey, *op. cit.*, p. 1502.

11. Bower, *op. cit.*, p. 30.

12. Jan Hogendorn, "The Origins of the Groundnut Trade in Northern Nigeria," see Chapter 3.

13. Charles Wilson, *The History of Unilever, A Study in Economic Growth and Social Change* (London: Cassell and Co., 1954), Volume I, p. 181.

14. Computed from data contained in P.N.C. Okigbo, *Nigerian National Accounts, 1950-57* (Enugu: Government Printer, 1962), pp. 20 and 79.

15. See U.N., Statistical Office, *Yearbook of National Accounts, 1964* (New York: U.N., 1965), pp. 457-460 and U.N., Department of Economic and Social Affairs, *Economic Survey of Africa Since 1950* (New York: U.N., 1959), pp. 16-17. Representative percentage figures for other African countries were: Belgian Congo, 11.8; Egypt, 8.6; Kenya, 10.8; Rhodesia and Nyasaland, 9.2. Some of the differences may have been due to the inclusion of small-scale industry in the data for other countries. Nevertheless, even if the value added for "crafts" is included in the Nigerian figures, the share of manufacturing increases to only 2.75 per cent.

16. M. Perham (ed.), *Mining, Commerce and Finance in Nigeria* (London: Faber and Faber Ltd., 1948), II, pp. 43-136.

17. *Ibid.*, p. 50. The majority of the remaining firms were engaged primarily in some form of trading activity.

18. *Ibid.*, p. 47.

19. *Nigeria Handbook* (Lagos: Gov't Printer, 1933), 10th edition, p. 125.

20. United Nations, Statistical Office, *International Standard Industrial Classification of all Economic Activities* (New York: U.N., 1968), pp. 45-46.

21. Divisions 2 and 3 of the International Standard Industrial Classification.

22. On the basis of an examination of the list of extra-territorial firms in the 1936 *Nigeria Handbook*, it would appear that there were eight enterprises engaged in the following activities: ginned cotton, lumber (2), aerated waters (2), cigarettes, soap, and boats. To this list of firms, one should add the Government Sawmill and Furniture Factory in Lagos (*Nigeria Handbook*, 1933, 10th edition, p. 114), the palm oil bulking plants of the United Africa Co. (U.A.C., *Statistical and Economic Review* [March, 1954] p. 33), and the four "mechanized," Lagos bakeries described in Peter Kilby's study *African Enterprise* (Palo Alto, California: Hoover Institute, 1965, p. 8). This list is still undoubtedly somewhat incomplete. It should be noted, however, that in the Gold Coast, in 1937, there were 13 such firms. Computed from: Gold Coast Government, *Gold Coast Handbook*, 1937.

23. To obtain these rights, the Government paid the Niger Co. £150,000 as well as half the royalties obtained from its former operating area. The agreement was to last for 99 years, but was redeemed by the Nigerian Government by a payment made to the U.A.C. in 1950. See Hailey, *op. cit.*, p. 1522.

24. In Northern Nigeria, the Land Proclamations of 1900, 1902 and 1910 established the principle; in Southern Nigeria, the principle was established in the Land Proclamations of 1900 and 1903 and the Land Ordinance of 1917. See McPhee, *op. cit.*, pp. 161-185.

25. For a complete description, see Imperial Institute, *Mining Laws of Nigeria* (London: Imperial Institute, 1937).

26. For an excellent discussion of this point, see W. K. Hancock, *Survey of British Commonwealth Affairs*, Volume 2 (London: Oxford Press, 1940), pp. 173-200. See also, C. K. Eicher, "The Dynamics of Long-Term Agricultural Development in Nigeria," chapter 1.

27. Bower, *op. cit.*, p. 21.

28. For a more complete description of this doctrine, see Lord Lugard, *The Dual Mandate in British Tropical Africa* (London: Frank Cass and Co., 1965), p. 348.

29. *Ibid.*, p. 348.

30. *Ibid.*

31. Mineral Proclamation, 1910, Section 14.

32. Mineral Ordinance, 1916, Section 22.

33. McPhee, *op. cit.*, p. 59.

34. For a more complete description of this ordinance, see Mars, *op. cit.*, p. 44.

35. In the South, for example, the Government would lease the land from the chiefs and then sub-let the land to the traders or manufacturers for periods ranging from 9 to 99 years. See McPhee, *op. cit.*, p. 167.

36. It should be stressed, however, that there were other important reasons for the lack of manufacturing activity in Nigeria prior to World War II. The lack of profitable investment opportunities in the manufacturing sector was undoubtedly an important contributing factor. Due to the lack of a skilled and disciplined labor force, for example, it was necessary to import foreign personnel at a very high cost. As Hancock noted, "the white man in the tropics was one of the most expensive of God's creatures." (Hancock, *op. cit.*, p. 193). Moreover, the small size of the Nigerian markets in relation to the minimum size of plant required for economic viability and the technical constraints on production imposed by the tropical climate, could also have limited the profit opportunities.

37. J. Mars, *op. cit.*, p. 74.

38. I.B.R.D., *op. cit.*, p. 387.

39. *Nigeria Handbook*, 1936, p. 67.

40. Calculated from price data contained in: International Institute of Agriculture, *International Yearbook of Agricultural Statistics, 1939-40* (Rome: Villa Umberto I, 1940), pp. 903-905. The palm kernel price was the delivered price in London, "in the hull;" the palm kernel oil price was the delivered price, in London, for refined and deodorized oil in barrels.

41. G. Helleiner, *Peasant Agriculture, Government and Economic Growth in Nigeria* (Homewood, Illinois: Irwin Co., 1966), p. 92.

42. Quoted in Leonard Woolf, *Empire and Commerce in Africa* (London: George Allen and Unwin, 1919), p. 7.

43. See, for example: *Report of the Indian Industrial Commission, 1916-1918* (Comd. 51 of 1919), pp. 245-300.

44. Lugard, *op. cit.*, p. 512.

45. *Ibid.*, p. 515.

46. *Ibid.*

PART TWO: *From Regionalism to the First Plan*

The period from 1950 to the launching of Nigeria's First Develop-ment Plan in 1962 includes two important political dates—1954 which introduced the Regional governments and 1960, the date of independ-ence. Nineteen fifty-four is of particular importance to economists because it introduced a new constitution which conferred "greatly in-creased fiscal and spending powers to the Regional Governments and converted Nigeria to a Federal system of government."[1] For example, the regions were given responsibility either wholly or concurrently for primary education, feeder roads, agriculture and modern manufactur-ing.[2] Moreover, the (National) Marketing Boards were transferred in 1954 to Regional Marketing Boards.

For the above reasons the six chapters included in Part Two focus on the transfer of substantial responsibility from the central to regional governments, marketing boards and their role in financing regional political parties, and the Ashby Report.

The 1954 World Bank Mission to Nigeria and their subsequent re-port of 1955 helped Nigeria define its planning and marketing board reserve strategy from 1954 to Independence.[3] However, since the World Bank Report is readily available, portions of it are not reprinted in this volume.

In Chapter 5 Berry and Liedholm analyze the overall performance of the Nigerian economy from 1950 to 1962. They point out that two of the most significant developments during the period were: 1) the emergence and subsequent rapid growth of the industrial sector and 2) the increased governmental participation in the economy. A large share of this increase in governmental activity was attributed to the regionalization of the marketing boards and development institutions and to the vigorous efforts made by the regions to promote economic development following the 1954 Constitution.

Charles Nixon, in Chapter 6, presents the results of his analysis of the Nigerian Federal and Regional Government's expenditures from 1950 to 1962. Nixon, a political scientist, utilized a functional method of analysis to trace the *actual* government expenditure patterns rather than expenditures which are promised by political parties or are pro-jected in a Development Plan. A functional analysis of expenditure is simply a method of tracing how the absolute and relative expenditures in a specific category such as agriculture change over time. Since expenditures in many categories are made by numerous ministries and quasi-autonomous agencies, e.g., Development Corporations, a functional analysis is of strategic value to economists because it supplements Accountant Generals' reports on how much money was spent by *all* ministries in a specific category or sector. For this reason, scholars have been unable to determine *actual* shifts in government development priorities over the 1950-62 period until Nixon's pioneering analysis. Previous functional analyses of the Nigerian government's expenditure patterns have omitted the expenditures of these semi-autonomous governmental institutions, despite their significant impact on the economy, and thus these earlier studies have provided a somewhat distorted picture of the government expenditure patterns in Nigeria.[4]

The marketing boards are the subject of the next two chapters. Since their inception during World War II, the marketing boards have controlled the local purchase and world market sales of all of Nigeria's major agricultural exports except rubber. Originally, the boards were established to assure a steady supply of raw materials to Britain during World War II and to serve as a mechanism for the orderly marketing of West African produce, the marketing of which had previously been controlled by a few large foreign firms.[5] After World War II, the stabilization of produce prices became the boards' major function, a function that received much scholarly attention.[6]

Gerald Helleiner called attention to the important fiscal role that the marketing boards were playing in the Nigerian economy in his *Economic Journal* article which is reprinted as Chapter 7. By maintaining a differential between the prices they paid to producers (or middlemen) and the prices they received on the world markets, the boards were able to accumulate trading surpluses, which were, in effect, taxes on peasant producers. Helleiner traces the evolution of official attitudes towards both the trading surpluses and their disposal; he then concludes by examining the efficacy of the marketing boards' fiscal role.

In assessing the performance of marketing boards, we should recall that the volume of Nigeria's agricultural exports grew at an annual rate of approximately 5 percent from 1950 to 1962,[7] even though the marketing board surpluses and other taxes removed from 20 to 30 percent of the potential producer income. Moreover, Helleiner notes that these trading surpluses were used for the most part to finance various types of development activities. Thus, it is not surprising that Helleiner concludes: "It can be unambiguously stated that Nigerian development has been aided through the device of channelling a portion of its export earnings via the marketing boards from the producer to other (governmental) decision-makers."

There are, however, several negative aspects of the marketing boards' fiscal role that are perhaps underplayed by Helleiner. The high "tax" on export and import substitution crops, for example, depressed the real incomes received by farmers producing these crops and thus served to widen rural-urban income differentials. This widening gap, which had been reinforced by the government's wage policy,[8] has served to intensify the rural to urban migration and the school leaver problems.

Additional evidence on the use of marketing board surpluses has been published since Helleiner's analysis in the mid-1960's. For example, the 1967 White Papers on the Northern Nigeria Development Corporation and the Northern Nigeria Marketing Board have called attention to the numerous examples of gross corruption and mismanagement in these institutions. The Government Committee investigating the Northern Nigeria Marketing Board, for example, noted that "the executive's incompetence and possible dishonesty has led to irrecoverable losses on a fantastic scale."[9] Correspondingly, the Commission investigating the Northern Nigerian Development Corporation, which has been a major recipient of the surpluses of the Northern Nigeria Marketing Board, concluded that of the twelve commercial projects wholly financed by the corporation "only one of them (The Tema Fiber Estate) is considered to be developing according to plan and to be worthy of every encouragement."[10]

In addition to the inefficient use of marketing board surpluses by government, it is also known that the marketing board surpluses have been used to finance regional political parties. Charles Nixon sketches the evolution of "The Role of Marketing Boards in The Political Evolution of Nigeria" in Chapter 6. In the light of the evidence available as of 1969, the fiscal role of the marketing boards is perhaps somewhat less impressive than Helleiner posited in the mid-1960's. Nevertheless, until the emergence of petroleum, as described by Pearson in Chapter 18, there was probably no effective substitute to the fiscal role of the marketing board for efficiently capturing a share of the agricultural surplus for use in financing structural change of the economy.

We pointed out earlier that the government greatly increased its role in the economy in the 1950's. In agriculture, the colonial government had restricted its activities in Nigeria until World War II to a limited amount of research and extension activities. However, after World War II there was fear by the colonial government that there would be a worldwide shortage of food, especially fat and oils. For this reason the colonial government selected Niger Province in Northern Nigeria as a site for a large-scale mechanized settlement scheme to produce groundnuts. (The Niger scheme is also often referred to as the Mokwa Settlement Scheme since it was located at Mokwa, a small village in Niger Province). The Mokwa land settlement scheme, which was liquidated in 1954 and subsequently turned into an agricultural experiment station in 1961, revealed that the resettlement of farmers on plots of 24 acres without adequate technical or social science research is doomed to failure. Since land settlements in Southern Nigeria and settlements in Tanzania, Kenya and numerous other tropical African nations are encountering many of the same problems common to the Mokwa scheme, we have reprinted as Chapter 9 the first and last chapters of K.D.S. Baldwin's important monograph—*The Niger Agricultural Project.*

Chapter 10 presents the conclusions and recommendations of the famous Ashby Commission Report (also called Investment in Education) on post-school certificate and higher education in Nigeria. Issued on the eve of independence, the report provided Nigeria with a logical and coherent strategy for its educational and manpower development even before it had a national development plan. Although the Commission admitted that its recommendations were "massive, unconventional, and expensive," the Nigerian Government not only accepted the report in principle, but even raised many of the Commission's targets upward.[11] An analysis of the Nigerian Government's implementation of the report as well as an evaluation of the current relevance of the Ashby Report's strategy can be found in Frederick Harbison's paper, "From Ashby to Reconstruction: Manpower and Education in Nigeria," which is Chapter 20 of this volume.

NOTES

1. Gerald Helleiner, *Peasant Agriculture, Government and Economic Growth in Nigeria,* (Homewood, Illinois: Richard Irwin, 1966), p. 33.
2. *Ibid.*
3. International Bank for Reconstruction and Development, *The Economic Development of Nigeria.* Baltimore: The Johns Hopkins Press, 1955.
4. See, for example, Nigeria, *Economic and Functional Analysis of Government Accounts 1958-59—1961/62* (Lagos: Federal Office of Statistics, 1964) and C. Nixon, "The Functional Analysis of Nigerian Government Expenditures, 1950/51—1961/62", unpublished manuscript.
5. For a description of the monopoly power exercised by these firms, see *Report of the Commission on the Marketing of West African Cocoa*

(the Nowell Report) Cmd. 5845, London: HMSO, September, 1938 and Sir Keith Hancock *Survey of British Commonwealth Affairs 1918-1939*, Volume II, Part 2, (London: Oxford Press, 1940), pp. 201-236.

6. P. T. Bauer in his classical work, *West African Trade* (London: Cambridge University Press, 1954), was the first writer to call attention to the accumulation and disposal of the marketing boards' vast trading surpluses (profits).

7. W. A. Lewis, *Reflections on Nigeria's Growth*, (Paris: OECD, 1967) p. 11.

8. In Nigeria, government minimum wage legislation determines for the most part, the wage scale for the urban economy. Government wages are established every few years by a commission of inquiry. For a description of this process see C. R. Frank. "Urban Unemployment and Economic Growth in Africa," *Oxford Economic Papers*, Volume 20 (July 1968), pp. 250-274.

9. Northern Nigeria, *A White Paper on the Northern Nigeria Military Government's Policy for the Comprehensive Review of Past Operations and Methods of the Northern Nigeria Marketing Board* (Kaduna: Government Printer, 1967) p. 11.

10. Northern Nigeria, *A White Paper on the Military Government's Policy for the Reorganization of the Northern Nigeria Development Corporation* (Kaduna: Government Printer, 1967).

11. Nigeria, *Educational Development, 1961-70*, Sessional Paper #3 of 1961, Lagos: Government Printer, 1961.

5. *Performance of the Nigerian Economy, 1950-1962*

SARA BERRY AND CARL LIEDHOLM

INTRODUCTION

During the first three decades of the twentieth century, the development of the Nigerian economy was shaped primarily by Nigerian farmers' and traders' responses to changing conditions in international markets. Agriculture and trading were the major economic activities; apart from handicrafts and mining, there was practically no industrial production in Nigeria.[1] The government played a conservative and essentially passive role in the economy; except for a few major outlays on transportation facilities, the colonial regime devoted itself to balancing the budget and trying not to interfere with the market system. After World War II, the production and distribution of agricultural products for domestic consumption and for export continued to dominate Nigerian economic activity, but the 1950's witnessed the beginnings of industrial devlopment and increasing government participation in nearly all sectors of the economy.

Available information unfortunately does not permit us to measure changes in the total level or the sectoral composition of economic activity in Nigeria with much precision,[2] although data on external trade and on the budgets of different levels of government and of various public corporations do reveal absolute changes in these particular activities. For example, exports of goods and services increased in value by 117 per cent between 1950 and 1962, while imports rose by 246 per cent during the same period.[3] Charles Nixon estimates that combined federal and regional budgetary expenditures tripled, in constant prices, during these years. (See Chapter 6.) However, our knowledge about private production for domestic use is much less satisfactory.[4] In particular, the estimates of domestically consumed agricultural output (which is generally believed to be the largest single component of GDP) are so unreliable that "one can have practically no confidence in the final absolute figures or annual changes therein."[5]

67

Hence "the Nigerian national accounts are not very useful for the purpose of gauging the level of aggregate economic activity or estimating growth rates thereof."[6] Similarly, one cannot attach much significance to estimates of the impact of rising levels of foreign exchange earnings or of government spending on the growth of aggregate output.

Although the Nigerian national accounts provide a poor basis for measuring the economy's aggregate rate of growth, they do constitute an interesting attempt to compile and quantify available information on the structure of the Nigerian economy in the early 1950's. In particular, Prest and Stewart's estimate of Nigerian national income in 1950-51, and Okigbo's *Nigerian National Accounts, 1950-57*, while they differ on both conceptual points and matters of fact, present broadly similar pictures of the composition of total product.[7] Both studies concluded that the Nigerian economy in 1950 was overwhelmingly agricultural, with agriculture, livestock, forestry and fishing contributing between two-thirds and three-fourths of GDP. They also assigned significant roles to distribution, although since this sector was treated as a residual it is difficult to judge the reliability of their ranking. Prest and Stewart ranked "building and civil engineering" as the next largest component of GDP; however, Okigbo's figure for this sector was much lower since he excluded all non-cement buildings. He ranked government (including net marketing board surpluses) as the third largest contributor to GDP. Both studies agreed that transport and communications came next and exceeded the combined output of mining, manufacturing, handicrafts and public utilities. In particular, the role of manufacturing in the Nigerian economy was negligible.[8]

In 1954, a World Bank Mission, which had visited Nigeria the previous year, proposed an "integrated development program" for long run economic expansion in Nigeria.[9] Although the Mission recommended a doubling of public expenditure between 1952/53 and 1959/60, their program was hardly a radical one: it envisioned neither rapidly accelerated growth nor significant structural change during the 1950's. Instead, the report concluded that it was essential to continue "strengthening the government services which will support an expansion of production."[10] In particular, it stressed the need for developing, through an expansion of educational facilities, a pool of skilled Nigerian manpower which would constitute the basis for Nigeria's future economic growth. It was also envisaged that other basic public services such as transport, communication, water supplies, and health would be expanded.

Accordingly, the report suggested that outlays on those basic public services, including education, should increase from 56 to 62 per cent of total government expenditure between 1952/53 and 1959/60. During the same period, expenditures on directly productive activities such as agriculture, industry, mining and power were only to increase from 15 to 16 per cent of total government expenditures.[11]

The government's development programs, however, appear to have exceeded the World Bank's expectations from 1955 to 1962. As Nixon shows, public expenditures not only rose faster than the Bank had proposed, but dramatic increases in government outlays on education and other basic services were to some extent balanced by rising expenditures on agricultural and industrial projects; thus, government spending did not favor the development of basic services over directly productive activities to quite the extent that the Bank had suggested. (See Chapter 6.)

The growth of public expenditures in Nigeria during the 1950's was greatly facilitated by the boom in world market prices for major Nigerian exports, which rose dramatically in the late 1940's and early 1950's.[12] Since, after the war, all of Nigeria's major agricultural exports were sold by publicly constituted marketing boards which kept producer prices substantially below world market prices, the prolonged price boom helped raise the revenues of the public sector as well as the incomes of the many farmers and traders engaged in producing and collecting export crops. Up until 1954, both public and private spending lagged behind the accumulation of foreign exchange earnings; the Nigerian balance of payments showed a surplus on both merchandise and current account. Thereafter, not only did the inflow of funds slack off, as world market prices for Nigerian exports stagnated or declined, but the rate of spending increased. From 1955 on, the Nigerian balance of payments showed a deficit on current account which consisted primarily of an excess of imports over exports of goods and services. The foreign assets of governments and semi-official bodies declined from a peak of £263.1 million on March 31, 1955, to £124.1 million on March 31, 1962.[13]

To understand the composition of government outlays and their relationship to the development of the economy, however, we must look beyond world market conditions and the aggregate balance of payments to the combination of political and economic circumstances which shaped both government policy and the pattern of economic activity during the 1950's.

Regionalization and Government Economic Activity

The increased pace of government spending after 1954 was associated with the transfer of substantial power from the central to the regional governments, a transfer effected by the Nigerian Constitution of 1954.

Not only did the 1954 Constitution expand the regional governments' responsibility for formulating and implementing economic policy in several areas (notably agriculture, education, regional roads and industry), but it also provided for substantial increases in the financial resources of the regions, both through the redistribution of government revenues and through the reorganization of the marketing boards and the public development institutions.[14]

As a result of the fiscal reorganization of 1954 (and subsequent modifications thereof), the regions' share of total budgetary revenues rose considerably after 1954. (See Chart I.) Much of the increase consisted of customs and excise duties collected by the federal government and then distributed to the regions according to the "principle of derivation."[15] At the same time the accumulated surpluses of the old commodity marketing boards were distributed to the new regional marketing boards, which were in turn responsible to the regional rather than the central government. The potential impact of marketing board surpluses on the regions' financial resources is suggested by Table 1. Finally, although most of the development corporations' funds continued to come in effect from marketing board surpluses, these funds now passed for the most part through the regional governments,[16] giving the latter increased potential control over development corporation finances.

TABLE 1. *Some Financial Resources of the Regional Governments* (£'000's)

Region	Assets Transferred from Commodity (National) to Regional Marketing Boards, 1955-60	Average Annual Current Revenue, 1955-60*
Eastern	11,464	11,742
Northern	32,652	12,804
Western	42,897	15,367

SOURCE: G. Helleiner, *Peasant Agriculture, Government and Economic Growth* (Homewood, Illinois: Richard D. Irwin, 1966), pp. 165, 286.
* Current revenue includes statutory transfers to the regions from the federal government.

The reorganization of the marketing boards and development institutions in the mid-1950's was accompanied by changes in the development expenditure policies of both institutions.[17] At various times during the latter half of the decade, each regional government announced its intention of employing marketing board surpluses primarily for development, rather than price stabilization. Moreover, the marketing boards continued to earn trading surpluses, although this necessitated reducing producer prices as world prices declined. Also, the development corporations began to expand the scope of their activities and to emphasize the development of large-scale agricultural and industrial projects, at the same time as the federal and regional governments were expanding outlays in developmental projects and facilities.[18] Thus, the combined resources of the public sector were, after 1954, increasingly directed towards modernizing and diversifying the economy. Nevertheless, as shall be seen later, the impact of the public sector on the growth and structure of Nigerian economic activity in the late 1950's was probably not very great.

CHART 1

Regional Governments' Share of Total Budgetary Revenues, 1952-1962

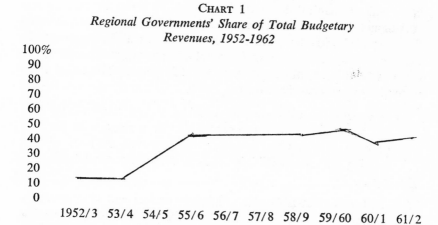

SOURCE: Calculated from G. Helleiner, *Peasant Agriculture, Government and Economic Growth* (Homewood, Illinois: R. D. Irwin Co., 1966), pp. 286-88.

Agriculture

Any discussion of trends in agricultural output and incomes in Nigeria inevitably concentrates on developments in production for export, since so little is known about the dimensions of production for the domestic market. Although recent research has begun to shed some light on, for example, the structure and volume of internal trade in foodstuffs, most findings so far relate to a single year in the mid-1960's and hence offer no basis for describing changes in agricultural output between 1950 and 1962.[19]

Spurred initially by soaring world market prices, Nigerian agricultural exports expanded rapidly during the 1950's. In fact, the growth in the volume of cocoa, groundnuts, cotton and rubber exported from Nigeria continued or even accelerated throughout the period under consideration, although world prices levelled off and/or declined after 1954.

This rapid growth of exports was accompanied by some important changes in government policy toward agriculture. Before World War II, the colonial government in Nigeria had confined its agricultural activities to a limited amount of research and extension work. Such programs were expanded in the 1950's, but in addition the government abandoned a long-standing policy and began to promote the development of large-scale agricultural enterprises.[20] In the south, these consisted of tree crop plantations;[21] in the north, the Niger Agricultural Project, a joint venture of the central government and the Colonial Development Corporation, sought to grow a variety of annual crops with mechanical methods.

Although increased government participation in agricultural production coincided with the rapid growth of Nigeria's agricultural exports, there is not much evidence that government plantations contributed to the growth of agricultural output during this period. The Niger Agricultural Project, conceived as

> an experiment in land settlement which incorporated a number of new methods which would provide a solution to the problem of combining modern and improved methods of farming with the traditional system of peasant land holding . . .[22]

failed both to attract a sizeable number of settlers and to demonstrate the superiority of "modern" over "traditional" methods of farming. With one exception, yields per acre never exceeded those obtained by local farmers, and revenue per acre was generally lower than the local average.[23] Total output on the Project's farms reached peaks of 199 tons of groundnuts in 1951 and 530 tons of guinea corn in 1953— obviously a negligible contribution to the growth of agricultural output in Northern Nigeria.[24]

Government-owned plantations in southern Nigeria did not fold, as the Niger Agricultural Project did in 1954, but they probably contributed little to total agricultural output from 1950 to 1962. Plantations were often located in response to the local political pressures, rather than in areas where the soil and rainfall were best suited to the proposed crops.[25] Planting proceeded slowly and was often ill-timed or improperly executed, so that some trees died and others' yields were reduced. And, of course, since most of the tree crops required several years to mature, those acres planted in the early 1950's did not begin to yield until the end of the decade. In 1958, the National Economic Council estimated that plantation output constituted less than 7 per cent of total export earnings for both Nigeria and the Southern Cameroons;[26] in 1961, plantations accounted for 5 per cent of the rubber and 3½ per cent of the palm oil exported from Nigeria.[27]

Thus, the sources of increased agricultural production for export during this period must be sought outside government owned or controlled plantations. Unfortunately there is little reliable data on increases in the acreage devoted to various crops during these years, and thus little basis for estimating changes in average yields.[28] However, there is some evidence that government programs designed to improve production methods for particular export crops may help to explain some of the increase in output. Beginning in 1956, the Western Region Marketing Board sold cocoa spray chemicals to farmers at subsidized prices. On the basis of farmers' consumption of these chemicals, it has been estimated that in 1962 between 115,000 and 230,000 acres were sprayed for black pod disease and 383,000 for capsids.[29] However, government efforts to train people in better methods of cultivation, tapping and processing of rubber probably had little effect on yields, although these programs reached over 50,000 persons.[30] According to one observer, the rubber improvement programs were designed to economize on trees rather than on labor and hence proved unprofitable to the average rubber farmer, whose chief cost is labor.[31]

In Northern Nigeria, farmers received cotton seed free from the marketing board; consequently, new higher yielding varieties were successfully introduced to most farmers growing cotton for export during the 1950's and are thought to have raised cotton yields during this period by over 20 per cent.[32] Also, the regional government built a number of "feeder" roads in groundnut growing areas which may well have induced farmers to extend the area under cultivation for export.[33] The regional government also successfully encouraged the substitution of mechanical groundnut decorticators for the traditional mortar and pestle; its efforts to sell fertilizer, on the other hand, were unsuccessful until it began to subsidize the price in 1961.[34]

In short, there is little reason to believe, at this stage, that government production replaced individual farmers' as the major determinant of observable trends in agricultural production for export during the 1950's and early 1960's. In the light of cocoa farmers' historical responsiveness to economic opportunity,[35] the substantial increase in cocoa output from 1957-59 on might just as plausibly be attributed to increased plantings during the post-war price boom as to the increased use of pesticides. Palm produce output actually declined in the late 1950's, as the marketing boards steadily reduced the price paid to producers. Without more information on trends in acres planted in various areas, it is impossible to weigh the relative contributions of farmers' response to changing market prices and of technical changes introduced through various government programs. However, even the effect of extension programs on output and yields may well have depended on farmers' economic calculations—as we have seen, there is evidence that rubber and groundnut farmers accepted those innovations in production techniques which proved profitable and rejected those which did not.

Industry

Although Nigeria's industrial sector—defined broadly to include manufacturing, mining, and public utilities—was extremely small and relatively stagnant prior to 1950, it grew very rapidly from 1950 to 1962. There were substantial variations, however, in the growth rates of the individual components of the sector, both timewise and between regions, and it is important to establish the reason for these variations.

The growth rates for the various components of the industrial sector can be ascertained from the following table:

TABLE 2. *Volume Index of Industrial Production (1957=100).*

Sector	1950	1951	1952	1953	1954	1955	1956	1957	1958	1959	1960	1961
Manufacturing	29	29	44	48	59	66	93	100	117	130	136	157
Mining	81	82	83	88	83	93	98	100	82	88	113	174
Public Utilities	41	42	51	59	63	75	95	100	116	124	151	228

SOURCE: O. Aboyade, *Foundations of an African Economy* (New York: Praeger, 1960), p. 134. These indexes were computed by Aboyade from the files of the Federal Office of Statistics. For manufacturing, 93 per cent of the value added in 1957 is included.

On the basis of these data, it is clear that the mining component was virtually stagnant until about 1960, when Nigeria's petroleum fields began to yield increasing amounts of crude oil. Public utilities, on the other hand, increased consistently during the fifties; indeed, from 1950 to 1961, utilities grew at a compound annual rate of 19 per cent, with the growth rate increasing sharply at the end of the period. Finally, manufacturing, which was virtually non-existent prior to 1950, also grew rapidly during this period, increasing at an average compound annual rate of 16.6 per cent.

There were substantial regional variations, however, in the growth of industrial activity in Nigeria. Although regional data are sketchy for all components of the industrial sector, it is possible to obtain some idea of the regional variations in at least the manufacturing component of the sector from the following table:

TABLE 3. *Regional Value Added by Manufacturing 1957 Prices*

Region	1950	1951	1952	1953	1954	1955	1956	1957
Lagos	767.7	1040.9	1594.2	1863.7	2074.8	2401.7	2893.7	2595.5
West	1921.9	1815.1	1795.7	2865.9	3700.9	3720.3	3724.8	3640.5
East	26.2	41.1	79.4	88.7	99.8	178.2	641.3	1713.5
North	408.7	221.5	346.8	389.8	571.9	926.3	2948.1	3091.8
Total	3124.5	3118.6	3816.1	5208.1	6447.4	7234.5	10207.9	11041.3

Computed from current price value added data in P. Okigbo, *Nigerian National Accounts, 1950-57* (Enugu, Nigeria: Government Printer, 1965), pp. 78-81. The constant value added figures were calculated by deflating the individual value added components by the implicit deflators used by Okigbo for each component.

In 1950, the majority of manufacturing activity was concentrated in Lagos and in the adjoining Western Region; indeed, these two areas accounted for 86 per cent of the manufacturing value added at that time.[36] From 1950 to 1954, manufacturing in all of Nigeria increased at a compound annual rate of 19.8 per cent, with Lagos and Western Nigeria still accounting for the majority of this growth.

From 1954 to 1957, however, the regional pattern of manufacturing changed markedly. Although manufacturing activity for all of Nigeria continued to increase at a compound annual rate of approximately 19 per cent, the most rapid growth now occurred in the Eastern and Northern Regions. The manufacturing sectors of Northern and Eastern Nigeria, for example, increased three and seventeen times respectively during this three year period. Lagos' manufacturing sector, on the other hand, increased by only 25 per cent and Western Nigeria's manufacturing sector remained stable during this same period.

The pattern of manufacturing growth in Nigeria during the fifties can be explained to a large extent by the changing role of the government with respect to the industrial sector. Prior to 1950, for example, the government did virtually nothing to promote development of this sector.[37] The Government did establish in 1946 a Department of Commerce and Industry, one of whose aims was "to accelerate the tempo of industrial development in Nigeria."[38] The 10-year Plan of Development and Welfare which was initiated the same year, however, envisaged that only 0.6 per cent of the total planned expenditure of £53.33 million would be devoted to industrial development.[39]

By 1950, however, the Government had become more actively committed to the development of Nigeria's industrial sector. According to Gerald Helleiner:

> the new interest was, to a great extent the product of the gradual transfer of governmental authority from representatives of the colonial power to Nigerians, who were, in general, far more anxious to attain rapid economic development, decreased dependence upon raw material exports, expanding urban employment opportunities, and 'modernity' for their economy.[40]

During the fifties, the Federal Government attempted to foster manufacturing activity, not primarily by establishing large numbers of publicly-owned and operated firms, but by providing incentives for private manufacturing establishments. In 1952, for example, legislation was passed that gave a 3 to 5 year income tax holiday to those firms engaged in "pioneer," or favored, industries.[41] In subsequent years, additional fiscal incentives were introduced, such as import duties relief, accelerated depreciation allowances, import duty drawbacks, and tariff protection. Moreover, the Government provided a number of non-fiscal incentives such as industrial estates, industrial and training research organizations and loan financing. Although the extent of their contribution is uncertain, these incentives, combined with the now more favorable "investment climate," contributed to Nigeria's manufacturing growth.

Another closely related factor explaining the pattern of industrial growth during the fifties was the partial transfer of responsibility for industrial development from the Federal to the regional Governments—a responsibility held solely by the Federal Government prior to 1954. The 1954 Constitution, which formed the basis of the pre-independence federal system, however, made industrial development and research "concurrent subjects." Although both the Regional and Federal governments thus had the joint legal responsibility for industrial development, the Federal Government, in fact, played a limited role in this sphere. The Federal Government, for example, admitted that "except in the Federal territory of Lagos, which is very small in comparison with the regions, a major part of government effort rests with the regional governments."[42]

With the regional governments thus assuming the major responsibility for industrial development, a keen inter-regional rivalry soon developed, as each region undertook extensive and vigorous efforts to attract firms to its particular area. Each of the regional governments, for example, sent economic missions abroad to attract both foreign and government investment. Other extensive promotional efforts, such as distributing elaborate brochures extolling the virtues of a particular region, were also undertaken.[43] This shifting of the responsibility for industrialization to the regions and the subsequent regional rivalry undoubtedly explains, to a large degree, the rapid spurt of manufacturing activity in both Eastern and Northern Nigeria after 1954.

Moreover, the ability of all the regions to assist in the financing of manufacturing activities substantially increased with the regionalization of the marketing boards in 1954. The funds of the regionally controlled marketing boards were now used, not only to assist the regional governments, but also to make loans and grants to both modern manufacturing concerns and to the regional development corporations.[44] These regional development institutions from their inception in 1949 to the mid-1950's devoted their efforts primarily to improving and diversifying peasant agriculture, to expanding the infrastructure, and to developing agricultural processing. In the latter half of the 1950's, however, they began to give greater emphasis to plantation agriculture and modern manufacturing.[45]

Although the government played an important role in stimulating the industrial sector during the fifties, it should be noted that much of the expansion was due simply to the increasing economic viability of industrial activity in Nigeria. The general growth of the economy after World War II, for example, increased the size of the Nigerian market and thus enabled those manufacturing enterprises requiring a large effective demand to become viable. Cement is an example of an industry whose establishment in Nigeria was delayed until the fifties because the Nigerian market was previously too small to support a plant of a viable size.[46] Moreover, during the fifties, the nucleus of a skilled Nigerian labor force was beginning to develop, thus reducing somewhat Nigeria's dependence on high cost, foreign personnel.

Infrastructure

Charles Nixon has calculated that between 1956 and 1962, about 20 per cent of the combined expenditures of the federal and regional governments and the public development institutions was devoted to transportation and communications. (See Chapter 6.) This figure does not include the operating expenses of the Nigerian Railway Corporation or the Nigerian Ports Authority—both federally owned corporations formed in 1955—but does cover their capital expenditures.[47] Thus, according to Nixon's figures, the development of transportation and communications facilities constituted the largest single component of public spending during this period.

Some of the principal developments resulting from these expenditures[48] were a substantial increase in road mileage (both tarred and untarred); the relaying of 400 miles of railway track and the construction of 400 additional miles of track into Bornu Province (completed in 1964); and the construction and improvement of numerous bridges and telegraph and telephone facilities. These developments not only laid the basis for rapid expansion of the transportation industry in Nigeria, but may also have facilitated increased production of other goods and services through the reduction of transport costs.

Trucking proved to be the most dynamic sector of the transportation industry during this period. The number of licensed commercial vehicles in Nigeria rose from 7500 in 1950 to 17,900 in 1958.[49] Despite substantial investment in both track and rolling stock for the railways, which were undertaken largely on the recommendation of the World Bank Mission, the National Economic Council estimated that the railway's share of total import and export traffic declined from over 90 per cent in 1948/49 to around 50 per cent in 1958/59;[50] most of this decline in the railway's share was absorbed by road transport. The increase in the proportion of freight hauled by road was no doubt partly due to the improvement of roads in areas not served by the railway; lorries also, however, offered faster and more flexible service. In addition, the railway's rate structure apparently failed to reflect the marginal cost of shipping.[51] In 1959/60, the Nigerian Railway Corporation actually ran an operating deficit for the first time in many years.

Other forms of social overhead facilities which expanded during the 1950's included electricity, airports and water supplies. Both electricity and air transportation are supplied by statutory corporations—the Electricity Corporation of Nigeria (ECN) and Nigeria Airways. The ECN expanded its output by over 400 per cent between 1951 and 1961; by 1956, the corporation was earning profits and financed some of its own capital expenditures thereafter.[52] The development of water supplies absorbed around 2 percent of combined government expenditures, most of which were undertaken by the regional governments.[53] Most of these water supplies went to satisfy household and industrial demand as there is little irrigated agriculture in Nigeria.

Education

In 1952, the Government of Western Nigeria applied to the Cocoa Marketing Board for a grant to build primary schools in the region. The marketing board rejected the application, on the grounds that primary education lay outside the range of development projects to be financed from marketing board surpluses. According to Chief Awolowo, then leader of the Western Region House of Assembly, "when my application was turned down, I threatened that I would agitate for the Cocoa Marketing Board to be controlled by the Western Region Government instead of by the Nigerian Government."[54] Whatever the importance of this incident in effecting regionalization of the marketing boards, it is clear that both the Eastern and Western Regional Governments were strongly committed to the development of primary education at the time their powers were expanded by the 1954 Constitution.[55]

Originally their goal was no less than universal free primary education for the entire region; later, difficulties in financing and staffing that many schools forced reduction in this goal. Nevertheless, both enrollment in and expenditures on primary schools increased dramatically, as Table 4 indicates. Between 1955 and 1962, the Eastern Region devoted between 37 and 49 per cent of its annual recurrent budget to education; in the West, and range was from 36 to over 47 per cent for the same period.[56] In the North, on the other hand, recurrent expenditures on education never absorbed more than 25 per cent of the region's budget during our period.[57]

TABLE 4. *Expenditures* on Primary Education and Primary School Enrollment in Eastern and Western Nigeria, 1952-1962*

Year	Eastern Nigeria		Western Nigeria	
	Expenditure (£'000)	Enrollment ('000)	Expenditure (£'000)	Enrollment ('000)
1952	1,059	519	1,034	400
1953	1,225	573	1,201	429
1954	1,283	665	3,668	457
1955	1,304	743	4,096	811
1956	3,893	904	4,082	908
1957	4,251	1,209	4,630	983
1958	3,201	1,221	4,612	1,037
1959	4,177	1,378	5,676	1,080
1960	4,912	1,430	7,281	1,125
1961	4,684	1,274	6,506	1,131
1962	4,168	1,267	6,200	1,109

SOURCE: A. Callaway and A. Musone, *Financing of Education in Nigeria,* Paris: UNESCO, International Institute for Educational Planning, 1968, pp. 15, 133.
* Expenditures include both recurrent and capital outlays.

In the short run, the rapid expansion of primary education in southern Nigeria contributed very little to economic development. Because of the acute shortage of trained teachers, the quality of education in

many primary schools was low. In 1960, the Ashby Commission found
that of the 80,000 primary school teachers in Nigeria

> nearly three-quarters of them are uncertificated; and among
> those who are certificated, two-thirds have had no more than
> a primary school education themselves. In brief, nine-tenths
> of the teachers in primary schools are not properly trained
> for the job.[58]

Moreover, there had been very little increase in secondary or higher
educational facilities, so that even qualified primary graduates might
have difficulty continuing their education long enough to assume technical, professional or administrative posts upon graduation. Unqualified
primary school graduates and those who dropped out before completing the primary course were not only unsuited for these occupations, but were frequently reluctant to take up less skilled and
correspondingly less glamorous ones.

> It was hoped that the literate primary school leavers would
> go back to be better farmers, carpenters, bricklayers, etc.,
> but all the pupils themselves want to be are junior
> clerks. . . . [59]

Because of these difficulties, the campaign for universal free primary
education has been criticized, in retrospect, as a "political" venture
which proved economically unwise and inefficient.[60] Certainly in the
short run, the expansion of primary schools made little contribution to
the Nigerian economy, aside from the dubious benefit of employing
large numbers of school teachers, and may have diverted public revenues from potentially more profitable projects. In the longer run, however, it might be argued that the attempt to offer primary education to
every child in the Eastern and Western Regions successfully stimulated
what Albert Hirschman has called "unbalanced growth." Insofar as the
very pace of expansion soon created intolerable strains which forced
the regional governments not only to stabilize primary school enrollment
and expenditures, but also to undertake vigorous efforts to expand secondary schools, universities and technical and teacher training facilities,
the campaign may have left Nigeria better able to meet her "high level"
manpower requirements in the long run than she might otherwise have
been. At least one observer who concluded in 1960 that "Nigeria has
not now, nor will she have in the next few years, the capacity to
generate the high-level manpower necessary to make rapid economic
growth possible . . ,"[61] could state in 1969 that *this* manpower problem had been pretty well solved. (See Chapter 20.)

NOTES

1. Carl Liedholm, "The Influence of Colonial Policy on the Growth and Development of Nigeria's Industrial Sector," Chapter 4 of this volume.

2. The uncertainty surrounding the population census of 1963 also makes it difficult to estimate *per capita* changes in GDP during the 1950's. See, for example, articles on the Nigerian census in J. C. Caldwell and C. Okonjo, eds., *The Population of Tropical Africa* (London: Longmans, 1968).

3. Trade data calculated from Gerald Helleiner, *Peasant Agriculture, Government and Economic Growth in Nigeria* (Homewood, Illinois: Richard D. Irwin, 1966), Table IV-C-1.

4. There were prior to the Federal Office of Statistics' assumption of this duty, two major attempts to estimate Nigerian national income. P. N. C. Okigbo, *Nigerian National Accounts, 1950-57* (Enugu: Government Printer, 1962), and A. R. Prest and I. G. Stewart, *The National Income of Nigeria, 1950-1951*, Colonial Office Research Studies No. 11 (London: H.M.S.O., 1953). Both studies are competent and imaginative but handicapped by the lack of information on many sectors of the economy.

5. Helleiner, *op. cit.*, p. 393

6. *Ibid.*, p. 394. There has been, in fact, a continuing debate over the aggregate growth rate of the Nigerian economy during the fifties. W. A. Lewis, for example, has recently argued that the economy grew steadily over the entire decade at a rate of approximately 4 per cent (See W. A. Lewis, *Reflections on Nigeria's Growth* [Paris: OECD, 1967], pp. 10-13). On the other hand, other scholars, basing their analyses on Nigeria's official national income statistics, have concluded that the economy did not grow at a steady pace during the fifties (See for example, W. F. Stolper, *Planning Without Facts* [Cambridge: Harvard Press, 1966] and G. Helleiner, *op. cit.* p. 25). They argue that the gross domestic product at constant prices grew at an average annual rate of approximately 6 per cent from 1950 to 1954, but at only one half that rate from 1954 to 1960. Much of the debate centers on the performance of the important, but difficult to measure "crops grown primarily for domestic use" component of the national income accounts.

7. There is a convenient summary of Okigbo's and Prest's sectoral breakdowns of GDP for 1950-51 in Helleiner, *op. cit.*, p. 390, which compares Okigbo's estimates both with Prest's original figures and with his figures adjusted for differences between his and Okigbo's definitions of the sectors. For discussions of both the conceptual and practical problems in the Nigerian national accounts, see Helleiner, *op. cit.*, pp. 387-94, and I. Eke, "Nigeria National Accounts—A

Critical Appraisal," *Nigerian Journal of Economic and Social Studies*, vol. 8 (November, 1966), pp. 333-360.

8. Indeed in 1950 Nigeria's manufacturing sector was one of the smallest in the world, if one considers manufacturing output as a per cent of total gross domestic product the relevant criterion. For the magnitudes involved, see Liedholm, *op. cit.*

9. International Bank for Reconstruction and Development, *Economic Development of Nigeria* (Baltimore: Johns Hopkins Press, 1955), especially Chapters 3 and 4. For an extensive criticism of this report, see P. T. Bauer, "The Economic Development of Nigeria," *Journal of Political Economy*, vol. 63 (October, 1955), pp. 398-411.

10. *Ibid.*, p. 34.

11. *Ibid.*, p. 79.

12. Helleiner, *op. cit.*, Table IV-A-9.

13. *Ibid.*, Table IV-D-1.

14. The fiscal and institutional changes involved in the 1954 rationalization of government economic activities are described in detail in Helleiner, *op. cit.* chapters 8-12. Cf. P. N. C. Okigbo, *Nigerian Public Finance* (Evanston, Illinois: Northwestern University Press, 1965), chapter II. Many of these changes were recommended by the World Bank Mission.

15. The "principle of derivation" is explained in detail in Okigbo's, *Nigerian Public Finance*, cited in the previous footnote.

16. Helleiner, *op. cit.*, p. 248.

17. The evolution of marketing board and development corporations policies is discussed in Helleiner, *op. cit.*, pp. 167-172, 250-253. For an evaluation of the political significance of these changes, see C. Nixon, "The Role of the Marketing Boards in the Political Evolution of Nigeria," Chapter 8 of this volume.

18. See C. Nixon, "An Analysis of Nigerian Government Expenditure Patterns: 1950-1962," chapter 6 of this volume.

19. A. M. Hay and R. H. T. Smith, "Preliminary Estimates of Nigeria's Interregional Trade and Associated Money Flows," *Nigerian Journal of Economic and Social Studies*, vol. 8 (March, 1966); R. Gusten, *Studies in the Staple Food Economy of Western Nigeria* (New York: Humanities Press, 1968).

    Several studies of the marketing of domestic food crops in each region of Nigeria, which were carried out in 1966 and 1967 under the supervision of the Food Research Institute, Stanford University, have recently been published.

20. Helleiner, *op. cit.*, pp. 250-252, 256-257; R. K. Udo, "Sixty Years of Plantation Agriculture in Southern Nigeria, 1902-1962," *Economic Geography* (October, 1965), p. 364; R. G. Saylor, *A Study of Investment in Oil Palm and Rubber Plantations* (C.S.N.R.D. Report No.

15), East Lansing, Michigan: Consortium for the Study of Nigerian Rural Development (August, 1968), pp. 13-14.

21. Before 1951 there were eight rubber and oil palm plantations in southern Nigeria—five of them owned by private expatriate firms. (Saylor, *op. cit.*, pp. 8-10a; Udo, "British Policy and the Development of Export Crops in Nigeria," *Nigerian Journal of Economic and Social Studies*, November, 1967, pp. 311-312.) During the next twelve years, twenty-seven more rubber and oil palm plantations and sixteen plantations growing other crops were established, principally by the Eastern and Western regional development corporations. Although plantation development started before the regionalization of agricultural policy-making in 1954, most of the expenditures on plantations were made after 1954, when the regional governments assumed control of the marketing boards. (Helleiner, *op. cit.*, p. 256.)

22. K. D. S. Baldwin, *The Niger Agricultural Project* (Oxford: Basil Blackwell, 1957), p. 21. A portion of this book is reproduced in the present volume, see Chapter 9.

23. *Ibid.*, p. 104.

24. *Ibid.*, p. 172.

25. The following discussion of government plantations in southern Nigeria is based on Saylor, *op. cit.*; Teriba, pp. 244-248; G. Helleiner, "The Eastern Nigeria Development Corporation: A Study in Sources and Uses of Public Development Funds, 1949-1962," *Nigerian Journal of Economic and Social Studies*, March, 1964.

26. Nigeria, National Economic Council, *Economic Survey of Nigeria 1959* (Lagos: Government Printer, 1959), p. 28.

27. Udo, *op. cit.*, p. 313.

28. Speculations on total acres under oil palm have always been based on assumptions about yield rather than *vice versa*, since much of Nigeria's palm oil and kernels are taken from wild trees scattered among other forest trees or farm crops. Essentially the same method has been used to estimate acreage planted in rubber, although Helleiner has also suggested that the substantial increase in export volume after 1955 was probably due to increased plantings in the early 1950's, since there was no apparent reason for a sudden increase in yields in 1955 and 1956. (pp. 121-122.) Even in the case of cocoa, for which we have the results of an extensive survey done in the late 1940's and early 1950's, there is no systematic record of acres planted since 1950. (Western Nigeria, Ministry of Agricultural and Natural Resources, *Tree Crop Planting Projects*, Ibadan, Government Printer, n.d., pp. 3, 16; U.N., FAO, *Agricultural Development in Nigeria, 1964-1980*, Rome, January, 1965, p. 53.)

29. *Tree Crop Planting Projects, op. cit.*, p. 13.

30. G. Helleiner, *op. cit.*, p. 123.

31. K. R. Anschel, "Problems and Prospects of the Nigerian Rubber

Industry," *Nigerian Journal of Economic and Social Studies* (July, 1967), p. 153.

32. Helleiner, *op. cit.*, p. 130.

33. *Ibid.*, p. 112; Nigeria National Economic Council, *op. cit.*, pp. 30-31.

34. Helleiner, *op. cit.*, p. 113; Nigeria, National Economic Council, *op cit.*, pp. 30-31.

35. Berry, "Cocoa and Economic Development in Western Nigeria, 1890-1940," Chapter 2 of this volume; cf. U.N., F.A.O., *op. cit.*, pp. 54-56.

36. Computed from Table VII.

37. The Colonial Government, in fact, may have actually discouraged the development of certain types of manufacturing activity. See, C. Liedholm, "The Influence of Colonial Policy on the Growth and Development of Nigeria's Industrial Sector," Chapter 4 of this volume.

38. Federal Government of Nigeria, Ministry of Commerce and Industry, *Handbook of Commerce and Industry* (1962), p. 27.

39. Government of Nigeria, *A Ten Year Plan of Development and Welfare for Nigeria, 1946-56* (The Nigerian Legislative Council Sessional Paper No. 24 of 1943), Lagos: Government Printer, 1946.

40. Helleiner, *op. cit.*, p. 311.

41. For a complete description of this fiscal incentive as well as others, see Samuel Suckow. *Nigerian Law and Foreign Investment* (Paris: Mouton, 1966) or Paul Proehl, *Foreign Enterprise in Nigeria* (Chapel Hill: University of North Carolina Press, 1965).

42. Government of Nigeria, House of Representatives, Sessional Paper No. 3, *The Role of the Federal Government in Promoting Industrial Development in Nigeria* (Lagos: Government Printer, 1958), p. 3.

43. See, for example, Government of Eastern Nigeria, *Investment Opportunities in Eastern Nigeria* (London: Whitefor Press, 1959).

44. See G. Helleiner, "Fiscal Role of the Marketing Boards in Nigerian Economic Development, 1947-1961," Chapter 7 of this volume.

45. Helleiner, *op. cit., Peasant Agriculture* . . . , pp. 250-56.

46. United Africa Co., *Statistical and Economic Review*, Volume 23 (September, 1959), p. 28.

47. We are defining transportation and communications to include expenditure on roads. The figures include expenditures by marketing boards and regional development corporations, but not statutory corporations such as the Railway or the Ports Authority.

48. Port facilities were also improved and expanded during this period, but the Nigerian Ports Authority financed most of its capital expenditures out of profits or by borrowing abroad, rather than from the government. Helleiner, *op. cit., Peasant* . . . , p. 301.

49. Nigeria, National Economic Council, *op. cit., Economic Survey*, p. 82.

50. *Ibid.*, p. 80. Stanford Research Institute, *The Economic Coordination*

of Transportation in Nigeria (Menlo Park, Calif.: S.R I., 1961), pp. 55, 59.

51. Stanford Research Institute, *op. cit.*, pp. 99-100, 102-104.

52. Helleiner, *op. cit., Peasant* . . . , p. 271.

53. C. Nixon, *An Analysis of Nigerian Government Expenditure Patterns, 1950-1962*, Chapter 6 of this volume.

54. Chief Obafemi Awolowo, *Awo: The Autobiography of Chief Obafemi Awolowo* (Cambridge: Cambridge University Press, 1960), p. 273. Cf. O. Teriba, "Development Strategy, Investment Decision and Expenditure Patterns of a Public Development Institution: The Case of Western Nigeria Development Corporation, 1949-1962," *Nigerian Journal of Economic and Social Studies* (November, 1966), p. 239.

55. See for example J. C. O'Connell, "The State and Organization of Elementary Education in Nigeria, 1945-1960," in H. N. Weiler, ed., *Education and Politics in Nigeria* (Freiburg im Breisgau: Rombach, 1964), pp. 188-210.

56. Capital expenditures on education were high up to 1957, then dropped sharply as construction of school buildings slowed down. Consequently, the share of total budgetary expenditures devoted to education in the Eastern and Western Regions was not so high as the share of recurrent expenditures.

57. A. Callaway and A. Musone, *Financing of Education in Nigeria* (Paris: UNESCO, International Institute for Educational Planning, 1968), p. 24.

58. Nigeria, Commission on Post-School Certificate and Higher Education, *Investment in Education* (Lagos: Federal Government Printer, 1960), pp. 4, 42. Cited hereafter as Ashby Report. A portion of this report is reproduced in Chapter 8 of this volume.

59. Western Nigeria, *Report of the Commission Appointed to Review the Educational System of Western Nigeria*, quoted in Helleiner, *op. cit., Peasant* . . . , p. 308.

60. Helleiner, *op. cit., Peasant* . . , pp. 308-309; Okigbo, *op. cit., Nigerian Public Finance*, pp. 171-179.

61. F. H. Harbison, "High-Level Manpower for Nigeria's Future," in Ashby Report, p. 63.

6. An Analysis of Nigerian Government Expenditure Patterns 1950-1962

CHARLES R. NIXON

Nigeria's six-year plan, 1962-68, is hailed as Nigeria's "first" development plan; indeed it is the first since the attainment of independence in
1960. The preparation of this plan was not, however, the first time
Nigerian governments concerned themselves with the problem of development or set long range goals to guide their day-to-day and year-to-year
activity. Nor was it the first time Nigerian political leaders, as distinct
from colonial civil servants, took a major responsibility for shaping the
government's role in development.

The Nigerian governments which issued and approved the 1962-68
plan had a past—a past in which they were concerned with and had a
responsibility for development. That past set a base line of achievement
as well as a political and administrative framework for development
which shaped the character of the 1962-68 plan. It is an examination of
that past to which this study is directed.

How can we summarize the development strategies of the past for a
country in which planning was elemental rather than sophisticated, was
largely carried out on a year-by-year basis, and in which governmental
responsibilities for development were not only fragmented among a
variety of government agencies, but steadily shifting from one set of
political decision makers to another? This is the context in which Nigerian development took place in the period 1950-62 and which conditions the kind of analysis of development policy presented here.

One way to summarize the development patterns of the past is to ask:
On what did Nigerian governments spend their money? Records of
governmental expenditures are a useful key to development patterns in
several ways. First, they do represent the actual commitments of governments rather than just promises of political parties or leaders.

Second, they also reflect not only the inevitable compromises among
possible alternatives urged by different political factions and interests,
but also the compromises between development objectives and the
constraints of a limited financial and executive capacity to which

governments are subject. In Nigeria, the gap between the promised governmental activity presented in the annual estimates and the delivered activity reflected in the actual expenditures was sometimes very substantial.

Third, actual expenditures, because they reduce various activities to common monetary units, provide a means of comparing the relative priorities given to these various activities and for identifying differences in these priorities—both differences of the same government over time and differences of several governments at the same period of time.

Fourth, because they provide a common unit of measurement, they make possible a comprehensive picture of overall development strategy at particular periods and a picture of changes in strategy from one period to another.

Fifth, this common measure makes it possible to sum into a composite picture the activities of several governmental units and the actions of several different sets of decision makers.

However, if one is to answer the question "What did Nigerian governments spend their money on," one must reorganize the data on expenditures in two distinctive ways.

First, actual expenditure data—available through the published reports of the accountants-general, the marketing boards and the development corporations—must be ordered in a way which is relevant to the analysis of development policy. This is done by a functional analysis of expenditures which distinguishes expenditures on *general services* such as defense, law and order and general administration from those on *community services* such as roads and water supplies, those on *social services* such as education and health, and those on *economic services* such as agricultural and industrial development. For a complete description of the activities within each category, see Appendix A.

Second, because the responsibility for financing various aspects of development is divided between the regular legislative appropriations, the marketing boards, and the development corporations, the expenditures of these various agencies need to be combined if one is to see the overall pattern of Nigerian expenditures on various aspects of development.

However, one should also be aware of some of the limitations of expenditure data as a key to development strategy.

First, the data on actual expenditures do not tell us why the government resources were allocated in this way. The pattern of expenditure is not an explanation of that expenditure. Rather, it is a picture which needs to be explained. Neither the economic, sociological or political factors which operated as constraints on policy making, the motives which led decision makers to make the choices they did, nor even a conception of the development strategy actually held by any individual person or any identifiable group of people are revealed by the pattern of expenditures which emerges from analysis of expenditure data. To get at these explanatory factors requires an examination and interpretation of other kinds of data.

Second, the data on actual expenditures do not tell us what was actually accomplished by the government in its efforts toward development. Was the money spent used effectively, constructively, productively? Did the government spend it in the best possible ways? Did the government and people get their money's worth for what they spent? These are also questions for which other kinds of information must be sought and interpreted if they are to be answered.

Third, the pattern of expenditure does not tell us the nature of the assumptions and the argument by which such a pattern could be justified. The formulation of the logical model which might have led to such a pattern may be stimulated by the evidence of the pattern and may be a useful exercise for revealing the policy problems expressed by the pattern of expenditure, but it is a hypothetical, imaginative and logical exercise which must draw on a range of theoretical materials which are not shown by the expenditure data itself.

In a sense it would seem that all the really interesting questions about development policy—Why was it adopted? What was accomplished by it? What are the theoretical implications of it?—are left unanswered by an analysis of actual expenditures. But though unanswered, they are not untouched. For basic to all of these inquiries are the questions: What did the governments of Nigeria actually do? In what sectors of development did they actually commit their resources?

Our interest here is in the general pattern of development policy in the years prior to the beginning of the six-year plan of 1962-68. In this period the spending agencies whose patterns are most relevant are the Federal and regional governments, the regional development corporations and the regional marketing boards. Though other agencies played important roles in the development process (agencies such as the Electricity Corporation of Nigeria or the Nigerian Railways), they either earned their own revenue and the accounts are best viewed as trading accounts, or they received grants or loans which came from or through the government agencies. Thus the additional investment in them is reflected in this analysis.

During the period covered here, government accounting procedures were changed from a single set of accounts for each agency under treasury control to divided sets which distinguished between recurrent expenditures, which include the personal emoluments (staff salaries and wages) along with normal operating expenditures of the agencies, and development or capital budget accounts including special expenses aimed at the development of new programs and activities. These were usually, but not exclusively, of a type which could be called capital expenditure—buildings or major equipment—but inasmuch as they sometimes included personnel and operating costs in starting new programs, they are not considered equivalent to "capital expenditure" in an economic sense and hence they are labeled "development expenditures." The expenditure for development purposes—as distinct from operating expenditures—made by the marketing boards and development corporations are all considered as part of the "development budget" when they are added to the accounts of the regional governments.

Though the distinction between recurrent expenditure and development expenditure was not formally introduced into the Federal and regional accounts until the period 1957-59, it was possible in the functional analysis of expenditure used here to simulate this distinction for earlier years by applying to those years the same principles which were used by the governments in restructuring their own accounts.

In the expenditure analysis presented here different terms are adopted to distinguish the types of information provided as follows:

1) "Recurrent expenditure" equals the expenditure included in the recurrent account reported by the Accountant-General.

2) "Development expenditure" equals the expenditure included in the development or capital account or simulated development account reported by the Accountant-General.

3) "Combined expenditure" equals the sum of the "recurrent" plus "development" expenditure.

4) "Composite development expenditure" equals the development expenditure reported by the Accountant-General plus the expenditure on development of the marketing boards and the development corporations or their equivalents.

5) "Composite combined expenditure" equals the sum of the "recurrent expenditure" plus the "composite development expenditure."

The government units treated are: the Federal Government, the Northern Region, the Western Region, the Eastern Region and Nigeria which treats the four actual governments as a single unit. The Accountant-General reports for each government cover the actual expenditures authorized by the annual legislative appropriations and subject to treasury control.

GROWTH OF AGGREGATE GOVERNMENT EXPENDITURE

A central aspect of Nigerian development policy in the transition period from colonial to independent status is the commitment to a great increase in governmental activity. The "combined expenditure" for Nigeria (Federal plus regional governments) increased from £24, 274,000 in 1950 to £165,173,000 in 1962. These figures exaggerate the real change because there was considerable price inflation in this period. If we adjust actual expenditure to a constant 1957 price basis (see Appendix A, Part B), however, and compare the growth of government expenditure to the growth of national income in this period, the very substantial growth of government expenditure is still clear, as the following table shows.

TABLE 1. *Nigeria: Change in Gross Domestic Product and Government Expenditure At Constant (1957) Prices (£ million).*

	1950	1962	Percent change (1950-1962)
GDP	688.7	1072.3	55.7
Government expenditures	34.7	137.1	295.10

SOURCE: Nigeria, *Digest of Statistics* (Lagos: Federal Office of Statistics 1965).

Thus "combined expenditure" for Nigeria grew at a rate more than 5¼ times the growth rate of the GDP. If we add the expenditure of the development corporation and the marketing boards to the government (treasury) expenditure, the growth of government expenditure would be even greater.

This growth of government activity was shared by both the Federal and Regional governments. But since the regions were only created as independent fiscal agents in the 1950's, the growth in regional activity was considerably greater than the growth in Federal activity as indicated by Table 2.

TABLE 2. *Nigeria: Growth of "Combined Expenditure" At Constant (1957) Prices (£ million).*

	1950	1962	Percent Change (1950-1962)
Federal Government	22,681.5	65,918.9	191
Western Region	3,067.6	27,692.8	803
Eastern Region	4,242.0	21,070.9	397
Northern Region	4,708.0	22,414.3	376
All Regions	12,017.5	71,178.0	492
Nigeria (All Regions plus Federal Government)	34,699.0	137,097.0	295

Again, the importance of the regions in this growth is even greater if one adds the expenditure of the development corporations and marketing boards, which were transferred from the central to the regional governments in 1954. It is worth noting that this probably represented a more rapid growth of governmental activity than any period of Nigerian development since 1910.[1]

When viewed against this increase in total spending in the period between 1950 and 1962, the projected increase in total spending envisaged by the 1962-68 plan appears as a continuation of an already established pattern rather than as a startling innovation. As the planners noted, the problems would be to hold down government consumption or to find the financial resources to meet the plan requirements.

PATTERN OF NIGERIAN GOVERNMENT EXPENDITURES, 1950-62

Whether the increasing expenditures for the period 1950-62 were spent wisely and productively is a question which cannot be answered directly. What can be examined however are the patterns of expenditure which were followed during the 1950-62 period as compared with the projected expenditures in the 1962-68 plan.

In presenting the patterns of expenditure during this period, a number of devices are used to simplify and summarize the data so that certain major aspects of the picture might stand out. Though the functional analysis of expenditure on which the tables are based originally used fifty-nine separate categories for the classification of expenditure as well as a number of summary categories, most of these categories were so small that they could be omitted.

A second device was to combine the expenditures of several years together. In the present analysis, the first period included the years 1950-51 through 1954-55, the second period 1955-56 through 1959-60 and the third period 1960-61 through 1961-62. The percentage of the total expenditure for the period spent on each type of service was then determined and used to present a picture of the priorities in expenditure for that period, and to serve as a basis for comparison of one period with another, as well as one government with another. Though this procedure has the disadvantage that our "priority" figures are not the actual percentage figures for any given year, it has several compensating advantages which seem important for our purposes.

To simplify the comparison by choosing selected years, e.g. 1953, 1958 and 1962 would be more misleading because of the highly variable nature of development expenditure. Recurrent budgets have a general pattern of steady incremental growth. New items are added, but relatively few are dropped. The development budgets, however, which provide largely for construction activity and capital expenditure, are of a different character. Once a building is completed, it disappears from the development budget. The next year quite different capital projects may receive priority. This high annual variability of development expenditure can be smoothed out by combining the expenditures of several years.

The particular grouping, 1951-55, 1956-60, 1961-62, was adopted for several reasons. First, these years correspond to the planning periods of the earlier five-year plans—periods during which Nigerian governments were shaping and reshaping the pattern of their own development efforts. Second, the fiscal year 1955-56 was the first full fiscal year in which the regions operated under the revenue allocations laid out in the Chick Report,[2] and agreed to at the Constitutional Conference in 1953. Thus the period 1956-60 shows the Nigerian federal system in full flower. Third, the years 1961-62 are the first years of sovereign independence for the whole country (though the Western Region and the Eastern Region had had internal autonomy since 1957 and the Northern Region since 1959). Thus, these divisions reflect significant points in the political and financial development of the country.

The third simplifying device is that in most tables "composite combined expenditure" figures are used. These figures include not only the recurrent expenditure and development expenditure appropriated by the legislature, processed by the treasury and accounted for in the Accountant-General's Report, but also the development expenditures of the regional development corporations and their predecessors and the development expenditures of the marketing boards. The administrative expenditures of these last two statutory boards and corporations however are not included. Thus the "composite combined expenditure" figures are designed to reflect the total development expenditure made by Nigerian government agencies from resources derived from taxes of various kinds, including marketing board profits.

If one adds together this total composite picture of the legislative budget plus the expenditure of the development corporations and the marketing boards, then it can be seen how Nigeria spent its money during these three stages of the period, 1950-1962. A simplified picture of the leading priorities is seen in Table 3. It lists in rank order all the specific and residual categories (omitting the summary categories) which received 2 per cent or more of the total composite expenditure.

If the percentage of the total expenditure is taken to be a measure

TABLE 3. *Nigeria: Rank Order of Priorities in "Composite Combined Expenditure"*

	1951-55		1956-60		1961-62	
	Type	Percent	Type	Percent	Type	Percent
1.	Education	17.1	Education	17.6	Education	16.4
2.	Trans. & Comm.	11.3	Other General	12.9	Trans. & Comm.	13.5
3.	Other General	11.2	Trans. & Comm.	11.9	Other General	12.7
4.	Other Unallocable	10.0	Other Unallocable	8.9	Other Unallocable	10.3
5.	Health	9.1	Roads	8.6	Roads	7.5
6.	Law & Justice	6.2	Health	7.0	Health	6.3
7.	Roads	5.8	Agriculture	5.9	Agriculture	6.2
8.	Agriculture	5.7	Law & Justice	5.3	Law & Justice	4.9
9.	Unalloc. Pub. Wks.	5.7	Unalloc. Pub. Wks.	5.0	Unalloc. Pub. Wks.	4.7
10.	Development Insts.	4.1	Defense	3.3	Defense	3.7
11.	Defense	3.2	Other Community	2.7	Water	2.5
12.	Water	2.2	Water	2.3	Other Economic	2.5
13.	Other Community	2.0	Other Economic	2.3	Other Community	2.3
14.	Other expenditures	6.4	Banking & Commerce	2.0	Other expenditures	6.5
15.			Other expenditures	4.3		
		100.0		100.0		100.0

of the relative priorities in development, then clearly the top priority
in all three periods was given to education and the second priority to
transport and communication. If roads were included as part of transport and communication, this category would equal or exceed the
expenditure on education.

Moreover, as shown in Table 3, there are few great shifts in the
overall priorities of "composite combined expenditure" over this
period of time. The most significant shifts which do occur are in the
relative growth in importance of transport and communications and
roads and a more modest rise in the expenditures on agriculture. The
most substantial decline is in the priority given to health.

The constancy in the pattern of expenditures is further shown in
Table 4. Economic services and social services together absorb over
half of the total composite expenditure with the social services showing a slight decline over the three periods analysed.

The relative constancy of these priority patterns in the "composite
combined expenditures" did not mean that each spending agency had
the same share of the composite budget and followed the same priorities
throughout this transition period. Rather, as we shall see in more
detail below, the changes which occurred tended to balance each other
off so that the net result was to produce this remarkably constant
overall pattern.

FEDERAL AND REGIONAL RESPONSIBILITIES

The major factor in the political development of Nigeria during
the period from 1950 to 1962 was the growth of the regional governments as semi-autonomous planning and decision making agencies with
substantial financial responsibilities. The expansion of their total expenditures has already been noted. What are particularly important in
examining the pattern of development and the problems of planning
are the areas of responsibility held respectively by the Federal and
the regional governments.

The constitutional division of responsibility is formulated by two
legislative lists: "The Exclusive Legislative List" of power to be exercised exclusively by the Federal Government and "The Concurrent
Legislative List" of powers to be exercised by either the Federal and/or
regional governments or both. Residual powers not on either list were
reserved to the regional governments. Many of the items on these
lists involve regulatory authority rather than responsibilities which require extensive expenditure.

The division of responsibilities outlined in the 1954 Constitution will
be employed here. The Exclusive List gave the Federal Government

TABLE 4. *Nigeria: Rank Order of Summary Categories of "Composite Combined Expenditures"*

SUMMARY CATEGORIES*

1951-55		1956-60		1961-62	
Type	*Percent*	*Type*	*Percent*	*Type*	*Percent*
1. Economic Services	27.0	1. Social Services	25.6	1. Economic Services	27.0
2. Social Services	26.7	2. Economic Services	25.5	2. Social Services	24.4
3. General Services	20.0	3. General Services	21.5	3. General Services	21.3
4. Unallocable	15.7	4. Unallocable	13.9	4. Unallocable	15.0
5. Community Services	10.0	5. Community Services	13.5	5. Community Services	12.4
	100.0		100.0		100.0

* See Appendix A for definitions of the summary categories.

95

sole responsibility for defense, aviation, railways, trunk roads, nuclear energy, maritime shipping and navigation, inter-territorial waters, posts and telegraphs, mines and minerals, and a number of specified institutions of higher education, including the University College at Ibadan with its teaching hospital and the Nigerian College of Arts, Sciences and Technology. Concurrent responsibility was extended to other higher education, industrial development, scientific and industrial research and water power. Agriculture, health, and education below the university level were not included on either list and therefore were reserved for the regions.

These legislative lists establish a distribution of authority; they do not establish a distribution of development priorities. The fact that industrial development is on the concurrent list does not mean that the Federal and regional governments made equal direct investments in industrial development.

In Table 5 a rank order listing is provided for each period of time for those services for which the Federal Government carried more than 50 per cent of the Nigerian expenditure and a similar listing shows those services for which the combined regions were responsible for more than 50 per cent of the expenditure. It is clear from Table 5 that the regional governments steadily expanded the number of areas in which they carried an extensive responsibility. We can define three levels of responsibility as follows: Primary responsibility when a level of government carried 80 per cent or more of the expenditure; large responsibility when a level of government carried 60-80 per cent of the expenditure; and shared responsibility when a government or level of government carried 50-60 per cent of the expenditure. On this basis, the Federal Government had primary responsibility only for defense, transport and communications and law and justice through all three periods of time, while the regional governments had primary responsibility for manufacturing and processing and water supplies through all three periods. Investment in banking and commerce which began as a primary Federal responsibility in the period 1951-55 had become a primary regional responsibility by 1961-62. Agriculture and education which had been largely regional responsibilities in the first period 1951-55 became primarily regional responsibilities in the second two periods, 1955-60 and 1961-62. And other economic services which was a shared responsibility of the Federal Government in 1951-55 became a primary responsibility of regional governments in the two later periods.

This information does not tell us where the development priorities lay, but it does give us some important insights into the structure of the Nigerian federal system and its meaning for development planning. To the extent that services were Federal responsibilities, commitments

TABLE 5. *Rank Order of Federal and Regional Expenditure As A Percent of Total Nigerian Expenditure For Each Category, 1950-62**

FEDERAL

1951-55 Type	Percent	1956-60 Type	Percent	1961-62 Type	Percent
1. Defense	100.0	1. Defense	100.0	1. Defense	100.0
2. Power	98.8	2. Trans. & Comm.	97.3	2. Trans. & Comm.	95.3
3. Trans. & Comm.	98.0	3. Law & Justice	84.2	3. Law & Justice	80.0
4. Banking & Commerce	81.9	4. Power	84.0	4. Power	76.9
5. Other Unallocable	81.3	5. Other Community	66.7	5. Other Unallocable	63.7
6. Other Community	59.8	6. Other Unallocable	58.5	6. Other General	52.6
7. Law & Justice	54.1	7. Roads	53.2		
8. Other Economic	52.2				
9. Unalloca. Pub. Wks.	52.2				

REGIONS

1951-55 Type	Percent	1956-60 Type	Percent	1961-62 Type	Percent
1. Mfg. & Processing	90.7	1. Mfg. & Processing	91.5	1. Banking & Commerce	97.3
2. Water Supplies	81.9	2. Agriculture	90.2	2. Water Supplies	87.8
3. Agriculture	76.4	3. Other Economic	86.9	3. Agriculture	85.2
4. Education	69.6	4. Education	83.0	4. Mfg. & Processing	84.9
5. Health	60.8	5. Water Supplies	81.4	5. Education	83.9
6. Other Soc. Ser.	58.9	6. Banking & Commerce	74.9	6. Other Economic	83.2
7. Roads	56.4	7. Health	66.2	7. Other Soc. Ser.	67.6
8. Other General	52.5	8. Other Soc. Ser.	65.4	8. Roads	67.0
		9. Public Works	55.6	9. Health	64.2
		10. Other General	55.1	10. Public Works	54.4
				11. Other Community	51.9

* The rank order is determined by dividing the Federal (or Regional) "composite combined expenditure" by the total Nigerian "composite combined expenditure" for each category. In addition it should be noted that the category "development institution" is not included in the table.

97

to them were made by a relatively unified and centralized set of decisions. To the extent that services were regional responsibilities, the overall commitments to them must be understood, not as a conscious set of unified decisions, but as the net product of a series of fragmented decisions. This fragmentation resulted not only from decision making by three different regional governments, but also from the fact that regional decision making was divided between three agencies, the regional government subject to treasury control, the development corporations and the marketing boards. Thus the commitments to manufacturing and processing, to water supply development, to agriculture, to education, and in the last period to banking and commercial activity and to other economic actions were widely distributed commitments whereas those made to defense, transport and communication and power development were relatively centralized.

PATTERN OF FEDERAL EXPENDITURE, 1950-62

There is an important difference between the location of responsibility for a service and the relative priority given to the service. The Federal Government may have 100 per cent responsibility for defense, yet this may have a low priority in the overall pattern of Federal expenditures. A picture of the major federal priorities is given in Table 6 which shows the rank order of all the specific and residual categories of expenditure receiving 2 per cent or more of the average annual expenditure by the Federal Government.

It is clear from Table 6, however, that the most important effort of the Federal Government was in the provision of transport and communication. Moreover, if the expenditure on roads is added to the expenditure on transport and communication, the total commitment would be 24.3 per cent in the first period, 33.3 per cent in the second, and 32.1 per cent in the third. Even if these figures are reduced by the revenue derived from post and telegraph earnings, the net roads-transport-communication commitment would be 20.8 per cent, 28.4 per cent and 26.6 per cent respectively.[3]

The Federal emphasis on transport and communications probably reflects not only the particular responsibility given to the Federal Government by the Legislative List, but a strong conviction that the strengthening of Nigerian unity would follow from improved communication and easier transport by both road and rail. In particular, the rise in expenditure on railways reflects the Federal Government's major single project—the building of the Bornu extension in an effort to open up the northeastern section of the country to the same kind

TABLE 6. *Federal Expenditure For Each Category As A Percent of Total Federal Expenditure*—Rank Order.*

1951-55 Type	Percent	1956-60 Type	Percent	1961-62 Type	Percent
1. Trans. & Comm.	19.8	1. Trans. & Comm.	23.9	1. Trans. & Comm.	26.9
2. Other Unallocable	14.6	2. Other General	12.1	2. Other General	13.9
3. Other General	9.6	3. Other Unallocable	10.8	3. Other Unallocable	13.7
4. Education	9.3	4. Roads	9.4	4. Law & Justice	8.2
5. Fed. Develop. Insts.	7.3	5. Law & Justice	9.2	5. Defense	7.7
6. Health	6.4	6. Defense	6.7	6. Education	5.5
7. Law & Justice	6.0	7. Education	6.2	7. Roads	5.2
8. Defense	5.7	8. Health	4.9	8. Health	4.7
9. Unalloca. Pub. Wks.	5.3	9. Unalloca. Pub. Wks.	4.6	9. Unalloca. Pub. Wks.	4.4
10. Roads	4.5	10. Other Community	3.7	10. Other Community	2.3
11. Power	2.8	11. Power	2.4	11. Power	2.2
12. Agriculture	2.4	12. Other Expenditures	6.1	12. Other Expenditures	5.3
13. Other Community	2.2				
14. Other Expenditures	4.1				
	100.0		100.0		100.0

* "Composite combined expenditure."

of economic development which followed the building of the railway in other areas in earlier decades. It is easy to argue that the single most important contribution which the British made to Nigerian economic development during the whole colonial period was the building of the railway which gave both the cocoa areas of the West and the cotton and groundnut areas of the North access to the international markets.[4] This took place of course before the advent of the lorry as a major transport vehicle. Whether in the 1960's and 1970's the railway extension is the most profitable or the most economical way to give a new area access to world markets is a debatable issue. However the objectives sought through the railway extension were certainly of great importance.

With the dominating position given to transport and communication it is not surprising that the provision of economic services ranks at the top of the summary categories for Federal expenditure. The relative priorities given to the major classes of services is indicated in Table 7.

What is somewhat startling, however, is the relative insignificance of all other specific economic services in the period 1956-60 and 1961-62. Only the supply of power, for example, rates as much as a 2 per cent commitment. Agriculture, manufacturing and processing, banking and commerce, and other economic activities accounted for only 4.5 per cent of the total Federal effort in 1956-60 and 3.6 per cent in 1961-62. If serious governmental attention was to be given to these areas of development, that attention would have to come from the regions.

PATTERN OF REGIONAL EXPENDITURE, 1950-62

The regions did give significant attention to a number of economic services which had been ignored by the Federal Government; but at no period, however, did economic services gain from the regions the high priority given them by the Federal Government. Where transport and communications had been the primary thrust of Federal development policy, education was clearly the dominant priority in regional development policies.

The regional commitments for all regions are seen in Table 8 which shows the rank order of specific and residual categories receiving 2 per cent or more of the total regional "composite combined expenditure" for each of the periods.

The most significant changes are the disappearance of law and justice from the list after responsibility for the police was transferred

TABLE 7. *Federal Expenditure Patterns By Summary Categories, 1951-62.*

1951-55		1956-60		1961-62	
Type of Service	Percent	Type of Service	Percent	Type of Service	Percent
1. Economic Services	35.4	1. Economic Services	30.9	1. Economic Services	32.8
2. General Services	21.2	2. General Services	28.0	2. General Services	27.8
3. Unallocable	19.9	3. Unallocable	15.4	3. Unallocable	18.1
4. Social Services	16.0	4. Community Services	14.0	4. Social Services	11.2
5. Community Services	7.4	5. Social Services	11.7	5. Community Services	8.1
	100.0				

TABLE 8. *Regional Expenditure (All Regions) for Each Category As A Percent of Total Regional Expenditure, 1951-62.*

1951-55		1955-60		1961-62	
Type	Percent	Type	Percent	Type	Percent
1. Education	26.9	1. Education	28.4	1. Education	26.4
2. Other General	13.3	2. Other General	13.9	2. Other General	11.5
3. Health	12.6	3. Agriculture	10.2	3. Agriculture	10.1
4. Agriculture	9.9	4. Health	9.0	4. Roads	9.7
5. Roads	7.4	5. Roads	7.8	5. Health	7.8
6. Law & Justice	6.4	6. Other Unallocable	7.1	6. Other Unallocable	7.2
7. Unalloca. Pub. Wks.	6.2	7. Unalloca. Pub. Wks.	5.4	7. Unalloca. Pub. Wks.	4.9
8. Other Unallocable	4.2	8. Other Economic	3.9	8. Water	4.2
9. Water	4.1	9. Water	3.6	9. Other Economic	4.0
10. Mfg. & Processing	3.7	10. Banking & Commerce	3.9	10. Banking & Commerce	3.0
11. Other expenditures	5.3	11. Mfg. & Processing	2.3	11. Mfg. & Processing	2.7
		12. Other expenditures	5.5	12. Other Community	2.3
				13. Other expenditures	6.2
	100.0		100.0		100.0

to the Federal Government; the steady decline in attention given to health from 12.6 per cent in 1951-55 to 7.8 per cent in 1961-62; and the shift of banking and commerce and other economic services from below to above 2 per cent.

Though agriculture was always the most important of the economic services supported by the regions, the level of commitment to it by all the regions remained fairly constant. The increase in total economic services came largely from the increases in banking and commerce and other economic services which, though still small, did become part of the pattern of significant expenditure.

As Table 9 shows, the social services, though they are always the top priority, are subject to a steady decline as are the general services whereas economic services enjoy a steady increase in priority.

Just as the pattern for combined Nigeria gave a somewhat misleading picture of the constancy of the country's commitments, so the pattern of expenditures for all the regions hides a considerable variation between regions and within each region over time. The pattern of each region's rank order of priorities is indicated in Table 10.

A comparison of the development of regional policies reveals some striking contrasts. In the Western Region education has by far the greatest commitment throughout the period from 1950 to 1962. But despite this the percentage of resources devoted to education declined from the first period to the second and from the second period to the third. On the other hand the commitment to agriculture which ranks fourth in 1951-55 is raised to second place in 1961-62, and its relation to educational expenditure is changed from being only 21 per cent of expenditure on education in 1951-55, to being nearly half of the educational expenditure in 1961-62.

In the Northern Region on the other hand the changes over time are made in the opposite direction. Though education is always given a higher priority than agriculture, they tend to diverge over time, with education steadily increasing in its importance and agriculture declining. Where agriculture gets 81 per cent of the amount spent on education in 1951-55, it gets only 46 per cent in 1961-62.

The Eastern Region shows a pattern distinct from either the West or the North. The commitment to education rises sharply from the first to the second period and then falls nearly as sharply again from the second period to the third. Agriculture drops off from 8.3 per cent in the first period to 5.7 per cent in the second, but remains nearly constant at 5.6 per cent for the third period.

These variations suggest fundamental policy differences between the regions as well as considerable revision of policy within the regions.

TABLE 9. *Regional Expenditure (All Regions) Patterns By Summary Categories, 1951-62.*

| 1951-55 | | 1956-60 | | 1961-62 | |
Type	Percent	Type	Percent	Type	Percent
1. Social Services	40.1	1. Social Services	38.5	1. Social Services	36.5
2. General Services	19.8	2. Economic Services	20.4	2. Economic Services	21.7
3. Economic Services	16.4	3. General Services	15.5	3. Community Services	16.3
4. Community Services	13.3	4. Community Services	13.0	4. General Services	13.4
5. Unallocable	10.4	5. Unallocable	12.6	5. Unallocable	12.1
	100.0		100.0		100.0

TABLE 10. *Regional Expenditures For Each Category As A Percent of Total Regional Expenditures, 1951-62.*

Type	1951-55 Percent	Type	1956-60 Percent	Type	1961-62 Percent
		WESTERN REGION			
1. Education	35.1	1. Education	31.2	1. Education	26.9
2. Other General	10.0	2. Agriculture	12.7	2. Agriculture	13.0
3. Health	9.8	3. Other General	12.7	3. Roads	9.9
4. Agriculture	7.5	4. Health	7.7	4. Other General	8.8
5. Roads	7.4	5. Other Economic	7.1	5. Health	6.9
6. Law & Justice	6.2	6. Roads	6.2	6. Other Economic	5.2
7. Unalloca. Pub. Wks.	6.2	7. Other Unallocable	4.6	7. Other Unallocable	4.6
8. Mfg. & Processing	5.2	8. Unalloca. Pub. Wks.	4.5	8. Water	4.5
9. Other Economic	3.6	9. Water	2.7	9. Unalloca. Pub. Wks.	4.5
10. Other Unallocable	3.6	10. Banking & Commerce	2.7	10. Other Social	3.5
11. Water	3.0	11. Mfg. & Processing	2.2	11. Banking & Commerce	3.3
12. Other expenditures	2.5	12. Other expenditures	5.7	12. Mfg. & Processing	2.9
				13. Other Community	2.7
				14. Other expenditures	3.3
	100.0		100.0		100.0
		EASTERN REGION			
1. Education	29.4	1. Education	38.2	1. Education	30.5
2. Health	14.2	2. Other General	12.0	2. Other General	13.7
3. Other General	13.0	3. Other Unallocable	11.3	3. Roads	8.5

4. Agriculture — 8.3
5. Law & Justice — 7.4
6. Roads — 5.9
7. Unalloca. Pub. Wks. — 5.5
8. Mfg. & Processing — 5.3
9. Other Unalloca. — 3.6
10. Other community — 2.9
11. Water — 2.2
12. Other expenditures — 2.3

100.0

1. Other General — 16.9
2. Education — 16.7
3. Health — 14.2
4. Agriculture — 13.6
5. Roads — 8.4
6. Unalloca. Pub. Wks. — 6.7
7. Water — 6.5
8. Law & Justice — 5.9
9. Other Unallocable — 5.4
10. Other expenditures — 5.7

100.0

4. Health — 9.0
5. Agriculture — 5.7
6. Roads — 4.8
7. Banking & Commerce — 4.6
8. Unalloca. Pub. Wks. — 3.3
9. Water — 3.2
10. Mfg. & Processing — 2.4
11. Other expenditures — 5.5

100.0

NORTHERN REGION

1. Education — 17.4
2. Other General — 16.6
3. Roads — 12.0
4. Agriculture — 10.9
5. Health — 10.4
6. Unalloca. Pub. Wks. — 8.2
7. Other Unallocable — 7.0
8. Water — 4.8
9. Law & Justice — 2.3
10. Mfg. & Processing — 2.3
11. Other expenditures — 8.1

100.0

4. Other Unallocable — 8.0
5. Health — 7.7
6. Agriculture — 5.6
7. Banking & Commerce — 5.0
8. Mfg. & Processing — 4.2
9. Water — 4.2
10. Unalloca. Pub. Wks. — 4.0
11. Other Community — 2.9
12. Other Economic — 2.7
13. Other expenditures — 3.0

100.0

1. Education — 22.0
2. Other General — 13.3
3. Roads — 10.5
4. Agriculture — 10.2
5. Other Unallocable — 10.1
6. Health — 9.1
7. Unalloca. Pub. Wks. — 6.3
8. Water — 4.1
9. Other Economic — 3.6
10. Law & Justice — 2.7
11. Other expenditures — 8.1

100.0

There are, however, some similarities between regional patterns of change. The relative commitment to health services declines from period to period in each region. In all the regions there are shifts from period to period in the percentages allocated to roads, manufacturing and processing and banking and commerce without there being a consistent pattern to the shifts. When policies are compared at the level of summary categories as in Table 11, the variations in commitment are also evident.

The difference between the Northern Region on the one hand and the Western and Eastern Regions on the other in their commitment to social services in the first two periods is striking. That this gap is substantially reduced in the third suggests what other evidence would also support—that the southern regions over-extended themselves in their earlier commitments to education and social services, while the North, feeling itself at a disadvantage, began to intensify its efforts to catch up to the other regions in this activity.

The Western Region was also the most aggressive in promoting economic services. The Western Region's outlay on economic services was to a great extent influenced by the availability of marketing board surpluses, which were considerably larger than those in other regions in 1954.

The Eastern Region, though it made much larger commitments to social services than did the North, ran slightly behind the North in its commitment to economic services. The North clearly leads the other two regions in the priority given to community services in the first two periods, reflecting a greater attention to the needs for roads and water supplies. It should be noted, however, that in the third period the East nearly meets the North's priorities for community services and the West surpasses it.

It would go beyond the limits of this discussion to explore what lies behind these figures, what explains the differences in priorities adopted by the regions, and whether the apparent investments in various economic services were really productive of economic growth or whether these were, as some investigating commissions have suggested, in part covers for diverting regional funds into political channels. The gross data on priorities in development presented here cannot answer such questions. But they do indicate that there were significant differences among Nigerians as to what should be the emphasis in development policy. The nature of these differences and the mode of their resolution may well pose one of the central problems with which the Nigerian political system had to cope—and with which it will still have to cope if some form of national unity is restored.

TABLE 11. *Regional Expenditure Patterns By Summary Categories, 1951-62.*

	1951-55		1956-60		1961-62	
	Type	*Percent*	*Type*	*Percent*	*Type*	*Percent*
WESTERN REGION						
1.	Social Services	45.4	Social Services	40.2	Social Services	37.3
2.	Economic Services	17.0	Economic Services	25.9	Economic Services	26.0
3.	General Services	16.1	General Services	14.0	Community Services	17.1
4.	Community Services	11.7	Community Services	10.8	General Services	10.5
5.	Unallocable	9.8	Unallocable	9.1	Unallocable	9.1
EASTERN REGION						
1.	Social Services	43.8	Social Services	47.6	Social Services	38.7
2.	General Services	20.5	Economic Services	15.3	Economic Services	18.8
3.	Economic Services	15.6	Unallocable	14.6	Community Services	15.6
4.	Community Services	11.0	General Services	13.2	General Services	14.9
5.	Unallocable	9.1	Community Services	9.3	Unallocable	12.0
NORTHERN REGION						
1.	Social Services	32.0	Social Services	29.5	Social Services	33.5
2.	General Services	22.8	General Services	19.0	Economic Services	18.4
3.	Community Services	16.6	Community Services	18.5	Unallocable	16.4
4.	Economic Services	16.6	Economic Services	17.9	General Services	16.0
5.	Unallocable	12.1	Unallocable	15.1	Community Services	15.7

PROJECTED GOVERNMENT EXPENDITURES IN THE
1962-68 PLAN

It is appropriate to ask at this point: What is the relation between these patterns of development as shown in the expenditure priorities during the period from 1950-62, and the Development Plan for 1962-68? In examining this relationship there are two important differences in the available evidence regarding the Plan and the evidence regarding the 1950-62 period.

First, the Plan shows the projected priorities of the planners rather than the priorities of actual expenditures in the period 1962-68. To the extent that these priorities of the Plan are different from those in the period of transition, they indicate how the planners felt that emphasis should be shifted as Nigeria moved into the planned period. Whether these objectives or new priorities were met is another question and one which will not be considered here.

The second difference is that the detailed breakdown of the Plan is in terms of what we call "composite development expenditure" only and does not include the recurrent expenditure which has been included in the figures presented so far. This difficulty can be overcome however by extracting from the actual expenditures during the 1950-62 period that portion called "composite development expenditure" which is comparable to the kinds of expenditure treated in detail in the Plan. In the tables which follow, the figures presented for various stages of the 1950-62 period are restricted to the "composite development expenditures" and their priorities.

The most striking feature of the regional plans for 1962-68 is not only the increased emphasis on economic services in general, but the differences in priorities among the various economic services compared to the earlier periods. The details of these differences can be seen in Table 12.[5]

In the Western Region, manufacturing and processing which ranked eighth in the period 1956-60 ranked first in the Plan with 24.6 per cent of planned expenditure. Agriculture ranked second as it had in the period 1961-62 but with a substantial increase in the percentage allocated to it. Other economic services, however, dropped below the significant 2 per cent level, having ranged from 8.5 per cent to 16 per cent in the earlier periods. Banking and commerce also dropped below the 2 per cent level, having ranged from 5 per cent to 7 per cent since 1956.

In the West, the compensating decline in priority is found primarily in the expenditure on roads which dropped from first place (19.3 per cent) in the 1961-62 period to fifth place (6.9 per cent) in the Plan.

TABLE 12. *Projected Regional Expenditure Patterns in the 1962-68 Plan As Compared With Expenditures* By Regions, 1951-62.*

Percentage

Type of Expenditure	62-68	51-55	56-60	61-62
WESTERN REGION				
1. Mfg. & Processing	24.6	13.7	5.2	6.1
2. Agriculture	20.4	11.6	16.6	15.8
3. Education	14.2	21.5	13.5	7.3
4. Water	10.9	8.0	6.5	9.8
5. Roads	6.9	13.5	10.4	19.3
6. Other Soc. Ser.	6.1	.6	2.4	6.7
7. Other Commun. Ser.	3.7	1.1	1.9	3.3
8. Other General	2.9	7.6	11.4	2.9
9. Other Unalloc.	2.9	.2	1.2	.5
10. Other Econ. Ser.	1.7	8.5	16.0	.1
11. Trans. & Comm.	.3	0.0	0.0	2.2
12. Health	1.8	6.2	4.3	3.7
13. Unalloc. Pub. Wks.	0.0	3.1	0.0	2.9
14. Law & Justice	.5	2.8	.6	1.0
15. Banking & Comm.	1.3	.5	5.7	7.2

Type of Expenditure	62-68	51-55	56-60	61-62
NORTHERN REGION				
1. Roads	22.8	13.7	27.6	24.5
2. Agriculture	22.3	18.9	7.8	7.0
3. Education	19.2	12.5	11.2	19.6
4. Mfg. & Process.	10.5	2.4	6.0	2.9
5. Water	9.4	14.4	11.4	10.6
6. Health	4.4	11.2	4.1	5.4
7. Other Soc. Ser.	3.8	2.2	.7	.7
8. Other Comm. Ser.	3.0	1.0	1.4	.2
9. Other Econ. Ser.	2.0	1.2	3.6	9.5
10. Other General	1.1	14.4	12.7	6.1
11. Unalloc. Pub. Wks.	0.0	3.9	5.8	2.0
12. Banking and Comm.	0.0	1.1	3.9	.9
13. Trans. & Comm.	0.0	1.3	1.7	4.5
14. Power	1.5	0.0	.7	3.2

Percentage

Type of Expenditure	62-68	51-55	56-60	61-62
EASTERN REGION				
1. Agriculture	40.4	17.6	10.2	7.4
2. Mfg. & Process.	17.0	17.2	9.2	11.3
3. Roads	11.8	12.0	14.5	20.5
4. Education	11.7	14.2	20.3	7.9
5. Water	6.8	5.0	10.7	9.7
6. Other Commun. Ser.	4.4	4.5	.2	5.4
7. Other General	3.3	8.3	4.8	8.6
8. Health	2.4	16.1	5.6	3.3
9. Banking & Comm.	.2	.7	15.5	12.7
10. Other Econ. Ser.	0.0	0.0	4.8	6.9

Type of Expenditure	62-68	51-55	56-60	61-62
ALL REGIONS				
1. Agriculture	26.8	16.0	12.3	11.3
2. Mfg. & Process.	17.2	9.9	6.3	6.6
3. Education	15.4	16.1	14.0	10.6
4. Roads	14.2	13.2	17.3	20.9
5. Water	0.2	9.9	9.0	10.0
6. Other Comm. Serv.	3.7	1.9	1.4	3.0
7. Other Soc. Ser.	3.7	1.2	1.4	3.6
8. Health	3.0	10.5	4.5	4.0
9. Other General	2.3	10.5	10.6	5.2
10. Other Econ. Ser.	1.3	3.7	9.5	9.1
11. Unalloc. Pub. Wks.	0.0	3.3	3.1	2.1
12. Banking and Comm.	.5	.8	6.9	7.0
13. Trans. & Comm.	.1	1.3	1.1	2.9

* Composite development expenditures (i.e. development expenditure reported by the Accountant-General plus expenditure on development of the marketing boards and the development corporations or their equivalent).

The most striking change of any of the governments, however, is the increased priority which the Eastern Region government gave to agriculture, raising it from 7 per cent in 1961-62 to 40.4 per cent planned for 1962-68. As with the Western Region, the critical reductions in priorities were in banking and commerce, other economic services, roads and other general services.

The North continued to give highest priority to roads as it had in 1956-60 and 1961-62. The most substantial change here was the increased priority to agriculture which rose from between 7 per cent and 8 per cent in the two periods 1956-60 and 1961-62 to 22.3 per cent in the Plan. Manufacturing and processing had the second largest increase in percentage commitment over 1961-62. The major reductions were in other economic services and other general services. In economic services it is clear that the effort of the planners in all the regions was to emphasize the production sectors of the economy by increasing investment in agriculture and manufacturing and processing.

It is also clear that though there was considerably more coordination of the regional plans than had occurred in 1956-60, there were still very substantial regional differences in the priorities selected—priorities which reflect real differences in what had been accomplished in earlier periods as well as differences in the problems and resources of the regions. For the first time, development expenditure on education has a higher priority in the North than in the East or West, suggesting its concern to catch up with the educational systems which the East and West had built in earlier periods. And the continued high priority given to roads compared to manufacturing and processing indicates that in the Northern view improving access to markets was still likely to be the most significant contribution to the economic development of the region.

In the Federal program, as Table 13 shows, the most dramatic change was in the new emphasis given to the development of electric power with the decision to build the Niger dam, the single most expensive project in the program. Transportation and communication other than roads dropped sharply though if the two were added together the total commitment to them would be slightly greater than that of the development of electric power.

The other important new area of Federal attention was manufacturing and processing. This category claimed nearly 10 per cent of the Federal Plan whereas in earlier periods it had always remained less than 1 per cent. The commitment of £30 million to the building of a steel mill was the most significant project here. Apart from the reduced priority in transportation and communication, the other major decline was in other general services.

TABLE 13. Projected Federal and Regional Expenditure* Patterns in the 1962-1968 Plan As Compared With Federal and Regional Expenditures, 1951-62.

	FEDERAL	Percentage				REGIONS	Percentage			
	Category	62-68	51-55	56-60	61-62	Category	62-68	51-55	56-60	61-62
1.	Power	25.9	4.8	5.3	5.3	Power	15.9	2.6	3.2	3.4
2.	Trans. & Comm.	17.7	17.8	32.3	41.6	Agriculture	13.5	8.8	6.3	6.4
3.	Mfg. & Processing	9.9	.2	.4	.9	Mfg. & Processing	12.9	4.7	3.3	3.8
4.	Roads	9.7	8.6	17.0	7.9	Roads	11.5	10.8	17.1	14.6
5.	Defense	7.8	.9	3.9	4.4	Education	10.8	16.4	9.7	7.4
6.	Education	7.7	16.6	5.4	4.0	Trans. & Comm.	10.5	10.2	16.8	21.8
7.	Other Social Services	4.4	.3	.9	1.4	Defense	4.6	.5	1.9	2.1
8.	Agriculture	4.2	2.5	.4	1.2	Other Social Services	4.1	.7	1.2	2.5
9.	Law & Justice	2.9	2.4	3.4	3.0	Water	4.0	5.4	5.4	5.6
10.	Health	2.7	10.4	2.4	1.7	Health	2.8	10.5	3.4	2.9
11.	Other General	2.1	5.2	11.3	14.9	Other General	2.2	7.7	11.0	10.3
12.	Development Institutions	1.8	21.4	3.9	.8	Other Community Services	2.2	1.6	3.5	3.3
13.	Other Community Services	1.1	1.4	5.6	3.6	Law & Justice	1.8	2.1	2.0	2.0
14.	Other Unallocable	.6	0.0	1.3	5.8	Development Institutions	1.1	11.5	2.0	.5
15.	Other Economic Services	.4	2.5	0.0	.2	Other Economic Services	.8	3.1	4.7	4.7
16.	Unallocable Pub. Works	0.0	2.7	3.5	2.2	Other Unallocable	.8	.1	1.1	3.2
17.						Banking & Commerce	.5	.7	4.1	3.6

* Composite Development Expenditures

111

For Nigeria the 1962-68 Plan doubles the 1961-62 commitment to agriculture, multiplies by nearly five the commitment to power development and more than trebles the commitment to manufacturing and processing. At the same time it reduces by half the commitment to transport and communication and continues to make substantial investments in roads and in education. All regions and the Federal Government planned to reduce development expenditure for general services though there is a substantial increase in the development expenditure for defense at the Federal level.

This shift in priorities is only part of the change in expectations revealed by the Plan. The other change of considerable importance is the change in the relationships between the regions and between all regions and the Federal Government as shown in Table 14.

TABLE 14. *Average Composite Development Expenditure for Consolidated Years 1951-55, 1956-60, 1961-62 and Plan Period 1962-68 By Individual Regions, All Regions, Federal, Nigeria. (£000.)*

GOVERNMENTS	1951-55	1956-60	1961-62	1962-68
Western Region	2,657.5	8,924.2	16,545.4	15,047.8
Eastern Region	1,688.3	3,733.1	9,019.6	11,283.3
Northern Region	3,012.6	6,969.7	8,906.2	14,816.7
All Regions	7,358.5	19,627.1	34,471.3	41,147.8
Federal	8,534.6	19,808.9	32,967.5	62,503.0
Nigeria (all regions plus Federal)	15,893.1	39,436.0	67,438.8	103,650.8
Regions as a percent of Nigeria	46	50	51	40

Throughout the period from 1950 to 1962 the most buoyant and the most energetic government in its development program had been the Western Region which expanded its activities much more rapidly in the period 1956-60 than either the East or the North and had the largest absolute gain in 1961-62. However, the East made a larger percentage growth in the period 1961-62 over the period 1956-60 while the North, which had a larger composite development expenditure in the first period 1951-55, expanded its development activities less rapidly in 1956-60 and 1961-62. An examination of the average annual composite development expenditure for the three periods of the transition and that projected for the years 1962-68 shows that the Northern Region Plan was the most optimistic in its expectations after 1962 with an expected increase of 66 per cent in average composite development expenditure. The Eastern Region was second with an expected increase of 25 per cent while the Western Region planners expected a decline of 9 per cent.

The government with the greatest expectations however was the Federal Government which contemplated an average annual composite development expenditure 90 per cent greater than in the 1961-62 period. If in reality the relationship between combined regional expenditures and Federal expenditures during the planned period 1962-68 were of the order comtemplated by the Plan, it meant a significant structural change in the relationship of the Federal and regional governments to the development process. For in the period of the full working of the federal system from 1956-62, the Federal and regional governments appeared to divide the financial burden of development expenditure on a 50-50 basis, yet the projections of the Plan anticipated that the Federal Government would carry the larger share of a 60-40 division.

It may be that an explanation of the changed relationship between the various regions and between the combined regions and the Federal Government was simply a matter of over-optimism on the part of some planners and greater realism on the part of others. On the other hand, it may be that the change in the relationship between the regional and Federal governments was related to the fact that substantial amounts of regional expenditure during the transition period (which appear in these figures as development expenditure of one sort or another) were in fact channeled into political activity and thus the figures inflate the real contribution which the regions made to development activity in the periods from 1956-60 and 1961-62.

THE CHANGING ROLE OF THE MARKETING BOARDS

One important factor in comparing the 1950-62 period with the 1962-68 Plan is the role of the marketing boards and their accumulated surpluses. Initially, these surpluses were used to support a policy of price stabilization. However, after 1955 these surpluses were converted into a general resource for development expenditures as shown by Helleiner. (See Chapter 7.) Certainly the buoyancy and aggressiveness of the Western Region is explainable in a significant measure by the greater resources it received from the Cocoa Marketing Board and the profits made by the Western Region Marketing Board after its organization in 1954-55. Table 15 shows the accumulated resources of the regional marketing boards for the years from 1956-61 and the distribution of these resources.

During the course of the years from 1956 to 1961, the Western Region Marketing Board was able to commit nearly £55 million to

TABLE 15. *Allocation of Regional Marketing Board Surpluses, 1955-61*

	WEST	EAST (£000's)	NORTH	ALL REGIONS
Accumulated Surpluses, 1954-61	62,550.2	23,919.2	31,900.3	118,369.4
Allocation				
Loans & Grants to Regional Govts.	35,589.1	7,500.0	6,811.2	49,900.3
Loans & Grants to Develop. Insts.	4,200.0	3,300.0	1,883.2	9,383.2
Direct Grants Loans & Investments	15,085.6	3,757.1	4,302.7	23,145.4
Total Contribution to Regional Develop.	54,874.7	14,557.1	12,997.1	82,428.9
U.K. & Fed. Nigeria Securities	1,721.6	33,202.2	9,603.1	14,526.9
Loans to Fed. Nigeria		1,816.9	3,323.6	5,140.5
Total Reserves in Govt. Securities & Loans	1,721.6	5,019.1	12,926.7	19,667.4
Balance of Other Assets	5,953.9	4,343.0	5,976.5	16,273.1

SOURCE: Gerald K. Helleiner, *Peasant Agriculture, Government and Economic Growth in Nigeria*, (Homewood, Ill.: Richard Irwin, 1966), pp. 166 & 173.

the development program of the Western Region through a series of loans and grants to the regional government, the expenditure of which can be accounted for in the recurrent and development budgets, as well as a series of direct grants, loans and investments to the development institutions and private or semi-private Nigerian enterprises which are accounted for in our "composite expenditures."

In contrast, the Eastern Region Marketing Board made a commitment of only £14.5 million and the Northern Marketing Board a commitment of nearly £13 million to the total regional composite development programs. This certainly is one significant clue to the differences between the regions in this period.

One consequence of this distribution of marketing board resources however is that the resources of the Western Region Marketing Board were practically exhausted by the beginning of the 1962-68 Plan, whereas the Eastern Region Marketing Board had reserves invested in United Kingdom securities and loans to the Federal Government of £5 million. The Northern Region had similar reserves of nearly £13 million. Though the Western and the East as well as the North might expect further marketing board resources from future earnings, clearly the Northern Region was in the most advantageous position so far as the backlog of reserves was concerned.

The role of the marketing boards and their surpluses in Nigeria's economic and political development is a problem which has yet to be subjected to a full scale analysis. What can only be suggested at this point is that they gave to the regions a financial resource and a development role which could not be sustained into the mid-1960's. Once the reserves were exhausted, the longer run trend was toward a larger Federal role in development programs.

What were the political consequences of this short term buoyancy of regional finances? Did it mean—despite the hope of those who designed it—that the 1950-62 period was not one in which the political leaders of the regional and Federal governments learned to live with and make work a federal system whose financial framework could be sustained in the period of complete independence? Or, rather, was it a period in which economic programs and expectations and initial political relationships were built on a financial base which was at best temporary and at worst illusory?

It is not now possible to say to what extent this experience contributed to the political stress which developed in the Nigerian system from 1963 onward. What is revealed by this analysis of the structure of the expenditure, however, is that the planners expected a change in the structure of expenditure which involved not only significant shifts in the direction of expenditure to different sectors of the economy but significant shifts in the financial structure of the federal system itself.

APPENDIX

Expenditure data used in this paper:
Recurrent and development expenditure of the various governments are taken from C. R. Nixon, "A Functional Analysis of Nigerian Governmental Expenditures 1949/50-1961/62" (privately distributed). This includes not merely all expenditures on goods and services but also grants, subventions, loans, etc. as part of the total governmental support for various services. Transfers between the Federal and regional governments or to government reserves are excluded however.
A. The functional categories were adapted from those developed by the United Nations. [United Nations, *Manual for the Economic and Functional Classification of Government Transactions* (New York, 1958).] The functional categories used in this analysis are as follows:
GENERAL SERVICES:
Defense
Law and Justice (including police and prisons)
Other (including legislature, governor, general administration)

COMMUNITY SERVICES:
   Roads
   Water Supply
   Other (including waterways, sanitation, town planning, community development, survey)
SOCIAL SERVICES:
   Education
   Health
   Other (including social welfare, public housing, recreation facilities)
ECONOMIC SERVICES:
   Agriculture (including veterinary and forestry)
   Power (primarily electric power via thermal units or hydro-electric investment in the Niger dam)
   Manufacturing and processing (including departments of industry, industrial promotion, oil mills, abattoirs, as well as modern manufacturing plants)
   Transport and communications (including railways, water and air transport, posts and telegraphs, broadcasting, subsidies to newspapers and publishers)
   Banking and commerce (including investments in banks, markets, insurance companies, and departments of trade and commerce)
   Development Institutions (including Federal Loans Board and other minor bodies. Does not include grants made to Western Region Development Corp., Western Region Finance Corp., Eastern Nigerian Development Corp., or Northern Region Development Corp., as their expenditures are included in the analysis.
   Other (including hotels, rest houses, cooperatives, construction companies, property investment companies)
UNALLOCABLE:
   Unallocable public works
   Other (including interest payments, pensions, passages, childrens' allowances)
B. The formulas for transforming "Current Price" expenditures into "1957 Price" expenditures were developed from the data on National accounts prepared by Dr. Pious Okigbo for the period 1950-57, [Pious N. C. Okigbo, *Nigerian National Accounts, 1950-57* (Enugu: Government Printer, 1962).] and that prepared by the Federal Office of Statistics for the period 1958-62. [Nigeria, *Annual Abstract of Statistics* (1964).]
Recurrent expenditures were transformed using a multipler obtained by dividing the 1957 price figures by the current price figures as shown in the national accounts for the item "government."
Development expenditures were transformed by a similar multiplier obtained from the data on "Gross Fixed Investment in Nigeria 1950-57" [Okigbo, *op. cit.*, Table IV.3 and Table IV.4, p. 22.] and on

"Gross Capital Formation" (private sector) 1957-62 [Nigeria, *op. cit.*, *Annual Abstract of Statistics* (1964), Table 13.2.] The multipliers obtained by this process for transforming actual expenditures at current prices into expenditures at constant 1957 prices are as follows:

Fiscal Year	Recurrent Expenditure multiplier	Development Expenditure Multiplier
1950/51	1.387	1.571
1951/52	1.388	1.579
1952/53	1.390	1.389
1953/54	1.099	1.359
1954/55	1.098	1.299
1955/56	1.099	1.197
1956/57	1.000	1.067
1957/58	1.000	1.000
1958/59	.9572	.9939
1959/60	.9166	1.0306
1960/61	.7795	.9886
1961/62	.7786	.9203

C. Development expenditures of the regional development corporations and their predecessors and the regional marketing boards and their predecessors are derived from the analysis made by Gerald K. Helleiner. [Gerald K. Helleiner, "A Wide-Ranging Development Institution: Nigeria's Northern Region Development Corporation, 1949-62," *The Nigerian Journal of Economic and Social Studies*, VI, 2 (July, 1964), pp. 239-57; Gerald K. Helleiner, "The Eastern Nigeria Development Corporation: A Study in Sources and Uses of Public Development Funds, 1949-62," *The Nigerian Journal of Economic and Social Studies*, VI, 1 (March, 1964), pp. 98-123; Gerald K. Helleiner, "The Fiscal Role of the Marketing Boards in Nigerian Economic Development, 1947-61," chapter 7 in this volume; and Helleiner, *op. cit.*, *Peasant Agriculture, Government and Economic Growth in Nigeria.*] These studies by Helleiner were supplemented by the Coker Commission Reports and by the annual reports of the various development corporations and the marketing boards.

D. In integrating the accounts of the governments' accountants-general and the development corporation and marketing board accounts, transfers between those agencies have been excluded. Grants, loans and investments in private enterprises have been included. The objective in integrating these various accounts was to obtain expenditures figures which represented the total contribution to various services made from financial resources derived from the various sources of public revenues, including marketing board profits.

E. The fiscal years of the various governments, boards and corporations do not coincide with the calendar years. We have adopted the practice of designating a fiscal year by the calendar year in which the fiscal year ends. Thus the year 1951 in our text and tables represents the fiscal year 1950/51, 1955 represents the fiscal year 1954/55, etc.

F. Unless otherwise noted, all tables are based on the sources described above. Those interested in the functional or economic analysis of Nigerian expenditures should also consult *Economic and Functional Analysis of Government Accounts, 1958/59-1961/62* (Lagos: Federal Office of Statistics, 1964). This analysis is done independently of the Nixon study and the rules for the classification of some items were not the same. Thus there are some differences between the two analyses due to differences in methodology. The F.O.S. analysis does not cover the period 1949/50-1956/57 nor does it include the accounts of the various development corporations or the marketing boards. It does, however, include local government expenditures, and does include an economic analysis as well as a functional analysis of expenditures.

NOTES

1. Gerald K. Helleiner, *Peasant Agriculture, Government and Economic Growth in Nigeria* (Homewood, Illinois: Richard Irwin, 1966).

2. Louis Chick, *Report of Fiscal Commissioner on Financial Effects of Proposed New Constitutional Arrangements* (Lagos, 1953).

3. Some inflation of the expenditure on communications results from the fact that Posts and Telephones and Telegraphs are operated as a Federal ministry instead of as a statutory corporation. The total P. T. & T. recurrent expenditure appears in the Federal Estimates and Accountant-General Reports as a legislative appropriation, and the earnings, which amount to about 75 per cent of the recurrent expenditure appear as government revenue. It would have been consistent with the objectives of this functional analysis to have deducted P. T. & T. earnings from recurrent expenditure and included in this analysis only the net nonearned recurrent expenditure. This was not done however.

4. Though the objective of those who promoted the building of the railway extension to Kano was to stimulate production of cotton, the real consequence of the railway was stimulation of groundnut production. An analysis of this relation between the railway, cotton, and groundnuts is provided by J. S. Hogendorn, "The Origins of the Groundnut Trade in Northern Nigeria." See chapter 3 in this volume.

5. The figures for the Development Plan 1962-68 are derived from *National Development Plan, 1962-68* (Lagos: Federal Ministry of Economic Development, 1963).

7. The Fiscal Role of the Marketing Boards in Nigerian Economic Development, 1947-61 *

GERALD K. HELLEINER

Much has transpired in the Nigerian economy since the debates of the early 1950s on the subject of the West African Marketing Boards.[1] The powers of the Regional Governments have been vastly extended; the markets for Nigerian exports have greatly weakened; manufacturing industry has expanded rapidly; oil has been discovered and exploited in the Eastern Region; nearly universal primary education has been introduced to the Southern Regions; and urban unemployment has begun to assume the dimensions of a major problem. Moreover, in the political realm, Nigeria has progressed through internal self-government to her present status as an independent republic in the Commonwealth. At present the Federation has nearly completed the second year of its first six-year national development plan. Yet some elements of the economic scene have undergone no essential change. Such an element is the dominance of the Marketing Boards, organised since 1954 on a Regional rather than a commodity basis, in the national economy. In 1962 the exports handled by these Boards still accounted for 63.2% of Nigeria's total exports.

Nigeria's Marketing Boards, it will be remembered, are statutory monopsonies handling Nigeria's major agricultural exports. They had their origins in war-time arrangements for the orderly marketing of West African produce and the protection of United Kingdom supplies of raw materials. After the war they assumed the responsibility for the stabilisation of producer prices and the development of the producing industries. The interpretation and implementation of the Marketing Boards' responsibility for stabilisation have received a great deal of attention from the economics profession. It is not, however, the most important aspect of Nigerian Marketing Board practices.

Stabilisation, of whatever sort, has never constituted the sole responsibility of the Nigerian Marketing Boards. That it has occupied so

* From *Economics Journal*, Vol. LXXIV, No. 295, September 1964, pp. 582-610. Reprinted by permission of the Royal Economics Society.

much of economists' attention indicates more about the main pre-occupations of the economics profession in the immediate post-war years than it does about its importance to the Nigerian economy. Growth should always have carried greater weight in Nigerian policy formation than stability, and there exists no conclusive evidence that the two are correlated. With the recent general revival of professional interest in the more "classical" problems of economic growth it seems particularly appropriate that the emphasis, as far as discussion of Nigerian (and other) Marketing Boards is concerned, should now be properly placed. The Marketing Boards have been and continue to be an extremely effective (though, of course, far from the only) instrument for the mobilisation of savings for government-sponsored economic development.[2]

They have had, since their very inception, considerable powers to accumulate and expend funds earned from their trading operations for development purposes. But the Marketing Boards have long since exceeded the limits originally set for their activities in this area. Within the last few years the Regional Governments of the Federation have stated quite explicitly that the Marketing Boards are an important source of revenues for their development budgets.

This paper will discuss the experience of the Nigerian Marketing Boards since their establishment with respect to the accumulation and disposal of the vast trading surpluses to which Bauer had already called attention and against which he had so effectively fulminated some years ago.[3] There has been remarkably little discussion of the Nigerian Marketing Boards since their regionalisation; Bauer's work, which has recently been reissued, has therefore remained the standard work on the subject, although it is now badly outdated. The discussion here will virtually ignore the questions as to how, what, or if, to stabilise—which were at the heart of the debates of a decade ago—in the belief that they are to-day, if not then, only of secondary interest. Its subject matters are, rather, the manner in which the trading surpluses were earned, the evolution of official Nigerian attitudes towards the resulting reserves and towards the accumulation of further surpluses, and the allocation of the eventual expenditures of the accumulated funds, together with some of the objections which can be raised as to the use of Marketing Boards as revenue collectors for governmental development programmes.

I. THE ACCUMULATION OF THE TRADING SURPLUSES

It is widely recognised that the period 1947-54 was one during which Nigeria's Marketing Boards acquired enormous reserves. Table 1

TABLE 1. *Total Accumulation by Nigerian Commodity Marketing Boards, 1947-54 (£ thousands).*

	Cocoa.	Palm oil.	Palm kernels.	Ground-nuts.	Cotton.	Total.
Initial reserves	8,896.6*		11,457.0†	4,487.8†	250.0‡	25,091.0‖
Net trading surplus§	33,797.4	2,269.7	18,790.8	22,483.6	6,968.6	84,310.1
Excess of other income over expenditures‖	3,349.3	2,497.3		3,563.9	1,102.7	10,513.2
	46,043.3	35,014.8		30,535.3	8,321.3	119,914.7

Sources: Annual Reports of Nigerian Marketing Boards.

* Reserves accumulated in respect of Nigerian cocoa by West African Produce Control Board before 1947 and turned over to the Nigeria Cocoa Marketing Board upon its creation in 1947.

† Reserves accumulated in respect of Nigerian produce by West African Produce Control Board in 1947-49 period and turned over to the Nigeria Oil Palm Produce Marketing Board and the Nigeria Groundnut Marketing Board upon their creation in 1949.

‡ Grant from U.K. Raw Cotton Commission to the Nigeria Cotton Marketing Board in compensation for previous under-payments to Nigerian cotton producers upon its creation in 1949.

§ Cocoa: 1947/48 to 1953/54 inclusive; palm oil and palm kernels: 1949-54 inclusive; groundnuts and cotton: 1949/50 to 1953/54 inclusive. Calculated from the original accounts of the Marketing Boards as follows: sales at f.o.b. prices less export duties, value of purchases, total expenses and decrease in stocks. The resulting figures for trading surpluses sometimes differ from those stated in the accounts.

‖ Calculated from the original accounts of the Marketing Boards. Primarily interest on reserves held in U.K. securities. The figure for groundnuts includes trading surpluses earned on other minor commodities under the jurisdiction and control of the Nigeria Groundnut Marketing Board (benniseed, sunflower seed, soya beans, groundnut oil and groundnut cake); that for cotton includes development premium paid by the U.K. Raw Cotton Commission.

shows the total accumulations of the four Nigerian Commodity Marketing Boards until their dissolution in 1954. By 1954 nearly £120 million had been mobilised by these four Boards, over £100 million (net) of which[4] had been realised as "trading profits" during this seven-year period alone. (For comparative purposes it may be worth observing that the two principal sources of government tax revenue at this time each earned less over the same seven-year period. Between 1947/48 and 1953/54 import duties accounted for a total of only £93.5 million, whereas export duties totalled only £56.7 million of revenues.)

The largest trading surpluses had been realised by the Cocoa Marketing Board, but all four had piled up substantial reserves. Only palm-oil producers, who received over £6.9 million in subsidies in 1953 and 1954, received any stabilisation benefits, in the form of price supports in lean years, during this period; and even these substantial subsidies could not alter the fact that they had already contributed far larger amounts to the Oil Palm Produce Marketing Board's reserves.

These accumulations were a not inconsiderable share of the total earnings on exported produce which could have been distributed to Nigerian peasant producers or what I have called "potential producer income."[5] Nor were they the only levy on this potential producer income. Further amounts were withheld in the form of export duties and, from 1953 on, Regional produce sales taxes, which were levied as specific duties upon each ton of produce sold to a Marketing Board. Table 2 summarises these government withdrawals from the Marketing Board agricultural sector during this and the subsequent period.

It can be seen that during the 1947/54 period over 42% of potential producer income earned from cotton, 40% of that from groundnuts, over 39% of that from cocoa, over 29% of that from palm kernels and 17% of that from palm oil were withheld by the Government through taxes and Marketing Board trading surpluses. By far the greatest share of this total in each case except that of palm oil, in respect of which, as has been seen, substantial trading losses were incurred in 1953 and 1954, was made up of Marketing Board trading surpluses. In peak years individual Marketing Boards alone withheld over 40, 50, and even 66% of potential incomes of producers of particular crops (see Appendix).

Less well known is the Nigerian Marketing Board experience since 1954. With the constitutional revisions of that year, which involved the devolution of considerable powers to the Regional Governments, there came a reorganisation of Marketing Board structure as well. Henceforth, instead of being organised on a nation-wide commodity basis, they conducted their operations on a Regional cross-commodity basis. Each Regional Marketing Board handled all the relevant ex-

Table 2. *Government Withdrawals from Major Components of the Marketing Board Controlled Agricultural Export Sector in Nigeria, 1947-62.*

		Export duties.		Marketing Board Trading Surplus.		Produce purchase tax.		Total withdrawals, £000's.	Potential producer income. £000's.	Total withdrawals as a % of potential producer income.
		£000's.	% of potential producer income.	£000's.	% of potential producer income.	£000's.	% of potential producer income.			
Cocoa										
1947/48 to 1953/54		27,565	17.6	33,797	21.6	390	0.2	61,752	165,829	39.4
1954/55 to 1961/62		36,917	17.9	12,841	6.2	4,163	2.0	53,920	206,216	26.1
	Total	64,481	17.8	46,638	12.8	4,553	1.3	115,672	363,046	31.9
Groundnuts										
1947/48 to 1953/54		11,329	11.5	27,797	28.1	425	0.4	39,549	98,776	40.0
1954/55 to 1960/61		20,825	14.0	-2,053	-1.4	3,574	2.4	22,346	149,660	14.9
	Total	32,154	12.9	25,743	10.4	3,998	1.6	61,895	248,436	24.9
Palm Kernels										
1947-54		11,872	9.4	25,096	19.9	—	—	36,968	126,438	29.2
1955-61		15,125	13.1	11,883	10.3	4,327	3.7	31,335	116,558	27.1
	Total	26,997	11.1	36,978	15.2	4,327	1.8	68,303	242,996	28.1
Palm Oil										
1947-54		7,356	9.0	6,544	8.0	—	—	13,899	81,608	17.0
1955-61		9,646	13.3	4,305	5.9	4,592	6.3	18,543	72,421	25.6
	Total	17,002	11.0	10,849	7.0	4,592	3.0	32,442	154,028	21.0
Cotton										
1949/50 to 1953/54		2,687	11.7	6,969	30.3	70	0.3	9,726	23,014	42.3
1954/55 to 1960/61		5,771	13.5	-1,696	-4.0	722	1.7	4,796	42,753	11.2
	Total	8,458	12.9	5,272	8.0	792	1.2	14,522	65,767	22.1

Source: See Appendix.

123

portable produce of its region of jurisdiction. Effectively, this meant that the Eastern Region Marketing Board did the bulk of its business in palm oil and palm kernels, the Northern Region in groundnuts and cotton and the Western Region in cocoa and palm kernels. These were not the only commodities handled by the Marketing Boards, but the remainder were of small relative importance. The Regional Marketing Boards took over the assets of the former Commodity Marketing Boards, their distribution being determined by the Region of origin of the products on which the surpluses had been earned. As can be seen in Table 3, this meant that the Eastern Region, dependent upon palm produce, came off very poorly, whereas the cocoa-producing Western Region received close to half the redistributed upspent total of £87 million. This table also shows clearly the pattern of Regional concentration in agricultural export production.

TABLE 3. *Total Transfer of Assets from Nigerian Commodity Marketing Boards to Nigerian Regional Marketing Boards* (£ thousands).*

Marketing Board.	Eastern Region.	Northern Region.	Western Region.	Total.†
Cocoa	176.1	135.5	32,625.1	32,936.7
Oil palm produce	11,248.4	484.5	10,199.0	21,931.9
Groundnut	39.6	24,722.6	—	24,762.2
Cotton	—	7,309.2‡	73.0	7,382.2
	11,464.1	32,651.8	42,897.2	87,013.0

Sources: Annual Reports of the Marketing Boards.
 * These transfers were not all made at the same time. The final allocations were not resolved for several years.
 † Excluding Southern Cameroons.
 ‡ Including development premia from the liquidation of the U.K. Raw Cotton Commission of £803.1 thousands.

The year 1954, which divides Nigerian Marketing Board history into two separate periods distinguished by different institutional arrangements, also marks the end of a period of export prosperity and the beginning of a period of declining barter terms of trade.

No longer was a large trading surplus to be relied upon year after year simply by the holding of the producer price line as commodity prices followed their standard post-war upward course; for world primary product market conditions had by now changed significantly in character. The usual instability of Nigerian export prices continued as before, but the price fluctuations were now about a steady or even declining trend.

Given that Nigeria's Marketing Boards began the period apparently still pursuing stabilisation as their principal objectives, it is noteworthy that they nevertheless continued, in the aggregate, to accumulate trading surpluses. Admittedly these accumulations were now much smaller in magnitude. Still, between 1954 and year-end of 1961, another £21.8 million was added to the Marketing Boards' resources through their trading activities. Although this amount is less than one-quarter the size of the aggregate trading profits of the previous seven years, it remains a sizeable sum. Earnings on the reserves accumulated earlier produced a net surplus on other operations of another £9.5 million (see Table 4).

TABLE 4.   *Total Accumulation by Nigerian Regional Marketing Boards, 1954-61 (£ thousands).*

	Eastern Region.	Northern Region.	Western Region.	Total.
Transfer from Commodity Marketing Boards	11,464.1	32,651.8	42,897.2	87,013.1
Net Trading Surplus* †	10,736.2‡	−3,202.7	14,303.9‖	21,837.1
Excess of other income over expenditure* §	1,718.9	2,451.2	5,349.1	9,519.2
Total	23,919.2	31,900.3	62,550.2	118,369.4

Sources: Annual Reports of the Marketing Boards.

* Eastern Region: 1955/61 inclusive; Northern Region: 1954/55 to 1960-61 inclusive; Western Region: 1954/55 to 1960/61 inclusive.

† Calculated in the same way as Table 1.

‡ Treatment of the produce sales tax has been altered so as to make the Eastern Region's trading results comparable with those of the other Regions.

§ Calculated in the same way as in Table 1. Principally interest earned on reserves. Includes trading results in minor commodities.

‖ This figure incorporates corrected trading results for year 1960/61, which were furnished by the Western Region Marketing Board. The originally published accounts were incorrect.

Aggregation of Marketing Board data for this period conceals, however, important differences between the experiences of individual Marketing Boards. One of the Marketing Boards, that handling the produce of the Northern Region, actually ran a net deficit on its trading operations. Indeed, it ran a net overall deficit as well, in spite of its earnings on assets during this period. From 1954 until 1961 this Marketing Board paid to agricultural producers £3.2 million[6] more than it earned from the sales of their produce. Moreover, these subsidies were paid both in respect of groundnut and cotton production.

The greatest trading surpluses over the 1954-61 period were earned by the Western Region Marketing Board, which, as was noted earlier, was already the wealthiest at the outset of the period. Over £14.3 million were withheld from Western Region producers, £9.7 million of which came from cocoa production. The remaining £4.6 million came from palm-kernel producers, who contributed in the East and West together over £10.7 million to total Marketing Board reserves. The Western Region Marketing Board's wealth also produced net income of another £5.3 million, mainly from interest on the securities held in its investment portfolio.

The proportions of Nigerian export producers' potential income which were withheld during the latter period were, in general, of course, rather smaller than they had been between 1947 and 1954. Palm oil was again the only exception to this rule. The most dramatic reductions in this proportion were those for groundnuts—from 40 to 14.9%, and for cotton—from 42.3 to 11.2%. (These percentages are still positive because of the withholding of export duties and produce sales taxes, which more than offset the Marketing Board trading losses.) These products are produced in the Northern Region, where the Marketing Board had not yet abandoned its policy of attempting to stabilise producer prices, and had therefore, as has been seen, actually incurred trading deficits. There was also a substantial drop in the share of cocoa producers' potential income which was withdrawn— from 39.4 to 26.1%. Export duties, in all cases, now not only removed a larger proportion of potential producer income than previously but also withheld a larger share than did the Marketing Boards in the form of trading surpluses. The higher export duties were the result of the shift from specific to *ad valorem* duties at the end of 1950 and the introduction of a progressive rate, increasing with the world price, together with a higher base rate, a few months later. Produce purchase taxes on groundnuts and cotton obviously also withheld greater shares of potential producer income than did the Marketing Boards (which ran deficits). What is notable is that in the Eastern and Western Regions the governments were able to continue the withdrawal of over 25% of total export producers' income even in a period of stagnant or deteriorating world export markets.

Some of the tax burden upon cocoa farmers was eased by the increasing productivity achieved through the use of insecticides during these years; but producers of palm oil and palm kernels enjoyed no such improvements and, in fact, suffered from steadily declining real incomes from 1954 onwards. While Marketing Board trading surpluses were no longer at this time the most important means of withholding income from export producers, it is with them that this paper remains primarily concerned.

II. THE EVOLUTION OF OFFICIAL ATTITUDES TOWARDS
TRADING SURPLUSES

Why were these trading surpluses earned? Through consideration of policy statements over the entire post-war period one can trace a steady evolution of official attitudes towards the role of the Marketing Boards in development. Prior to Regionalisation the accumulation of large reserves was primarily fortuitous and unpremeditated. It was at that time sincerely intended by the governmental authorities that they should be used for stabilising purposes. From 1954 onwards the earning of trading surpluses became, more and more, a matter of conscious design. The surpluses were now to be used for the intensified development effort. Only in Northern Nigeria has this change of attitude not quite been completed.

Nigerian Marketing Boards have borne a degree of responsibility for the support of research and development ever since their formation. At the time of its inception in 1947 the Nigeria Cocoa Marketing Board was assigned the duty "to assist in the development by all possible means of the cocoa industry of Nigeria for the benefit and prosperity of the producers."[7] Similar provisions were included in the ordinances which set up the other three Nigerian Marketing Boards two years later. The funds required for the performance of these duties were clearly to be provided by the Marketing Boards themselves.

Whereas the intention to use reserves accumulated through trading operations for purposes other than stabilisation was thus acknowledged from the outset, these purposes clearly did not constitute at that time a first priority claim upon them:

> "The first charge on the [Groundnut Marketing] Board's funds must be for working capital to finance its purchases of groundnuts. . . . Price stabilisation must always constitute the primary claim on the Board's actual and prospective resources after the critical requirements of working capital have been met."[8]

Almost identical statements may be drawn from the early Annual Reports of the Nigeria Cocoa and Oil Palm Produce Marketing Boards.[9] Only after working capital needs and stabilisation reserves had been provided for was significant consideration to be given to research and development allocations. This principle was embodied in a rule which the Groundnut and Oil Palm Produce Marketing Boards (and after 1951, the Cocoa Board as well) adopted to govern the distribution of whatever trading surpluses they might earn. After setting aside the estimated requirements for working capital the remainder was always to be allocated, on a product-by-product basis, in the following proportions: 70%—to be retained for stabilisation purposes; 22½%—to be allocated to development; 7½%—to be expended upon research.

The development allocations were to be turned over in the form of grants to the three Regional Production Development Boards which had been set up at the same time as the Marketing Boards to further "the development of the producing industries and . . . the economic benefit and prosperity of the producers and the areas of production."[10] The size of the grant to each Region's Production Development Board was to be determined by the share which the Region in question had contributed to the total sales of the product on which the trading surplus had been earned.

The Nigeria Cotton Marketing Board differed from the others in that it did not adopt the "70-22½-7½" formula and seemed to regard the accumulation of development funds for its programme of doubling the exportable surplus of Nigerian cotton as of equal importance to its stabilisation responsibilities.

> "The keynote of the [Cotton Marketing] Board's present policy is the accumulation of funds during the present (1949-50) period of high selling prices. These reserves are the best guarantee of the Board's ability to carry out its main objects of giving maximum price to the producer [sic] and at the same time contributing to the development of the cotton-growing industry and areas."[11]

Even the Cotton Marketing Board, however, was far from giving prime emphasis to development.

There can be little question, then, that the huge trading surpluses earned in the first few years of the Marketing Boards' operations were with the possible exception of those earned on trading in cotton, not primarily or originally intended to be used for purposes other than stabilisation.

The accumulation of these reserves was, in large part, accidental. There could have been no means of predicting the tremendous commodity price increases of the post-war period or, more particularly, the devaluation of sterling or the outbreak of the Korean War. And, even if there had been, there was considerable question as to whether the raising of producer prices to any higher levels would, in fact, have benefited them or, with the existing inelasticities of food supplies and shipping space for the transport of imports, merely produced price inflation. In any case, there remained in the background the fear of a post-war collapse which had, after all, been nearly universally predicted. The reserves were earned, therefore, from peculiarly favourable world market conditions coupled, perhaps inevitably, with conservative producer price policies.

Since, according to the prescribed formula to which rigid adherence was given 70% of these accumulating reserves were to be retained for stabilisation purposes, inordinately high stabilisation reserves were soon accumulated. By the year-end of 1954 Nigerian Marketing Boards held upwards of £66 million of investments in the United Kingdom which were specifically allocated to the provision of "economic security" to the farmers. As Marketing Board reserves mounted, some modifications to the system of distribution of trading surpluses were introduced. In order to enable the Production Development Boards to plan their pro- grammes more effectively the Oil Palm Produce Marketing Board guaranteed them a minimum allocation of £800,000 for each of the years 1950-55, thus abandoning in principle the "70-22½-7½" for- mula. In order to fulfill this obligation during its two years of trading losses it was necessary actually to reduce reserves which were not originally to be employed for development purposes at all. This may be said to mark a major breach in the idea that the Marketing Board's assets were purely stabilisation reserves. The Groundnut Marketing Board made a similar guarantee of £500,000 per annum for each of the seasons 1950/51 to 1954/55, but at no time was this guaranteed minimum greater than 22½% of that year's trading surplus. More significantly, perhaps, the Marketing Boards undertook to lend to the Central Government "a sum which they can be reasonably certain they will not require within the next fifteen years"[12]—ultimately placed at £14 million.

Reserves of the size which had been accumulated by 1954 con- stituted a very great temptation to the Regional Governments, which had been granted vastly increased responsibility for the promotion of economic development following the constitutional revisions of 1954. The World Bank Mission estimated that liquid reserves of £25 million were adequate for the fulfillment of the stabilisation responsibility and recommended that the remaining surplus (or "second line reserves") be "loaned on a long-term basis to government for development pur- poses."[13] At the same time it recommended that no further stabilisation reserves be accumulated.

The World Bank was taken at its word—and considerably more than its word! But a further recommendation to the effect that the Marketing Boards henceforth confine themselves to the stabilisation of producer prices and the improvement of quality it was found more convenient to ignore. Having seen, semi-accidentally, the enormous potential for the raising of revenues which the price-fixing function of the Marketing Boards offers, first the Western Region, and then the Eastern Region as well, began consciously to take advantage of it for development purposes. Both the Western and the Eastern Region Mar- keting Boards continued to earn trading surpluses after 1954 which cannot reasonably be regarded as accidental or intended for stabilisation.

The altered views of the Regional Governments with respect to the primary functions of the Marketing Boards can be seen in their planning documents. The Western Region's 1955-60 development plan announced final abandonment of the "70-22½-7½" formula for distribution of the Western Board's trading surpluses, offered a strong defence of the Marketing Board's right to contribute to development, and provided for £20 million in loans and grants to come from the Board for the use of the Regional Government during the plan. This was about two-thirds of the total capital funds expected and nearly 20% of the total capital and current revenues anticipated for the planning period.[14] The 1960-65 Western Region plan called for a further contribution of £21 million from the Western Region Marketing Board over the course of the five-year period;[15] and, with over £14.5 million already having been granted under the former plan, another £10 million was called for in the 1962-68 plan. In the latter it is stated boldly that, "In the public sector, the Marketing Board is the main source of savings for the improvement of agriculture and allied industries and the provision of social services."[16] The Marketing Board's contribution is, in fact, 40% of the total available domestic finance for the capital programme.[17] By this time these savings could no longer refer merely to the running down of previously acquired assets. It was now obviously intended to run trading surpluses to finance the Regional Government's programme. The Western Region Marketing Board had by now become, apart from its other responsibilities, a fiscal arm of the Western Nigerian Government. This emphasis upon using the Board as a supplier of savings for development purposes has, incidentally, been very much underplayed by the Annual Reports of the Board itself; this seems to indicate that the Board is somewhat sensitive to producer complaints on the matter.

The operations of the Eastern Regional Marketing Board were evolving in much the same manner during this period, although the amounts which it now accumulated from trading surpluses were somewhat smaller than those piled up in the West. To be fair, an allowance should be made for the fact that the Eastern Region Marketing Board began with by far the lowest reserves; but it also had the smallest need for them—with respect both to working capital requirements and to stabilisation reserves.

The Eastern Region's development programme for 1958-62 already showed that the Marketing Board was expected to contribute £5 million towards the construction of the new University of Nigeria at Nsukka, and a further £500,000 to the Eastern Region Development Corporation.[18] The current (1962-68) plan lists not only the Marketing Board reserves but also "Marketing Board's earnings in the Plan period"[19] as a source of finance. Altogether, the Marketing Board's contribution to the present plan is to be £13.6 million, a large share of total available domestic resources for the capital programme. Thus, the Eastern Region Government is also employing the Marketing Board as a revenue raiser.

By 1962 even the Northern Region Government was consciously employing the Northern Nigeria Marketing Board as an important source of revenues for its development effort, though in a much modified fashion. That it was the Northern Regional Marketing Board which had formerly taken its stabilisation responsibility most seriously and has consequently been the weakest accumulator of reserves is reflected in its aggregate trading losses and its policy statements. As late as 1958 it was still saying that, "The main object of establishing Marketing Boards was to ensure stable prices for produce."[20] Subsequent Annual Reports modified this approach, emphasising that stabilisation constituted only "one of the principal objects"[21] of the Board. By 1962, however, the Northern Nigerian Government had announced its intention of "relieving the Board of its liability for subsidizing the producer prices of crops in lean years, and fixing producer prices annually at such a level in relation to world prices as to anticipate a surplus on the year's operation to cover operating costs."[22] All of the Northern Nigeria Marketing Board's reserves above and beyond its needs for working capital (about £6 million) are to be mobilised for the use of its proposed "Development Bank." Even with the explicit abandonment of year-to-year stabilisation, the Northern Nigeria Marketing Board remains the only one which has at no time stated its intention of running current trading surpluses for the purpose of contributing to regional economic development. Government attitudes in the Northern Region, in this as in most other matters, have been more conservative than those in the Eastern and Western Regions, where the Marketing Boards had abandoned their role as trustees for the farmers and assumed that of tax collector in the mid-1950s.

III. THE DISPOSAL OF THE MARKETING BOARD TRADING SURPLUSES

How were the vast reserves accumulated by Nigeria's Marketing Boards ultimately employed? During the period before their Regionalisation, as has been seen, the Marketing Boards held the bulk of them as stabilisation reserves in the form of United Kingdom and Commonwealth securities. Some of their profits, however, were spent upon or reserved for research and economic development. As has been seen, this was in keeping with announced policy.

TABLE 5. *Disposal of Funds of Nigerian Commodity Marketing Boards: Cumulative Grants, Investments and Loans Outstanding, 1947-54* (£ 000's).*

	Cocoa (Sept. 30, 1954).	Oil-palm produce (Dec. 31, 1954).	Ground-nut (Oct. 31, 1954).	Cotton (Oct. 31, 1954).	Total (Sept. 30-Dec. 31, 1954).
Cumulative grants to Production Development Boards†	8,851.4	8,357.7	6,178.3	271.0	23,658.4
Cumulative research and development expenditure†	2,051.8	2,469.0	86.0	1,328.4	5,935.2
Loans outstanding to Government of Nigeria	2,494.0				2,494.0
United Kingdom Securities	24,119.1	23,775.1	13,570.0	4,920.8	66,385.0

Sources: Annual Reports of the Marketing Boards.
* This is not a complete listing. Current assets and current liabilities are excluded.
† Further allocations were made from Commodity Marketing Board funds after this table's 1954 cut-off date, in the extended period during which their affairs were finally wound up.

By year-end of 1954 (see Table 5) over £23 million had been granted to the Regional Production Development Boards. With the final allocation of the dissolved Commodity Marketing Boards' assets, their total contribution to the Production Development Boards reached £24,666,700. The latter Boards were not able to spend these amounts as quickly as they were received, and therefore accumulated substantial reserves of United Kingdom securities themselves. The amounts which were spent or lent until the mid-1950s were concentrated in agricultural development projects (including government-owned plantations in the Eastern and Western Regions), small-scale processing of agricultural produce both for home consumption and for export, and roads.

In addition to these allocations, the Commodity Marketing Boards also spent nearly £6 million on their own research and development schemes. The largest items of this type were the support of the West African Institute for Oil Palm Research and the West Africa Cocoa Research Institute, grants in support of the Faculty of Agriculture at the University College, Ibadan, and expenditures on roads, distribution of improved seed, stores, etc., in connection with the development of cotton production in the Northern Region. Smaller sums were spent upon other research institutes, surveys, experiments and investigations, co-operative marketing schemes and so forth.

A further commitment had been entered into by the Marketing Boards to lend £14 million to the Federal Government. By 1954 only £2.5 million had been lent (by the Cocoa Marketing Board), and the remaining obligations were assumed by the successor Regional Marketing Boards.

A completely different pattern of disposition of Marketing Board funds emerged following their Regionalisation. Led by the Western Region Marketing Board, the Boards began to supply funds in the form of grants and loans to the Regional Governments, directly to purchase equity in and offer loans to private companies, and to purchase Nigerian Government securities. At the same time expenditures for research and development were continued and expanded in amount. Grants to the successors of the Regional Production Development Boards, now renamed Development Corporations, and to the similarly organised Regional Finance Corporations, on the other hand, were sharply curtailed. These Corporations sharply accelerated their own development expenditures, however, by running down their unspent reserves accumulated from earlier years' Marketing Board grants. By 1962, as a result of these new investments and expenditures, Nigerian Marketing Board holdings of United Kingdom securities had been all but eliminated (see Table 6). Nor was there much left in any other reasonably liquid form of investment which might be employed for stabilisation. By 1961 even working capital requirements for one of the Boards were being supplied through the banking system rather than from the Marketing Boards' own reserves.

By far the greatest beneficiaries of this reserve disposal programme were the Regional Governments. Grants totalling over £33 million had been made by 1961, and loans of a further £16.8 million were outstanding at year-end. Some of these (grants of £1.4 million, loans of £6.4 million) may be considered merely as continuations of the Marketing Boards' allocation of funds to the Development Corporations, since, particularly in the Western Region, where grants from the Marketing Board to the Development Corporation ceased as a matter of policy in 1955, the Regional Governments now became key sources of the Development Corporations' finance. Of the remainder, much was allocated to specific projects: notably the building of the University of Nigeria in the Eastern Region and the University of Ife in the Western Region, and a road-construction programme in the Western Region. But the bulk was turned over or lent to the Regional Governments for general use in the accelerated development effort.

Grants and loans to the Regional Development and Finance Corporations, even allowing for those which were made through the medium of the Regional Governments, were much reduced in the post-1954 period, totalling about £17.2 million.[23] These institutions, however, were much more active during the latter period; by 1962 they had

TABLE 6. *Disposal of Nigerian Regional Marketing Board Funds: Cumulative Grants, Investments and Loans outstanding, 1955-61* (£ 000's).*

	Eastern Region (Dec. 31, 1961).	Northern Region (Oct. 31, 1961).	Western Region (Sept. 31, 1961).	Total (Sept. 30- Dec. 31, 1961).
Cumulative Grants to Regional Government	7,500.0	—	25,589.1	33,089.1
Cumulative Grants to regional development and finance corporations	2,800.0	1,883.2	—	4,683.2
Other Cumulative Grants and expenditures	212.1	3,226.7	5,717.4	9,156.2
Loans outstanding to Federal Government	1,816.9	3,323.6	—	5,140.5
Loans outstanding to Regional Government	—	6,811.2	10,000.0	16,811.2
Loans outstanding to Regional Development and finance corporations	500.0	—	4,200.0	4,700.0
Equity investment in Nigerian private companies	3,545.0	276.0	3,080.0	6,901.0
Loans outstanding to Nigerian private companies	—	800.0	6,288.2	7,088.2
United Kingdom Securities	3,202.2	6,578.0	1,721.6	11,501.8
Federation of Nigeria Securities	—	3,025.1	—	3,025.1

Sources: Annual Reports of the Marketing Boards.
* This is not a complete listing. Current assets and current liabilities are excluded.

totally exhausted their 1955 reserves of £ 13 million. In the second half of the 1950s a large proportion of their funds went into loans to and equity in modern manufacturing enterprises, construction and real-estate firms, and indigenous banks, as well as into the government plantations and other schemes which had been begun earlier.

Other grants and expenditures totalling £ 9.1 million were in continuation of the "own account" research and development activities begun in the earlier period. The Western Region spent the greatest amount in this way, the bulk of it (nearly £ 5 million) going for support of cocoa research and extension work by the Regional Department of Agriculture; a further £ 591,000 was employed to subsidise the sale of chemicals used for spraying cocoa trees against capsid and black pod. The Northern Region spent over £ 1.6 million on the development of an agricultural research station (at Samaru, now a part of the new Sir Ahmadu Bello University) and a further £ 1.2 million on the continued development of cotton production, as well as further amounts upon a variety of experimental schemes and investigations in river transport, textile production, groundnut decortication, and cocoa and palm produce production. The Marketing Boards also continued to support such research institutes as the West African Institute for Oil Palm Research (which received the largest share of the Eastern Region Marketing Board's other grants and expenditures) and the West African Stored Produce Research Unit.

A major innovation in the 1955-62 period was the increasing use of Marketing Board funds for the purposes of loans to and purchases of equity in Nigerian private companies. This occurred at the same time as the Regional and Federal Governments and the Development and Finance Corporations (using funds previously acquired from the Marketing Boards) were also embarking on this course. It is this area in which the greatest possibilities for misuse of funds have been located.

These funds were concentrated in a very few indigenous financial institutions, a real estate concern and two successful industrial enterprises—a cement plant and a textile factory. Of the three Boards, the Western Regional Marketing Board channelled the largest amounts into private enterprise, quite exclusive of those grants to the Development and Finance Corporations which, as has been seen, were actually indirect investments in private enterprises.

The bulk of these went to a bank and a real-estate concern, the affairs of which were closely bound up with those of the political party then in power in the Western Region and its leading members. While it is in any case worth questioning the wisdom on development grounds of devoting £6.7 million for the purpose of "preventing the complete domination of expatriate firms and individuals in the field of real property,"[24] and a further £3.1 million "to assist the growth of well established indigenous banking institutions so that they might be able, if placed on a strong financial position, to assist in the private sector of the country's industrial and commercial activities,"[25] there can be no doubt as to the impropriety of these investments.[26]

The propriety of the largest investment in a private concern by the Eastern Region Marketing Board is also subject to question. This was an investment of £3 million in a bank with a record of connections with the former leader of the political party in control of the Region. As in the West, the Development Corporation of the Eastern Region was also beginning to invest in private enterprises of questionable worth at this time. From a development point of view it is less a matter for concern that ethical standards were not maintained in these instances than that these funds might have been allocated more rationally.

There were, however, more worthwhile undertakings in the area of Marketing Board support of private ventures, notably the taking up of shares in two of the most successful manufacturing enterprises to have been set up in Nigeria; the Nigerian Cement Company at Nkalagu (Eastern Region) and Kaduna Textiles (Northern Region); but the amounts involved in these totalled only £2.2 million.

The recent practices of Nigeria's Marketing Boards with respect to the making of loans and investments in private companies illustrate both the opportunities and the dangers of activities of this sort. On the one hand, government loans to, and investment in, the desired type of private concern is a useful means of achieving expansion and diversification of the economy while maintaining indigenous participation and the commitment to private initiative in a situation where the supply of domestic capital and entrepreneurship is limited. On the other hand, the probability that there will arise from such activities conflicts between public and private or political interests, with the possibility of resulting investment misallocations, is great; particularly is this so where, as in Nigeria, the standards to be expected from those in public life are less than clear and where the number of persons sufficiently wealthy and sophisticated to be engaged in activities of the type which it is intended to encourage is very small.

It would be difficult to summarise the wisdom or foolishness of Marketing Board allocations in a phrase or two, particularly in view of the fact that much was merely passed on to other decision-making authorities. On the face of it, however, the Marketing Boards performed reasonably well. The allocations the wisdom of which it is necessary seriously to question were not, after all, large relative to the total development loans and expenditures made. Disappointment over the misuse or misallocation of some of the funds accumulated should not therefore be permitted to destroy one's perspective on their overall performance as contributors to the development effort.[27]

IV. THE CASES FOR AND AGAINST THE FISCAL ROLE OF THE MARKETING BOARDS

Given the need for revenues to finance the Government's development effort, is the earning of trading surpluses by monopsonistic Marketing Boards the optimal means of obtaining them? In the first place, the objections are frequently raised that the Nigerian Marketing Boards were originally established for the benefit of (or as trustees for) the producers, and that their activities should not, in any case, infringe upon the general revenue-raising and development-promoting responsibilities of the governments concerned.

> "One cannot have it both ways; if an organization is to have taxation rights it should be integrated with the Government and if it is not to be integrated it must not act so as to be a permanent instrument of taxation of the producer groups it is supposed to represent."[28]

From the point of view of general principles and both administrative and intellectual tidiness, this cannot be disputed. Moreover, the present untidiness is easily remediable. Since both the largest share of trading surpluses and 100% of export duties now return to the Regional Governments, changes in export duty rates could quickly rectify the situation by converting trading surpluses into export taxes. But this is obviously not the central issue.

The main question concerns the general suitability of taxes, regardless of whether they are called "trading surpluses" or "export duties," levied upon export producers. The Marketing Board system of earning continual surpluses is institutionally different but does not, after all, alter the fact that an export tax is being collected; trading surpluses which are subsequently spent upon general development projects, as far as producers are concerned, are identical to export duties. The principal ground for heavy taxation of exports is its convenience. In a country where *per capita* income is very low, administrative personnel are scarce, modern accounting practices are nonexistent and much of the population is self-employed or engaged in "traditional" (and therefore unrecorded) economic activity, recourse must be had to maximum revenue collection in the few sectors where it is possible. In that it must pass through only a very few ports, foreign trade is easily measured, controlled and taxed.

From the point of view of equity, the case for heavy taxation of export production is a shaky one. One cannot, of course, adequately discuss the equity of one particular tax without considering its place within the whole tax structure. It is nevertheless clear that export taxation, in the Nigerian context, constitutes an extra burden for one type of productive activity which is not borne by others. The other principal sources of government revenues (import and excise duties, income taxes, property rates, etc.) are taxes which are levied upon all incomes, those of export producers as well as of others; but these export producers' incomes have already borne export tax. Export production is thus subject to double taxation. In some instances this may be quite fair, representing, among other things, a means of achieving some "progressiveness" of the tax burden. It is altogether likely, for instance, that many of the highest incomes earned in Nigeria have always been attributable to export cropping. It is also true that the huge post-war export price increases involved a large element of windfall gain. But there can also be little question that many, if not most, export producers conduct operations on a tiny scale and can only be depicted as extremely poor. The burden of the tax on the latter seems unreasonably heavy when compared with that borne by non-export producers. It may also be considered unfair when compared with that borne by larger producers of the same export crop, for the tax is withheld to an equal extent on the sale of each individual ton of the export crop. The rich peasant who owns several acres and produces relatively large quantities has the same proportion of his export crop income withheld as does the poor one who sells very little. Export taxation may not therefore be the most equitable revenue-earner imaginable.

Far more fundamental issues are involved in a consideration of the overall development effects of export taxes. There remains considerable disagreement as to the desirability, from a development point of view, of their imposition. The principal questions at issue are two: (1) the extent of supply elasticity with respect to prices on the part of the peasant producers; (2) the uses to which marginal increases in peasant incomes are put. Both are questions of fact, but neither have received a degree of empirical investigation sufficient to justify the making of very firm statements.

As soon as it is granted that there exists positive price-elasticity of supply, it must also be granted that the taxation of the sale of the commodity concerned reduces these sales, and therefore, given the elastic world demand curve facing Nigeria for all its principal exports, because of its small relative importance in world markets, reduces export proceeds and domestic product. In most less-developed countries lack of foreign exchange and the inadequacy of savings out of a very low domestic product are significant constraints upon the development effort. These effects cannot therefore be taken lightly.

Price-elasticity of supply is extremely difficult to establish in Nigeria, where disease, pests and weather are such important and largely uncontrollable variables, and where data are, in any case, so sparse and unreliable. As far as tree crops such as cocoa (and rubber, which is not sold through Marketing Boards in Nigeria) are concerned, it is clear that short-term supply elasticity must be very small, if not non-existent. Some such response may be possible through varying attention to disease and pest control and changing intensity of harvesting, but this is not likely to be very important. The important supply responses are longer-term ones, resulting in increased output only after a lag of several years. There is evidence that cocoa-tree planting in Nigeria has responded to changes in producer prices.[29] Thus, all other things being equal, export proceeds from cocoa will be greater in six or seven years time in the absence of the export tax than they would have been with its imposition.

There do exist substantial opportunities for more immediate supply responses on the parts of other peasant producers—those selling palm oil, palm kernels, groundnuts and cotton. Palm oil and palm kernels are obtained from wild trees which grow profusely in the southern parts of Nigeria without human involvement in plantings, cultivation or care of any sort. It is unlikely that the harvest of palm fruit ever approaches the potential total available from the wild trees. One would therefore expect to observe substantial price-elasticity of supply of palm produce. Particularly is this so in the case of palm oil, which is consumed locally as a cooking fat, an illuminant and an input for soap-making, as well as being exported. The recent reduction in overall sales of kernels and oil which coincides with the sharp reduction in real producer prices tends to confirm the suspicion that there exists a positive supply response in this sector. Far more striking, however, is the clear relationship between the proportion of palm oil produced which is sold to the Marketing Board and the real producer price.[30] There seems little doubt that export sales could be increased by raising producer prices.

The production of groundnuts and cotton is similarly potentially price-responsive in that they are annual crops, the acreage of which can easily be altered from year to year. Moreover, there exists the possibility of domestic consumption, particularly in the case of groundnuts, where about 30% of total production is normally not sold for export. But sales to the Marketing Boards are the only data available, and they are greatly affected by weather and other food crops' experiences. Price responses are not therefore observable from existing statistical sources. There exists little reason, however, to doubt that peasant producers of groundnuts react to price changes much as do those of cocoa and palm produce. Supporting evidence is provided by the swift response which has been observed to the introduction of quality differentials in groundnut prices; within three years of the introduction of differentials between special and standard grade, Kano area sales to the Marketing Board of special-grade nuts rose from 2 to 99% of the total.[31]

Export taxation therefore clearly may produce current foreign exchange earnings and a domestic product lower than they might be in its absence. This implies an unfavourable distortion of the production structure away from the export production in which the economy is most efficient. At a time when the Regional Governments are all anxiously trying to persuade the urban unemployed to return to the land and farmers to stay there, such a distortion away from agricultural production should be viewed seriously. But this in itself is not sufficient objection to the use of export taxes. There remains the crucial question as to what would be done with the extra income which the peasants would enjoy in the absence of the tax.[32] It is possible that all of it would be spent upon increased imports of consumer-goods— either directly or after a couple of income "rounds." If this is the case a higher immediate level of peasant (and perhaps other) living is attained but there is no gain whatsoever from the higher income from the point of view of capital accumulation and the raising of future incomes. If, on the other hand, the increased income were all saved, the development potential of the country could be greatly increased. This could, of course, occur in a variety of ways. The increased income could be ploughed right back into agriculture either through local investment expenditure such as land clearing or through imports of capital equipment. Alternatively, it could be mobilised in other sectors through direct branching-out of their activities by farmers, direct loans (often to relatives), or deposits with financial intermediaries; or it could, if hoarded, merely free scarce resources (notably foreign exchange) for employment by others in investment activities.

What sort of evidence do we possess on this question? The paucity of research on farm expenditure pattern forces reliance upon three out-of-date studies. An investigation of Yoruba cocoa farmers in 1951-52 showed clearly that, once a family net income of £100 had been reached (below which savings were zero), the percentage of disposable income saved increased with the size of income.[33] Most of these savings in the year of study went into hoardings of cash, or what may be regarded as private stabilisation and development reserves, rather than productive investment;[34] but this year may well have been unrepresentative. Very little ever makes its way into the banking system, but considerable sums are lent and borrowed among neighbours and relatives. To the extent that savings are ultimately reinvested the principal outlets for cocoa farmers are into clearing and planting operations (both in cocoa and in food) and houses. More occasionally, investment in transport and business equipment, such as lorries, bicycles, sewing machines and corn-mills, takes place.[35]

A roughly concurrent study of Ibibio oil-palm farmers in the Eastern Region also showed that savings were occurring even at low incomes. It indicated, moreover, that local (indigenous) credit institutions played a large role in their mobilisation. The uses to which they were put were mainly housing, education and such business equipment as bicycles, hand-presses and sewing machines.[36]

Similar findings were made in a study undertaken in the Zaria area of Northern Nigeria. Only after a certain (unspecified) level of income is reached do more "productive" expenditures, such as the hiring of more farm labour, the building of new housing or the purchases of bicycles, corn-mills, sewing-machines, sugar-crushers or lorries, take place. For the majority, it is usual to spend all of the cash income upon consumption goods.[37]

As far as the increased peasant income which would accrue from reduced export taxes are concerned, two conclusions seem inescapable: (1) the largest proportion would be consumed; (2) of the amounts which were saved, most would be directed to agricultural improvements or extensions at the local level, residential construction, small-scale purchases of equipment, such as sewing-machines and bicycles, and private expenditures on education. Furthermore, it is unlikely that the factors freed by the hoarding of savings, to the extent that this is a significant outlet, would ever be employed at all, given the limited credit availability characteristic in underdeveloped areas and the fact that the size of the government programme is predetermined.

It remains to be demonstrated that the employment of the taxes collected by the Government from export production was, in some sense, preferable to the consumption and investment expenditures which would have taken place in their absence. This paper will not attempt to demonstrate that this has, in general, been the case. Since the arguments with which it is concerned have to do with Marketing Boards, the discussion here will be confined to the uses which were made of Marketing Board funds. Discussion of the disposal of export duties, so called, cannot, in any event, be separated from a general discussion of the composition of total government expenditures.[38]

Can it be said that the uses to which the trading surpluses earned by the Nigerian Marketing Boards were put were superior to those to which the peasant farmers would have put them had they been given the opportunity? Since a much larger proportion of the increase in peasant income would have been consumed than that which was actually consumed out of Marketing Board trading surpluses, the rates of return on peasant investments would have had to be much greater than those on Marketing Board ones if peasant uses of the funds in the aggregate were really to have been considered superior. The disposition of Marketing Board surpluses may not have been perfect, but the rates of return from their investments in research, roads, agricultural schemes, universities, modern manufacturing plants and so forth are unlikely to have been any lower than those on housing, sewing-machines, land clearing and the other small-scale outlets for peasant funds discussed above, let alone so much lower as to offset the difference between consumption ratios.[39] It can therefore unambiguously be stated that Nigerian development has been aided through the device of channelling a portion of its export earnings via the Marketing Boards away from the producer to other (governmental) decision-makers.

Nigeria's Marketing Boards have collected over £106 million in trading surpluses and have earned (net) a further £20 million on the assets thus accumulated during the fourteen years since the first Nigerian Board was formed. These are considerable sums in an economy as poor as Nigeria's; they are sufficient to make these Marketing Boards pivotal elements in any governmental stabilisation or mobilisation policies. Originally earned primarily for the purpose of stabilising producer prices, in anticipation of future declines in world prices, they were ultimately used for public developmental expenditures. Moreover, since the mid-1950s the Eastern and Western Region Marketing Boards not only employed their former stabilisation reserves for development purposes but also began consciously to earn current trading surpluses for the same purposes. In these Regions there can no longer be any question that the role of the Marketing Boards has changed from those of protector of the farmer's interests and stabiliser of his prices to that of collector of a portion of his income as taxes for the use of the Regional Governments.

Nigeria's use of the Marketing Boards as collectors of the revenues so desperately needed for its public development effort can be neither wholly commended nor wholly condemned. Against their remarkable success as revenue collectors in an environment where revenues are hard to find must be set the doubtful suitability of these institutions for such a role, the unquestionable inequities of export taxation, the probable distortions in the production structure which such taxation introduces and the losses incurred through improper timing of expenditures. To this list are frequently added further general reservations applicable to any form of taxation and government activity as to the desirability of reducing private incentives and opportunities for saving and small-scale investment; and as to the likelihood that governments ever spend the revenues more intelligently than the tax-payers would have. On the latter counts it has been argued that the Nigerian economy has benefited from more rather than less taxation.

The Marketing Boards' uses of the earnings from their trading operations, while subject to question in some particular instances, notably those involving equity investment in and loans to private companies, have clearly promoted economic development. Such diverse activities as agricultural research and experimentation, the construction of universities, road-building and modern manufacturing have all benefited from the Marketing Boards' support. On balance, it would be difficult not to conclude that the earning and subsequent spending of trading (and other surpluses) by the Marketing Boards were beneficial to the economic development of Nigeria.

If this is true, and if it can confidently be expected that the wisdom of governmental expenditure policies will not deteriorate, there are clear policy implications. Marketing Boards, the principal objects of which are to mobilise savings (tax revenues), should obviously not be worrying unduly about stabilising producer prices or incomes, matters with which too much public discussion has been concerned. Nor should they be seeking to maximise export earnings, as many others have urged. They should, rather, be exerting all their monopsony power to the full so as to maximise their own trading profits. A profit-maximising strategy, of course, calls not simply for the minimisation of producer price. Too low a producer price may result in supply reductions which more than offset the lower price paid, and thereby produce smaller absolute trading surpluses; this is a possibility to which particular attention should be devoted by the Eastern Nigeria Marketing Board, for the reductions in supplies of palm oil and palm kernels in recent years have been substantial. The appropriate strategy for the profit-maximising Marketing Boards, as for monopsonists anywhere, is to set the producer price so as to equalise marginal revenue, as derived from the relevant world demand curve facing Nigeria, and marginal cost, as derived from the relevant Nigerian producers' supply schedule.

A few other policy recommendations also derive from the above discussion. In the first place it seems reasonable that, for as long as heavy reliance must be placed upon export taxation, the Marketing Board trading surpluses should be converted, through appropriate adjustments of the fiscal structure, into export duties and treated identically with other government revenues. In this way the development responsibilities of the Government will be clearly separated from those other functions now being performed by the Marketing Boards, such as intra-season price stabilisation, orderly marketing and so forth, which can more reasonably be considered to reflect the farmers' interests. Secondly, as the opportunities for direct taxation of other sources of income appear, one would hope for a gradual shift to a more equitable (and less distorting) tax structure. This may, unfortunately, be a long time coming. Last, but probably most important of all, greater attention must be devoted to the economic rationality of the allocation of government expenditures. The mechanism of export taxation through the earning of Marketing Board trading surpluses has worked well, but there remain opportunities for considerable improvement.

APPENDIX

Taxes and Marketing Board Trading Surpluses Earned on Major Types of Nigerian Marketing Board Controlled Agricultural Produce, 1947-62

Sources: (1) *Annual Reports of the Marketing Boards.*
(2) *Report(s) of the Accountant-General of the Federation of Nigeria with Financial Statements for the Year(s) ending March 31st, 1955-61.*
(3) Federation of Nigeria, *Digest of Statistics.*
(4) *Marketing Board Statistics* (Lagos, mimeo).

TABLE A-1. Cocoa.*

	Export duties.†		Marketing Board Trading surplus.		Produce purchase tax.‡		Total withdrawals, £000's.	Producer income,§ £000's.	Potential producer income,‖ £000's.	Total withdrawls as % of potential producer income.
	£000's.	% of potential producer income.	£000's.	% of potential producer income.	£000's.	% of potential producer income.				
1947/48	307.1†	2.2	9,201.8	66.2	—		9,508.9	4,380.4	13,889.3	68.5
1948/49	700.1†	5.1	420.6	3.1	—		1,120.7	12,589.3	13,710.0	8.2
1949/50	608.1	3.4	6,479.4	36.2	—		7,087.5	10,792.4	17,879.9	39.6
1950/51	4,461.8	15.2	10,549.6	36.0	—		15,011.4	14,316.6	29,328.0	51.2
1951/52	5,494.2	21.9	1,438.7	5.7	—		6,932.9	18,164.5	25,097.4	27.6
1952/53	4,527.5	19.6	87.3	0.4	—		4,614.8	18,435.1	23,049.9	20.0
1953/54	11,466.0	33.8	5,620.0	16.6	389.7	1.2	17,475.7	16,398.9	33,874.6	51.6
Subtotal, 1947/48 to 1953/54	27,564.8	17.6	33,797.4	21.6	389.7	0.2	61,751.9	95,077.2	156,829.1	39.4
1954/55	5,569.8	21.0	5,025.8	19.0	334.3	1.3	10,929.9	15,540.5	26,470.4	41.3
1955/56	3,844.5	19.0	-4,169.0	-20.6	423.9	2.1	99.4	20,101.4	20,200.8	0.5
1956/57	3,223.1	14.8	-1,266.0	-5.8	513.7	2.4	2,470.8	19,231.1	21,701.9	11.4
1957/58	4,153.3	20.8	4,916.3	24.6	294.6	1.5	9,364.2	10,583.8	19,948.0	46.9
1958/59	7,504.5	21.4	7,830.6	22.4	526.1	1.5	15,861.2	19,116.0	34,977.2	45.3
1959/60	5,484.7	18.5	1,098.6	3.7	585.4	2.0	7,168.7	22,471.3	29,640.0	24.2
1960/61¶	3,938.5	14.1	-3,752.9	-13.5	727.7	2.6	913.3	26,952.3	27,865.6	3.3
1961/62	3,198.1	12.6	3,157.2	12.4	757.5	3.0	7,112.8	18,299.7	25,412.5	28.0
Subtotal, 1954/55 to 1961/62	36,916.5	17.9	12,840.6	6.2	4,163.2	2.0	53,920.3	152,296.1	206,216.4	26.1
Total	64,481.3	17.8	46,638.0	12.8	4,552.9	1.3	115,672.2	247,373.3	363,045.5	31.9

144

* Up until 1953/54 inclusive statistics refer to all Nigeria (plus Southern Cameroons); from 1954/55 on they refer only to the Western Region.

† Includes a small element of "inspection fees."

‡ Obtained by applying tax rate of £4 per ton to tonnages purchased.

§ Derived directly from Annual Reports of the Marketing Boards. Where necessary, estimates of buying allowances have been made.

‖ Defined as producer income (actual, excluding produce purchase tax) *plus* export duties *plus* produce purchase tax *plus* Marketing Board trading expenses (trading expenses only) *plus* increase in stocks.

¶ Results published in the Annual Report for this year were inaccurate. Correct results have been furnished by the Western Region Marketing Board.

145

TABLE A-2. *Groundnuts.*

	Export duties.†		Marketing Board Trading surplus.		Produce purchase tax.‡		Total withdrawals, £000's.	Producer income,§ £000's.	Potential producer income,‖ £000's.	Total withdrawals as % of potential producer income.
	£000's.	% of potential producer income.	£000's.	% of potential producer income.	£000's.	% of potential producer income.				
1947/48	873.6	8.3	4,267.2	40.5	—		5,140.0	5,376.0	10,516.0	48.8
1948/49	1,065.9	8.0	6,137.0	45.7	—		7,202.9	6,201.6	13,404.5	53.7
1949/50	620.4	8.8	2,444.0	34.6	—		3,064.0	3,985.6	7,049.6	43.4
1950/51	675.9	10.9	3,002.7	48.5	—		3,678.6	2,513.5	6,192.1	59.4
1951/52	2,524.5	14.4	4,851.3	27.6	—		7,375.8	10,185.7	17,561.5	42.0
1952/53	2,638.9	13.5	3,505.8	17.9	—		6,144.7	13,449.7	19,594.4	31.4
1953/54	2,929.9	12.0	3,588.6	14.7	424.6	1.7	6,943.1	17,515.0	24,458.1	28.4
Subtotal, 1947/48 to 1953/54	11,329.1	11.5	27,796.6	28.1	424.6	0.4	39,549.1	59,227.1	98,776.2	40.0
1954/55	2,633.0	16.6	−133.1	−0.8	372.8	2.4	2,873	12,969	15,842	18.1
1955/56	3,314.0	14.3	1,075.5	4.6	530.2	2.3	4,920	18,303	23,223	21.2
1956/57	2,554.0	13.6	3,075.0	16.3	357.9	1.9	5,987	12,812	18,799	31.8
1957/58	3,059.0	13.6	−4,041.5	−18.0	714.7	3.2	−268	22,686	22,418	−1.2
1958/59	3,195.0	13.6	−1,970.2	−8.4	533.4	2.3	1,758	21,675	23,433	7.5
1959/60	2,686.0	13.2	828.4	4.0	445.4	2.2	3,960	16,464	20,424	19.4
1960/61	3,384.0	13.3	−887.4	−3.5	619.1	2.4	3,116	22,405	25,521	12.2
Subtotal, 1954/55 to 1960/61	20,825.0	14.0	−2,053.3	−1.4	3,573.5	2.4	22,346	127,314	149,660	14.9
Total	32,154	12.9	25,743.3	10.4	3,998.1	1.6	61,895	186,541	248,436	24.9

146

* Up until 1953/54 inclusive figures include all Nigeria; from 1954/55 on they refer only to the Northern Region. Figures for 1947/48, 1948/49 and 1949/50 are calculated from figures in P. T. Bauer, *West African Trade*, p. 401. His figures for later years do not agree with mine, but they are usually not far off; in the absence of any substitutes I therefore employ his annual figures. This produces a slight discrepancy between the relevant total Marketing Board trading surpluses shown in this table and those shown in Table 3 in the text, which was derived directly from Marketing Board Annual Reports.

The 1947/48 and 1948/49 figures refer to Nigerian operations of the West African Produce Control Board (W.A.P.C.B.). The 1949/50 figure is partly W.A.P.C.B. and partly Nigeria Groundnut Marketing Board.

† From 1950/51 until and including 1953/54 the export duty figures are taken from the Annual Reports of the Groundnut Marketing Board. For subsequent years there are only calendar-year figures available. I have therefore employed the calendar-year figures for the latter years of the two stated in the crop year; as stated in the Digest of Statistics (revenues due at time of shipment). Figures for these latter years include duties on groundnut oil.

‡ Obtained by applying tax rate of £1 per ton to tonnages purchased.

§ Same as footnote § to Table A-1.

‖ Same as footnote ‖ to Table A-1.

147

TABLE A-3. Palm Kernels.*

	Export duties.†		Marketing Board trading surplus.		Produce purchase tax.‡		Total withdrawals, £000's.	Producer income,§ £000's.	Potential producer income,‖ £000's.	Total withdrawals as % of potential producer income.
	£000's.	% of potential producer income.	£000's.	% of potential producer income.	£000's.	% of potential producer income.				
1947	347.6	4.4	2,433.2	30.7	—		2,780.8	5,150.8	7,930.9	35.1
1948	784.8	7.9	2,550.6	25.5	—		3,335.4	6,638.1	9,973.5	33.4
1949	827.2	5.5	4,512.0	29.8	—		5,339.2	9,776.0	15,115.2	35.3
1950	1,080.4	7.9	2,553.7	18.7	—		3,634.1	10,000.3	13,634.4	26.7
1951	1,805.1	10.3	4,818.2	27.5	—		6,623.3	10,901.1	17,524.4	37.8
1952	2,361.0	11.0	4,044.5	18.9	—		6,405.5	14,963.5	21,369.0	30.0
1953	2,280.1	11.4	2,538.4	12.7	—		4,818.4	15,096.5	19,915.0	24.2
1954	2,385.7	11.4	1,645.1	7.8	—		4,030.8	16,944.3	20,975.1	19.2
Subtotal, 1947-54	11,871.9	9.4	25,095.7	19.9	—		36,967.6	89,470.6	126,437.5	29.2
1955	1,874.7	12.9	523.1	3.5	593.0	4.1	2,990.8	11,573.4	14,564.2	20.5
1956	2,123.3	13.1	260.6	1.6	657.5	4.1	3,041.4	13,131.5	16,172.9	18.8
1957	1,734.8	11.9	−257.9	−1.7	596.3	4.1	2,073.2	12,393.1	14,466.3	14.3
1958	2,286.5	14.2	635.0	3.9	647.9	4.0	3,569.4	12,508.9	16,078.3	22.2
1959	2,864.8	13.4	5,780.4	27.1	620.0	2.9	9,265.2	12,050.7	21,315.9	43.5
1960	2,292.7	12.0	4,379.2	23.0	611.5	3.2	7,283.4	11,774.7	19,058.1	38.2
1961	1,948.3	13.1	562.1	3.8	601.2	4.0	3,111.6	11,790.8	14,902.4	20.9
Subtotal, 1955-61	15,125.1	13.1	11,882.5	10.3	4,327.4	3.7	31,335.0	85,223.1	116,588.1	27.1
Total	26,997.0	11.1	36,978.2	15.2	4,327.4	1.8	68,302.6	174,693.7	242,996.3	28.1

* Up until 1954 inclusive, statistics refer to all Nigeria (plus Southern Cameroons); from 1955 on, they refer only to Eastern and Western Regions except in the case of export duties. Figures for 1947, 1948 and 1949 were calculated from figures in P. T. Bauer, *West African Trade*, p. 407, 1947 and 1948 refer to Nigerian operations of the W.A.P.C.B. The year 1947 is partly W.A.P.C.B. and partly Nigeria Oil Palm Produce Marketing Board. Other comments in note 1 to Table A-2 apply.

† From 1955 on, sum of surpluses earned on palm kernel trading by Eastern Region and Western Region using the latter year of the two included in the Western Region's fiscal year to correspond with the calendar year followed by the Eastern Regional Marketing Board.

‡ Obtained by applying tax rate to tonnage purchased. The 1961 figure, however, is my rough estimate.
§ Same as footnote § to Table A-1.
‖ Same as footnote ‖ to Table A-1.

149

TABLE A-4. *Palm Oil.**

	Export duties.†		Marketing Board trading surplus.		Produce purchase tax.‡		Total withdrawals, £000's.	Producer income,§ £000's.	Potential producer income,‖ £000's.	Total withdrawals as % of Potential producer income.
	£000's.	% of potential producer income.	£000's.	% of potential producer income.	£000's.	% of potential producer income.				
1947	75.6	1.8	995.4	23.7	—		1,071.0	3,124.8	4,195.8	25.5
1948	347.5	4.4	3,169.2	40.3	—		3,516.7	4,336.8	7,853.5	44.8
1949	660.1	6.8	2,511.6	26.1	—		3,171.7	6,440.0	9,611.7	32.9
1950	694.4	7.3	1,996.9	21.1	—		2,691.3	6,792.9	9,484.2	28.4
1951	1,167.1	10.5	2,301.3	20.7	—		3,468.4	7,643.7	11,112.1	31.2
1952	1,753.8	10.7	2,508.3	15.3	—		4,262.1	12,081.4	16,343.5	26.1
1953	1,285.1	11.8	-4,647.1	-42.7	—		-3,362.0	14,247.2	10,885.2	-30.9
1954	1,371.9	11.3	-2,292.0	-18.9	—		-920.1	13,041.8	12,121.7	-7.6
Subtotal, 1947-54	7,355.5	9.0	6,543.6	8.0	—		13,899.1	67,708.6	81,607.7	17.0
1955	1,350.0	13.3	377.7	-3.7	658.4	6.5	1,630.7	8,511.9	10,142.6	16.1
1956	1,736.3	14.3	1,669.8	13.7	654.6	5.4	4,060.7	8,094.7	12,155.4	33.4
1957	1,426.8	12.9	1,694.8	15.4	616.9	5.6	3,738.5	7,300.3	11,038.8	33.9
1958	1,343.9	13.3	263.5	2.6	667.9	6.6	2,275.3	7,816.2	10,091.5	22.5
1959	1,416.3	13.6	853.1	8.2	678.9	6.5	2,948.3	7,453.7	10,402.0	28.3
1960	1,270.7	13.6	6.0	0.00064	676.6	7.3	1,953.3	7,377.5	9,330.8	20.9
1961	1,102.4	11.9	195.7	2.1	638.4	6.9	1,936.5	7,323.0	9,259.5	20.9
Subtotal, 1955-61	9,646.4	13.3	4,305.2	5.9	4,591.7	6.3	18,543.3	53,877.3	72,420.6	25.6
Total	17,001.9	11.0	10,848.8	7.0	4,591.7	3.0	32,442.4	121,585.9	154,028.3	21.0

150

* Until 1954 inclusive (1957 inclusive for export duties), statistics refer to all of Nigeria; after, only for the Eastern Region. Figures for 1947, 1948 and 1949 were calculated from figures in P. T. Bauer, *West African Trade*, p. 407. 1947 and 1948 refer to Nigerian operations of the W.A.P.C.B. The year 1947 is partly W.A.P.C.B. and partly Nigeria Oil Palm Produce Marketing Board. Other comments in note * to Table A-2 apply.

† From 1950 to 1954 inclusive, export duty figures are taken from *Digest of Statistics* (various issues). From 1955 to 1960 inclusive, they are from the *Reports of the Accountant-General of the Federation of Nigeria* (various issues) using the former year of the two calendar years included in its fiscal year to correspond with the calendar year followed by the Eastern Regional Marketing Board. The 1961 figures are taken from the accounts of the Eastern Regional Marketing Board.

‡ Same as note † to Table A-3.
§ Same as note § to Table A-1.
‖ Same as note ‖ to Table A-1.

TABLE A-5. Cotton.*

	Export duties.†		Marketing Board trading surplus.		Produce purchase tax.‡		Total withdrawals, £000's.	Producer income,§ £000's.	Potential producer income,‖ £000's.	Total withdrawals as % of potential producer income.
	£000's.	% of potential producer income.	£000's.	% of potential producer income.	£000's.	% of potential producer income.				
1949/50	—		1,185.9	48.4	—		1,185.9	1,266.6	2,452.5	48.4
1950/51	386.0	9.6	2,077.6	51.5	—		2,463.6	1,569.1	4,032.7	61.1
1951/52	713.7	13.6	1,028.5	19.6	—		1,742.2	3,509.5	5,251.7	33.2
1952/53	812.2	16.1	1,440.0	28.5	—		2,252.2	2,795.2	5,047.4	44.6
1953/54	775.1	12.4	1,236.6	19.9	70.3	1.1	2,082.0	4,147.3	6,229.3	33.4
Subtotal, 1949/50 to 1953/54	2,687.0	11.7	6,968.6	30.3	70.3	0.3	9,725.9	13,287.7	23,013.6	42.3
1954/55	813.6	10.3	1,672.1	21.2	92.1	1.2	2,577.8	5,303.1	7,880.9	32.7
1955/56	1,058.2	17.6	500.7	8.3	75.4	1.3	1,634.3	4,378.9	6,013.2	27.2
1956/57	751.1	15.1	230.7	4.6	68.1	1.4	1,049.9	3,934.3	4,984.2	21.1
1957/58	756.3	11.4	−949.5	−14.4	115.6	1.8	−77.6	6,687.6	6,610.0	−1.2
1958/59	918.8	19.4	−983.3	−20.7	81.5	1.7	17.0	4,729.8	4,746.8	0.4
1959/60	693.6	15.4	−990.5	−22.0	80.2	1.8	−217.6	4,726.7	4,510.0	−4.8
1960/61	779.4	9.7	−1,176.5	−14.7	208.7	2.6	−188.4	8,196.5	8,008.1	−2.4
Subtotal, 1954/55 to 1960/61	5,771.0	13.5	−1,696.3	−4.0	721.6	1.7	4,796.3	37,956.9	42,753.2	11.2
Total	8,458.0	12.9	5,272.3	8.0	791.9	1.2	14,522.2	51,244.6	65,766.8	22.1

* Until and including 1953/54, statistics refer to all of Nigeria; from then on, they refer only to the Northern Region, except in the case of export duties.

† Up until and including 1953/54, from Annual Reports of the Nigeria Cotton Marketing Board. From then on, export duty figures were taken from the *Annual Reports of the Accountant-General of the Federation of Nigeria* (various issues).

‡ Calculated by applying tax rate to purchases data.

§ Same as note § to Table A-1.

‖ Same as note ‖ to Table A-1.

152

NOTES

1. This study was prepared under the auspices of the Economic Growth Center at Yale University. Most of the research underlying this paper was undertaken while I enjoyed an Associate Research Fellowship at the Nigerian Institute of Social and Economic Research in Ibadan. I am grateful to Mr. M. O. Kayode for statistical assistance, to the officers of the three Nigerian Marketing Boards for their co-operation, and to Professors Donald Mead, Hugh Patrick and Donald Snodgrass of Yale University, who offered comments on an earlier draft.

2. Stabilisation and mobilisation of savings are not the only possible aims of Marketing Board policies. In a discussion of the Ghanaian experience with Marketing Boards Reginald Green also lists the establishment of confidence in the future of the industry, the pursuit of general fiscal and price policies for the entire economy, income redistribution and the pursuit of international price stabilisation. Reginald Green, "Ghana Cocoa Marketing Policy, 1938-1960," *Nigerian Institute of Social and Economic Research, Conference Proceedings*, December 1960, pp. 132-60. One might also add the improvement of marketing facilities and quality of produce.

3. P. T. Bauer, *West African Trade* (1964), chapters 23, 24.

4. Including the accumulations in respect of Nigerian oil palm produce and groundnuts by the West African Produce Control Board during the 1947-49 period before the creation of the Nigerian Marketing Boards for these products.

5. "Potential producer income" is defined here as actual producer income plus export duties, Marketing Board trading surplus and produce sales tax. Strictly speaking, the potential for producer incomes is actually higher than this if, as is likely, there exists positive price-elasticity of supply and greater than unit elasticity of world demand for Nigerian produce.

6. Only groundnut and cotton trading are included in this figure. Rough calculations suggest that a further large deficit was encountered in groundnut trading during the 1961/62 season, but there are as yet no figures to confirm them.

7. Nigeria Cocoa Marketing Ordinance of 1947, section 16.

8. *First Annual Report of the Nigeria Groundnut Marketing Board*, p. 16.

9. Although not, as will be seen, from those of the Nigeria Cotton Marketing Board.

10. The Cocoa Marketing Board spent its own development allocations until 1951, but thereafter it, too, turned them over to the Production Development Boards. The Cotton Marketing Board never did transfer any development funds to the latter Boards, retaining its authority to

spend them itself because of "the facts that the present main area of cotton production is a confined one, and that the industry is still relatively small and requires separate and special fostering care" (*Second Report of the Nigeria Cotton Marketing Board*, p. 16).

11. *First Annual Report of the Nigeria Cotton Marketing Board*, p. 21.

12. *House of Representatives Debates*, First Session, 1952, I, p. 46.

13. International Bank for Reconstruction and Development, *The Economic Development of Nigeria* (1955), p. 88.

14. Western Region of Nigeria, *Development of the Western Region of Nigeria, 1955-1960* (Sessional Paper no. 4 of 1955), p. 15.

15. Government of Western Nigeria, *Western Region Development Plan 1960-1965* (Sessional Paper no. 17 of 1959).

16. Government of Western Nigeria, *Western Nigeria Development Plan 1962-1968* (Sessional Paper no. 8 of 1962), p. 12.

17. *Ibid.*, p. 50.

18. Eastern Region, Nigeria, *Development Programme, 1958-62* (Eastern Region Official Document No. 2 of 1959).

19. *Eastern Nigeria Development Plan, 1962-68* (Official Document No. 8 of 1962), p. 17.

20. *Fourth Annual Report of the Northern Regional Marketing Board*, p. 8.

21. *Fifth Annual Report of the Northern Regional Marketing Board*, p. 7.

22. Government of Northern Nigeria, Ministry of Economic Planning, *Development Plan, 1962-68*, p. 44.

23. Some of this amount, moreover, was immediately on-lent to private companies. In this case the Development Corporations were little more than intermediaries.

24. Federation of Nigeria, *Report of Coker Commission of Inquiry into the Affairs of Certain Statutory Corporations in Western Nigeria*, 1962, I, p. 65.

25. *Ibid.*, p. 26.

26. Nor was this the whole story. The activities of the Western Nigeria Development Corporation also involved gross improprieties and carelessness, the whole of which are documented in the Coker Report cited above.

27. One further minor point concerning the expenditure of these funds should be made in passing. This concerns the losses incurred through the delay between the dates at which the bulk of the trading surpluses were earned and the dates at which they were expended. These losses took two forms. As a result of the timing pattern of the Nigerian investments in and sales of United Kingdom securities, considerable capital losses were suffered. At the same time, increases in the prices of Nigerian imports probably diminished the real value of the proceeds of the securities' sales. Neither of these losses were large enough, however, to alter the conclusions which can be reached

on other grounds concerning the success of Nigerian Marketing Board experience; and neither relate to the more general issues discussed below.

28. A. R. Prest, *Public Finance in Under-Developed Countries* (1962), p. 71. See also International Bank for Reconstruction and Development, *The Economic Development of Nigeria* (1955), p. 88.

29. R. Galletti, K. D. S. Baldwin and I. O. Dina, *Nigerian Cocoa Farmers, An Economic Survey of Yoruba Cocoa Farming Facilities* (Oxford University Press, 1956), pp. 3-4.

30. A correlation coefficient of $+0.96$ was found between the annual Eastern Nigeria producer price for palm oil deflated by consumer price index, and the annual proportion of Eastern Nigeria palm oil production (implicit in export sales of palm kernels, which are jointly produced with palm oil from the palm fruit and have no domestic use) which was sold to the Eastern Regional Marketing Board between 1949 and 1961.

31. Similar experience with quality differentials has been encountered with other Nigerian peasant-produced commodities.

32. This extra income may be greater than the mere amount of the tax collected, particularly if there has been some leisure foregone as a result of the changed terms of trade between leisure and production.

33. R. Galletti, K. D. S. Baldwin and I. O. Dina, *op. cit.*, pp. 462-73. This study showed remarkably high savings, averaging about 40 per cent of disposable income, but these were attributed to a large and unexpected increase in producer incomes to which final adjustments had not yet been made (p. 461).

34. *Ibid.*, pp. 279, 571, 601.

35. *Loc. cit.*

36. Anne Martin, *The Oil Palm Economy of the Ibibio Farmer* (Ibadan University Press, 1956), pp. 18, 21-22.

37. M. G. Smith, *The Economy of Hausa Communities of Zaria, A Report to the Colonial Social Science Research Council* (H.M.S.O., 1955), pp. 165-68.

38. It can be argued that Marketing Board trading surpluses should also be considered as part of general government revenues and that discussion of their uses alone is impossible. Such an approach would require that the activities of the Development Corporations and their predecessors, and the research and development responsibilities of the Boards themselves, also be included with those of general government. Since these institutions are, in fact, separate and ostensibly bear responsibilities different from those of the government, narrowly defined, it seems worthwhile to consider their activities separately.

39. It is probable that even if the total economic returns from such items as universities and manufacturing plants were zero, the Governments would, in the present climate of opinion, have regarded them as inherently desirable.

8. The Role of the Marketing Boards in the Political Evolution of Nigeria

CHARLES R. NIXON

What has been the impact of the marketing boards on the *political* development of Nigeria? This is a question which has largely been ignored by both the political scientists who have examined the political evolution of Nigeria as well as by the economists who have examined the functioning of the marketing boards as an aspect of Nigeria's economic development. This is not surprising in view of the distinctiveness of the main interests of the two disciplines, and in view of the fact that the marketing boards were originally established as economic agencies rather than political.

Yet the question is important. If we are to have a full understanding of either Nigeria's economic or political system we must also have some understanding of the interplay between economic and political institutions in the emergence of modern Nigeria.

The marketing boards grew out of administrative arrangements created by Britain in 1939 in order to assure a steady supply of Nigeria's major export crops to Britain during the war, stabilize prices, and provide for the orderly management of export trade. In time, they also became significant sources of revenue for development projects.

In the first ten years of their operation, the marketing boards were managed by the same British administrators who were responsible for the management of Nigeria. It was assumed that they had a technical and not a political role and in the political discussions of the nationalist movement and the series of constitutional reforms proposed during the period 1945-1951, they were largely ignored. During this period however, their price stabilization policy, carried on during a time of substantial increase in world prices, meant the accumulation of considerable financial reserves so that by 1951 their foreign reserves of approximately £60m constituted about 43% of Nigeria's total foreign assets and were over twice the £25m held by the Federal Government. By the time of the constitutional conference of 1953 the use of these reserves posed political problems.

The years 1951-54 mark the critical period in which the basic pattern of Nigerian federalism was set. In this period the major political parties were formed and each established itself in control of a region. The regions were thus transformed from administrative units to fundamental bases of political power, and the major party leaders became the leaders of regional governments—Chief Obafemi Awolowo of the Action Group in the Western Region, Nnamdi Azikiwe of the National Council of Nigeria & The Cameroons (NCNC) in the Eastern Region, and Alhaji Ahmadu Bello, Sardauna of Sokoto, of the Northern Peoples Congress (NPC) in the Northern Region.

This regionalization of politics brought the Commodity Marketing Boards with their accumulated surpluses to the attention of political leaders who were seeking the financial resources to support the expanded service programs they were promising their people. When the Cocoa Marketing Board refused to make a capital grant to the Western Region to finance the expansion of the school building program required by the Action Group's new policy of universal primary education, Chief Awolowo threatened to have control of the marketing boards transferred from the Federal Government to the regional governments. This threat was made good at the London Constitutional Conference in 1953 which agreed to the creation of new regional marketing boards to replace the existing commodity marketing boards, and distribution of the latters assets to the new regional boards. The regional marketing boards were organized in 1954 and the assets of the commodity marketing boards were allocated as follows: £42.9m to the Western Regional Marketing Board, £11.5m to the Eastern Region Marketing Board, and £32.7m to the Northern Region Marketing Board.

It is difficult to say what part, if any, this financial windfall played in winning support for the new federal system from those Southern leaders who previously were committed to a stronger central government. Up to this point, federalism had often meant to them a system of many small regions, based on ethnic groupings, which would not have extensive financial jurisdiction or responsibility. Such a fragmented regional structure would inevitably require a fairly strong central government to carry out major development programs. In the political context of 1953, however, it seemed clear that Northern leaders would not accept such a fragmented system with a strong central government because they feared the North would be dominated by the Southern groups which had much broader and longer established educational programs and a university-trained cadre of leadership. Indeed the Southerners hoped to be able to provide the effective leadership for an independent Nigeria. Faced with a choice of either further delaying independence, or accommodating the Northern demand for substantial Northern regional autonomy under the proposed federal scheme, the Southerners accepted this plan for three strong regions with residual powers.

Under the new system in which a new revenue allocation plan assured regional governments of substantial recurrent financial resources, in which responsibility for major agricultural, educational, and industrial growth rested with the regions, and in which the regional governments were to attain autonomy from British control prior to national independence, regional leadership and regional programs became the major focus of attention of political leaders.

Control over the marketing board reserves gave Nigerian leaders a capital resource for supporting new policy commitments without having to rely entirely on new taxes. Thus, the new federal system combined with the financial resources of the marketing board reserves meant that the Eastern and Western regions could proceed with their development programs without having to be held back by what they viewed as the retarded state of Northern development and Northern thinking.

Each region treated its marketing board reserves somewhat differently than the other regions, but there were certain basic patterns in the use of these resources, some of which were derived from British policies and commitments made while administering the earlier commodity marketing boards. Before regionalization, one of the basic policies of the commodity marketing boards was that a certain limited percentage of marketing board profits would be used for development programs to benefit the producers. In each of the regions, production development boards were to be financed through marketing board grants. Thus a distinction between marketing boards and development corporations was already drawn prior to Nigerian control of administrative structures and policies. Though the marketing boards did not necessarily confine their development expenditure to grants to these regional production development boards, the major development commitments were made through these corporations.

Following the division of the produce marketing boards into regional marketing boards this same pattern of grants from marketing board resources to the development corporations was followed. What was changed in a very fundamental way however was the earlier notion that only a certain limited percentage of the profits should be used for development purposes. There was a basic shift from the concept that the marketing board reserves should be retained for purposes of price stabilization to the view that marketing board reserves should serve primarily as capital resources for development programs. This commitment was much stronger in the West and the East than it was in the North, and over the whole period through 1963 the North used somewhat less of its resources for development and returned more of its resources to the farmers in price stabilization programs than did the boards in the East and West.

In all regions one important aspect of the structure was that the marketing boards and the development corporations operated outside the legislative budgetary process. They were not subject to treasury control. This was important because the major technical competence within the governments lay in the high level civil servants who were by and large still expatriates. This meant that when the regions became autonomous, (in 1957 in the East and West and 1959 in the North) and control over the marketing boards and the development corporations fell to the Nigerians, it was possible to have political direction of marketing board and development corporation policies without these policies being subjected to the same procedures used in evaluating ministry programs dependent on legislative appropriation.

In the Western region the impact of the marketing board reserves can be seen in several aspects of development policy and political action. In the first place, the decision to establish universal primary education was based on the presumed availability of marketing board reserves as a fundamental capital resource with which to build the school system necessary for universal primary education. Secondly, it was possible for the Western region government to make commitments in 1954 and 1955 to a broad capital expenditure program in areas other than education on the promise that there would be a loan or grant from the Western Region Marketing Board once those reserves came under effective regional control. (The details of these other areas appear in an appendix to the accountant general's report which lists those capital expenditure projects to be covered by a loan or grant from the marketing board.)

Political direction of marketing board investments as well as development corporation investments in the Western region meant that some of these reserves could be invested in enterprises which proved to be covers for what were essentially political expenditures. In the Western region the most significant agency which received money for this purpose was the National Investment and Properties Co. Ltd. (NIPC) which received something like £7m in loans from the Development Corporation or the Marketing Board. This company bought and sold properties in price inflated agreements so that although the books appeared to be perfectly straight, much more was actually paid for properties than they were worth, and the excess payment was then funneled over into party treasuries to finance political activities.

In the Eastern region the Marketing Board, the Eastern Nigerian Development Corporation and the African Continental Bank constituted a triangular relationship which some people in the government called "a state within a state". Their activities and financial relationships were not subject to examination by the permanent civil servants in the treasury. What many people suspected was going on however was that the Development Corporation or the Marketing Board or both would put substantial deposits in the bank, and the bank could make loans to various persons or agencies against these deposits. As long as the Marketing Board or the Development Corporation did not withdraw their deposits, they served as a basic resource which the bank could use for what might be viewed as political loans. A politician who wanted to borrow money in order to carry on a campaign might do so without having to put up anything of real value as collateral. If he won his campaign he might be able to pay back the bank from the financial resources he accumulated while in office. If he did not win his campaign, the bank might extend his credit over a long period and not collect from him. Also it is important to remember that this provided a certain sanction on politicians—if they wished to break with the party leadership, the bank could call in the loan.

Certain commitments made by the Eastern Region Marketing Board such as those for building the University of Nigeria at Nsukka were essentially commitments made by Azikwe. A total of £3½m Marketing Board resources were committed to this purpose—an expenditure which was not matched by the Western Region Marketing Board.

In the North the Marketing Board and the Development Corporations took a little longer to become so political because Northern regional autonomy did not come until 1959. Also the British colonial civil servants probably played a larger role in the Northern Marketing Board. Yet after an inquiry when the military government of the North issued a white paper in 1967 regarding the affairs of the Northern Nigerian Development Corporation it was quite clear that they too had bought up enterprises at inflated prices.[1] And it is probably valid to assume that the excess payment over the real value was returned to the NPC in some form of kickback or donation.

The marketing boards and their financial reserves were clearly only one factor in a complex picture of political evolution; nevertheless they were an important factor and their role might well be summarized in the following broad general terms.

With the coming of independence one of the major political problems was the establishment of a pattern of political relationships between various interests and forces in the society and between the various regions. One of the underlying assumptions of the Nigerian federal system as a way of dealing with the conflicting cultural groups was that there would be three regions with internal political autonomy and no one region dominating the others. However, the Western Region had available substantial financial resources through the Western Region

Marketing Board and was able to finance a very extensive political campaign in Northern Nigeria during the federal election of 1959. There is no doubt that the Western Action Group carried on a much more intensive campaign in the North than the North carried on in either of the regions or than the NCNC carried on in the North. In the North, for example, the Action Group used helicopters, they imported poll watchers, and they had Western Region ministers speaking in Sokoto and Maiduguri. The amount of money spent by the Action Group was obvious to many people in the North and the NPC adopted the tactic of telling people to accept the money, use it, but vote for the NPC. This Action Group campaign, however, angered the Northerners and may well have been one of the roots of the deep antagonism between the NPC and the Action Group, between the Sardauna and Awolowo in the period following the election. It might be said that this was the first violation of the presumption that the leadership of one region would not interfere seriously in the political life of another region. This, of course, was not a legal principle of the constitution but rather one of the underlying political presuppositions of Nigerian federalism. There was clearly no bar to a certain amount of campaigning throughout the country. However the marketing board reserves provided the Action Group with the financial resources for a level of campaigning, of political activity and of attempted political interference which went far beyond that of the other political parties and far beyond that which had been recognized as generally acceptable by other political leaders in the country.

Because these resources did not depend upon immediate taxes but had been accumulated ahead of time, they could be drawn on for political purposes without raising an immediate public hue and cry about taxation. There was, of course, a hue and cry about taxation anyway but it was not specifically tied to the marketing board resources. These resources moreover meant that political relationships in this early period were built on an unusual and short-term financial basis which could not be continued into the future. The fact that it was a short-term foundation for political relationships may have distorted their character rather than helped build permanent patterns of political relationships.

Whatever the future of Nigeria may be once civilian political life is restored, there will probably be one great difference compared to the period we have examined. Money will certainly play its role in the society. But there will be no extensive marketing board reserves which can be tapped for political purposes and thus distort in the same way the character of the new political relationships.

NOTES

1. [Editor's Note: See *A White Paper on the Military Policy for the Reorganization of the Northern Nigeria Development Corporation* (Kaduna: Government Printer, 1966), and *A White Paper on the Northern Nigeria Military Government's Policy for the Comprehensive Review of the Past Operations and Methods of the Northern Nigeria Marketing Board* (Kaduna: Government Printer, 1967).]

9. The Mokwa Land Settlement Scheme*

K. D. S. BALDWIN

In 1947, the West African Oilseeds Mission had drawn attention to several areas where it seemed that groundnuts and other oilseeds might be profitably grown by mechanical methods. Two of these areas were in Nigeria and after careful consideration the Nigerian Government selected one of them as likely to warrant immediate development. This particular area was a virtually uninhabited tract of land near a small town named Mokwa about 325 miles north of Lagos and 25 miles north of the Niger River.

In 1948, various plans were examined and at the end of the year one was finally decided upon involving a farming area of some 32,000 acres, or about 50 square miles. The recently established Colonial Development Corporation was invited to take part in this project and finally it was agreed that the Nigerian Government and the Corporation should undertake it jointly. The Corporation realized, however, that the scheme was only likely to be of marginal profitability. A limited liability company known as the Niger Agricultural Project Limited was formed to operate the scheme, having a capital of £450,000 which was subscribed in equal parts by the Corporation and the Nigerian Government.

Owing to the local land tenure laws, plantation farming was not possible. A solution was found by the declaration of the area by the Government as a Settlement Area. The Company's function was to clear the land and to plan and control the agricultural operations. The farmers, however, were to be peasant settlers who, it was hoped, would be attracted from more densely populated localities. The whole system was based on that evolved in the Gezira area of the Sudan.

In practice it seems that settlers from outside the Emirates where the Project was situated were discouraged on political grounds. Steps, therefore, had to be taken to induce settlers to come from within the Emirates and these felt that they already had enough land of their own. The number of settlers was 78 in 1951 and increased to 135 in 1952 and 163 in 1953.

---

* From *The Niger Agricultural Project: An Experiment in African Development*, B. H. Blackwell and Harvard University Press, 1957, chapters 1 and 14.

The Project had as its aim a contribution to the increase in the production of groundnuts for export and of guinea corn (sorghum) for local consumption. It was at the same time to demonstrate better methods of farming. These methods, however, demanded a very high degree of mechanization. Mechanization, in turn, required very strict control by the management of the activities of the farmers.

In the early days land was cleared rapidly but the rapid regeneration of the undergrowth and small trees showed that the clearing, which was almost entirely by hand, had to be more thorough and therefore slower. Even then, the prolific lateral root-system just below the surface of the ground caused severe losses from breakages of agricultural implements. The acreages cleared were as follows:

1949	1816
1950	3187
1951	1906
1952	1755
1953	810
1954 (to June 1st)	178
Total	9652

Unfortunately it became clear after about three years that the Project was not, and could not be in the near future, a financial success. Inquiries in the area showed that the average amount of farm land cultivated by an adult man was about four acres. On the Project each settler was asked to cultivate twenty-four acres and it was thought that mechanization would make this possible.

It was soon found that it was only possible to make use of machines for ploughing and ridging the ground; no machine capable of doing the other necessary farming operations could be found. In particular the time taken for weeding after planting amounted to about 17 man-days per acre. Since each settler had to weed his entire 24 acres by hand, he had the impossible task of doing 408 days' work in 6 weeks. Furthermore there were no casual labourers in the district who could assist him.

The situation was complicated by the introduction of a share-cropping system under which two-thirds of the production was kept by the Company for services rendered and the remaining third by the settler. This was a major disincentive to work hard since the settler only received one-third of the reward for all his effort. Since there was ample land in the area where farmers could work in their old traditional way there was nothing to induce them to remain. The system, moreover, was a standing temptation to cheating and pilferage.

Besides this attempt to make the settler take up a new agricultural technique, an attempt was made by the Nigerian Government to bring

about a change in his manner of living by trying to make him live in
model villages. These bore little resemblance to the type to which he had
been accustomed.

The initial enthusiasm and subsequent disillusionment is shown in the
following extracts from the Annual Reports of CDC:

1950   The agricultural programme is still experimental—
       will be so for some years yet—so that the right types
       and varieties of crops, suitable for mechanical cultiva-
       tion, may be chosen.

            From every point of view—political, social, agri-
       cultural, economic—this is one of the most interesting
       and satisfactory of the Corporation's projects.[1]

1951   During 1951 capital development was slowed down;
       progress purposely restricted to the rate at which
       work could be done thoroughly and economically.

            Agricultural programme is still experimental.

            It was anticipated Company would incur losses at
       least until end 1952; now seen they will continue
       some considerable time and anyhow until average
       yields are increased above level of best holdings in
       1951 and production costs can be reduced through
       greater efficiency of Company and tenants.

            Social and political progress has been satisfactory
       but it will be more difficult than originally expected
       to make a scheme of this kind pay.

1952   Revenue per acre would have to be quadrupled or
       more to make project pay.

            No higher value crop yet in sight; many of settlers
       unsatisfactory.

            Mechanized cultivation probably uneconomic while
       yields still on level of subsistence agriculture.

            Discussion initiated with Nigerian Government as
       to future.

1953   At end 1952 some information gained but com-
       mercial prospects bad; Government still regarded
       scheme as valuable contribution to rural welfare
       despite prospect of continuing trading losses; but this
       put it outside Corporation's terms of reference.

            Early in 1953 Corporation notified Government of
       intention to withdraw; board (controlled by Cor-
       poration) continued to administer project on re-
       stricted scale on funds provided by Government after
       July 1st, 1953.

Implementation of Corporation's 1952 desire drastically to reduce operations pending experimentation (which should have been done in 1949), and subsequently to withdraw from participation has been impeded by political happenings in Nigeria.

1954 Company is now to be liquidated; assets purchased by Northern Regional Government (of Nigeria) who will carry on an experimental farm and training centre.

Central Government and CDC withdrew from scheme at June 1st, 1954.

Project was well and economically managed but more experiment is needed to prove crops, methods of cultivation and economics of mechanization; Overseas Resources Development Act, 1948, Section 15 (I), puts such projects beyond CDC as long as millstone of abandoned projects has to be borne.

Net loss to CDC at December 31st, 1954, at £123,494.

It is always tempting when things go wrong to seek scapegoats and to blame individuals for failure. Any organization is bound to contain or be affected by persons unsatisfactory for various reasons such as conceit, obstinacy, over-enthusiasm, inefficiency or short-sightedness. This Project was no exception. Interesting as a psychological analysis may be, it would do no more than show how certain individuals reacted to the situations in which they found themselves, and to what extent they affected progress. The reasons for failure were far more fundamental.

As Professor Frankel wrote of the Kongwa Experiment in the East African Groundnuts Scheme: 'It cannot be too strongly emphasized that those who were asked to implement the plan were unable at any time to escape from the fundamental concepts on which it was originally based. Whatever mistakes were made were due primarily to the nature of the task, not to the men who had to try to carry it out, and who, indeed, laboured with great zeal, determination and much self-sacrifice.'[2] These words are equally true of the position at Mokwa.

THE LESSONS OF MOKWA

After the sombre results described above, it might be thought that the Project was a very expensive failure. Certainly it was a commercial failure, but the scheme was in fact one vast set of experiments. Considered from the point of view of research, the half million pounds spent on the Project was money put to good use. The urgency of 'getting the job done' forced to light many problems which might well have become obvious only many years later on a normal experimental station. Whether the experience could have been gained more cheaply is a moot point; human nature being what it is, it is unlikely. But the money will have been completely wasted if the lessons to be drawn are not carefully studied and remembered in the future. From the experience at Mokwa we can now determine some of the major problems which are likely to face those concerned with setting up agricultural schemes in undeveloped areas, especially in the tropics.

Initial Planning

The Project was originally planned as an attempt to combine the advantages of plantation and peasant production. It was generally accepted that West Africans would object most strongly to the establishment of plantations. It was felt that, no matter what assurances Africans were given that the Project was entirely in their interest, they would be most suspicious that this was an attempt to introduce European settlement. The Oilseeds Mission therefore proposed that there should be as rapid a transition as possible from paid labour, which it felt was the only practical method of operation in the early stages, to a participating peasantry. The Nigerian Government went further; it aimed at securing peasant participation from the very start and set about collecting relevant data in the Sudan.

The essential successive stages of sound development were not appreciated. These must be:

(1) Investigations by persons or missions to ascertain what data are already available.

(2) Experiments to provide answers to questions on which information is not available.

(3) A pilot scheme to test at small expense whether plans work out as expected. (This cannot be started, or even planned, until basic data are provided from stages (1) and (2).)

(4) Commercial or large-scale development. (This cannot be undertaken unless the pilot scheme points to its practicability.)

The veto by the Nigerian Government on the paid labour stage, although given with the best intentions, was a major reason for the failure of the Project. It eliminated the crucial stage at which the results of agricultural research elsewhere might be tested locally. As a result the Project jumped from stage (1) to stage (4). It can hardly be said even to have jumped only from stage (1) to stage (3). Though it was called a pilot scheme, it was a pilot scheme on an unduly large scale. But whichever view is taken, the fact remains that the planning omitted the vital stage (2). As a result the Project failed as a self-supporting enterprise because it rested on numerous assumptions which proved unwarranted.

In agriculture an increase in production may be obtained either by more extensive or more intensive cultivation. This first involves an expansion into a marginal area, that is, one which may be beyond the present settled limits, farther from or less accessible to markets, or with less good soils. The second involves the use of more labour, mechanical methods or improved techniques such as the provision of fertilizers. The Project at Mokwa was a mixture of both methods.

It does not seem to have been realized until much too late what a vast amount of data was lacking to make either of these methods successful. Pioneering in a marginal area is an uncertain business at the best of times and there is no justification for assuming without trial that methods proved successful in one area will automatically prove successful in another. Yet, the choice of crop, the variety, planting dates, use of fertilizer, weed control, practicable size of holding, suitable type of tractor, cost of mechanized operations, marketing of produce and attraction of labour were all matters on which no information was available in the Mokwa area. Other data were incomplete or misinterpreted: thus, though it is true that many Northern Nigerians leave their farms to seek work elsewhere every dry season it is not correct that they are necessarily available all the year round. Some knowledge was available but was apparently not used. Whether it was not offered, whether it was ignored or whether its importance was not appreciated, it is difficult to say, though it was probably the last. Examples of this were the need for a contour layout and the difficulty that settlers would have in controlling by hand, weeds on large acreages.

The unfortunate Company was therefore forced to try, without adequate knowledge, to ensure that such settlers as were induced to come had a reasonable income. It was virtually precluded from experimenting except at the cost of endangering the settlers' livelihood. It is not surprising that dissatisfaction resulted; the settlers were in general no better off than they had been before and the management was working in the dark.

The scheme should never have been started until, first by experiment, and secondly by small-scale pilot operations, reasonably certain answers had been obtained to many of the basic questions. It would then have been clear what revenue per acre could be expected and a scheme could have been worked out to take account, for example, of the amount of mechanization and of European supervision which the estimated revenue would justify.

The Corporation stressed from the beginning that the scheme was expected to be one of the most marginal. The Corporation was wrong: the scheme proved to be quite sub-marginal. Even though the Nigerian

Department of Agriculture was the largest and reputedly one of the best in the Colonial Empire, the knowledge at its disposal before the scheme started was insufficient to enable sound plans to be drawn up. The lesson is that far too large an element of guesswork was tolerated to support an investment of £500,000.

Utilization of Local-Knowledge

The Corporation seems to have tried its best to ascertain and make full use of available knowledge. At the higher levels, Nigerian Government officials, agricultural and administrative, helped to draw up the working plans for the Project; half the directors of the Company were Nigerian Government representatives; there was a Government liaison officer living on the Project and an advisory committee, including the local Emirs and Government officers. Such people do not necessarily have the local knowledge requisite for such a scheme, and too much should not be expected from them. As it transpired, none of them knew enough about basic questions to offer really sound advice. None, for example, are on record as objecting to the rectangular layout of the farms regardless of the contours.

At lower levels, little attempt seems to have been made to utilize the local farmers' knowledge. Virtually nothing was known about the customary sizes of the local farms; the labour units and amount of work performed; the crops grown and yields obtained; and the reasons for adhering to a particular calendar of farming operations. Without this knowledge it is impossible to tell whether the farmer is better or worse off than before and whether the new methods are ever likely to be more profitable and acceptable. The local farmers are most likely to know what crops can be grown best; newcomers are liable to waste their time experimenting with crops which the local farmers already know do not grow well.

The Human Problem

In the absence of solutions of fundamental agricultural and economic problems, the oft-repeated assertion that 'the settler is the real crux of the problem' was erroneous. One hundred of the best farmers in the world set down at Mokwa with the same lack of knowledge of soils, crop and mechanization potentialities, could not have made a success of the scheme. It is clear that the settlers were asked to do the impossible. Even if they had been asked to do something more reasonable, they would still have failed. Some of the principal factors overlooked or insufficiently appraised were:

(a) The restriction in the choice of settlers to those only from the Bida and Kontagora Emirates in which the Project was situated. Indeed, in the Bida Emirate the choice was further restricted in the first two years only to those from the Mokwa District. They had, therefore, to come from areas where they already had more than enough land for their needs and from which they had no desire to move. It would clearly have been better to start with people from over-populated areas where they are at present only making a precarious livelihood, but it is impossible to plan resettlement schemes for them if they are to be refused entry into under-populated areas.

(b) Even if the local people were willing to move, the new villages and facilities in the settlement were not adapted to suit their local customs.

(c) Farm work was not varied in accordance with their capacities. The size of the holding did not vary with the size of the family and consequently there were usually too many acres for such operations as weeding to be carried out satisfactorily.

(d) The feeling of insecurity and regimentation. The settlers did not feel that the farms and the produce belonged to them; in other words they felt that the scheme was forced collectivization, not voluntary co-operation.

Nevertheless, the settlers at Mokwa were a very important element in the scheme and there appears to have been failure from the beginning to secure their enthusiastic co-operation. In any land settlement scheme, the human element is vital. Before the project was started there clearly ought to have been a prolonged study of the local Nupe, from whom the great majority of the settlers were to be drawn, and their traditions and customs.

Someone knowing their language and capable of gaining their confidence should then have been given the task of explaining and demonstrating the possibilities of new methods. This would have taken time; it could probably only have been done by working for two or three seasons with no more than three or four carefully selected settlers and a single tractor. It would either have delayed the start of the larger scheme or have proved that it was not worth starting. In the event of expansion to the full scheme it would, together with other research work, which could have proceeded at the same time, have provided a sounder foundation. Experiments elsewhere in Community Development and other schemes have shown that Africans, like most other people, respond much more readily when the right psychological approach has been made and when they have been allowed to feel that the proposed scheme is one of their own choice which they want badly enough to work for.

It is, however, by no means clear that a large-scale mechanized agricultural scheme is compatible with the settlement on it of peasant farmers. Peasant farmers are usually thought of as growing what crops they like, how they like and when they like on land over which they have undisputed right of usufruct. Large-scale mechanization demands agreement to grow crops which can be cultivated by a uniform method over a wide area. Any attempt by an individual farmer cultivating part of the area to grow a different crop, or to neglect any part of the sequence of agricultural work might jeopardize the success of the whole scheme. His rights must therefore be severely curtailed and only those willing to accept such curtailment can be admitted to take part in the scheme. Such 'settlers' must be willing to accept the status virtually of a paid labourer. Whether they are willing to do so will depend on the 'real' income they obtain compared with that obtained in their former way of life.

The Use of Machinery

The use of machinery is to increase the output per head of labour. It will not be economic where labour is cheap and abundant. Unskilled labour is normally highly mobile and willing to move in search of work. Mechanization often occurs in times of high prices when heavy capitalization is profitable and initial expenses of installation can be covered. It may then result in a permanent change of technique when its success and profitability have been demonstrated in times of lower prices. The original expectations of the innovators may, however, turn out to be unrealistic, either because they have overlooked some relevant factors or circumstances later have completely changed. It is essentially a matter of experimenting with various techniques and their success or failure is equally important to those who follow them.

Knowledge in agricultural engineering has advanced rapidly in recent years. In spite of this it would not be true to say that suitable machinery and implements have yet been developed for all operations in the agricultural year in the tropics. Owing to the many variations and unknown factors in local conditions, it may well be that a tractor or implement that has given excellent service in one place is quite useless in another. The abrasiveness of the soil, for example, in some particular place may well lead to unexpectedly rapid depreciation.

Equipment may have to be scrapped rapidly as it is found unsuitable for the work for which it was designed or as other more efficient equipment becomes available.

Technical progress may result in rapid obsolescence and the burden of this expense cannot fall on an ordinary commercial enterprise.

The size of the workshop staff, the stock of spares, the ordering preparation of indents and accounting arrangements all depend on the amount of work to be done. This work consists broadly of normal servicing and maintenance and repairs. Reduction in the amount of repairs necessary depends partly on the skill of the tractor drivers and partly on the removal of obstacles on the farms such as roots and stumps of trees and ant-hills.

The difficulties of clearing the prolific lateral roots found at Mokwa in order to make ploughing possible were not expected to be so serious. Europeans are particularly prone to overlook such difficulties since they are accustomed to farm on land which has been cleared over many centuries as the pressure of increasing population dictated. If it is considered necessary to clear tropical farms thoroughly, then it is urgent to find the best types of machinery to locate or remove hidden obstacles such as roots and stumps. No one, however, can yet say with any certainty what damage is done to tropical soils by wheels and tracks as compared with human feet or oxen hooves. Neither does anyone know the effect of removing the roots which hold the soil and prevent erosion.

To determine the economics of mechanized agriculture, accurate cost accounting is vital. It is most disappointing to find how little has yet been done on this. Perhaps this has been due to concentration on the problem of finding whether particular machines have any chance of functioning at all under tropical conditions rather than examining the profitability of their use relative to other methods. Even if the figures are available they are liable to serious misinterpretation. Attractive propositions may turn out to be illusions. In particular, fixed costs are particularly important in the tropics where there is only a short farming season. At Mokwa the work had to be concentrated during the period March to June but for the rest of the year drivers and tractors were largely unemployed.

Management and Overheads

It is a tribute to the skill of the management that it kept its direction costs per acre lower than, and its other overheads in line with, other schemes in Nigeria even though it had to assume greater burdens. The Project had, for example, to pay half the salary of a full-time doctor, the salary of a qualified accountant and the costs of the Demonstration Farm, which was in fact a miniature research station, including the salary of a full-time agriculturist in charge of it. In addition, it was necessary to run a catering rest-house to cope with the innumerable visitors and passing travellers, and a shop to cater for the needs of the staff and the settlers. The rest-house and shop were, however, virtually self-supporting.

Far more important were the costs of maintaining and running the workshop. There is no possibility in any underdeveloped area of sending a tractor into the nearest garage for repair. The nearest workshop was 80 miles away and the nearest of commercial size was 200 miles. There is no question of connecting up to the nearest power supply. If electricity is required then a separate plant has to be installed as was done at Mokwa.

In a country where the standard of education is very low and mechanical equipment is rare, it was only to be expected that the number of trained workshop personnel was very limited. Again owing to lack of experience, the average level of skill was poor. There was nothing for it but to take such men as were available and train them to the standard required. The Project therefore was forced into running a kind of technical school at its own expense. The same considerations applied to drivers, who caused unnecessary wear and tear or damage by their lack of skill or experience. This is no reflection on the innate ability of the men to learn such work but it takes time to teach them and the teaching is costly.

The training of staff is not only expensive in terms of damaged equipment but also in terms of the senior staff who must be imported to do the training. The European in the tropics has been aptly described as 'the most expensive of God's creatures'. This is due to the necessity of paying him a higher salary than he would obtain in his own country (an expatriation allowance) in order to induce him to go overseas; paying his passage from and back to his own country; providing him with a house of a standard to which he is accustomed and providing him with medical facilities and social amenities. The United Africa Company found in 1949 that the cost of maintaining the most junior European employee in West Africa was not far short of £1250 per annum.[3] Since then, of course, the figure has increased considerably. Commercial firms, which are interested in their profits clearly do not incur such expense unless they have to in the absence of local people of the necessary technical and managerial ability.

To support such heavy costs an enterprise must therefore be exceptionally profitable or have a very high ratio of unskilled labour to skilled and supervisory staff. It is most unlikely that a commercial concern, or a Government-sponsored body like the Colonial Development Corporation attempting to operate on commercial lines, will embark upon such an enterprise. In more developed countries, repair costs will be much lower owing to the much greater division of labour and hence more trained staff, and to easier access to the manufacturers. Power supplies will be cheaper for the same reasons. Technical education is normally provided by the state and finally expatriate staff are unnecessary. Such development expenditure is uneconomic to a firm or any enterprise which is to be run on commercial lines. There is a strong case for as much of it as possible to be regarded as a normal charge on government in the interests of rapid advancement.

In spite of all these difficulties, the day-to-day management was cheap and conscientious and most visitors were very favourably impressed by the lack of extravagance. Mr. W. T. Newlyn in a study of the costs of mechanized agriculture in Nigeria concluded:

The final point which is established by the analysis is that the facile popular conclusions regarding the Niger Agricultural Project are not well founded. A Colonial Development Corporation scheme is a convenient whipping boy, and the failure of Mokwa has been persistently ascribed to prodigiously high overheads and direction costs. In fact direction is a less costly item per acre at Mokwa than on any other [official and partnership] scheme and overheads compare quite well with the schemes in these groups for which such data are complete.[4]

Incidentally, Newlyn also found that the Project was better recorded and documented than any other scheme he investigated in Nigeria.

It might, however, be argued that this proves nothing since the other Nigerian schemes were on a much smaller scale and therefore carrying a relatively much heavier burden. There was, for example, considerable argument in 1951 over the reduction in the rate of clearance of land at Mokwa. On the one hand it was considered that this would increase losses since the Project would still have to carry the same overheads. On the other hand the staff, from the Manager downwards, were fully occupied with the problems that had already arisen, and no equipment was standing idle. There can be no doubt now that the policy of reduction in the rate of clearance that was decided upon was the right one and reduced losses to a minimum.

Frankel, in his criticism of the East African Groundnuts Scheme, has already drawn attention to the curious, but common fallacy in thinking that agricultural operations lend themselves to economies on a very large scale. 'This', he says, 'is surprising because it runs counter to the accepted principle that agriculture is generally the least likely form of economic enterprise to yield considerable large-scale economies; its factors of production cannot be readily centred and supervised, nor in general are they sufficiently homogeneous to allow easily organized repetitive processes of production.[5]

Innovations

The administrative organization of a scheme such as the Project, or indeed the Gezira Scheme, must inevitably be very expensive. This can only be afforded where productivity can be raised significantly in comparison with the achievements of existing local methods. The same is true for mechanization: it is usually more expensive per acre than hand methods and again can only be afforded if productivity per acre can be increased significantly. There may not be very many conditions in which such a complicated, expensive organization can be justified as a method of development. Wide departures from established systems of agriculture, whether African or any other, are seldom immediately practicable. It may often be that there is one limiting factor which once it can be recognized can be put right by simple and relatively inexpensive methods.

Schemes designed to do everything at once may be dangerous. An arrangement to make fertilizers available or to make mechanized ploughing available may achieve much better results economically than a grandiose scheme designed to organize farmers from A to Z. Such a comprehensive scheme is more likely to be practicable where irrigation water is being made available, for this is more likely than anything else to increase productivity above previous levels. But the Project was not one of these.

Dr. Nash wrote in 1948 about the very successful Anchau Rural Development and Settlement Scheme in Zaria Province, farther north in Nigeria:[6]

> Europeans are far too prone to consider that their own methods are best and therefore must be introduced. When one studies native methods—the inherited wisdom of generations —one finds how sound they are in many things, and how wrong are our preconceived ideas, based subconsciously on our European experience.
>
> The object of rural development should be to graft on to native life those things which it lacks, not to attempt to revolutionize it. The northern native (of Nigeria) has learnt from experience not to accept everything we say and is fortunately very cautious in adopting new ideas. But this caution means that the native cannot be hurried and will not accept innovations until he is satisfied of their efficacy. Hence time, and continuity of staff, form the essence of successful development. A steady drip, drip, is far better than a sudden deluge.

This is probably true of almost any peasant community and failure to take account of it was one of the reasons for many of the troubles at Mokwa.

Undue haste at Mokwa gave the farmers no time to satisfy themselves that the new methods were better than their own. Furthermore, none of the senior staff had worked in Nigeria before. None spoke Nupe or even Hausa, hence all their dealings with the farmers had to be through interpreters. Finally there was a serious break in the continuity of staff at the end of 1950. It is difficult to see how this could have been avoided. If no senior staff were available in Nigeria, they had to be recruited from somewhere else. The Sudan would appear to be an obvious choice, at least for the Managers, since its Agricultural Service had such a high reputation and physical conditions were not unduly dissimilar to those in Nigeria. No imported foreign expert is likely to speak the local language; the most that can be hoped for is that he will learn it as soon as possible.

Less haste would have enabled the staff to gain some experience of local conditions and establish friendly relations with the farmers. As it was, the farmers were simply told to give up their own methods and adopt new ones, not yet proved sound. Their traditional methods had at least given them a modest livelihood; there was no proof that the new methods would give them any at all.

Conclusion

The failure of the scheme at Mokwa was not due to the lack of any one of the factors of production—land, labour and capital—but to the inability to combine them into an economic unit. There was adequate land but it was virtually uninhabited and no information was available about its potential. Preliminary investigation suggested that it was suitable for growing groundnuts and it had the very great advantage of not interfering with the existing rights of the local people.

Labour was difficult but not impossible to obtain. It is clear that much further work has yet to be done in determining the volume of labour seeking employment in Northern Nigeria. Much more has also to be done in determining what rates of pay, and possibly conditions, would provide sufficient incentive to attract adequate labour to the places where it was required. Direction of labour by administrative action has little to commend it except in emergency. On the other hand it is absurd to think that men are going to travel 100 miles or more only to obtain work at the same rate as they could obtain at their starting point. It is noticeable in the inquiries already made that men are only willing to travel long distances to areas where the rates of pay are known to be high. The same considerations apply to both unskilled and skilled workers. A particular case is that of overseas staff whose knowledge and skill are essential to the success of the scheme, but even these should be obtainable though expensive.

There was no question of any shortage of capital in the form of money; but money is only of value for what it can buy. In an agricultural scheme it has to be converted into 'real' capital in the form of such things as seed, fertilizer, tractors, ploughs and so on. It is now clear that very little was known about the type of equipment required. Such experience as there had been in areas in any way comparable was negative. Optimistic assumptions that the right type of machine would be found were not realized. Makeshift arrangements had to be made mostly with equipment designed for conditions other than those in which it was used.

Even the best management could only combine these factors into a highly expensive organization. If it was to be self-supporting prices must be high; if not, it must be subsidized. A subsidy at the expense of the community as a whole would be difficult to justify. The original purpose of the Project at Mokwa was to provide the settlers with more food to eat and more crops to grow. Since the local farmers were already growing enough for their own needs a subsidy could not be justified on that score. A subsidy for cash crop farming could only be justified if there was urgent need for the crop elsewhere in the country or for the obtaining of foreign currency.

The aim of such a scheme can clearly not be limited to the establishment of a self-supporting subsistence economy for the benefit only of the people in the immediate neighborhood and to the exclusion of others. Such an economic microcosm must always remain backward unless integrated within a wider economy. By remaining outside it must lose the advantage of trade with other areas and fail to enjoy the benefits of the division of labour on which economic progress depends.

On the other hand cash crop farming assumes the existence of a market. The most profitable crop at Mokwa turned out to be guinea corn—a basic food in Northern Nigeria. This would suggest the possibility of certain areas specializing in the growing of food for cash. Unfortunately there is a tendency in Northern Nigeria, as in many other parts of Africa, to feel that it is necessary to husband stocks of food crops in the areas in which they are grown so that supplies are adequate and prices low. Such a parochial attitude is incompatible with economic development. The limitation of markets limits production.

As the specialization of labour increases, the proportion of the population employed in food production will fall. An increase in productivity per head will then be essential to maintain the present level of consumption. This, however, is most unlikely by the traditional local methods. The problem is aggravated by the rate of increase of the local population, though the exact rate is unknown. The present state of general welfare and nutrition of the West Africa peasant populations is far higher than that of many others elsewhere.[7] Soon, however, they may well be hard put to it to maintain, let alone improve, their existing standards.

It is therefore becoming urgent to test the possibilities of the introduction of new techniques found successful in other parts of the world. It would be wise to approach these problems in a spirit of humility. We may think, quite honestly and without deliberate self-deception, that we know enough to deal with them. Searching cross-examination soon reveals many lacunae in our knowledge which we had never realized before. We should do well to remember with Whitehead that 'our knowledge of scientific laws is woefully defective and our knowledge of the relevant facts of the present and the past is scanty in the extreme'.[8]

We may sum up by saying that the history of the Project at Mokwa is

a sharp lesson that successful economic development depends on adequate knowledge. The Project, even though a commercial failure, has
been valuable in that it has shown the many questions that must be
asked before the establishment of similar kinds of mechanized agricultural and settlement schemes. An abundance of money, machinery
and technical skill is no substitute for answers to these fundamental questions. If the answers are not known, there is nothing for it but to wait
until they are. This is no excuse for dilatory behaviour. On the contrary,
there must be all the more emphasis on the urgency of scientific and technical research and experiment. This will take time, but knowledge and experience can only be accumulated and not bought. Socrates once made
the sardonic remark: 'I have no doubt that if you only give him money
enough, he will make you wise too.' To this his friend replied: 'I would,
ye gods! it only depended on this: if it did, I would not spare the last
farthing of my own fortune, or of my friends' either.'[9]

NOTES

1. A Government-appointed director of the Niger Agricultural Project
   stated at the Board meeting on June 29th, 1951, that he felt the unin-
   formed, reading this report, might take an unduly optimistic view of the
   Project. He asked for restraint in all public utterances concerning the
   Project until tangible results could be shown.
2. S. H. Frankel, *The Economic Impact on Underdeveloped Societies*
   (Blackwell, 1953), p. 144.
3. F. Samuel, "Economic Potential of Colonial Africa," an Address to the
   Royal Empire Society Summer School (1949), circulated privately.
4. W. T. Newlyn, "Report on a Study of Mechanized Agriculture in
   Nigeria" (duplicated and circulated by W.A.I.S.E.R.), p. 22.
5. Frankel, *op. cit.*, p. 149.
6. T. A. M. Nash, *The Anchau Rural Development and Settlement Scheme*
   (H.M.S.), 1948), p. 5.
7. B. M. Nicol, "Food, Population and Health in West Africa," *West
   African Medical Journal*, II, 3, New Series (September, 1953).
8. A. M. Whitehead, *Adventures of Ideas*, Pelican edition, p. 107.
9. E. Lowes Dickinson, *Plato and his Dialogues*, Penguin edition, p. 42.

10. Investment in Education

(The Ashby Report)*

CONCLUSIONS AND RECOMMENDATIONS

1. Our Report rests upon three foundations: our conception of Nigeria in 1980, Harbison's estimates of Nigeria's needs for high-level manpower by 1970, and our estimates of the present capacity of the educational system. Our recommendations aim at two objectives: (i) to upgrade Nigerians who are already in employment but who need further education, and (ii) to design a system of post-secondary education which will, as estimated to need; and to design it in such a way that it can be enlarged, without being replanned, to meet Nigeria's needs up to 1980.

2. We believe it would be a grave disservice to Nigeria to make modest, cautious proposals, likely to fall within her budget, for such proposals would be totally inadequate to maintain even the present rate of economic growth in the country. Accordingly we reject this approach. Our recommendations are massive, unconventional, and expensive; they will be practicable only if Nigerian education seeks outside aid and if the Nigerian people themselves are prepared to accord education first priority and to make sacrifices for it.

Primary Education

3. Enough children are completing primary education to provide the flow of recruits for post-secondary education which our proposals demand; but they are very unevenly distributed through the country. In the Northern Region the first step must be to increase, by 1970 if possible, the numbers completing primary school until they reach about 25 per cent of the age-group. A massive effort to improve standards everywhere, particularly in English, is necessary.

* From *Investment in Education* (*The Report on the Commission on Post-School Certificate and Higher Education in Nigeria* (Sir Eric Ashby) Lagos: Federal Govt. Printer, 1960, pp. 41-48. Reprinted by permission of the Federal Ministry of Education, Lagos.

Secondary Education

4. In order to provide an adequate flow of recruits for post-secondary education there must be at the earliest opportunity an increase in secondary school intake from the present level of 12,000 per annum (1958) to more than 30,000. We recommend that this should be accomplished through the creation of some 600 more secondary school streams (section 5), both in new institutions and through the enlargement of some of the stronger secondary schools already in existence. This recommendation is linked to our proposal for the expansion of sixth forms.

5. The bias of the present primary and secondary curricula toward literary and academic subjects should be corrected by the introduction of an obligatory manual subject. In some secondary schools, technical subjects should be included among those which may be carried to School Certificate level. We recommend that some girls' secondary schools should provide a one-year, post-School Certificate commercial course to prepare for secretarial employment. We further propose that vocational agricultural courses be offered by some schools.

The Educational Pyramid

6. Our aim is to design a balanced system of post-secondary education. Education in the East and West is unbalanced and education in the North is too meagre at all levels. To remedy these defects we recommend that for the next ten years the pyramid of education should have one shape in the Northern Region and another in the other Regions.

Sixth Forms

7. We estimate that of 29,000 children who will complete School Certificate courses each year when the rate of flow we recommend is established, some 21,000 should seek employment, and some 8,000 should go on to further training. This of course is only a first objective. Of these 8,000, some 3,500 should study for the Higher School Certificate or General Certificate of Education Advanced level in sixth forms, including 500 planning to enter teaching careers.

We recommend that sixth form work be carried on both in existing secondary schools and in new National High Schools, and be Federally financed and directed. These High Schools should be planned to serve also the function of community colleges. Opportunity for adult students, who have left school and are in employment, to study for the General Certificate of Education Advanced level should be provided in the technical institutes.

8. There will have to be 150 streams of sixth form pupils to fulfill our objectives by 1970. At present there are sixth forms in 22 schools, not all of which can now take 40 pupils a year. We therefore recommend that at least 110 additional sixth form streams will have to be established. Federal funds will be needed and should be provided.

Teacher Training

9. *Special programmes for present primary and secondary teachers.* Something like nine-tenths of the primary teachers and over half the secondary teachers are not adequately educated or fully trained for their work. Our first proposals refer to the upgrading of these teachers. We recommend that the target by 1970 should be a staff for the secondary schools, technical institutes and teacher training colleges that is half graduate and half Grade I. At least one teacher in fifteen in the primary schools should be Grade I. The critical need of improving the quality of English used in the schools causes us to recommend a programme of vacation courses lasting one month in English and other relevant subjects, to be taken by some 3,000 teachers a year at the universities. The teachers for these vacation courses would have to be imported for the month from overseas countries. The aim should be that by 1968 at least one teacher from each of the 17,000 primary schools in Nigeria will have attended a vacation course. For secondary teachers we recommend vacation courses lasting two months, in the subjects taught to School Certificate level.

10. To consolidate the programme proposed above, we recommend that the supervising teacher service be enlarged to perhaps 1,000 by 1970, to include experienced teachers who would travel from school to school to maintain and to improve standards of teaching.

The Supply and Training of Teachers over the Next Ten Years

11. The training colleges will have to undergo great expansion and will need both graduate and Grade I staff. For Grade I teachers we estimate that the annual output must rise, as a first objective, to 3,000 a year as soon as possible. Over 18,000 will be needed by 1970. Roughly 1,000 a year of these would be Grade II teachers selected for their special merit; the balance of 2,000 a year would be recruits direct from secondary schools. These are minimum estimates and they take little account of the migration of teachers into other professions which is such a feature of the Nigerian teaching profession at present.

12. We recommend that all candidates who wish to qualify as Grade I teachers should pursue a 2-year full-time course of post-secondary education. The present arrangements are wholly unsatisfactory. We have in mind two kinds of Grade I certificates: those designed for secondary school teachers without university degrees, and those designed for primary school teachers. We recommend that there should be three channels for the education and training of Grade I teachers: (i) for those who will teach in primary schools some 2,000 per annum when the rate of flow is established) there should be eight Grade I training colleges, of the kind shortly to be established in Lagos and in the Western Region; (ii) for those who will teach in secondary schools (some 1,000

per annum) there should be an intake of some 500 per annum in technical institutes (for teachers of technical subjects and mathematics) and
(iii) an intake of some 500 per annum in sixth forms where pupils would
get a Grade I certificate by taking Higher School Certificate together with
some pedagogic training and teaching practice.

13. Although we believe that the main cost of teacher training should
fall upon the Regions, we recommend that the Federal Government
should offer grants-in-aid for the training of Grade I teachers in sixth
form streams and in technical institutes, and for the special Grade I
colleges which we believe should be associated with university institutes
of education.

14. We feel strongly that the salary scales of Grade I teachers compare
very unfavourably with the scales of graduate teachers and we recommend that the Grade I scales start at a higher figure and be revised so
that there is a considerable overlap.

15. We recommend that all Ministries of Education should have a
vigorous public relations department which will create in the public a
respect for the teacher and an interest in his work.

16. For our recommendation on the training of graduate teachers, see
paragraph 39.

Technical Education

17. Plans should be made for the development of post-secondary
courses for the training of technicians in some half dozen technical institutes, building up to a flow of about 2,500 per annum. For the next
ten years, the Institutes at Enugu, Ibadan, Kaduna and Yaba, together
with that planned for Benin City, one at Port Harcourt, and we hope one
at Kano, will probably suffice if appropriately expanded.

18. As the technicians' courses should preferably be taken concurrently with industrial training by students already in employment, they
should wherever possible be conducted either on the sandwich or the
part-time day-release basis. They should lead mainly to Certificates of
the City and Guilds Institute.

19. The technical institutes, we believe, should be mainly non-residential, though we would expect some hostel accommodation to be available in the smaller cities. We recommend that each institute should have
good catering arrangements and generous work space where students
can study in the evening.

20. We propose that the technical institutes, in co-operation with
employers, should provide short courses for potential supervisors and
foremen.

21. Associated with each technical institute there should be an advisory committee composed of representatives of leading employers. We

recommend also the establishment by the Federal Government of a Standing Conference for Technical Education to facilitate co-operation between the technical institutes, to advise the Governments on their needs, and to enlist the interest of employers.

22. We recommend that the technical institutes should be mainly the responsibility of the Regional Governments, but the Federal Government should be prepared to make grants-in-aid.

23. We draw attention to the very great difficulty of recruiting and retaining adequately qualified staff for the technical institutes, and we emphasise that Nigeria will for some years to come have to recruit staff from abroad, on attractive conditions of contract and on better salaries than are paid at present.

24. Our recommendations in regard to technological education at the professional level are in paragraph 40.

Commercial Education

25. The technical institutes should provide full-time post-secondary, general commercial courses; also sandwich and part-time day and evening courses of a similar kind, and others designed to meet more specific needs of employers.

26. Our recommendations with regard to higher commercial education at the professional level will be found in paragraph 37.

Agricultural and Veterinary Education

27. We emphasise that the crucial importance of agriculture to Nigeria is not reflected in its Federal Government organisation, in education, or in the scale of its research and advisory work in the field of agriculture. All these activities need to be strengthened. To enlarge the scope of agricultural education will not be enough: it will be necessary, too, to create a greater variety of posts in which men trained in agriculture can be employed, and to attach more attractive salaries to these posts. At present there are vacant places in agricultural schools, because the conditions of employment for agricultural assistants and superintendents are not sufficiently attractive.

28. We recommend that as a first objective agricultural assistants and superintendents should be produced at the rate of not less than 200 a year from the four existing agricultural schools at Akure, Moor Plantation, Samaru, and Umudike and that plans now be made to double this output. The posts open to the products of these schools should be made attractive enough to persuade School Certificate holders to apply to enter the schools. The schools should also be prepared to conduct sandwich courses, short courses (*e.g.* for young farmers) and even extra-mural courses.

29. We recommend, too, that as soon as possible vocational agri-

cultural streams should be added to some secondary schools. Those who teach in these schools should preferably be graduates; but for some years to come it may be necessary for agricultural teachers of Grade I status to staff these schools. These should be produced by the four agricultural schools.

30. For the training of veterinary assistants at sub-degree level the Veterinary Research Institute at Vom should remain the national centre, but we recommend that its annual output should be doubled as soon as possible.

31. Our recommendations on agricultural and veterinary education at universities are in paragraphs 42 and 43.

Universities

32. University development in Nigeria should be so planned as to ensure that by 1970 there will be an enrolment of at least 7,500 students, with a substantial growth beyond that figure in the decade 1970-80.

33. All universities in Nigeria should be national in outlook and general policy. Each university should admit, without discrimination and on the criterion of merit alone, students from any Region or tribe.

34. Care should be taken to avoid unnecessary and uneconomical duplication of expensive courses.

35. There should be wider diversity and greater flexibility in university education if it is to be relevant to the needs of Nigeria. The whole intellectual and professional life of the country depends for its quality on sound university standards. Paragraphs 36-46 offer examples of the needed changes of attitude toward the content of university studies.

36. It should be the duty of all Nigerian universities to promote work and research in the field of African studies. We recommend that every university in the country should have an Institute of African studies, which co-ordinates research being conducted by various university departments.

37. Professional qualifications in subjects like accountancy, banking, secretaryship, insurance, and transport should be gained through university courses in commerce and business administration leading to a degree of Bachelor of Commerce, B.Com. To provide an appropriate combination of academic study and professional training, some of these should be sandwich courses (see paragraphs 46 and 53).

38. Provision should be made at a university for courses at the postgraduate level in higher management studies (see paragraph 53).

39. In order to assist in the preparation of graduate teachers we recommend the introduction of a Bachelor of Arts degree in Education, B.A.(Ed.), in all Nigerian universities; the degree course would consist of four subjects in the first year, and three in each of the second and third years, with some pedagogical instruction.

40. A degree of Bachelor of Engineering, B.Eng., should be instituted which is biased toward the practical side and is of a standard equivalent to that required for membership of the professional engineering institutions of the United Kingdom. Post-graduate courses leading to masters' degrees in special subjects could be added in due course.

41. We propose that medical education should cease to be bound to the requirements for medical practice in Britain and that the medical degree course should be so modified when University College, Ibadan, achieves university status, as to emphasise some of the major medical problems of Nigeria, *e.g.* public health, preventive medicine, and paediatrics. We further propose that for the students who are unsuccessful in qualifying for a medical degree, a locally recognised examination should be instituted which, if it is passed, will entitle them to practise medicine under such conditions as may be prescribed. The output of the University College Hospital Medical School at Ibadan should be doubled.

42. Veterinary education should not be tied to the requirements of overseas professional bodies but should be closely related to the special needs of Nigeria. It should particularly emphasise animal husbandry, animal nutrition and preventive medicine.

43. Agriculture, being the largest element in the Nigerian economy, should have a much greater part in university education. We recommend that, in addition to the present faculty of agriculture at University College, Ibadan, schools or faculties of agriculture with research and extension programmes should be established in a university in each Region. In due course, departments of home economics could well be added.

44. We are in general agreement with the proposals of the special committee which recently reported on legal education in Nigeria, and we accordingly support their recommendation that the road to legal practice should be through a university degree.

45. We recommend that each university in Nigeria should organise extension-work on a large scale in its own Region.

46. In order to open up further opportunities for university study, we propose (*a*) that one university should offer evening courses leading to degrees; (*b*) that one university should organise and conduct correspondence courses leading to degrees in a limited range of subjects (paragraph 53).

47. We recommend that Nigerian universities should be independent of one another and that each should offer its own degrees.

48. We propose that new Nigerian universities should seek sponsorship from well-established universities overseas, in order to gain international currency for their degrees.

49. We recommend that the Federal Government should concentrate its resources for the time being around existing centres of academic

activity, with the addition of Lagos to their number, and that the Nigerian College of Arts, Science and Technology should be integrated into the university system of Nigeria.

50. We recommend that the Federal Government should give full support to the development of the new University of Nigeria and should make available the buildings and equipment of the Enugu branch of the Nigerian College of Arts, Science and Technology for university work under the aegis of the University of Nigeria. Failing this, an alternative but more costly proposal would be for the University of Nigeria to be developed with reduced Federal participation and for the buildings at Enugu to be used as the nucleus of a separate university financed by the Federal Government.

51. We recommend that steps should be taken toward the establishment of a university in the Northern Region with its headquarters at Zaria in the buildings now occupied by the Nigerian College of Arts, Science and Technology. We hope that there will be links with the Ahmadu Bello College in Kano, with the Agricultural Research Institute at Samaru, with the Veterinary Research Institute at Vom, and with the Institute of Administration at Zaria.

52. We recommend that the Ibadan branch of the Nigerian College of Arts, Science and Technology should be incorporated into University College, Ibadan.

53. We recommend that a university should be established at Lagos with day and evening courses leading to degrees in the fields of commerce, business administration, economics and social science, and courses at post-graduate level in higher management studies. We further recommend that the university should have a department for correspondence courses leading to degrees in a limited range of subjects.

54. Grants should be made from Regional or Federal funds to all students who are accepted for admission to Nigerian universities and who are not able to pay for their university education themselves.

55. The Federal and Regional Governments should continue their present policy of offering scholarships for undergraduate study abroad, and we recommend that a substantial proportion of these awards for some years should be for intending teachers.

56. We recommend that there should be post-graduate scholarships tenable in Nigerian universities, both for Nigerian graduates and for graduates from overseas.

57. Those who plan and finance universities in Nigeria should provide opportunities for research in both the humanities and the sciences.

University Government and a National Universities Commission

58. We recommend that each university should be governed by its own autonomous Council, which should have undisputed control over

the affairs of the university: the appointment of staff, the content of the courses, and the admission and examination of students. The Council of University College, Ibadan, presents a good model of an effective govern- ing body.

59. We recommend that governing bodies of Nigerian universities should negotiate for funds not directly with the Federal Ministry of Edu- cation, but through a National Universities Commission whose establish- ment is fundamental to all our proposals about higher education.

60. We therefore recommend that a National Universities Commission should be established without delay under the chairmanship of an out- standing Nigerian citizen. The Commission will play a vital part in secur- ing funds for universities and in distributing them, in co-ordinating (with- out interfering with) their activities, and in providing cohesion for the whole system of higher education in the country.

International Aid

61. We recommend that the Federal Government explore the possi- bility of international aid for Nigeria's schools and universities. The greatest need in the schools is a corps of graduate teachers for all post- primary institutions. We propose a co-ordinated programme for the coming decade involving (i) scholarships for Nigerians to prepare for teaching in universities overseas, where places will have to be reserved for them, and (ii) the importation of young graduates from many parts of the world, to be recruited and selected by an organisation representing the voluntary efforts of educators and leading citizens from many nations. It is possible that the overall cost of this programme might be £15 million to £20 million by 1970.

62. New universities are expensive under any circumstances, but particularly under present conditions in Africa. An estimate of the capital costs of our university proposals might approach £20 million, though some parts of this development might attract international aid. We hope particularly that support for Institutes of African Studies can be obtained.

63. The total cost of the programmes we recommend in this Report will be very great. The projects mentioned in paragraphs 61 and 62 are intended only to illustrate aspects of our overall design that might attract international aid. Still larger amounts will be required for capital and recurrent costs from Nigeria's own budget.

Inter-Regional Manpower Board

64. We strongly support Harbison's recommendation that an Inter- Regional Manpower Board be established. This Board should include members from the appropriate Federal Ministries, the Regional Govern- ments, and representatives of employers, trade unions and the general public. The duties of the Board should be to review continuously the

nation's manpower needs and to formulate programmes for effective manpower development throughout the Federation.

RESERVATION
by S. D. Onabamiro

I agree with the recommendations in this Report subject to the following reservations:

(a) *Number of universities.*—I do not agree that four universities financed by the Federal Government will adequately meet the needs of Nigeria during the next ten years. I favour the creation of an additional Regional university in each Region which will bring the total to seven. In my view the University of Nigeria at Nsukka and the proposed Ahmadu Bello College at Kano should be allowed to develop into full universities owned respectively by the Eastern and Northern Regional Governments but with Federal financial support if required. The university which the Western Regional Government proposes to build somewhere in the Region should fall into the same category.

(b) *Composition of the National Universities Commission.*—I am of the opinion that the proposed Commission should in its composition follow the present pattern of Regional representation in the Councils of the existing Federal institutions of higher education; two members should be appointed by the Governor-in-Council of each of the three Regions. It is only in this way that the interests of the Regions can be safeguarded by ensuring that the Regions are represented on the Commission by persons in whom they have confidence.

(c) *Sixth-form work.*—As secondary education and community development are matters for the Regional Governments in their own Regions, I am of the view that the proposed National High Schools should be owned and directed by the Governments concerned but with Federal financial support. I suggest that there should be six such High Schools within the next ten years each with an enrolment of 500 students; two in the Eastern Region, two in the Western Region, one in the Northern Region, and one in the Federal Territory of Lagos.

14th September, 1960.

PART THREE: *Planning and Implementation of Development in the 1960's*

Nigeria's 1962-68 National Development Plan represented that country's first attempt at comprehensive, integrated planning.[1] The plan envisaged that the economy would grow at a rate of at least 4 percent per year and that priority would be given to agriculture, industry and to technical training.[2]

An excellent discussion of the formulation of the Plan, its main features, and the planner's intentions are provided in Wolfgang Stolper's *Planning Without Facts*.[3] As Head of the Economic Planning Unit of Nigeria from 1960-62, he played an important role in the preparation of the Plan and thus is able to provide valuable insights into the planning process in Nigeria.

One of the key themes which was used in the formulation of the Plan was that of selecting projects on the basis of "economic profitability." A detailed account of the procedures and reasoning underlying this investment criterion is Chapter 11, Lyle Hansen's article, "Comprehensive Economic Planning in Nigeria." One of the most useful aspects of Hansen's chapter is its detailed presentation of the methods and calculations actually employed in assessing the economic profitability of the Nigeria Ports Authority.

The criterion of economic profitability was not applied to the social sectors such as health and education in the Plan for numerous reasons as Stolper points out in his "Social Factors in Economic Planning" which is reprinted in Chapter 12. In fact, Stolper contends that such calculations of economic profitability are "repugnant" when applied to potential expenditures in the social services.[4] Stolper's discussion of these points is particularly valuable in view of the large expenditures for health and education—usually 40-60 percent of recurrent budgets—in the new states of Nigeria.

Although the agricultural sector receives priority in the Plan, there were few feasibility studies of agricultural projects by Planners during the Plan preparation period from 1960-62. For example, Professor O. Aboyode has noted, "It would have been far more useful to have some idea of the anticipated returns ... 'from the white-elephant farm settlement schemes' ... than say the elegant economic analysis of Lagos Island Sewerage System."[5]

Professor Jerome Wells, in Chapter 13, however, provides useful insights into agricultural planning and its implementation during the 1962-

68 Nigerian Development Plan. He points out the lack of coordination between project studies and the budgetary process within the agricultural sector. Moreover, Wells' study reveals that, except for the North, the bulk of agricultural investment went into large "government directed projects" such as plantations and "settlement projects" rather than into extension services to support traditional farming. Wells concludes that this composition of agricultural investment was inconsistent with the planners' original goals and that this investment was much less effective than it could have been.

In Chapter 14, however, Malcolm Purvis reports on one of the most successful agricultural projects in the Plan, the Eastern Nigerian Oil Palm Rehabilitation Scheme. On the basis of one of the most detailed economic analysis of small-holder oil palm production ever undertaken in any African country, Purvis was able to spotlight how new hybrid palms were successfully grafted onto an existing smallholder oil palm tradition.

Turning to the implementation of the Plan, Edwin Dean has pointed out that there was a significant amount of underspending for development during the first four years of the Plan, an underspending that he attributed primarily to a lack of executive capacity within Nigeria.[6] The most serious shortfall, however, was foreign aid; indeed, during the first four years of the Plan, Nigeria received only 29 percent of the total foreign aid receipts that it had expected to receive over the period from 1962 to 1968.[7]

One result of the foreign aid shortfall was that Nigeria had to place a greater reliance on short-term credit arrangements such as contractor finance and supplier credits. A. A. Ayida, Permanent Secretary, Federal Ministry of Economic Development, presents in Chapter 15 an excellent discussion of the role played by such borrowing. He calls particular attention to the potential dangers and the limitations in utilizing these forms of international finance. In view of the recent debt servicing problems encountered by Ghana and Liberia, Ayida's warnings are timely.

Although there were admitted difficulties in implementing the Plan, the Nigerian economy performed extremely well during the years prior to the outbreak of the Civil War in 1967. The gross domestic product in constant prices, for example, grew at an annual rate of 4.7 percent from 1962 to 1966, thus exceeding the Plan's aggregate growth target.[8] Moreover, this growth was accompanied by important structural changes in the economy. Both the petroleum and modern manufacturing sectors of the economy grew rapidly and, in W. A. Lewis' terminology, joined agricultural exports as the leading "prime movers" of the Nigerian economy.[9] The growth of Nigeria's petroleum industry is analyzed in detail by Scott Pearson in Chapter 18. The modern manufacturing sector of the Nigerian economy grew at a rate in excess of 15 percent during the early sixties.[10]

Although the major impetus for manufacturing growth was still provided by foreign entrepreneurs, Nigerian entrepreneurs played an increasingly important role in this sector. In Chapter 16, John Harris examines the performance of Nigerian entrepreneurs in the manufacturing sector of the economy. His study is of particular importance because it is the first broadly based analysis of entrepreneurship in Nigeria. One of the key findings of his study is that the most important bottlenecks to an expansion of Nigerian entrepreneurship are the limited markets and the shortage of personnel with technical and managerial skills.

NOTES

1. For an excellent discussion of the institutional background connected with the Nigerian planning process, see Peter Clark, "Economic Planning for a Country in Transition: Nigeria" in E. Hagen (ed.) *Planning Economic Development* (Homewood, Illinois, R. D. Irwin, 1963), pp. 252-293.

2. Nigeria, *National Development Plan, 1962-68* (Lagos, 1963), pp. 21 and 22.

3. Cambridge: Harvard University Press, 1966.

4. *Ibid.*, p. 73.

5. O. Aboyade, "A General Critique of the Plan," *Nigerian Journal of Economic and Social Studies*, Volume 4, (July, 1962), p. 112.

6. See E. Dean, "Factors Impending the Implementation of Nigeria's Six Year Plan," *Nigerian Journal of Economic and Social Studies*, Volume 8 (March, 1966), pp. 113-128 and E. Dean, "Nigerian Plan Implementation, 1962-1966," (manuscript prepared for a Workshop on Economic Growth and Political Instability, held at Michigan State University, 1968).

7. Dean, *op. cit.*, "Nigerian Plan Implementation," p. 11.

8. Nigeria, Federal Office of Statistics, *Gross Domestic Product of Nigeria, 1958/59—1966/67* (Lagos).

9. W. A. Lewis, *Reflections on Nigeria's Economic Growth* (Paris: OECD, 1967), p. 15.

10. *Ibid.*, p. 11.

11. Comprehensive Economic Planning in Nigeria*

LYLE M. HANSEN

A specific comprehensive economic plan is as much the result of the influences generated by the type of staff, procedures, and organization of the Government originating the Plan as the influence of the technical methods employed or the characteristics of the economy being planned. In my judgment, and this paper expresses only my views and not the views of any Government of Nigeria, this was certainly true in the preparation of the National Development Plan 1962-68 for the Federation of Nigeria. A brief description of how the Plan was prepared must, therefore, take into account the influence of these three sets of factors upon the final product, although the primary purpose of this paper is consideration of the technical methods employed.

The policy directive to the planners from the National Economic Council stated "that a National Development Plan should be prepared for Nigeria with the objective of the achievement and maintenance of the highest possible rate of increase in the standard of living and the creation of the necessary conditions to this end, including public support and awareness of both the potential that exists and the sacrifices that will be required."[1] The schedule for independence and termination of existing economic programmes required that both planning staffs be organized and the Plan formulated, adopted, and printed in a little over two years' time. The Federal and each of the three regional governments had to prepare and adopt plans for themselves, and then co-ordinate these into a national Plan. As it is a comprehensive Plan, the task also involved study of, and consultation with, non-government individuals and agencies.

The decisive factor influencing the final shape of the Plan was the procedural element involved in processing a comprehensive plan through

* An article originally prepared under the same title for The Economic Commission for Africa, Addis Ababa, 1962 (mimeographed.) Reprinted by permission of the United Nations.

192

four Governments and their inter-Government machinery within a tight time schedule. No full length book could do justice to this aspect of Nigerian planning.[2] An insight can be gained from appreciating the implications when Nigerian planners accepted as a cardinal procedural principle that the Plan should be realistic, and this would best be achieved *inter alia*, when all Government agencies were fully consulted and completely understood and supported those parts of the Plan they would be responsible for executing. This meant repeated discussions with and among well over one hundred agencies as the Plan evolved. This work was in addition to the day to day tasks of governments operating a newly independent country with a rapid turn-over of personnel. Professional planners can judge the final Plan document for the amount and quality of effort required in its production. I believe that one of the major difficulties in economic planning in Africa is that not only many civil servants but most junior or beginning planners do not appreciate the sheer amount of effort and time involved in a commitment to comprehensive economic planning.

The general policy directive given to Nigerian planners was initially and authoritatively spelled out to mean achieving a growth rate at least as high and preferably higher than that achieved in the past decade with, at the same time, avoidance of inflation; maintenance of the international value of the currency and avoidance of a balance of payments crisis; expansion of economic opportunities for citizens in all fields of endeavor; and modernization of the economy. These qualitative directives with their quantitative implications derived from existing government policies at the time.

The planning task involved a simultaneous study of the aggregate economic structure including the foreign trade and payments sector; aggregate and detailed foreign and domestic financing on both public and private account; detailed investment plans of Government and private sector; and the institutional and policy framework for development. Attention was first directed to an analysis of existing and past trends to provide the basis for evaluating future estimates and desires. It might be best to treat each of these studies separately although I want to emphasize that the inter-relationships between the aggregate and detailed aspects of the economy was our primary concern, and much of our work was shaped by the results of one study interacting on others.

Nigeria was fortunate in having a set of national accounts in current and constant prices covering the seven years 1950-57.[3] One of the first tasks was to bring these accounts up to date, 1960, in constant prices, and analyze the trends in the aggregate structure of the economy. These patterns of resource production and use established the aggregate conditions on which growth must be built. The significant features were (all in constant prices or real terms):[4]

(i) The predominance of gross domestic production (GDP) deriving from primary production, but an average aggregate annual increase of both domestic and export crops above the estimated population growth rate.

(ii) GDP increasing at an average annual rate of 4%.

(iii) Gross fixed investment (GFI) increasing as a share of GDP from 7% in 1950 to 15% in 1960. This implied a trend of decreasing productivity in the existing pattern of GFI.

(iv) Consumption relatively constant at 90% of GDP, but Government consumption increasing rapidly from 3.4% to 7.5% while private consumption declined from 87% to 85% of GDP.

(v) Gross domestic savings relatively constant at 10% of GDP. This meant that Nigeria had a net export surplus in the early fifties and import surplus in the late fifties. In short, increased resource use attributable to constant rate of private consumption and increasing GFI and Government consumption was financed from past savings with a resultant drawing down of foreign exchange reserves.

Nigerian planners followed no specific aggregate model when considering aggregate projections for the future. The major influence might be termed a pragmatic adaptation of Tinbergen and Chenery concepts.[5] The object of aggregate projections was to determine whether simultaneous achievement of the targets of aggregate resource use were *consistent* and *feasible* with a *complete* accounting of aggregate resource availability within the conditions set by policy directives.

The known variables were Government gross fixed investment and consumption; policy direction that private consumption increase 3% per annum (average) as an incentive or slightly above an estimated population growth rate of 2% to 2½% per annum; and detailed calculation of foreign trade and balance of payments. The major assumption was that a 4% average annual increase in GDP could be achieved by leveling off GFI at 15% of GDP provided the composition of GFI was shifted sharply to more productive investments. A calculated estimate was that private GFI would maintain at least current levels given establishment of selected policies and organizations, and that foreign private investment would increase as a share of this total private investment. Inventory accumulation was taken as a ratio of projected GFI from comparative experience.

The procedure was to make alternative projections and test their consistency and feasibility with known facts.[6] One alternative was to project GDP at 4% increase per annum with known government and private investment as a residual of GFI at 15% constant share of

GDP; private consumption increasing at 3% per annum and known government consumption to arrive at the import surplus required to achieve the above targets. This import surplus was in turn tested for consistency and feasibility with detailed balance of payments calculations and detailed estimates of foreign public and private financing possibilities. Foreign public investment possibilities were determined by discussions with potential donors, and analysis of the time lags in preparing projects for financing and implementation against known donor country lending and aid policies. The increase in foreign private investment was tested against existing patterns and knowledge of probable and possible projects involving this type of investment.

An alternative projection took the estimated feasible import surplus including allowance for terms of trade; known government investment and consumption plans; private investment as a residual of GFI at 15% of GDP; assumed inventory accumulation, and GDP increasing at 4% per annum average to test whether resource availability would permit an average annual increase of 3% for private consumption.

A third alternative projection calculated resources required if inflationary price movements emerged, and tested this against estimated resource availability if GDP increased at 4% per annum plus the estimated feasible import surplus.

These aggregate calculations resulted in a range of alternative magnitudes. The selection of the Plan magnitudes was further refined by examining financial considerations. Government adopted the principle that all recurrent and one-half of capital expenditure must be financed by Nigerian sources. This was also in accord with common foreign financing policy which usually covered only the off-shore component of investment projects, and this ranged generally between 40% to 50% of government investment. This implied that recurrent expenditure was a crucial variable as its growth determined budget surpluses given a specific revenue forecast. Analysis of continuing and planned government expenditure revealed the recurrent expenditure component.

Significantly, the desire to control recurrent expenditure in order to generate surpluses for development reinforced the desirability of shifting the composition of government investment sharply into economic sectors. It was established that a Nigerian Pound (N£) invested in economic, social, and administrative sector projects generated two, four, and six shillings respectively of recurrent expenditure each year thereafter. In short, investment in administrative sectors not only is less directly productive economically, but reduces budget surpluses by a factor of three compared to economic sector projects in generating recurrent expenditure. The revenue-generating capabilities of these three sectors also sharply favored investment in economic sector projects.

Another gauge of feasibility was to test the capacity of government to increase revenues, and of the economy to save. We calculated the marginal rate of increase for public and private saving separately and combined. We judged that a marginal rate of increase of public savings of 20% or more would not be feasible, nor for aggregate savings given the institutional and structural character of the economy. We also tested whether increased public savings was consistent with private savings with allowance for foreign private investment.

Another test of the over-all size of investment was what would be a prudent level of foreign debt repayments. The calculations of feasible levels of total foreign financing also included estimates of the share of loans and grants and the possible terms and build-up of debt repayments. This was added to existing foreign debt commitments, and the totals compared to past trends in debt payments in Nigerian balance of payments.

A final and most important test of the over-all size of GFI was derived from the analysis of specific investment plans of governments. With scarcities of staff and institutions, a major test was the feasibility in implementing projects. This, as described below, involved analysis of time lags or flows in investment programs. This was especially true in primary production, industry, and technical education which were identified as the first priority programs. When a country such as Nigeria seeks major foreign financing for its development, it must demonstrate the feasibility of implementing the projects for which foreign funds are requested. This sets limits on the size of investment in the early stages of development.

A corollary influence of government investment plans is in determining the strategy of development. These investment plans plus the aggregate economic and financial structure of the economy largely determine the strategy of development. The leveling off of GFI made a shift in investment to more productive sectors mandatory, given past Nigerian and comparative experience. Leveling off GFI followed from the estimated savings and import surplus available. The feasibility of the pattern of investment could only be judged project by project, and by inspection, where estimated rates of increase in agricultural cash crops equalled or exceeded 4% per annum on average. Given the share of agriculture in GDP and higher rates of growth in other sectors, we believe the pattern and size of GFI will produce the estimated increase of GDP.

Capital output ratios were not employed in determining the size of investment over-all or by sectors. It was our belief that we lacked the data to employ this technique, and we questioned the validity of such a technique in a changing economy. We only employed capital output ratios as an *ex post facto* external check on aggregate projections.

We did not have data on distribution of income that would permit linking aggregate disposable income to specific economic sectors and investment programs, much less the data for an input-output matrix. We did test this linkage selectively whenever possible as is described below.

We viewed the function of aggregate projections as providing an over-all sense of direction and, more important, a test of the economic consistency and feasibility of the desired targets. Professor Stolper has ably described this conception, and I recommend his papers for a more complete coverage of the function of aggregate estimates in comprehensive economic planning.[7]

The discussion above illustrates the crucial role of systematic detailed studies of foreign trade, balance of payments, and government finances. The foreign trade studies involved a detailed commodity by commodity approach.[8] Exports began with detailed examination of production estimates including effects of planned investment; estimates of domestic consumption or processing; costs of distribution, transport and storage; effect of producer prices on production and sales and the relationship to export taxes; and finally, estimates of world demand, price, and competition including effects of institutional changes in marketing or world economic organizations. Imports were estimated first with no substitutions taken into account; then known domestic production plans or substitutions were deducted; and finally, wherever possible, import needs of import substitutions were added. Careful consideration was given to import price estimates, and terms of trade were then calculated. These studies involved detailed consultation with all affected or informed parties at home and abroad. Major tests of these estimates resulted from reconciling our estimates with those made independently by international agencies and several foreign aid missions.

Balance of payments calculations followed a similar method except that item-by-item analysis was more difficult to obtain. We described above how we calculated net inflows of foreign capital as related to known projects and lender-donor policies, and the calculation of remittance of profits and debt repayments abroad. A double-check was provided by extrapolating existing indices of invisible payments into the future.

It is at this point that one observes how the linkages within the Plan are established. The detailed foreign trade estimates had to be not only consistent with aggregate economic projections, but also with detailed agricultural, mining, and industry development programs, as well as with traffic estimates for transport and revenue forecasts for government, and so forth. Any change in one of these variables required adjusting the others until a consistent and feasible pattern of inter-relationships existed.

Government finance was analyzed in a similar detailed item-by-item approach in the analysis of budgets. This is indispensable to translating government budgets into national income terms for testing consistency with aggregate projections. It is also crucial if one desires to make full economic cost studies of development projects as part of economic evaluation of projects. Conversion of budget data into performance accounting provides a basis for evaluating agency performance and achievement, as well as suggesting methods of improving unit efficiency. We found it worthwhile, for example, to establish a continuing review of staff requirements and availabilities per unit of work, as staff patterns of the past might not be valid when functions change. Another by-product of budget analysis was an inquiry into ways of improving government purchases, both to reduce costs and to channel this demand into the domestic market as a stimulus for investment. These were all efforts to contain recurrent expenditures and, as described above, the estimates of recurrent expenditure were vital in determining the size of over-all investment.

Revenue estimates were first of all made consistent with detailed development plans that affected the specific revenue base. Major effort was directed to examining possibilities of expanding existing or introducing new sources of revenue. One result was adoption of the principle that where the benefit of investment was primarily and directly for one community or group of users, it should pay fees or rates related to the full economic cost of such services, unless social justice made such payments repugnant or impossible. In many cases, this will result in increasing revenues instead of a substitution. For example, most of the Federal Government investments in the Lagos area were shifted from a grant to loan basis where residents of Lagos were the primary beneficiaries of the investment, e.g., markets, streets, sewers, water, etc.

A major source of income for government investment was found in the depreciation and capital reserves of statutory corporations and government-owned companies, either by requiring these agencies to use such funds to finance their own development, or occasionally by investment in government securities. These resources are, of course, found only by a careful analysis of the budgets of every agency.

I would like to turn now to the project and action program side of the Plan to illustrate our methods of planning. When a government plans, as in Nigeria, the major preoccupation is and was with detailed projects and policies. How one proceeds is largely governed by the past and present experience, and the ideas of government agencies. We always proceeded on the assumption that the final resulting investment programs must be understood and supported by the executive agencies if the plan was to be realistic.

A federation such as Nigeria, with its constitutional division of development functions (e.g., agriculture was essentially regional while seaports and defense were federal) results in a division of labor where the planners undertake to evaluate and organize the investment program for their respective governments, and then for the total government sector. This requires constant close consultation if the planners are to arrive at coordinated and consistent calculations and conclusions. This was achieved in part by the fact that all planners submitted their work and met in an all government Joint Planning Committee (JPC), but much more by direct contact—both formal and informal. In part, Federal responsibility for power, all transport except some types of roads, and communications facilitated coordination, as Federal planners linked these sectors to others.[9]

Space does not permit describing the methods employed in analysis of all the investment sectors for all governments. Therefore, I will concentrate on one program in some detail to illustrate our methods for determining investment projects within coordinated programs. I shall take the Nigerian Ports Authority, as this will illuminate the entire transport sector. This sector accounts for a significant share of Government investment and, if realistic, has multiple linkages throughout a plan.

We began by requesting all agencies to analyze their past programs in a systematic fashion. The objective was to persuade the agencies to stop concentrating on budgetary estimates and expenditure, and to think systematically about their programmes, e.g., the basis for selection of, and inter-relationships between, targets, policies, institutions, costs and returns. This evaluation of the past also was to concentrate on the lessons learned in implementing old programs. Together, these would provide the basis for projecting future agency programs in a similar systematic fashion. Unfortunately, time and staff available prevented completion of these evaluations by all agencies. Nigerian Ports Authority (NPA), however, presented a complete evaluation in their annual reports, in special presentations for the Economic Planning Unit and in loan applications to the World Bank. The NPA had already worked out a ten year expansion program in early 1960. The basic features of this plan were a ten year statistical extrapolation of past traffic trends, and with some exceptions for Port Harcourt, the assumption of constant unit efficiencies of facilities for Lagos, e.g., tons per shift, per quay, shed, etc.

The first step taken by the planners working with NPA personnel was to re-calculate traffic estimates, as this is the crux of transport analysis. Here the first step was to establish production estimates for exports and future demand for imports. Production estimates involved working back to calculations of each important commodity. Each

region had analyzed the production of all their important commodities
by first systematizing knowledge of each crop, e.g., acreage per crop,
output per acre and farm worker; influence of inputs like weather
cycles, improved seeds, fertilizers, improved husbandry, prices and
other variables. Then the effect of the projected feasible expansion of
agriculture programs was introduced and production estimates were
prepared, e.g., effect of larger extension services on crop output. These
estimates were then checked with as many informed people as possible
both at home and abroad.

These production estimates were then analyzed in terms of their
probable use at home and abroad, e.g., how many tons of palm oil
or groundnuts would be marketed or consumed on the farm; what
tonnage of groundnuts or cotton, tin, timber, etc. would be processed or
not processed; what tonnage would be consumed domestically or exported? An identical analysis was applied to imports, and the impact
of import substitution on domestic production was taken into account.
One result of this analysis was our foreign trade estimates, and all of
our traffic estimates were consistent.

From past experience of NPA with composition of traffic, we
paid most attention to groundnuts, cocoa, palm products, cotton,
rubber, iron scrap and tin on export traffic. Timber and petroleum
were separate problems as they do not move over the quays, but
are loaded directly aboard ship or into special company-owned facilities. Regarding imports, attention was focused on cement, salt, flour/
wheat, sugar, textiles, iron, steel and machinery.

We had to pay attention to trans-shipment to and from Dahomey,
Niger, Chad and Cameroons especially regarding petroleum, groundnuts
and cotton. This meant attempting analysis of economic conditions
and transport in these countries and estimation of probable trends for
each factor that would influence traffic through Nigeria. Details on
the new port to be built in Cotonou, Dahomey, had to be obtained
and an estimate made as to the effect this port would have on existing
trans-shipment via Lagos to Cotonou of individual commodities—in
this case, petroleum. Other major developments included the possible
extension of the Dahomey railroad North to connect with an improved
road East through the southern and populated areas of Niger. This
would offset groundnut shipments from Niger, which are important to
Nigerian road and rail operations. Ultimately, such a development
would influence river traffic upstream from the new Niger Dam at
Kainji and thereby the benefits from the locks of the dam. This affects
a £7.0 million investment. A third potential development is the expansion of the railway and road system to the North of the Cameroon
Republic connecting to Chad, or the river-railroad extension via Gabon/

Central African Republic/Chad. If either project matures, it will affect traffic through Nigeria via the Benue River or the new Bornu Railway extension with road to Chad and Northern Cameroons. The Government of Nigeria attached great importance to these inter-state transport links, hence planners took these into account in the project analysis.

Another prerequisite of this exercise was obviously an analysis of industrial growth in Nigeria, and making traffic and foreign trade estimates consistent with industrial production estimates. This meant frequent analysis of the prospects of entire industrial complexes, e.g., demand for and economic costs of production, competitive supplies; status of new projects and time lags in reaching production levels, etc. One of the major by-products of this enquiry was a full-scale analysis into petroleum production, refinery, consumption, and transport. This and other industrial analysis, therefore, contributed to building the industrial programs just as it did for agriculture. These were in turn linked to the other sectors, and our aggregates and vice versa in the effects on traffic.

Given estimates of basic export and import tonnages, the next question was what share of each commodity would move in what direction— to Lagos, Port Harcourt, Niger Delta, or to a lesser extent, Calabar ports? This in turn raised the question of the relationship between Nigerian Ports Authority ports and the total transport situation. The answer turned in part on factors of physical of location, on the time pattern in a transport year, on the economics of alternative forms of transport, and on habits and institutions established to handle imports and exports. Above all else, it raised the issue of government transport policy.

The critical problem was to what extent Lagos and Port Harcourt ports should be developed compared to the Delta ports. Lagos was already crowded and experiencing traffic delays, and trends indicated the same situation for Port Harcourt in two or three years. At first, a shift of traffic to the Delta ports seemed most rational, with excess capacity available at Warri and Burutu, and a new port under construction at Koko. However, further questions had to be answered. What was the capacity and costs of the Niger/Benue river and road access to these ports, and what would be the implications for railways and roads serving Lagos and Port Harcourt? Alternatively, what would be the direct and indirect benefits and costs of developing Lagos and Port Harcourt?

Briefly, we established that inland waterways would confront limitations of channel depths at Delta ports until completion of Escravos Bar in 1964/65, which would limit ship cargoes to 2000 tons (normal is 9000 to 10,000). Also, there will only be an eight-month shipping season upriver (2½ months Benue, and 5 Niger river) until the completion of the Kainji Dam in 1967/68. This meant that use of these waterways was only practical in special locations (e.g., Iddah) or where timing was compatible with movement of bulk commodities as with groundnuts. Furthermore, on a full cost basis, meaning total public and private costs, the waterways costs[10] of 2.08d per ton-mile would exceed railways costs where underutilized capacity means roughly a marginal cost of 1.4 and as low as 0.4d per ton-mile. Road costs are in excess of 4.0 pence per ton-mile. These considerations indicated the use of railways until 1966 when their capacity would be full and their average economic costs would be close to 3.0d per ton-mile. Thereafter, waterways would become the lowest cost carriers.[11] On the other hand, we had to balance the effect of such things as institutional habits—like Marketing Board transport policy in their shipping allowances—plus effects of commercial rates and net cost to shippers. Here, waterways could sometimes close the cost gap with railways.

Given the structure of the economy and the necessity to maximize returns, we accepted the Stanford Research Institute recommended principles that transport policy should be designed to meet demand with the minimum expenditure of resources, and be coordinated to obtain the lowest costs in terms of real expenses and service considerations.[12] This follows from the fact that *transport facilities commonly are heavy and capital intensive investments with low and long-term rates of return.* This means not creating facilities before anticipated traffic emerges, but rather relating investments to firm forecasted traffic. Therefore, timing of transport invesments was crucial. This would differ from the implications of some economic history studies. We did recognize the exception however where there was evidence that a transport facility would encourage new production and/or marketing of existing production, as with feeder roads.

The importance of relating transport investments to traffic can be seen in Table 1. The difference in total cost per ton-mile varies 27% between the two estimated river traffic forecasts for 1968. If the lower cost per ton-mile obtained, then river transport would be cheaper than railways. If the higher river transport cost prevails, the cost relationship with railways reverses.

The result was that we did not expect waterways and Delta ports to increase their share of total import-export traffic, nor would it be economic to induce such a shift before 1966. This, of course, would not apply to special developments on the river such as a potential steel mill, or evacuation from areas adjacent to the delta such as the completion of the Benin-Ijebu-Ode road. Incidentally, the analysis of a steel mill project turns very much on detailed knowledge of both

TABLE 1. *Niger and Benue River Traffic and Cost.*

	1962-3	1964-5	1967-8	1971-2
Traffic based on known projects (million ton mile)	120	135	160	240
Traffic if potential developments mature (million ton miles)	120	156	243	293
Total cost per ton mile (pence) known projects	2.08	2.17	2.05	1.66
If potential developments mature	2.08	1.92	1.68	1.10

present and future transport economic policies—another type of linkage in the Plan.

The problem of road, as opposed to rail, share of this traffic was less significant to ports' investments once total directions were determined as Delta ports are supplied primarily by water transport. However, we again made separate studies of each consistent with the foreign trade and port traffic estimates. We then had estimates of total traffic through Lagos and Port Harcourt by commodity, direction and year.

The next step was to determine to what extent existing facilities could handle the projected traffic and at what costs, and what new facilities would be required with what economic and financial implications. The former is a question of the characteristics of the traffic, and the efficiency and potential improvement in use of existing ports. Economists will recognize the benefit of reduced costs and increased returns in higher levels of utilization of existing facilities, and especially where fixed costs are a large share of total costs. Converted into a planning rule of thumb when evaluating capital intensive facilities, this comes to a question of how production can be increased with little or no additional investment through better organization, etc. With ports, the evaluation of past performance referred to above was of immense assistance in focusing on obstacles to efficiency, as well as a means of measuring efficiency.

Statistics revealed that ship delays in waiting to load or discharge, and average ship turn around times were constantly reducing over past years. This was confirmed by an increase in tons moved over the quays per year and month, and especially per lineal foot of quay in these time periods. Here, the economist must depend on comparative studies and technical knowledge of the work process of a facility to measure its efficiency—it is a job of accumulating what I like to call "economic development" detective devices. The conclusion was that the harbour operation and movement over the quays was highly efficient. The ports were fully mechanized and, combined with staff turnover due to Nigerianization, it was agreed that there was little room for improvement on the quays themselves.

Like most ports, however, access to and evacuation of port storage space leaves much room for improvement. Unlike many ports, custom clearance was judged to be relatively efficient. The problem was limitations in access roads (e.g., delays on Apapa Road) and especially the fact that importers and, therefore, lorry operations work on an eight-to-twelve-hour day, whereas the ports could work twenty-four hours. An interesting complication was that storage fees bring one of the highest revenues to cost operations in the port, which led us to suspect that NPA had mixed feelings on quicker clearance. One result of exploring the possibilities of quicker clearance was the priority given to the Second Mainland Bridge—Apapa Road and Western Avenue High-speed road system in the Federal road program as this would facilitate movement to and from the Lagos port areas—another planning linkage.

NPA also agreed to review their storage fees schedule as the old system contained a possible inducement not to clear storage up to two weeks. Importers could in effect obtain cheap storage depending on their timing in storing and removing their cargoes. However, there was a limit to increasing fees to induce quicker clearance. We had to enquire into what would be the implications of increased storage fees to lorry operators, importers, wholesalers, retailers and ultimately the consumer. For example, what happens to road transport rates when shifted on to a twenty-four hour basis; did importers have storage capacity or would this mean additional costs; what was the incidence of transport costs—would consumers bear all or part of any increased rates? NPA is still exploring these possibilities as an entire institutional complex is involved in any changes.

A special problem was raised by the customs quays in Lagos. The traffic demand is primarily a problem of imports, and customs quays handle only imports. However, the quays are so old that they must be renovated or replaced within the next ten years. This meant linking this issue with comparative costs of new facilities, and to plans for land use and traffic on Lagos Island itself, e.g., to Town Planning sector of the Plan.

We finally come to the question of investment in new facilities. Agreement was made that the Plan should cover at least ten years given the permanency of ports and time lag in construction, and it should be in two phases: up to 1966-67 and thereafter. The two-phase idea followed from our awareness that after completion of Kainji Dam and Escravos Bar mole, a shift to the Delta ports—river complex was a real possibility as it probably would then be the least cost transport system. In addition, further expansion at Lagos after Phase I would not only involve expensive filling of land in the harbour for replacement and/or renovation of customs quays, but would probably imply double-tracking of the railways to evacuate future port traffic—in short, a decision involving major investments and a commitment to a transport system far into the future. Readers of the Plan will recall the difficulties of the railways and the total emphasis therein on modernization and improved efficiency and not on expansion of the system. No one wanted to take a decision at this time to expand the railways after 1966 especially when it would only be an indirect result of deciding on port expansion beyond 1966.

Investment in new port facilities was now estimated. First we returned to the traffic data to determine its annual and monthly variations or periodicity. Secondly, NPA converted the traffic estimates into a weight-bulk ratio which defined the space capacity required. Thirdly, the question was, given peak periods of traffic, at what level should port capacity be developed—50, 80 or 100 per cent of these peaks? We had made very conservative traffic forecasts. What about emergencies like breakdowns, or the impact of traffic like the 450,000 tons of materials for Kainji Dam?

We decided, on NPA advice, to add a 20 per cent margin to the annual traffic estimates to cover these considerations. This was judged to be conservative as it was less capacity than the highest monthly traffic peaks, but we have a safety margin in existing Port Harcourt import capacities until 1964, and in the Delta port capacities up to 1967. Finally, we decided after reviewing manpower training and availability, that we would assume present unit efficiencies. The resulting calculations of port capacity requirements may be seen in Table 2.

The NPA then prepared a capital construction and cost schedule, and a financing forecast showing the results of anticipated operations. We always attempted to isolate the effect of price inflation, but not uniformly as the composition of project costs varies too much. Costing capital projects really involves costing past and existing activities, and each component for comparative purposes, e.g., cost per lineal foot of quay, etc. At this point, we had staff and materials for construction and operation analyzed in order to be able to assess the import component for foreign trade and aid calculations; to assess demand for standard commodities like cement and steel construction roads for industrial planning, and to measure the employment effect of the investment. The last was divided into net increase by type of staff, and net increase in Nigerian staff. We attempted a foreign exchange cost and benefit analysis, but with less success due to the difficulty in tracing ultimate source of payment. All are links in the Plan inter-relationships.

TABLE 2. *Expected Traffic at Ports of Lagos and Port Harcourt.*

Present capacity	Forecast tonnages	Weighted Bulk/ general cargo	120 per cent to avoid congestion	Excess tonnage	Short- age of berths	Addl. berths planned
(a) Port Harcourt import capacity available with 7 berths						
1961-2 480	520	515	618	138	1	—
1962-3 660	536	541	649	—	—	—
1963-4 660	566	580	696	36	—	—
1964-5 660	579	606	727	67	⅓	—
1965-6 660	613	654	785	125	⅔	1
1966-7 710	694	735	882	172	1	—
(b) Port Harcourt export capacity available with 7 berths						
1961-2 440	321	—	385	—	—	—
1962-3 450	333	—	400	—	—	—
1963-4 450	345	—	414	—	—	—
1964-5 450	358	—	430	—	—	—
1965-6 450	369	—	443	—	—	—
1966-7 450	382	—	458	8	—	—
(c) Apapa import capacity available with 9 berths and lighter berths						
1961-2 735	865*	838	1006	271	2	—
1962-3 910	865	866	1039	129	1	—
1963-4 910	924	948	1138	228	2	2
1964-5 910	941	1009	1211	301	2	1
1965-6 910	1004	1106	1327	417	3	1
1966-7 910	1169	1268	1522	612	4	—+
(d) Apapa export capacity available with 9 berths and lighter berths						
1961-2 790	735	—	882	92	—	—
1962-3 1000	762	—	914	—	—	—
1963-4 1000	790	—	948	—	—	—
1964-5 1000	820	—	984	—	—	—
1965-6 1000	838	—	1006	6	—	—
1966-7 1000	870	—	1044	44	—	—

1. Figures cover the five years 1962-7.

* All figures for Lagos imports less 375,000 tons at Custom Quay.
+ Plans now call for another berth in 1967-8, the last year of Plan. Also replacement or renovation of Customs Quay must be decided by 1966.

The crucial analysis was, however, the calculation of economic and financial costs and returns. With agreed traffic and operating costs plus known rate schedules, the NPA had prepared financial budget results. We did not question the price effect of NPA rates on demand as ports are a monopoly, but we did question the financial viability and whether there was a reasonable rate of return on a "utility" type investment. NPA financial calculations were on an "actual" basis, and are what we call a commercial balance sheet or pay-off calculation. Thus, they show the cost of capital loan repayments and interest as charged by a probable loaner (in this case, the World Bank rates) or no charge if equity. They charge for initial capital allowances and taxes. Depreciation charged may or may not be equal to the useful life of the asset. We used past NPA balance sheets and knowledge of commercial accounting and known variables to check the validity of these financial forecasts.

A planner has two main interests in financial or commercial balance sheets. First, he must determine the financial viability of a program and the projects within the program. This is where the Plan principle of having direct beneficiaries of a service pay for that service may, in part, be tested. More important, however, is to convert the balance sheet into a "cash flow" analysis in order to determine what financial resources are available to an enterprise. The procedure is to take total estimated receipts and then deduct the actual payments that must be made by the enterprise. This means deducting from gross receipts actual operating costs, interest and amortizing repayments on loans, taxes, rents, insurance, etc. Usually, some provision must be made for working capital balances although these can be reduced when temporary or short term loan facilities are available. Sometimes contractual sinking funds require cash contributions. The remainder is cash available for development expenditure and typically includes profits plus reserves for depreciation and capital allowances.

The difference between balance sheet profits and cash available is frequently large, e.g., between £400,000 and £1,000,000 annually for NPA over the Plan period. This is why a nominal deficit operation, as with the railways, is consistent with the ability of the railways to finance a large share of its own development. Railways show a cumulative financial deficit over 5 years at the same time as showing they can finance £12.2 million of their £20.1 million development programme.[13] We applied the principle of maximizing the mobilization of such resources to all government statutory corporations and companies. We thereby generated 40 per cent of the Nigerian share of financing the Federal Development program e.g., £80 million of the £200 million Nigerian resources. Some might question this on the grounds of invading the autonomy of statutory corporations. This, however, does not follow, as these methods of financing expansion are common to prudent enterprise around the world, and, of course, a developing country must mobilize every possible financial resource.

Financial viability, however, does not tell one whether a project is economically viable, and, therefore, its rating as a growth inducing investment. Here we get to the heart of the economic analysis. The first step is to determine economic costs. We insisted first on considering full or complete costs, and although NPA covers total costs in a port operation, some costs like the costs of roads would not be covered unless Government and private expenditure were combined. A major question in economic costing itself is what costs to include and at what prices. Unlike commercial balance sheets, economists charge an interest rate for all capital employed whether equity or loan, and do not charge for loan repayments as capital supply is assumed infinite at some interest rate. Taxes are not charged as a cost or grants as a receipt to eliminate positive or negative subsidies. Depreciation is taken at the true or "useful" life of the specific capital asset. Needless to say, there was difficulty in explaining this distinction between economic and commercial costs to the layman.

Pricing costs and receipts is still more difficult. Obviously the Nigerian economy is not perfectly competitive, and, therefore, market prices reflect structural distortions of the Nigerian market. We, therefore, attempted to impute prices that would more closely resemble true prices (values) given actual supply and demand relationships without such distortions in the market.[14] I must immediately confess that we simplified this exercise, and related prices to levels familiar to our audiences. Thus, interest rate on transport and utility type capital investments was taken at 6 per cent because this was the bank rate in the United Kingdom at the time, and, therefore, related to the price Government would pay for funds in that market. Six per cent was also the rate used by Stanford and, therefore, familiar to, and associated by, our audience with transport. Finally, 6 per cent is roughly World Bank rates for transport loans. We took 8 per cent for commercial type investments like steel and ships as this reflected loan terms then prevailing.

I would be the first to admit that true interest rates in Nigeria should be imputed at higher levels.[15] If we followed the traditional method of taking the interest rate charged for capital for marginal projects, the rate would easily exceed 15 per cent. Some loan funds to Government actually cost this much as in supplier credits. Local bank rate for prime loans is still over 8 per cent, and I suspect that in private personal loans interest rates rise over 100 per cent. A planner, however, takes one step at a time in presenting a new subject to a non-specialized audience. Similar considerations led us to take wages at actual cost, knowing that this undervalued highly skilled and overvalued unskilled labor given the supply and demand of each. In order to double-check, we ran "spot checks" or trial balance sheet calculations with "weighted" and different interest rates and wage levels. Alternatively, one may discount or appreciate results by some percentage figure imputed to value wages, interest rates, or foreign exchange as Bryce does in his valuing of industrial investments, e.g., inflate all foreign exchange by 10 per cent as a cost or receipt.[16] I believe the essential point is explicitly to reason out a rational set of prices and then consistently follow them so that comparisons can be made between projects.

The importance of variations between nominal and imputed interest rates, and charging interest on all capital employed compared to only loan funds and not equity capital, is illustrated in Table 3. This shows the familiar phenomena where a typical company following normal commercial accounting practices shows a net return of 7 per cent (+140) based on nominal market interest rates (6 per cent).

TABLE 3. *Variations in Economic Rate of Return with Variations in Capital and Interest Rates Employed.*

	CAPITAL EMPLOYED			Market interest rate 6%	Imputed interest rate 12%	Gross receipts before interest	Net return after int. charged 6%	12%
	Loans	Equity	Total					
1. Commercial accounts	1000	1000	2000	60	120	200	+140	+80
2. Economic accounts			2000	120	240	240	+ 80	−40

Whereas a full economic cost of capital at the same interest rate reduces the net return to 4 per cent, if an imputed "scarcity" value of capital expressed as interest is charged, then the enterprise shows a net return of −2 per cent. Needless to say, we had some difficulty in explaining this difference when a government-owned company revealed this variation. This is also an illustration of the familiar fact that the success of a government economist turns more frequently on his ability to explain basic economic concepts to a non-specialized audience, rather than the more complex formulations and methods.

A more concrete illustration of these differences in apparent and imputed interest rates and "commercial" financial profitability compared to full economic rate of return, may be seen in the Analysis of the Railways in Table 4. Note the difference in interest rates charged in lines 4, 5 and 6, and the resulting difference between financial and economic rate of return in lines 8 and 9.

Another problem in calculating economic costs and returns is what capital base to use to relate to the net economic income for purpose of calculating economic rate of interest.

TABLE 4. *Economic Analysis of the Nigerian Railway Corporation (NRC)*
All figures in £ million unless otherwise stated

	1960-1	1961-2	1962-3	1963-4	1964-5	1965-6	1966-7
1. Gross Income	—	15.406	15.793	15.950	17.941	18.562	19.870
2. Operating Costs including depreciation but excluding interest	—	14.860	14.861	15.083	15.680	15.937	16.365
3. Depreciation Charges	—	2.484	2.701	2.728	2.792	2.823	2.832
4. Interest Charges, actual	—	1.650	1.962	2.154	2.207	2.182	2.156
5. Actual Interest Charges at percentage of depreciated value of capital	—	2.13	2.38	2.57	2.63	2.59	2.57(%)
6. Interest Charges calculated at 6 per cent of depreciated value of capital	—	4.652	4.940	5.024	5.059	5.046	5.030
7. Net Income if economic rate of 6 per cent were charged	—	−4.106	−4.008	−4.157	−2.798	−2.421	−1.525
8. Economic rate of return (item 7 as percentage of depreciated value capital)	—	−5.29	−4.86	−4.96	−3.31	−3.11	−1.81(%)
9. Financial rate of return (net income of NRC as given by NRC as percentage of depreciated value of capital	—	−1.42	−1.54	−1.54	+0.64	+0.53	+1.60(%)

Notes: Items 1, 2, 3, and 4 given by NRC.
           Item 5 calculated.
           Item 7 Gross Revenues (Item 1), less costs (Item 2), and 6 per cent interest (Item 6).

Taking only new capital means treating existing capital assets as "sunk" costs and of no value, and overvalues the rate of return. Fortunately, we could generally calculate depreciated value of existing capital assets using original costs and true depreciation although original cost may undervalue existing capital. A further complication is that income returns related to capital *undepreciated* understates the true rate of return, and if against depreciated capital (on an annual average) generally overstates the rate of return.[17] We sometimes averaged the two or followed the latter as a more valid method. A more precise method would be to use discounted cash or income flows, but this requires a long time series. This method was applied to electricity, steel mills, and inland water transport, e.g., "present worth" of present and future income is a more relevant measure of return on capital in a capital scarce economy.[18]

The results for NPA may be seen in Table 5.

TABLE 5. *Nigerian Ports Authority Expected Financial and Economic Returns.*

	Depreciated Value of Capital	Net[1] Income	Economic Rate of Return	Net[2] Financial Income	Financial Rate of Return
1962-3	13,468	741	5.50	571	4.2
1963-4	15,967	779	4.88	636	4.0
1964-5	18,328	549	3.00	175	0.9
1965-6	21,653	351	1.62	595	2.7
1966-7	23,852	369	1.55	845	3.5
1967-8	27,755	398	1.43	1011	3.6

[1] Gross Surplus minus 6 per cent interest on depreciated value of capital useful life of asset depreciation.
[2] Gross Surplus minus actual interest and amortization payments.

In fact we ran several "trial" alternative calculations, and this is only one selected as representative for presentation purposes. Other variations included rates of return with and without Phase 2 capital costs; with and without depreciating new capital, and with a variation in depreciating and valuing capital used for replacement works as distinguished from new capital works. The variations are illustrated in the appendix.

Table 5 may be misleading in that the time span is too short, and the "bunching" of new investment cost during this period is not counterbalanced by increasing income in later years against a depreciating capital base, nor is the time lag between investment cost and use of the facility taken into account. The long term calculations show a more positive rate of return. I have not described the Bonny Bar dredging project for petroleum tankers which, although a major exercise in itself, came after publication of the Plan. This, if it matures, will increase the returns of NPA.

It does not follow that a project like ports development would receive an allocation only because its economic rate of return was positive. Economic analysis does not result in decisions, it is only a hand maiden in facilitating more rational decisions. Many other factors influence the final decision by Government. The constraints of politics and administration figure large in allocation decisions. Frequently programs and projects are already underway—spillovers, as it were, from older decisions, and it is most difficult to persuade governments to stop a project underway, even if it is a loss. At best, one seeks to reduce additional investment. In addition, the practice of log rolling or "everybody gets a bit of the cake" constitutes a powerful force on allocation decisions. The original request of agencies stake out a claim in resources, so to speak, and allocation decisions generally are a matter of whether a bit more or less should be given from these original requests. As budgets evolve, they become "sticky or frozen" due to vested interests, and the discretion left open to the planner is marginal. The priority needs in an underdeveloped country can quickly block out one's resources even on a rational economic basis, e.g., £100 million for electricity plus £75 million for roads, £50 million for education and telephones each, and £40 million for ports and railways, etc., quickly commits £400 million.

For example, the strategy dictated by the structure of the economy collided with the total requests for transport investments by all governments in that transport investment should increase less rapidly than that for primary production, trade and industry. Our first attempt was, therefore, to reduce the total for the sector. Here our recommendations sought to eliminate what we considered the low priority projects. Usually, with transport it was a question of deferring investment, as timing in relation to traffic is crucial. However, how could one set a ceiling on roads when £100 million could be usefully invested? In this case we attempted to define a "hard core" below which Federal roads would deteriorate at a disastrous rate based on anticipated traffic, plus a notional percentage ceiling for all road investments for all governments. With agreed priority on feeder roads, we reasoned from the Regional road allocations which include feeder roads down to a level for Federal roads.

The over-all priorities implied that greatest reductions should fall on the administrative sector followed in turn by the social and then transport-communications sectors. The more or less reasoned marginal reductions followed as with transport.

As described above in relation to foreign trade or transport, the primary production sector was planned on the basis of a systematic inventory of agricultural production, e.g., acreage per crop, and per workers; output per acre; then the effect of each element of the development program was introduced, e.g., increase in output per acre due to units of fertilizer; improved seeds; improved husbandry, etc. These inputs were then programed backwards to ensure that the inputs would materialize, e.g., production schedule of schools for extension workers in turn related to schedule of training school staff, etc. The final annual production estimates were then adjusted for the impact of weather based on historical patterns, and then discounted over-all by an arbitrary factor to allow for disasters and unknown failures.

We attempted to include calculations of rates of returns based on these inventories. However, our only systematic calculations were those of known government investments such as farm settlements, plantations, and rehabilitation of natural oil palms and rubber groves.[19] Our major concern was to maximize primary product output unless sufficient data indicated long term negative results, and establish consistency with the Plan by way of linkages. Hence, the size of investment was largely determined by estimates of maximum rates of feasible implementation of agriculture projects. Considerable attention went into the question of institutions such as agricultural credit, research, or extension workers, and basic policies such as producer prices, export taxes, and savings. We feel confident concerning all significant cash crops which we believe accounts for a major but unknown share of agricultural output. Their average rate of increase is approximately 4 per cent which indicates that the entire economy will grow by this much as other production sectors are increasing at faster rates. On the other hand, we are organizing a two-year enquiry into a national agricultural plan, and this comments on the gaps and inadequacies of the existing Plan.

Industrial planning focused primarily on policies and building organizations. Several surveys were conducted into potentials and problems of manufacturing. The foreign trade studies included calculating production plans and, as a by-product, an estimate of the market in dynamic terms. Indeed, a considerable appreciation of the market emerged when raw material processing possibilities and investment induced opportunities were added to imports. This data was shared as widely as possible with investors, but more important, organizations are planned which will regularly collect and distribute such information. As with agriculture, therefore, much of the significant development expenditure is recurrent expenditure for technical staff operations in these fields.

The size of Government investment in industry was determined primarily by the capital concomitant by staff expansion; estimates of how fast credit organization staffs could expand and process prudent investments; and the Government share of large known projects such as petroleum refining; sugar plantations and steel mills; and coal mining plus an estimate of additional funds for such direct investments. Direct Government investment involved studies of the economies of textiles;

oil seed crushing; construction materials including steel, cement, aluminum, and fertilizer and chemicals to mention a few.

Power and electricity investment was an outcome of commissioned studies—going back eight years—of the Niger and Benue river systems, and the national fuel and energy industry. Comprehensive and sophisticated studies were made of hydro, coal, natural gas, and oil as alternatives for generating electricity as part of the Niger Dam's feasibility studies. A discounted cash flow method was used as the studies were designed to meet World Bank criteria. This, in turn, led to studies of development in the Niger and Benue river valleys in order to assess navigation benefits of alternative dams. Another linkage was that of producing and/or transport of construction materials for the Kainji Dam which was the final selected alternative. The size of investment was determined by the maximum present worth alternative for generating electricity to meet estimated demand for power. The latter was estimated in terms of both end users, and aggregate demand extrapolations. End use analysis included alternatives when major users projects like steel or aluminum smelting were included or not.

Transport studies benefited from several commissioned expert studies including a major study of domestic transport co-ordination by Stanford Research Institute.[20] The planners, therefore, had an advanced level on which to build their studies and recommendations.

Communication was like transport, built around estimated demand, and calculation of both commercial (in this case government budget) and economic rates of return and market considerations. The implementing schedule plus the requirements of a target of self-financing in five years largely determined the investment program.

Considerable effort was put into the Federal town planning program to illustrate the value and methods of co-ordinated metropolitan planning. All programs began with estimates of users based on alternative population growth rates, and their stratification into user units, e.g., number of family units. A major analysis was made of Lagos traffic and transportation relating all users (numbers and location, etc.) and methods of existing and possible transport. The housing program focused on a self-financed solution to low-cost urban housing. This ultimately involved detailed analysis of land availability, alternative development costs, disposal policies, user location and density policies; construction methods and costs; and marketing and finance organization and policies. A third key segment was water and sewerage programs. These were related, in turn, to other land use projects, e.g., schools, hospitals, markets, etc. Finally, alternative methods were explored to discover ways that the local community could assume the costs of these projects based on charges related to the full economic costs. This was one point where local government revenues and expenditures were analyzed and linked to the over-all national Plan.

Health programs were built around targets relating to availability of services measured by staff or beds, etc., and to population estimates. Priority was given to preventive medicine, and with the service targets generally involved calculating schedules and costs of training health staff. Considerable attention was given to unit efficiencies such as nurse-to-bed or patient ratios; costs of alternative construction methods or building sites, etc. The staff training schedules had to be linked to education plans and, as with all ministry programs, construction schedules co-ordinated with capabilities and commitments of public works.

Indeed, several common inquiries covered all ministry programs. One was the linkage of required staff to education plans and overseas recruitment. This is being systematized by a National Manpower Board into annual manpower surveys. A second linkage was of construction schedules with public works capabilities. A special study was also made into ways of containing or reducing government construction costs, and new staff and policies emerged covering design, tendering, and construction methods, e.g., standardized designs and bulk purchase or production for similar structures. This was part of the third common inquiry which was into unit efficiencies. Here, I should note that we made special study of staff housing with the view of reducing considerable use of government resources for this purpose.

Educational planning began with a ten-year National Educational Plan prepared by a National Commission.[21] This was organized around population growth rates; manpower estimates based on comparative experience and large user demand; estimates of building of pipelines of trained staff and students; and financing capabilities. One of the first steps was to budget the staff availability, construction, and costs elements of this Plan, and then test feasibility of each. Unit efficiencies are examined as projects evolve. Size of investment was determined by feasible rates of construction and training of staff or recruitment overseas as this is a critical sector for overall development.

An interesting sidelight is the studies being made of training projects where foreign aid is involved. Here we calculate economic cost per net graduate in Nigeria, compared to education abroad, to judge whether to undertake the project in Nigeria and when. The method is to calculate interest and depreciation on capital and total recurrent costs, and then attribute this to net graduates. If, as is common, several types of students are produced, then common costs are attributed in terms of the ratio of each type of student or instructor to the total. The crucial measurements are the cost per graduate the first year of full operation, and the first year after foreign aid ends. Naturally, the overseas training costs must be selected with care to account for differing wage rates or term lengths, and qualitative judgments of ways of achieving effective training must be included, as well as the political and social benefits, if a regional African institution is involved. We are finding initially some striking cost differences for projects that at first appear very attractive.

Information services were determined in part, by measuring opportunity costs of investment here against other sectors, and evaluation of variables such as multiplication ratios of recurrent expenditure. High levels of subsidy in existing programs led us to a careful inquiring into ways of reducing unit costs and increasing revenues from users.

The planners left administrative sector projects largely to finance and establishment staff and the ministries concerned. An economic planner has little to say about police, defense, judiciary, etc., except for the larger economic and financial implications in terms of resource availability, use, and opportunity cost.

Policies are, of course, crucial in a comprehensive plan as they provide the framework to guide an evolving economy. We treated most policies in the context of each problem within the relevant investment sector. For example, the policy towards the private sector is difficult to generalize, and is more accurately seen in the context of each sector of the economy, e.g., private efforts differ in agriculture and transport. A few major policies could be generalized and warranted statement in the Plan. These covered such subjects as policy regarding inflation; balance of payments; manpower; organizational efficiency; construction costs; private sector; and savings.[22]

I must point out that the analysis of the NPA was one of our best in the sense of completeness and reliability although I believe that much of the electricity, energy, transport, and communications analysis approached this level. However, frequently analysis revealed gaps in our knowledge, and we had to "make do" with whatever we could devise as rational criteria of analysis. A proposed national inquiry into agriculture speaks of the gaps in that vital sector. We are only now obtaining a systematic analysis of the economics of the cotton textile and oil seed crushing industries. For the latter, we had to work with reconnaissance analysis where a quick set of calculations revealed magnitudes and tendencies, not precise costs and rates of return. Estimated air traffic was a reasoned compromise between the ranges given by informed people with few statistics, etc.

Indeed, one of the major characteristics and difficulties in planning is the uneven quality of data and analysis. We found it useful to make several distinctions. If we had only an "idea" project with no data and analysis, we would seek a reasoned qualitative evaluation. We made inclusion of such a project in the Plan contingent both on a study and study results that indicated a viable project. If at all possible, we would specify the minimum criteria of what constituted viability. Sometimes we had rough data or time only for a quick reconnaisance analysis. This provided an indication of gross magnitudes, but again required a contingent acceptance calling for a confirmation study based on given criteria. More common was data carefully worked up by technical people based on recent comparable or known experience but lacking final architectural designs and tender document cost estimates. These could be denoted as planning or pre-investment analysis. Here, the acceptance contingency is that final actual tender costs do not significantly alter planned results in a negative direction. More rare is to have costs based on final designs and tender documents. A simple reason underlies this in that such final designs are expensive in time and money, and are not prudently incurred before the decision is taken to include the project in the Plan and an actual budget.

In conclusion, we planners always operated on the assumption that our function was to identify alternatives, and present systematic objective and wherever possible quantitative analysis of all alternatives. If, as was common, non-economic factors were introduced, then we attempted to ensure that these were made on an explicit and reasoned basis, and that debate followed reasoned lines.

Our major concern, however, was to calculate the economic implications of a decision including both direct costs and returns, and the indirect inter-relationships. I believe this brief overview of these programs illustrates our methods. Our direct concern essentially was whether to expand, and with what economic and financial results. In order to answer this, we had to trace out the inter-relationships of, for example, alternative forms of transport, the relationship between traffic and production trends in the economy, and finally, what share of aggregate investment would be devoted to transport and with what overall results. The analysis is not complete or perfect. Planning is a continuous process, and we expect future Nigerian planners to make these studies more complete and accurate.

APPENDIX

NIGERIAN PORTS AUTHORITY

Trial Calculations of Economic Rates of Returns
1. Rate Return: Net income where interest charged on depreciated value of capital throughout includes works for post 1968 plan.

A. Depreciated Value Capital (base)   B. Adjusted Value Capital (base)

Net	Capital	Rate	Net	Capital	Rate
766	13,229	5.79	766	13,690	5.59
823	15,515	5.30	823	16,518	3.98
602	17,828	3.37	602	19,050	3.16
397	21,233	1.86	397	23,270	1.70
413	23,451	1.76	413	26,453	1.56

Average rate of return = 3.61 p.a.   Average rate of return = 3.39 p.a.

2. Rate Return: Net income where interest charged on adjusted true value of capital. No depreciation charged on 1962-67 capital expenditure. Includes works for post 1968 plan.

A. Depreciated Value Capital (base)   B. Adjusted Value Capital (base)

Net	Capital	Rate	Net	Capital	Rate
738	13,229	5.57	738	13,690	5.39
764	15,515	4.92	764	16,518	4.62
528	17,828	2.96	528	19,050	2.77
274	21,233	1.29	274	23,270	1.17
233	23,451	0.99	233	26,453	0.88

Average rate of return = 3.15 p.a.   Average rate of return = 2.96 p.a.

3. Rate Return: Net income where interest charged on depreciated value of capital adjusted exclude expenditure in 1962-67 for works for 1968-72 period.

A. Depreciated Value Capital (base)   B. Adjusted Value Capital (base)

Net	Capital	Rate	Net	Capital	Rate
766	13,229	5.79	766	13,690	5.58
823	15,515	5.30	823	16,518	4.98
699	16,868	4.14	699	18,850	3.87
614	19,112	3.21	614	22,020	2.78
747	20,221	3.69	747	25,203	2.96

Average rate of return = 4.42 p.a.   Average rate of return = 4.03 p.a.

4. Rate Return: Net income where interest charged on adjusted true capital. No depreciation charged on 1962-67 capital expenditure. Excludes works for post 1968 plan period.

A. Depreciated Value Capital (base)			B. Adjusted Value Capital (base)		
Net	Capital	Rate	Net	Capital	Rate
738	13,229	5.57	738	13,690	5.39
764	15,515	4.92	764	16,518	4.56
628	16,868	3.72	628	18,050	3.47
439	19,112	2.29	439	22,020	1.99
448	20,221	2.21	448	25,203	1.77

Average rate of return = 3.74 p.a   Average rate of return = 3.43 p.a.

Note: Alternative A depreciated value capital base is where depreciation charged throughout.

Alternative B adjusted value capital base is where no depreciation is charged, but replacement was excluded.

NOTES

1. Subsequent to writing this article, my colleague, Wolfgang Stolper has written such a book. See his *Planning Without Facts: Lessons in Resource Allocation From Nigeria's Development.* Cambridge, Mass: Harvard University Press, 1966.

2. Federation of Nigeria, *National Development Plan, 1962-68.* Apapa: Federal Ministry of Economic Development. Nigerian National Press Limited, Apapa, 1962. Chapter 6, p. 1.

3. P. N. C. Okigbo, *Nigerian National Accounts, 1950-57,* Enugu: Government Printer, 1961.

4. *Op. cit., National Development Plan, 1962-68,* Chapters 2 and 3.

5. J. Tinbergen, *The Design of Development,* Baltimore, Maryland, 1958, pp. 99. H. B. Chenery, "The Application of Investment Criteria," *The Quarterly Journal of Economics,* Vol. LXVII, No. 1, February, 1953; and "Development Policies and Programmes," *Economic Bulletin for Latin America,* Vol. III, No. 1, March, 1958.

6. W. F. Stolper, *Prospects for the Nigerian Economy: Principles and Procedures Adopted in Projecting National Accounts.* Lagos: Nigerian National Press, 1961. This paper should be read in conjunction with Chapter 5 of *The Nigerian National Development Plan, 1962-68.*

7. See W. F. Stolper, "The Main Features of the 1962-68 National Plan," *Nigerian Journal of Economic and Social Studies,* Vol. IV, No. 2 (July, 1962), pp. 85-91 and W. F. Stolper, "Notes on a Method of Comprehensive Planning in Tropical Africa," *Economic Bulletin for Africa,* Vol. II, No. 2 (June, 1962), pp. 45-58.

8. W. F. Stolper assisted by P. Clark, "Prospects for the Nigerian Economy—Technical Appendix on Exports, Imports and the Balance

of Payments Gap," (unpublished). This should be read in conjunction with Chapter 5 of the *National Development Plan, 1962-68*.

9. See Peter Clark, "Economic Planning for a Country in Transition: Nigeria," *Planning Economic Development*. Edited by Everett Hagen, Homewood, Illinois: Richard D. Irwin, 1963, pp. 252-293 and O. J. Aboyade, "A General Critique of the Plan," *Nigerian Journal of Economic and Social Studies*, Vol. IV, No. 2 (July, 1962), pp. 110-115.

10. *Op. cit., National Development Plan, 1962-68*, Chapter 6, p. 26, footnote 1.

11. *Ibid.*

12. Hamlin Robinson, Stanton R. Smith, Kenneth G. Clare, *The Economic Co-ordination of Transport Development in Nigeria* (prepared for the Joint Planning Committee, National Economic Council, Federation of Nigeria), Menlo Park, California, Stanford Research Institute, 1961. Also *op. cit., National Development Plan, 1962-68*, Chapter 6, p. 25.

13. *Op. cit., National Development Plan, 1962-68*, Chapter 6, p. 33 and tables XX, XXI, XXII.

14. There is an extensive literature on this subject. For an illustrative statement see Otto Eckstein, *Water Resource Development: The Economics of Project Evaluation*, Cambridge, Mass: Harvard University Press, 1961.

15. One of the most reliable methods at the micro level is to use the implicit interest rate found by discounting the stream of costs and benefits.

16. M. Bryce, *Industrial Development—A Guide for Accelerating Economic Growth*. New York: McGraw-Hill, 1960.

17. Strictly speaking it is only the returns on new capital that matter in the economic analysis.

18. Using discounting methods avoids the problems in alternative methods of calculating depreciation.

19. *Op. cit., National Development Plan, 1962-68*, Chapter 8, pp. 28-34 and Chapter 9, pp. 80-84.

20. *Op. cit., The Economic Co-ordination of Transport Development in Nigeria*.

21. Federal Government of Nigeria, *Educational Development, 1961-70*, Sessional Paper No. 3 of 1961, Lagos: Government Printer, 1961.

22. *Op. cit., National Development Plan, 1962-68*, Chapter 10.

12. Social Factors in Economic Planning with Special Reference to Nigeria*

I

The present working paper is written by an economist, not an anthropologist or sociologist. It is written primarily from the standpoint of an economic planner who has to deal with an existing situation which is characterized by particular facts and ambitions, by a limited knowledge, and by the need to make decisions in very imperfect circumstances. Although the achievement of economic purposes cannot present an aim in itself but is mainly a means for the achievement of other and higher aims, the emphasis must, nevertheless, be economic.

While economists necessarily stress profitability and other mundane matters, this does not mean that they are unaware of the ultimate objectives of economic development, and it is the purpose of this paper to indicate how the other objectives have entered into the planning process and planning decisions. Thus problems of income distribution, equity, slums and urban problems are not discussed as such, but only how they enter the final solutions proposed for economic problems.

It is important to keep in mind this viewpoint, which amounts to a limitation on the paper. Yet it should be stressed at the outset what will be a major purpose of the paper to point out: that assumptions which might be too easily made, namely that economic purposes of profitability and social objectives of justice and equity, to say nothing of charity, are necessarily conflicting, is fortunately not necessarily true in practice. It will be argued that the ultimate aims of society can be met better and faster by more attention to economic solutions proper.

* From "Social Factors in Economic Planning, With Special Reference to Nigeria," *The East African Economics Review*, Vol. II, No. 1, June 1964, pp. 1-17. Reprinted by permission of the East African Economics Society.

II

Economic Planning has the purpose of mobilizing and allocating resources as efficiently as possible to achieve the best results obtainable in a given situation. From the standpoint of the present paper it is necessary to define more closely both what is meant by "results", and what is meant by "planning". The "special reference to Nigeria" can be explained simply by the fact that I was for eighteen months Head of the Economic Planning Unit in the Federal Ministry of Economic Development, Lagos, and as such responsible for much of the staff work that went into the formulation of the First National Development Plan, 1962-1967. It is hoped, however, that the comments that will be made are of wider use to planners in Africa and beyond.*

It is characteristic of all problems, economic or otherwise, that they represent conflicts among many aims, all of which are desirable and many of which are equally desirable so that it is impossible to establish clearcut priorities among them. The aims are normally not themselves economic. A better life, raising standards of health and education, achieving increased national coherence, increasing the power of old and new nations, ensuring the internal and external security of the nation, are all aims that are in their nature not economic. The economists' contribution becomes essential, however, because all of them require real resources. And as long as real resources of all kinds are scarce it is not possible to achieve all of them simultaneously to the desired degree. Nor is it possible to achieve all of them to the desired degree very quickly. The essential role of the statesmen and politicians consists precisely in mediating among the conflicting aims. The role of the economists, though more modest, is as essential; they alone can and must point to the cost of achieving aims not so much in terms of money, as in terms of alternative desirable ends forgone. Money simply becomes the common denominator by means of which the various costs can be compared, and by means of which the total cost can be evaluated. No other method of doing this has thus far been invented.

From the standpoint of the economic planner, development planning involves planning for as rapid an increase in per capita production as possible. This aim itself is nothing but a shorthand description of certain basic facts.

First, the total amount of real resources available should be raised as quickly as possible so that they become available for the achievement of

---

* Because of my official position in the past, it is necessary to state that all views expressed in this paper are mine alone and do not necessarily reflect those of my colleagues of the Government of the Federation of Nigeria.

more and more aims. It stands to reason that the more resources are available the easier the choices among conflicting ends become.

Secondly, the problem of achieving growth and what to do with the growth once achieved are logically and factually separate. It is a misunderstanding of the essential contribution of the economist to accuse him of seeing only economics; of seeing everything in terms of profits, in terms of money; and of being apparently impervious to non-economic factors as well as non-economic ends. This accusation is possibly deserved in a few cases. Normally the economist is as human as the rest of mankind. However, unless resources are available, they cannot be used for any ends, economic or non-economic. Only by raising the amount of available resources will it be possible to achieve non-economic ends. There is no real conflict here. It may be best to consider the achievement of growth and the uses to which it is put as interdependent but logically separate.

Thirdly, the achievement of increased per capita *production* involves the recognition that production and income, though not indentical, are in fact closely linked. Economists cannot promise happiness. They know as well as the next man that many of the best things in life are free. But they know also that people in the emergent nations are not content with the happiness that can be found from free goods. No further apologies for the emphasis on production seem therefore needed.

Fourth, the emphasis on production rather than income or consumption is intended to emphasize that the decisions as to how much of the production should be used for the further increase in the productive capacity of the nation, and how much should be allowed to be currently used to raise standards of consumption are separate.

Fifth, the emphasis on per capita production is meant to bring into the open the proposition that the maximization of the numbers of people that can be maintained at the existing level of per capita production is not among the aims of the emergent nations. This is by no means a self-evident proposition. Moreover, it raises questions of population policy and theory as well as of economic theory, and it should bring out the fact that, in Africa and at the present time, a population problem of the Malthusian type, such as is found in India or China, fortunately exists only in relatively few areas. It also should bring out that within, say, two generations such Malthusian problems could easily arise unless steps are taken *now* to make total resources grow at a rate that stays ahead of the inevitable population increase that follows any improvement in public health.

Before analyzing how the various social factors enter into the picture it is necessary to outline the manner in which the problem of development planning is viewed in this paper. The precise methods that can be used to achieve the aims of economic development must depend on the particular time and place in which they are used. To be realistic and workable, planning must not only aim at certain ends that are likely to be largely extra-economic, but it must start with an existing situation. It is no use, for example, to insist that such market prices as exist in under-developed countries at best reflect an existing situation (and only imperfectly at that) and hence are useless in planning, since the plans aim at a very different situation. Such a statement implies—unconsciously, no doubt—that the desired situation can be achieved by wishing it to be so. If the plans are not to hang in the air, they must start with where an economy is and then must specify the paths which will get the economy to the point desired.

In the case of Nigeria, planning was visualized as involving:
  (a) the formulation of governmental capital budgets in as integrated a manner as possible in the circumstances;
  (b) a careful development of the implications of all governmental capital expenditures and policies for the ordinary (recurrent) budgets;
  (c) the development of policies for the economy as a whole, and specifically towards the private sector; for governmental budgets (i.e., tax policy) and towards foreign capital;
  (d) the building of institutions that could be used increasingly to execute policies and to increase the flexibility of the economy.

In many respects, the ordinary (recurrent) budget is of central importance to planning. All uses of resources compete for all available resources at any moment so that from the standpoint of the best allocation of resources, there is no sense in distinguishing between ordinary and capital budgets. The ordinary budget more than any other single place, puts a limitation on the extent to which *social* objectives can be satisfied. And the ordinary budget, more than any other document reflects economic and social policies. This is a central point of my argument to which it will be necessary to revert again at some length.

III

Social factors enter the planning process at several levels. Most obviously, they largely determine the ends of economic development: a better life, more schools, more hospitals, better housing, more leisure and less back breaking work and so forth.

It should be pointed out as strongly as possible, however, that the decision to have development and to change from traditional ways of living and of doing things, to modern and continuously changing ways is itself a political and social decision which, however, has definite and inescapable economic implications. The major implication of this decision is that investments must be profitable and that no resources must be squandered. It is no use to assert that "profitability" is a "narrowly economic" concept, that it omits consideration of social factors and so forth. Such arguments reveal a fundamental misunderstanding of the *social* implications of *economic* profitability, and of the economic implications of social decisions. Simply wishing them to be will not make social aims to come into existence. Economic profitability will.

Social factors enter the formulation of plans through policy decisions. It is commonly agreed that too uneven an income distribution is not tolerable and that the poorest should not carry the main burden of development. These two propositions are, of course, not self evident. In fact, a very good case can be made that premature preoccupation with equity problems will backfire and prevent any development from taking place. Furthermore, in no African country do we have really good information on existing distribution of income or wealth. Nevertheless, equity considerations do play a part in the formation of both economic and tax policies, and in the decisions on the final structure of any investments.

An example of the kind of policy decision that has been made with considerations of equity in mind is: of those investment projects that are subject to economic calculations, only those are *socially* (i.e., from the standpoint of equity) justifiable that will after a reasonable time lead to an increase in available resources. Economically unprofitable investments are not only economically nonsense, but are likely to be socially and politically pernicious. They are financed by the taxes exacted in Nigeria from farmers by means of low producer prices set by marketing boards. They will benefit very few people directly employed, who are being subsidized by the tax payer at large, i.e., in the existing situation by the bulk of the farmers. Unprofitable investments not only do not benefit the economy—subsidies mean that real resources are used not to increase the productive capacity of the economy but to make it go backward!—but involve a redistribution of income from the poorer farmers (if they are poor) to the relatively well-to-do city workers and businessmen owning the subsidized investments; or in the case of government investments to subsidize a relatively well-paid civil service—relatively to the rest of the tax-payers—and relatively well-paid workers.

A second example of social considerations entering policy decisions is given by the decision made by the Nigerian cabinet and announced by the

Federal Minister of Finance in the budget speech made during the budget session of 1962 when the Plan was laid on the Table of the House of Representatives, that on principle road users and the users of economic services ought to pay for the services they receive. This refers primarily to electricity and telephones, railroads, etc. but with modification it is also applicable to water, the provision of sewerage services, the provision of markets, and so forth.

The Nigerian Plan contains calculations that indicate, for example, that the provision of water to Lagos could be made to pay for itself, that markets should be able to pay the running cost and more, and that Lagos sewerage could be installed without requiring subsidies from the Government. These points may seem petty, compared to calculations of economic and financial profitability for, say, the railways or the telephone system. The points, however, that the inclusion of these calculations wants to make, are not. They deal precisely with questions of equity and income distribution that would be intractable when attacked frontally.

Specifically, the problems involved are: should certain services be provided? If so, how can they be financed? Who will benefit by them? Who should pay for them? Are subsidies necessary, or are they desirable whether necessary or not?

In the first place, it should be clear as has been stressed, that only a productive economy is in a position to pay subsidies. It is therefore necessary to make the economy productive by stressing directly productive investments as far as possible.

In the second place it is obvious that resources required for subsidies are not available for an addition to the productive capacity of the economy. It follows that subsidies must be specially justified as doing one or more of the following:

(a) In the case of projects or programmes that are amendable to the economic calculus, the subsidies must be smaller than the economic gains. This means primarily that the persons benefitting from an investment that in itself is profitable are not expected to bear the cost. Or it may mean also that society at large pays the cost of waiting for an investment to bear fruit.

(b) In the case of expenditures in which it is either impossible or repugnant to make economic calculations, the subsidies should be deliberate and not accidental; they should be given for particular ends and suitable to achieve their aim; and they should at the very least not involve a redistribution of income from the poor to the rich or of the tax burden from the rich to the poor.

In the third place, in poor economies all means available must be used to maximize the mobilization of resources. The policy decision that users of *economic* services should pay for them on principle involves therefore a decision (a) to maximize resources; (b) to allocate them as economically as possible; and (c) to ease the tax burden on the poor.

The last point deserves further explanation. It is all too frequently assumed, (a) that there would be many investments that would make economic sense, but that are unprofitable financially; (b) that subsidies are automatically "good" because they always involve a redistribution of income from the rich to the poor and tax burdens from the poor to the rich. Both statements involve questions of fact, not of theory. The question alluded to under (a) can be resolved by making the necessary calculations. The questions alluded to under (b) require logically a sophisticated system of data involving the distribution of the tax burden by income groups, the distribution of the benefits from government expenditures, and the likely tax shifting that is taking place in the economy, and a wealth of facts that are simply not available nor are likely to be available for the foreseeable future.

As to (a), the Nigerian Plan contains at least two calculations for economic and financial returns, both showing that financial profits are turned into economic losses when proper prices and indirect effects are allowed for. Specifically they show that in the past, the tax payer at large subsidized the railway users and the telephone users. Calculations for other services were made, including a notional road fund, which showed similarly that the presumption of economic feasibility with financial losses was the reverse of the truth.

This raises question (b). The following reasoning has to suffice in the absence of the data mentioned above. The people who can afford cars and telephones are not likely to be among the poorest in Nigeria. Subsidies in these fields are therefore likely to redistribute income from the poor to the rich. The insistence that users *as a group* pay for the services they receive is likely to satisfy social criteria, particularly as individual subgroups can continue to be subsidized. Thus it is not necessary that every mile of roads pays for itself, etc. Even though it is not possible to make a systematic study of the incidence of taxation among various income groups it is nevertheless possible to make statements in important individual cases that have a good chance to be of more general validity.

Similar ideas underlie the mentioned calculations of the returns for Lagos water, Lagos sewerage, and Lagos markets. As long as resources are scarce and real resources are involved in achieving any end, such calculations are unavoidable if only because of the need for a rational basis for policy decisions.

However, more is at stake here. Lagos is the Federal capital with perhaps 400,000—600,000 inhabitants out of perhaps 40 million*; concentrated in it is a relatively large share of total investment expenditure, and it attracts increasing numbers if people. The drift to towns which raises the problems of urbanization, unemployed school leavers and so forth has been extensively studied, and it has of course been considered in the formulation of the Plan. In fact, the problems of urbanization illustrate a third level at which social factors interact with economic ones: any decisions made by economists and executed in the Plan will, whether we like it or not, have important non-economic effects.

There are several social and political problems involved here that must be disentangled. Compared to the size of the Regional Plans, the Federal Capital Budget is relatively large: £412½ million for the Federal Plan against £263.2 million for all three Regional Plans. Much of these £412½ million must of necessity be spent in Lagos. Expenditure on the Ports must be of necessity where the Port is. Nevertheless when the Federal expenditures on Health are £10.3 million most of them in Lagos, while the three Regions together spend less than £7 million, or if the Federal Government plans to spend £23.2 million out of a total of £41.7 million on Town and Country Planning, questions as to the legitimacy of spending so large a portion of the total on so small a fraction of the population must be answered.

Part of the answer is that certain health expenditures, say, on a teaching hospital and doctor training, must be concentrated and are logically located in Ibadan, and the capital itself, which can make use of existing facilities. But part of the answer must be that no tax funds are diverted to provide certain services: tax funds that from an equity standpoint might more legitimately be diverted to other purposes. It is therefore the awareness of these difficult political problems involving also problems of equity, that have led to the inclusion of calculations of economic returns on such social expenditures as sewerage and water. In effect the Plan also contains a discussion of low cost housing that also makes the same point, and which shows that attention to economic problems could provide more housing cheaper than the previous subsidized housing.

The urbanization problems involved relate, of course, to overcrowding, slum formation, unemployment among school leavers, and certain health problems that arise with particular severity when large numbers of people congregate. These problems tend to feed upon themselves. They also have the most explosive political implication. An unemployed urban proletariat, politically organized as a pressure group, can cause troubles to governments; the pressure to do something can and does lead to increasing amounts being spent in cities to solve these problems which

---

* This was written before the results of the 1963 census were announced.

nevertheless succeed only in making them worse. Subsidies that in turn achieve and perpetuate standards higher than in the country, lead to further migration, to further problems which lead to further political pressures and so forth. If there is sufficient pressure to use inflationary finance it is the cities where the ill effects first appear, further aggravating the pressures. If slums are cleared—at horrendous cost that someone has to pay—and subsidized housing is erected, living conditions in the cities become yet more attractive; still more people move in and cause the congestions and problems that the expenditures were intended to solve in the first place. If epidemics are to be avoided, water and sewerage become necessary, and the heavy capital expenditures—which some one has to pay—which make life in the city more attractive, themselves lead to further inflows of people.

Economics alone can hardly be expected to solve this kind of problem which has very deep social roots. It should be clear, however, that it is socially and politically unbearable to have a population of 40 million subsidize 600,000 people, however important their problems look when seen in isolation. The funds expended on alleviating urban problems in a few spots must compete with similar uses all over the map. The problems of Lagos do not become less urgent, because Kano, or Port Harcourt also have urban problems. Nevertheless it should be clear that if water or sewerage could be made to pay at least to the extent that the running cost plus depreciations plus a rational rate of interest on capital could be recovered, this would not only raise the rate of resource mobilization, but would help in a rational allocation of resources, and would ease political and social problems.

Thus far I have discussed how certain non-economic aims and some social factors have affected planning decisions in the face of a virtually complete absence of necessary facts to make a general assessment. I hope to have shown two things: first, it turns out in many cases that there is no necessary conflict between various economic and non-economic aims. Thus the condition of achieving a cetain growth rate involves the economic decision to invest the resources in a manner that will produce *economic* profits to the extent of the growth rate desired or more. This is quite consistent with the wish to maximize the mobilization of resources by making the people benefitting from economic services pay for them, and this in turn is quite consistent with the social aim that the cost of development should be equitably distributed.

The second point is related to the first. We do not possess the necessary information to set up a general planning system in a mathematical form that is also operational—that is, not simply in the form of an abstract model that pays prime importance to completeness and internal consistency but which is not formulated in terms of parameters that can actually be measured or affected by policies. Nevertheless, it is possible to take out certain important sectors about which we do have adequate information and use this information for policy purposes.

The case of car owners or telephone users is obvious. They are clearly not among the poorest. There are, of course, indirect repercussions that the only method that is feasible to deal with the problem must neglect. Thus the principle that road users should pay for the roads in the first instance neglects initially the fact that if, say, gasolene taxes are raised, this will increase the cost of transporting goods to the market, and there will be thus shifts in unknown directions.

All of this is true. But observe that when the principal outline is adopted, it is possible to allow for social factors by such means as making truck and bus licences relatively cheap and private car licenses expensive; of making the former pay little or no import duties and the latter pay much, and so forth. Observe further, that in fact *partial* consideration of the market is put into a *general* context by asking successive questions. Thus the problem of whether or not we have to worry about effects on cost of transportation raises the next question: Why or why not? Heavy trucks tear up roads much more than light ones, and require heavier roads that are much more expensive to build. If we subsidize the heavy trucks and build expensive roads, who pays for it? Does not the farmer pay for it by lower producer prices? Would he and everyone else not be better off by making road transport a little more expensive, forcing the use of lighter trucks and of a more rational road system, making the richer car owners pay for it, etc.?

I turn now to another aspect of social factors in planning which in many respects is the most difficult and the most important. Granted that economic services should be treated primarily from an economic view point and not from a social one, there are many non-economic services that are commonly agreed upon and that must be provided at great cost. How big should a hospital programme or a school programme be? How do *these* important social factors enter into the planning process?

Assuming that the people really want the hospitals and schools, and hopefully assuming that they want them for what they can give, the general answer is: the health and school programme should be as big as the economy can afford. The difficulties that such a statement encounters in the process of being made operational are as follows:

(a) First, there is a problem of time sequences.
(b) Second, there are problems of staffing in the broadest sense.
(c) Third, there are problems of the kind of services that should or can be provided at any moment of time.

(d) Fourth, there are problems of the capital cost of providing the services.

(e) Fifth, there are problems of the running cost in order to maintain the services, once they are established.

(f) Sixth, there are the vexing problems of who should pay for both the capital and the running cost of the services.

Before taking up these points, it should be noted that thus far I have *not* mentioned that a healthy and educated population is also necessary to produce a productive economy. This is perfectly true but not very helpful in the planning process because it is next to impossible to quantify the problem. To take American attempts and apply their results to African conditions can be extremely dangerous. It is even more dangerous to take the results of American studies, which indicate that much of the rise in American productivity has been due to technical progress and has in turn been the result of education and research, and to offer these findings to Africans with the expectation that results can be quickly and relatively painlessly achieved. Few "processes of production" are as time-consuming and as capital-intensive as are education and research. Their results will be spectacular, but only after a long period of waiting and after many sacrifices.

The economic justification of education should be rationally confined to establishment of manpower boards that will make specific estimates for an economy of the manpower needs of the immediate future and that link *initially* training to the *immediate* needs of the economy; "immediate" being defined as, say, ten years. I stress "initially", because, useful though this approach is, it clearly does not really come to grips with the problems of: How much education? What kind? For whom? When? Nevertheless it seems to me an essential *first* step. In the absence of a manpower board at the time at which the Nigerian Plan was formulated this reasoning led to establishing technological training among the top priorities. The National Plan has formulated this point as follows:

> In the Plan, the highest priority has been given to agriculture, industry and training of high and intermediate level manpower. It is realized that there is only a limited amount of capital which can at any one moment of time be put into the expansion of agriculture and the establishment of new industries. Much of the expenditure by governments in agriculture and, to a similar extent, in industry is necessarily in the form of the recurrent expenditure on extension and advisory services and supervision. In order to provide extension services and supervision, training is necessary and education for these activities is therefore of high priority. This is

particularly true of technical education at various levels; training of extension workers, supervisors, foremen, technicians, administrators and managers. The extension of primary and secondary education has the double function of providing the informed electorate without which a democratic state cannot survive and of providing a pool of school-leavers from which, subject to further training, the future managers, foremen, administrators and technicians are drawn.

In the meantime, a manpower board has been established and has begun to function.

Economic reasoning by itself would similarly lead to giving priority to preventive over curative medicine, even though the former is in most cases not strictly medicine at all but public health, and closer to engineering. The major preventive measures of health are the provision of pure water and of sewerage, both essentially engineering problems. Malaria eradication also has substantial engineering rather than medical aspects. The reason for this priority is simply that it seems more sensible as well as more humane to keep people well in the first place rather than cure them after they have fallen sick. It seems a waste of human resources to have people born only to die before they have reached their productive age in which they contribute more to the economy than they consume, as well as before they reach the adulthood for the full enjoyment of life. The emphasis on preventive medicine shows no conflict of economic and non-economic aims.

Nevertheless, economic justifications for educational and health expenditures hardly come to grips with the real problems. It will not do to provide only that amount of education and health that is needed for strictly economic purposes in the near future. The economists role in establishing educational and health goals for the economy can be best defined as attempting to establish (a) the limits of resources available at any one time for achieving the desired social aims which he shares with the rest of the community; (b) the best use of the available resources so as to maximize the results achieved.

Having disposed of the narrowly economic justification for social expenditures on health and education as relatively unimportant, I now turn to the six points raised above. I pointed out that it was desirable to plan for as much education and health as the economy could afford.

First, time sequences. Not everything can or should be done at once. The point is, initially, that the more resources that can be pushed into directly productive investments that will raise income, and the faster this income is raised, the more resources will become available for the social expenditures that are the proper aim of society, and the more quickly they will become available. Hence, *in the interest of achieving non-economic ends* it is essential to create as fast as possible a productive economy and to push as many of the resources as possible into directly and quickly productive enterprises. It is characteristic of under-developed economies that the amount of resources that can be so employed is limited at any one time, and it is the major problem of development planning to widen as quickly as possible the range of available rational choices.

In education, it is clear that general literacy is essential before high schools can be established, and that one must have high school graduates to produce college students; college students to produce graduate and post graduate work. Moreover, you can't have schools without teachers, and teachers without teachers' colleges, with teacher training being linked to higher education. This does emphatically not mean that one should wait with a university until everyone can read and write. On the contrary, I believe that a university should be established as soon as sufficient students become available. Mission teachers have for over a century helped break bottlenecks in teachers, and Peace Corps, the UN and its sister organizations are all available to help.

The problem of time sequences is intimately connected with, *second, the staffing problem,* and *third, the kind of services to be provided.* Though logically separate, it is best to discuss them together. All of these problems are, of course, equally related to cost, but that discussion must be postponed. The reason is simple that although everything depends on everything else, one can talk and write only of one thing at a time. Much of reality is circular in nature, but writing and talking are necessarily one-directional processes.

In Nigerian planning, the economists' initial reaction to any proposals involving health or education was: if you can staff it, you can have it. As economists we are not competent to criticize curricula, nor can we tell a doctor what to do. We can, however, raise questions as to cost. And we must ask whether a hospital, say, can be staffed with doctors, nurses, radiologists, pharmacologists and the rest. We must ask not only whether the buildings proposed are suitable for their ends, for future additions; and are reasonable in cost. We must also insist that a proposal has been thought through. This will be the case only if we can get details on the number of staff required, and if we can get the assurance that the staff will be forthcoming. In the case of schools, we must also ask where both the teachers and the students are to come from.

These questions are essential for two reasons. First, hospitals that cannot be staffed, equipment that cannot be used for lack of competent staff, are clearly a waste of resources that poor economics can ill afford. Do not think that it doesn't matter because the equipment might have been a gift. The donor will point out that he has already done so much for you, and can't reasonably be expected to do more. Gift or purchase, poor economies cannot afford waste. And wasted equipment will not heal people. This kind of questioning is essential to ensure that proposals are suitable to achieve their ends, ends which themselves are not questioned by the planners.

Secondly, the answer to these questions is essential because staffing involves recurrent cost for ever. There will be a limit to what can or should be done *at any moment of time* because recurrent costs build up rapidly and compete for the resources that are available for all purposes, economic and social.

Thus the questions after staffing, etc. serve to limit what can be done at any moment, and to establish rational sequences for the development of social expenditures in terms of both the growth objectives of the economy and its social objectives. The time sequences will depend on the manner in which resources become available as the economy grows and in which they are being increasingly absorbed by rapidly rising expenditures to run social institutions. The desirable and feasible time sequences will also depend on the rapidity and sequence in which the necessary staff and students are being turned out.

I turn now to the capital and running cost of social institutions. It should be recalled that on principle the social expenditure on health and education should be as large as the economy can afford. This is not proposed as a general law applicable at all times and in all places. It is simply a recognition of the fact that in Africa, both health and education are and will for the foreseeable future be woefully inadequate, and that even the maximum effort that can be made will not satisfy the aspirations of the people.

How much the economy can afford will utimately find its reflection in the ordinary recurrent budget. A moment's reflection will show why this must be so, and why the ordinary budget rapidly must become the central concern of the planners. Budgetary surpluses are the major source, or at least one major source of domestic public capital formation whether public or private. For if they are achieved by raising taxes substantially (or by lowering producer prices to farmers), this will immediately and adversely affect private capital formation. How high the level of taxes can safely be raised is a question of degree, of course, but the whole complex of problems cannot be ignored.

Now, two facts become quickly apparent. First, it is relatively easy to borrow or get gifts from abroad for capital expeditures. With few exceptions it is next to impossible to get loans or gifts to finance running expenses involved in capital expenditures. For these reasons, the Nigerian Plan, as far as the governmental capital budgets were concerned, was based upon the assumption that governments had, on balance, to finance, *all* recurrent cost and half the capital cost out of local resources. There is also the political aspect of the matter that, to say the least, it is uncomfortable if the day-to-day running of government in all its ramifications depends on the goodwill of agencies outside of its control. Thus the resources that can be domestically raised will provide one, though not the only, limit to the size of the governmental capital plans.

Second, it is equally obvious, that current expenditures for health and education build up very rapidly, and hence diminish the possibilities of achieving the necessary budgetary surpluses for capital expenditures. In some of the Regions of Nigeria, the recurrent cost of education is already over 40 per cent of the total ordinary budget, an enormous amount. It is obvious that this proportion cannot be further raised if the whole development of the Region is not to be jeopardized. It follows that the rapidity with which recurrent cost will build up will limit *the size and will (or ought to) determine the time sequence* of social investments. For, if so much is spent on running the institutions that surpluses become impossible to achieve, the economy will come to a grinding halt. Capital formation to employ school leavers will not be forthcoming, nor will the the resources needed just to maintain the institutions that have been built up. If, therefore, social institutions are built up too rapidly they will lead to a waste of resources and not to a satisfaction of the very real social needs. It is no use to accuse the economist of having a "purely economic" view point. Nothing in the world can change the fact that doctors are needed to run hospitals, that doctors are scarce, that doctors must eat and must be paid, and hence require resources, and that resources are scarce, and when used to pay doctors are not available to create the capital which will employ people.

The point cannot be overstressed. It would be fatal to put resources into the provision of schools and hospitals and other social institutions, whose exceedingly great desirability is not only conceded but emphasized, without providing simultaneously for a productive and growing economy that can support the great running cost that these social expenditures entail.

This leads to the final point: who should pay? It goes without saying that a person who is sick should be treated whether he can pay or not. But this sort of argument misses the point. As long as real resources are involved, someone has to pay. The question then becomes: if the taxpayer at large is to provide the resources, which group of taxpayers? In advanced countries, where there are not only better statistics, but where the collection of progressive income taxes is administratively feasible, the answer would be fairly simple, though to get political action is another matter as an American citizen has every reason to know. In African countries, progressive income taxes cannot conceivably raise the money needed, and most income taxes are administratively not feasible. Most revenues that are feasible are either import duties, oil revenues if the country is fortunate enough to have found oil as is the case in Nigeria, income taxes on expatriate businesses, export taxes including the control of producer prices by Marketing Boards, and producer sales taxes, on export products.*

Oil revenues and income taxes on expatriate businesses (including expatriate staff) may or may not be so high as to restrict production, but they are not likely to hit the poorest. Whether import duties are or are not progressive depends on their structure. Export duties are likely to hit not only the relatively well-to-do cocoa farmers, but also the very much poorer farmers of other agricultural export products such as groundnuts or palm oil. Oil revenues are not common in African countries South of the Sahara, and new in Nigeria. Income taxes are a very small portion of total actual or potential tax receipts. This means in effect that export taxes are the major means of hitting the poor, and import duties are the major means of hitting the well-to-do, who cannot easily be touched by income taxes.

If this brief analysis is accepted the problem then becomes: how can we finance more health and education in such a manner to (a) increase the available resources; (b) not make the tax structure more regressive than is absolutely necessary, given the unavoidable fact that we know very little about the progressivity or regressivity of the tax structure in the first place, and the equally inevitable fact that it is impossible to avoid taxing the poor if resources for our ambitious development programmes are to be raised.

Both questions lead inevitably to suggest (a) that more of the financing of schools is shifted to local authorities and parents; and (b) that this shift should be accompanied by a scholarship programme based on ability both to learn and to pay. As education is undoubtedly a potent incentive good, shifting the cost increasingly to local authorities and parents is likely to induce larger efforts and hence will raise the resources available to the economy. A scholarship programme in conjunction with school fees will also tend to shift the cost of the schools to the shoulders better able to afford them and will also help to raise the mobilization of resources.

The discussion should have made plain why there must be major emphasis on the budgetary implications of all governmental expenditures. This also explains the major emphasis on economic profitability

---

* There are sound reasons why Marketing Boards should not be used as a taxing device if alternatives are available. The size of oil discoveries allows some optimism in the future.

of those government investments that are amenable to the economic calculus. Profitability must be achieved; and subsidies for private or public enterprises must be given only when there is a chance that profitability will be achieved in a reasonable time. This limitation on subsidies is essential for social as well as economic reasons. This is *not* a matter of ideology; nor is it a question of private versus public consumption or investments. It is simply due to the recognition that anything which is decided upon requires real resources which someone has to furnish for the purpose and which are then not available for other purposes.

Tax concessions, import duty relief, guaranteed markets at guaranteed prices for selected manufacturers, are all expressions of policies that have direct budgetary implications. They must therefore be justified in that their cost will raise the available resources, and that the benefits expected will really accrue. It would be tedious to develop this point further.

IV

There is one further major complex of problems through which social factors enter economic planning. The data available or to be collected for planning, the policies to be developed, the institutions to be built; they all have to be collected, developed, built, and interpreted in a particular context that is very different from the one in which modern economic theory or modern economic institutions were developed. Now the *theory,* being an abstraction, is not very different in different parts of the world. However, modern economic theory, like all modern theories is defined in operational terms. Economists have learned that it is not sufficient to count the number of equations and of unknowns and rest content that the system they have set up is determinate. They want to know the nature of the parameters that determine the manner in which a particular economy will react to changes that are introduced. The parameters reflect the social and historic uniqueness of an economy as far as the economist must know it. Economists want to know something of behavior patterns, and they try to distinguish carefully their definitional from their behavioral equations. They talk about stability conditions, which basically means that they talk about paths of adjustments, about the time sequences mentioned above. When they have determined to suggest the establishment of new institutions they want to make sure that the institutions do what is expected of them, and the same institutions can perform their identical function in a different form in different parts of the world. Although the theory underlying the Federal Reserve System of the United States and the Bank of England is the same, the manner in which it works itself out differs because of non-economic factors. The sheer size of the US, for example, has made decentralization natural.

It should not only be admitted but stressed that this is one of the many areas in Africa (and elsewhere) where the uncharted areas of our knowledge are bigger than the charted areas. Nevertheless, the planner must continuously make the best decisions he can. If he has any sense he will continuously ask people with much wider knowledge than he has whether some policies or institutions have a chance to work and how they can be made to work; how the existing features of society can be utilized to change it to something better.

For example, in Nigeria there is every evidence that farmers are susceptible to new ideas provided that they work. All too frequently, however, "work" is interpreted purely technologically. But this is only half the problem. The other half is that they must make him better off economically, either by increasing his income or by reducing his effort, or by doing both. The fact that Nigerian farmers are susceptible to new ideas if they work means that the Nigerian planner can work with indirect means and incentives, and need not worry unduly about why people react. In other parts of the world we are told this is quite different. Some—not all by any means—Indian farmers will not use improved methods of production even if they do make them better off or at least so we are told. The planner has then the very serious problem of how to overcome these inertias which usually have deep social roots.

Again, Nigeria is fortunate in a strong co-operative spirit of its people in some of the Regions. This has been used in the past to build schools and even some roads without burdening the capital budget—the ordinary budget remains heavily charged, of course. It also can be used to introduce modern technologies and combine them with co-operative developments, raising of local resources, and drawing the local people directly into the development process. An excellent example is the introduction of hydraulic handpresses in Eastern Nigeria that are efficient enough to produce the best quality palm oil; cheap enough to be purchased co-operatively by a relatively small number of people; simple enough so that both a loan to a new co-operative and the working can be effectively supervised and administered.

A strong saving habit already exists in many parts of Nigeria. It is a well-known and truly admirable phenomenon that villages have got together to send their promising youths to school. In fact, there is very much evidence that at least in Nigeria people will work and save and pay for something that seems worthwhile to them. The development problem then becomes to widen the opportunities. Nigeria has developed indigenous banks collecting local funds and making them locally available.

Again, the major problem confronting African businessmen and farmers is less that of capital shortage, however important that may be, than of productivity of labour and management. The establishment of good accounting systems adapted to local needs of a *small* man— the problems of the big man may be technically more difficult, but they are socially easier to handle, since all he has to do is to hire himself an expert or two—is a difficult task of industrial extension services. The fact that buying machines will *not* raise productivity at all unless this is accompanied by radical changes in the attitudes of the businessman, raises serious social questions. A machine must be continuously employed and continuously watched and tended. It requires new kinds of organizing arrangements for a constant supply of fuel and other materials, moving the product, marketing, and the rest, without which it will make the businessman worse off than he was before. All of this is not merely a new technique but a new attitude to life. It can be learned and it is being learned. But it would be extremely foolish to ignore the fact that this learning process must take place.

Planners like to use concepts like saving and investment. I do not want to stress the fact that these concepts are frequently illegitimately used even in contexts in which their meaning is clear. In many African countries their meaning is far from clear as research workers have found out when they have tried to measure investment or consumption. It is not even always easy to find out what a particular year's production of some agricultural products is because they can be stored in the ground.

It follows that economists in planning do well to steep themselves as much as possible in the local customs and histories, manners of doing things and modes of thinking and reacting. That this is not easy to do under any circumstances, and particularly when the planner himself is an expatriate whose stay in a country is relatively short, goes without saying. Yet without some such sensitivity, it is impossible to make even a start with the necessary creative transformation of local societies into the kind of modern societies they wish to become. Suggestions for changes will backfire in the sense that, at best they will not work, and at worst they will achieve the opposite of what they are intended to achieve. Yet economists are economists, and not anthropologists or sociologists, and economic planning and economic development remains, whether we like it or not, primarily an economic problem.

13. Issues in Agricultural Policy During the 1962-68 Nigerian Development Plan

JEROME C. WELLS

This Chapter is directed at a number of issues in agricultural policy and economic planning suggested by Nigerian experience in the 1962-68 Development Plan.[1] The terms "planning" and "policy determination" carry quite different connotations in economic theory and in planning practice, and the distinction between them affects the range of tasks which are given priority in plan formulation and the extent to which various aspects of government activity in a particular sector of the economy are reviewed in the planning process. The issues raised here relate to this distinction and involve the techniques used for formulating and appraising different types of policy decisions.

The definition of "agricultural policy" to be used is a broad one, incorporating not only the specific allocation of resources through the budget and Plan, but also the rule-making activities of government which affect resource allocation. The discussion is organized around three major issues related to planning: (1) the range of activities involved in planning and policy making, (2) the components of program and project evaluation, and (3) the relation of the budgeting process to the appraisal of investments and of other aspects of policy.

It is necessary at the outset to agree upon what constitutes the "agricultural plan" and to indicate the point of view from which the planning process is to be examined. The plan document itself provides the starting point for any review of agricultural policy during the 1962-68 period. It outlines a general approach to agricultural development—assigning agriculture, along with industry and the development of high level manpower resources, "priority"—and lists a series of expected government capital allocations totalling approximately £90 million. These allocations are subdivided, on a regional basis, between a number of individual investment projects which are briefly described, and the project descriptions are supplemented by listings of regional goals with respect to agricultural development, an occasional reference to output targets, and thumbnail sketches of the major problems in the agricultural sectors of the regional economies.[1]

240

The allocations recorded in the basic plan document represent a series of choices about the allocation of resources during the plan period. They incorporate the political goals sought in the plan and the relative power of various interest groups involved in planning. They have been subjected to at least rudimentary tests to insure they are not inconsistent, and they involve commitment of resources rather far beyond the capital allocations included in the plan. All of these elements may be in part inferred from the discussion of the plan document, but they involve much more than it explicitly records. To define the "plan" requires an examination of these additional aspects.

1. Agricultural Policy and the Planning Process

The first aspect which deserves specific consideration is perhaps the most general: it involves the relation of planning to the formulation of "economic policy."

The concept of "policy"—as noted above—carries a variety of connotations, and confusion over what elements of policy are implied in a given context makes discussion of the relation between "policy formation" and "planning" rather difficult. On the one hand there is a tendency—most evident in the formal theoretical literature on economic planning—to equate planning with the determination of policy. Operational discussions of planning, in contrast, tend to restrict the term to forms of government decision-making which do not involve resource allocation through some form of budgetary process. The broader, former definition will be used in this discussion, but policy thus defined should be seen as consisting of two related but separable components, one dealing with the allocation of resources directly and the other with the institutional framework within which resource allocation takes place.[2]

The process of allocation may involve physical quantities (as in manpower planning) or generalized economic resources (as in the budgeting process). The "qualitative" elements of policy include the activities not directly related to agricultural budgeting, such as government's approach to land tenure, marketing, price policy, taxation, and the points at which it chooses to intervene in the agricultural sector. The two forms of policy might be termed "allocational" and "institutional" to distinguish between the forms of their impact on agriculture. Both forms imply the full range of activity associated with government policy-making. Goals to be achieved (and the trade-offs between them) must be specified, either explicitly or implicitly. Information on possible courses of action must be gathered and available options defined, evaluated, and selected. Finally, decisions which have been made must be implemented through the use of appropriate means. The process in both cases may be stated in terms of the target and instrument variables of formal planning theory, though the instruments for allocational policy almost always involve specific resource allocations as in the items of a budget or economic plan. The instruments for institutional policy are usually more diffuse; they may involve laws or administrative rules, or even decisions about which sector of government is to intervene in the agricultural sector.

For a number of reasons the typical development plan tends to focus largely on the allocative aspects of policy. There is still a tendency to envision planning as a process essentially involving the allocation of capital resources, and the types of variables involved in allocative policy are more easily specified and lend themselves more directly to quantitative examination and prescription. The need for consistency between quantitative resources allocations is apparent; discrepancies between allocative and institutional policies are less obvious. Even the way in which planning tasks are divided within government tends to strengthen the bias toward allocative policy. While the preparation of the budget and capital allocations is clearly seen as the task of the agencies dealing with planning, the origins of institutional policies are more widely spread throughout the governmental structure and are not automatically assumed relevant to the planning process.

The focus on allocative policy extends to most discussions of planning, especially those which deal primarily with agriculture. These tend to be divided between sections on "policy" and on "planning" (or programming), but rarely are the links between the two specifically discussed. So far, studies on planning fail to recognize that the policy considerations noted elsewhere must be incorporated in the procedures for determining and reviewing specific resource allocations.[3] The results of this bifurcation strengthen the impression that planning is involved with resource allocation and that the consideration of policies dealing with institutions within the agricultural sector is at best a supplement to the resource allocations derived in a development program.

What elements of institutional policy are involved in the agricultural sector and how can these elements be effectively examined? Here the qualitative nature of institutional policies and the lack of information about their impact on agricultural institutions pose considerable problems. Perhaps the most that is possible, given our state of knowledge, is a taxonomic approach. Planning might be envisioned as involving determination of (a) the points at which government will intervene in the economy (or agricultural sector), (b) the extent to which it will intervene, and (c) the ways in which it will intervene. It is the third point which spells out the options of allocative and institutional policy. Government may intervene through the allocation of specific resources, or through rule-making affecting the conditions under which agricultural production is organized and carried out and agricultural goods are traded. The typical development plan, envisioned in this manner, involves the following components:

(1) a set of resource allocations to increase directly productive and infrastructural capacity within the agricultural sector;

(2) a set of policies toward land tenure and individual rights with respect to agricultural land;

(3) a set of policies toward the forms of economic organization to be promoted in the agricultural sector— individual enterprise, cooperative organization, etc.;

(4) a set of policies toward the marketing of agricultural produce;

(5) a set of policies related to the international factors affecting agricultural growth—food imports (including surplus food distribution), export promotion, and the like;

(6) a set of policies toward agricultural taxation;

(7) a set of trade-offs or priorities toward regional development within agriculture;

(8) a set of policies on income distribution within agriculture and between agriculture and other sectors;

(9) a set of policies toward rural-urban migration; and finally

(10) an overall examination of the points at which government will intervene—and refrain from intervening—in the agricultural sector.

To what extent can the elements of institutional policy be said to have been incorporated in the agricultural components of the 1962-68 Plan? This question is difficult to answer, for problems of institutional policy do not—for reasons of specificity of sensitivity—lend themselves to explicit discussion. The major descriptions of the planning process[4] cover a variety of issues in institutional policy, but their treatment of agricultural topics is limited to a few general observations and leaves the impression that issues of agricultural policy were not widely examined at the level of the national plan. This is not surprising in view of the primary responsibility of the regions for agriculture and the relatively greater need for coordination between regional industrial programs. The regional agricultural plans—as presented in the plan document—stress the goals of agricultural development in general terms, but contain no evidence that a comprehensive review of institutional policies affecting agriculture was undertaken in connection with the planning exercise.[5] The impression left by both the documents covering the planning process and subsequent discussions of plan implementation is that while the Plan recognized the importance of institutional as well as allocational elements of policy, the allocative elements received the main focus of attention.

Thus the framework presented, while suggestive of the elements relevant to agricultural planning, is far too elaborate to apply with any confidence to the Nigerian experience. While informal consideration of aspects of policy listed above in items (2) through (10) undoubtedly took place, and in some cases debates over aspects of policy can be inferred from the published descriptions of plan formulation, it is clear that no systematic review of the various aspects of institutional policy relevant to agriculture was carried out. Such a review would have been useful, but limitations of time and manpower precluded it; and the issues of institutional policy have largely been considered in connection with the specific resource allocations to which they were directly relevant. This practice will be followed in the discussion here, but it is important to note the broad issues of policy implicit in the discussion of resource allocation.

2. *Project and Program Evaluation*

Another source of supplementary evidence on the agricultural development program is to be found in the economic analyses of the various project allocations listed in the plan document. The potential allocations of resources omitted from a plan are perhaps as revealing as those included, and the quality of evaluative procedures used is the major determinant of the potential economic impact of a plan. Project analysis is primarily the baliwick of the economist and it is in this area that most economic discussion of the Nigerian development plan and its agricultural components has taken place. The analyses of agricultural allocations at the time the plan was formulated were extremely cursory, and the limited time available for plan formulation restricted the planners' analysis of economic projects to large allocations mostly outside of the agricultural sector. The original analyses for plan projects were generally provided by the operating ministries which proposed them and provided only sketchy estimates of costs and expected returns.

This weakness has been mitigated considerably since the beginning of the plan period, as more and more of the projects included have been examined through benefit-cost analysis and other forms of specific economic studies.[6] These have added considerable information about the nature of government effort in the agricultural sector to the capital allocations of the plan, and in some cases have led to changes in the ways particular projects are implemented. But both the form of analysis and the ways in which it is applied deserve careful scrutiny in the context of

Nigerian planning. The range of agricultural projects which can be effectively examined through the use of benefit-cost analysis is rather limited, and there is a great danger that the economic tools available have dictated too narrow an approach to investment evaluation and led to misspecification of the decision making context in which government investment is determined.

As the benefit-cost studies of particular projects indicate, the amount of resources committed in the Plan considerably exceeds the capital allocations listed in the plan document. Resources allocated through the recurrent sector of the government budget are required in almost every project and program; substantial quantities of resources are thus committed and in some projects the implicit value of recurrent resources required exceeds the capital allocations themselves. This is especially true in the agricultural sector of the plan where development efforts involve long lead periods and where the staff personnel of the respective ministries of agriculture will be responsible for developing and carrying out the plan allocations. The extent to which plan allocations involve future streams of recurrent resources was of course recognized by the planners, and considerable emphasis was given in the Plan document to the problem of growing recurrent budgets in the government sector.[7] The extent to which the budgetary implications of specific agricultural components of the plan were recognized by the agencies proposing them is less clear, for the form in which recurrent budgets are presented does not facilitate easy identification of the impact of specific capital projects. Certainly, however, the Plan must be defined to include the recurrent implications of the programs and projects listed in the plan document. The relation of recurrent budgeting to the planning process is a subject on which little published material exists and economic studies since the original planning exercise have been remarkably scarce. Access to the decision-making processes underlying recurrent budgeting is limited, especially to students working outside the government agencies, but it is interesting to note that the major effort to define the allocative implications of the recurrent budgets represents the work of a political scientist, Charles R. Nixon. (See Chapter 6.)[8]

The relation of recurrent budgets to the capital allocations of the plan document leads to another component of the development plan not developed explicitly in any great detail: the consistency of plan allocations. Consistency tests are the crucial part of any planning exercise, for they define the options with respect to the scope and composition of efforts to which resources may be allocated and impose upon the political decision-makers the necessity of setting priorities. Two different types of consistency tests were included in the 1962-68 Plan, but discussion of these is rather limited in the plan document and it is necessary to go to the subsequent writings of the planners themselves to gain some impression of what was done. The overall consistency of resources available with proposed resource uses was explored at the budgetary level in the plan and in terms of national income in a small paper appended to it.[9] Consistency tests between specific projects of an infrastructural nature are outlined by Hansen,[10] and Stolper[11] but the extent to which the consistency of agricultural allocation was explored is not clear. The F. A. O. study of Nigerian agricultural development[12] provides a series of projected increases in output from the major investments in export crop development and similar estimates are occasionally provided by the regional ministries, but otherwise there is little in the way of compresensive examination of the effects of chosen allocations on output and prices. As in the case of recurrent budgets there is little to indicate that the specific resource requirements (manpower, etc.) of particular projects included in the plan received any extensive examination when the projects were proposed,[13] and analyses of individual investments indicate that the extent of substitution possible between different programs did not receive much consideration.

Though the impact of consistency tests upon the selection of individual allocations constitutes a crucial dimension of any development plan, this is not a subject which is particularly tractable in terms of the economist's frame of reference. The economist can stress the need for a consistent set of allocations—and there is considerable evidence that the economic advisors involved in the Nigerian planning process did this—but the trade-offs between inconsistent proposals and the extent to which inconsistent elements will be removed from a proposed set of allocations essentially results from processes which are political and administrative. The ways in which these influences determine the final composition of a development plan are not readily accessible to those outside the decision-making process and can at best be inferred from reasonable knowledge of the political and administrative context within which a particular plan is developed. Yet it is these decisions, more than the particular allocations or analysis presented in a planning document, which define the essential character of a development plan.

There is little firmly documented discussion about the nature of the trade-offs made between inconsistent claims upon resources, the locus of decision making, or the processes involved in determining the agricultural components of the 1962-68 development plan. Stolper[14] and Clark[15] have described the institutional framework within which planning decisions were made; both of these discussions imply that much of the decision making with respect to capital allocations took place in the Joint Planning Committee and the National Economic Council, agencies composed of regional and federal civil servants and politcal leaders, respectively. The decisions taken in these bodies must have dealt largely with coordinating and resolving conflicts between federal and regional allocations. The majority of agricultural allocations probably did not come within their purview.

This discussion may be supplemented with some general observations based on the process of resource allocation associated with implementation of the plan. It would appear that most decision making with respect to individual agricultural allocations took place within the agencies responsible for agricultural development—the various ministries of agriculture and development corporations. The allocations finally determined reflected the decision making processes of these agencies, subject to political demands and to review by the ministries of finance and economic development.[16] How particular decisions were determined and particular programs chosen is probably a topic which will be most adequately described in the memoirs of the senior civil servants (though the published reports of the various commissions of enquiry established after the demise of the civilian regime give some idea of the political pressures involved). One generalization about this process does seem justified—it was far more closely associated with determination of the annual budgets and the allocation of scarce manpower within ministries than with any once and for all analysis of the potential projects—either before or after the writing of the plan document. As implementation of the plan proceeded, the process of review and initiation of programs also became more closely associated with budgeting.[17]

3. Allocative Decisions and the Budgeting Process

It is clear to anyone who has examined government activities in Nigerian agriculture that the budgeting process provides the central nexus for allocative decision-making. The budget covers all allocations for government efforts at agricultural development, and the annual process of budgeting provides the point at which different efforts are reviewed, expanded, or cut back. The annual capital allocations to various lines of activity show the process of review and implementation explicitly, while the process of determining recurrent allocations and distributing them *within* the agencies involved in agricultural development determines in large measure the extent to which the explicit priorities of Plan and capital budgets will be effectively carried out.

The budgeting process has several advantages as a base for the study of allocative decision-making, especially in the agricultural sector. Because the budget must be made up and approved annually, it tends to provide the focal point for political review of the allocative process and the major point of administrative reference in implementing various programs. The publication of the annual *Estimates* and audits provides a continuous record of allocative activities.

In fact, the importance of budgeting as the locus of allocative decision-making during the 1962-68 Plan contrasts rather strongly with the lack of effective interest shown by decision-making agencies in the project studies which became increasingly available throughout the plan period. The numerous project studies—often commissioned by the various ministries and development corporations—were rarely taken very seriously. Where they confirmed projects already accepted in the Plan allocations they were cited in support of these projects, and where they evoked interest on the part of aid-giving agencies they also received support. But generally the results of these studies circulated more widely among the research agencies which performed them than they did among the agencies whose projects they studied.

The lack of coordination between project studies and budgeting is at least as much the fault of those (in government and out) involved in project analysis as it is of the government agencies themselves, and stems from several severe limitations on the application of benefit-cost analysis to allocations within agriculture. Although the form and application of investment criteria are too complex to be discussed here,[18] two of these limitations deserve mention. The first of these is the serial form in which Nigerian agricultural projects have been proposed. The form of evaluative criterion cannot be divorced from the selection process in which it is employed, and most discussion in the economics literature assumes this to be a ranking process involving potential allocations of some scarce resource over a given time period. In fact project studies in Nigerian agriculture have rarely been used to rank and select allocations from a set of simultaneous proposals. The process is more a serial one with projects coming up for acceptance or rejection on a one at a time basis. This factor, rarely recognized explicitly in project studies, renders the traditional form of project analysis relatively ineffectual as a guide to decision-making.

The second limitation relates to the range of activities typically encompassed in an agricultural development program; this range is too great and the activities involved are too varied to permit examination of all allocations within the common framework of project analysis. The range of activities involved in the Nigerian agricultural Plan can be at least partly represented by a framework used to classify expenditures in the development program.[19] It distinguishes between:

(1) Government Directed Projects, defined as directly productive investments where government plays the major entrepreneurial and managerial role (e.g. plantations, settlement projects);

(2) Investments in Processing and Marketing; including

food storage depots, market construction, and various processing plants or centers;

(3) Extension Activities, including a wide range of activities directed at a peasant farmer, such as fertilizer distribution, smallholders tree crop development, demonstrations, pest and disease control, publicity on crop and animal husbandry, soil conservation, and the general development of extension services;

(4) Research and Investigations; including the total range of agricultural research as well as soil and water surveys not directly tied to irrigation schemes;

(5) Education; comprising the training of both extension personnel and special courses for individual farmers; and

(6) Credit provision, where it can be separately identified.

Of these six forms of investment only the first is really easily tractable within a framework of discrete project analysis. Forms (2), (3), and (6) can be appraised by benefit-cost tests when inputs and expected outputs of the projects can be reasonably clearly identified, but—except for processing activities—this is usually not the case. Investments in research and training are of course impossible to appraise in advance on an individual investment basis. Both of these forms of investment constitute a vital part of any agricultural development program and a fairly important task of decision-making in agricultural investment involves setting the division of effort between this form and the more directly productive types of investments of the other categories.[20]

The limited range of investment forms to which benefit-cost analysis can be applied carries one crucial implication: this form of analysis can never serve as the major means of directing government participation in the agricultural sector. Benefit-cost studies can fulfill an important supplementary role in appraising certain types of investments, but even to perform this role well they must be integrated with a much broader review of allocations and policy. These considerations make a strong case for a more functional recasting of the annual budgets—a radical change considering the evolutionary nature of most government accounting processes, but one which could be accomplished within the current limitations of ministry personnel. There are two ways in which this could be done; first in the establishment of the new states' budgetary reporting frameworks and second, in supplementary budgets made up on a functional basis. Neither approach would be novel: the functional casting of all budgetary allocations by Charles Nixon[21] and Roider's work in compiling farm settlement data shows that establishing budgetary frameworks and collecting data broken down by activity is possible. The former Eastern region had started on this process in its listing of "development expenses," and in the Northern Ministry of Agriculture, attempts to allocate personnel charges to functional categories have been reasonably successful. The framework noted above could provide a basis for project reporting well within the scope of current accounting procedures, and to demonstrate its usefulness, it will be employed as a base for reviewing government activity in agriculture during the first 5 years of the development plan.

4. A Budgetary Review of the Agricultural Plan: 1962-67

Although the budgetary framework provides perhaps the best base for analyzing government's activity in agriculture during the plan, it is not without its shortcomings, and several caveats needs to be appended to the discussion which follows. The figures cover only the budgetary allocations of the Federal and Regional governments, and some fairly important components of government effort in agriculture are omitted. These include the spending of local governmental units, an undetermined amount of the resources channelled into agriculture through aid-giving agencies,[22] and some educational spending on agriculture not presented separately in the budget documents.[23] A second limitation to the analysis stems from the lack of functional categories for budgetary reporting. The framework presented in Section 3 above is used to classify capital allocations, and the application of this framework to the capital accounts involves a number of arbitrary conventions and imputations. For recurrent expenses, the framework can not be applied, and our discussion here is limited to a few general observations.[24]

In spite of these weaknesses the analysis provides a much better estimation of the level and composition of government effort in agriculture than does the original list of allocations in the plan document or the subsequent revisions of these lists in the various *Progress Reports*. In addition it permits a comparison between the policies of the former regions and provides a base for a few generalizations about the nature of government effort in agriculture during the 1962-68 Plan.

4.1 The Level of Government Activity in Agriculture

The most commonly used measure of government effort in agriculture is derived from the allocations of the 1962-68 Plan document, where a total of £91.76 million out of a total investment allocation of £676.8 million (13.6%) is devoted to "primary production."[25] Table 1 summarizes the total estimated expenditures[26] of the Federal and Regional governments from 1962/3 to 1966/7, the first 5 years of the plan period. By the end of 1966/7 £41.94 million, or about half

TABLE 1. *Estimated Government Expenditures in Agriculture: 1962/3-1966/7*

(£ millions)

	East	Midwest	West	North	Federal	Total
I. Estimated Expenditures						
Capital	18.25	1.34	11.16	8.00	3.19	41.94
Recurrent	7.67	1.48	10.97	12.37	4.80	37.30
	25.92	2.82	22.13	20.37	7.99	79.23
II. Plan Allocations: Capital	30.36	—	18.44[a]	22.49	9.29[b]	80.55[b]
III. Recurrent Expenditures:						
1962/3	1.16	—	2.31	1.99	.62	6.60
1966/7	2.00	.513	2.43	3.31	1.62	9.93
IV. Agricultural Allocations as Proportion of Allocations for all Sectors:						
Plan Allocations	40%	—	20%	23%	2%	12%
Estimated Capital Expenditures	20%	14%	19%	14%	2%	13%[a]
Estimated Current Expenditures	7%	7%	10%	8%	1.2%	5%[d]
Estimated Combined Expenditure	15%	9%	14%	10%	1.5%	7%[d]

Sources: Calculated from Federal and Regional *Estimates*, 1962/3-1966/7, and *National Development Plan*, Table 5.9, p. 41.

Notes:

a. Includes original allocation for both West and Midwest.
b. Federal total in plan document reduced by £10 million (transfers to regions) and £1.17 million (geologic survey and mineral exploration).
c. Includes only 1965/6 and 1966/7.
d. Agricultural proportions for combined Regions are as follows: capital, 21%; recurrent, 8%; combined, 12%.

of the allocation for agriculture presented in the Plan document, had been spent. Agricultural capital spending proceeded at about the same rate as all capital expenditure, and about 13% of the total spending was devoted to the agricultural sector.

One's impression of the level and nature of government effort in agriculture is considerably modified when the impact of recurrent expenditures is taken into account, for during 1962-67 estimated recurrent expenditure in agriculture (£37.3 million) almost equalled the total capital expenditure. When recurrent expenditures as well as those on capital account are included, the proportion of government effort going in to agriculture is seen to be considerably less than in the plan allocations; only about 7% of total government spending went into agriculture during the first 5 years of the plan. Whether or not this level of activity substantiates the Plan's claim that "priority" has been given to the agricultural sector cannot be determined, but if the capital budget is supposed to reflect the governments' development effort while the recurrent reflects its day to day administrative operations (as some people suppose), the claim that the weight of agriculture increased can be at least in part substantiated.

The relationship between capital and recurrent spending is far more complex than this assumption indicates and the two cannot be separated—either at the project or plan level—in appraising government efforts directed at "development." If anything, the division between "capital" and "recurrent" expenditures in agriculture conforms to a rather rough distinction between allocations in the form of services and goods. The recurrent budget measures largely the costs of "establishment" (personnel), while the capital budget reflects the purchase of goods valued at over a few thousand pounds. One serious problem of this division, coupled with the emphasis on capital allocations made in the plan document, is that it draws attention away from the personnel requirements necessary for many of the "capital" items proposed in the plan. Even in many project studies recurrent resource requirements appear as an afterthought, rather than an integral part of the analysis.

The relation between recurrent and capital allocations is apparent in the path of recurrent allocations over the 5 year period (Section III of Table 1). Recurrent expenditures on agriculture in the regions increased by 30-50% of their original levels since the start of the plan period, and the proportion of increase is even greater if the base year is taken as 1961-62, the year before the Plan went into operation. Federal recurrent allocations in the same period tripled and total recurrent expenditures increased by about 50%. The combination of rapidly increasing recurrent expenditures with shortfalls in the rate of capital expenditure is perfectly consistent with the impression gained from project studies that availability of recurrent resources (in the form of personnel) constituted the effective limit on the rate of capital expenditure.

4.2 *The Composition of Government Effort*

The composition of effort directed at agricultural development is shown by both the capital and recurrent budgetary allocations. Although the lack of a functional budgeting framework precludes detailed analysis of the recurrent component, the differences in Regional policies appear to show up most strongly in the capital allocations (which are linked to projects in the development plan), and recurrent allocations do not appear to vary as greatly as do the capital allocations between the Regions.

The framework for classifying allocations is that described in Section 3, and distinguishes between (1) government directed investments, (2) processing and marketing allocations, (3) extension activities, (4) research and investigation, (5) education, and (6) the provision of credit.[27] The resulting classification is presented in Table 2.

What can be learned from this categorization of expenditures? By far the most useful comparison is that between relative effort going to the two major types of direct output raising activities, categories 1 and 3. At the beginning of the Plan period, there was considerable interest in the difference between "transformational" and "improvement" types of activities, and a tendency to regard emphasis on extension alone as an outmoded feature of colonial agricultural policy. The extent to which this feeling was translated into planned—and implemented—projects is probably the most useful item of information to be obtained from this analysis. Also of interest is the extent to which credit projects were implemented in actual expenditure and the division of effort between activities directed at production and supporting (educational and research) activities.

The figures show about 13% of capital allocations going to the supporting forms of activity (categories 4 and 5), and even if ⅓ of total university capital expenditure is assumed to be for agricultural purposes, this proportion would not rise above 18-20%. The weight of these categories is undoubtedly higher in recurrent expenditure: excluding university expenditure they appear to account for about 25% of the recurrent agricultural allocations. Processing and marketing facilities absorb a small proportion of allocations and expenditures recorded;[28] and although the credit allocation accounts for 14% of allocated funds the slow implementation (or reduction) of Western and Federal programs reduced the weight of credit in capital expenditure to less than 5%. Effective ways to administer the distribution of

TABLE 2. *Proportional Distribution of Capital Allocations and Expenditure: Revised Plan Allocation and Estimated Expenditure 1962/3—1966/7*

	East	Midwest^a	West^b	North	Federal	Total
I. Revised Planned Allocations by Type of Spending						
1. Directed Investment	59%	38%	53%	18%	—	40%
2. Processing and Marketing	4%	6%	—	4%	19%	5%
3. Extension	23%	30%	18%	55%	53%	25%
4. Research & Investigation	3%	2%	2%	8%	—	11%
5. Education & Training	4%	N.A.	—	5%	28%	2%
6. Credit	5%	24%	27%	6%	—	14%
7. Misc. & Unclassified	2%		—	4%	—	2%
Total: %^d	100%	100%	100%^b	100%	100%	100%
Total: Amount in £ millions^d	28.25	2.39	18.44	14.99	10.52	74.58
For Comparison: Original Plan Allocations (£ millions)	30.36	—	18.44	24.99	9.29	80.55
II. Estimated Actual Expenditure to 1966/67						
1. Directed Investment	70%	59%	71%	23%	—	59%
2. Processing and Marketing	4%	11%	—	6%	1%	3%
3. Extension	18%	18%^c	16%	46%	99%	21%
4. Research & Investigation	2%	3%	3%	10%	—	11%
5. Education & Training	2%	—	2%	8%	—	3%
6. Credit	4%	—	5%	4%	—	4%
7. Misc. & Unclassified	1%	9%^c	4%	4%	—	2%
Total: %^d	100%	100%	100%	100%	100%	100%
Total: Amount in £ millions^d	18.25	1.34	11.16	8.00	3.19	41.94

Source: Compiled from Federal and Regional Estimates, 1962/3 to 1966/7. Section 1, last line derived from Estimates and National Plan document.

Footnotes: a. Midwest figures derived from listing of projects' estimated total costs, 1966/67 budget.
 b. Western figures derived from plan document, since no later listing of estimated total costs is printed.
 c. If staff housing removed from Category 3 and placed in 7, proportions becomes Category 3—12%, Category 7—18%

credit and to employ it in increasing output apparently have yet to be devised.

The major forms of government activity directly focussed at increasing output come under categories 1 and 3: government directed investments and extension activities within traditional farming patterns. The former constituted the 40% of all revised allocations, and the latter 25%, but rates of implementation varied so that over half the resources allocated through capital budgets went into directed investments. Spending on extension types of activities lagged behind the average spending rate, and constituted only 21% of total capital expenditure in the first five years of the plan. The different rates of implementation are not difficult to understand; the "directed projects" usually involve significant amounts of construction, land clearing and the like, and these forms of expenditure—especially when confined to a few locations—are somewhat simpler to plan and get underway. Extension activities require more personnel spread over wider areas; thus it takes longer to develop effective extension programs and the rate of expenditure on them is more sensitive to personnel shortages and other bottlenecks. Whether returns on these projects are more sensitive to shortfalls in personnel and administration than they are on the directed type of investments is open to question. Expenditure upon the directed investments can simply proceed at a more rapid rate.

Expenditure on government directed investments not only constituted the major total capital expenditure in agriculture, it also accounted for the largest difference between regional investment policies in the North and the South. Sixty percent of total regional capital spending in agriculture was for government directed investments, and the East, West, and Midwest were largely responsible for this emphasis; their proportions of spending on category 1 projects ranging between 60 and 70%. The North took a completely different approach, putting almost half of its expenditure in the extension type of activity, and less than ¼ into directed investment. Within the South, this ranking was completely reversed, and category 3 received less than 20% of total expenditure in every case. The difference in emphasis was reflected in plan rates of implementation; the East and West, concentrating heavily on their priority investments in category 1, spent 60-65% of the totals allocated, while the North spent only 53% of a revised plan allocation (£14.99 million) vastly scaled down from the original amount allocated (over £20 million). The directed investment component includes four major types of projects: settlement schemes, plantations, irrigation projects, and cattle ranches. The pattern of allocation between these types also varied widely between the regions with the North spending most of its much smaller allocation to directed projects on irrigation while the South concentrated on the settlement schemes and plantations. Within the East and West there was a further difference in emphasis; the West's settlement program absorbed the largest share of its inputs to directed projects while plantations are in second place and in the East the plantations received priority.

How effective have these types of investment been? This question cannot be fully answered on the basis of current data, nor without an examination of all elements of agricultural policy, but some observations can be recorded. The farm settlement programs appear to be the weakest of the four forms. Originally defended as a means of introducing "modern" agricultural techniques and a cooperative form of organization, they involved high capital costs per settler and fairly complex administrative requirements. The level of costs—over £2000 per farmer in the original estimates—subverted any possibility that the schemes, if successful, could be imitated by other farmers and forced them to specialize heavily in a few crops which at the time of their inception, promised the highest returns.[29] In practice, the settlements in 1967 appeared to be turning in a worse performance than the marginal one predicted. Settler turnover had been high, costs were considerably higher than the original amount predicted, and the schemes had absorbed considerable numbers of agricultural staff from other activities. Their net impact on the economy beyond their confines appeared to be limited to providing opportunities to increase the government labor rolls.

The plantations by 1967 represented a form of investment which was at least potentially successful, but they faced administrative and cost problems similar to those of the settlements. Government's comparative advantage in plantations appears low: government plantations were frequently the highest cost producer of the crops they raised. The Northern irrigation projects were perhaps slightly less plagued by difficulties, though the more ambitious of these were marked by development costs of over £120 per acre and it was not clear by 1967 whether cropping patterns promising yields high enough to cover these costs could be devised. But the irrigation schemes encompassed a variety of types and the lower total amount of resources going into them (£1.37 million in estimated expenditure for the Northern irrigation projects vs. almost £10 million for Southern settlements) at least partially justified their claim to being "pilot" investments.

The major forms of extension activities displayed considerably more variety than the directed investments and, although implementation lagged throughout the period, they appeared to show more promise than the investments of Category 1. With the exception of smallholders tree crop development and the North's fertilizer program they are relatively small schemes, that hold out prospects of affecting a larger number of farmers. The major forms of this type of investment in the South are the smallholder tree crop schemes promoted after 1964 by the IBRD; these attempt to provide technical advice and small amounts of capital to encourage smallholders to replace ageing trees or to expand their tree crops. An even lower cost scheme aimed at tree crop planting together with development of arable cash crops was that of the Eastern Region's Ministry of Rural Development, incorporating land consolidation (through the use of cooperative holdings released to individual planters), community effort, and technical expertise provided by the Ministry. By 1967 one modest experiment in relocation was taking place under this scheme. Other schemes which appeared to be meeting with limited success in the South were those directed at expansion of the poultry industry through the sale of day old chicks and poultry batteries and the provision of information on the operation of such commercial poultry units. Expansion of domestic egg production was considerable during the plan period and local eggs had replaced imports by 1965. Oddly enough, the ministries did not consider their efforts successful because the increased supply of local eggs depressed prices below their former high levels.

The difference between Northern and Southern policy extended to the types and varieties of investment undertaken in extension activities as well as in government directed investment. The major Northern extension effort was based on widespread distribution of subsidized fertilizer backed by an extensive program of on-the-farm demonstrations of recommended cropping practices. Totalling over 5000 in 1966, these demonstrations served to show farmers the potential gains from fertilizer use and modest changes in crop husbandry which can be applied under existing patterns of land use and tenure. They showed that considerable gains are possible from use of these practices, as well as providing a good measure of response to new seeds and fertilizer under actual field conditions. The extent of the scheme's success in establishing widespread use of recommended practices can not yet be predicted, but sales of the subsidized fertilizer increased fivefold between 1961 and 1965. The other Northern extension efforts were smaller in scale but covered a wide range of activities, from provision of grazing lands and water for cattle to an attempt to establish tractor hire units and introduce use of mechanical cultivation.

The extension activities in all regions have been much more difficult to appraise than the directed investment projects; in most cases their success will depend on peasant response to the government efforts. Although they do not involve government control of the entire productive environment they have a number of strong points in their favor. They are much less expensive per farmer affected than the directed investments; this permits the possibility of widespread emulation (with or without additional government effort) if they prove successful, as well as the commitment of a smaller level of government resources to projects for which returns are uncertain. Furthermore, the extension projects are usually more flexible; because they do not involve large components of fixed assets they can be changed as conditions dictate. The pace of their expansion is not, in general, a crucial determinant of their level of total returns.

The patterns of recurrent expenditure between 1962-3 and 1966-7 are more difficult to ascertain. The framework presented above cannot be applied, but a rather impressionistic breakdown of recurrent allocations can be summarized as follows: About half of recurrent expenditure during the period went to productive services (irrigation, engineering, field services), about 25% to research and educational activities, and about 25% to administration produce inspection, and miscellaneous items. Underspending ranged between 6 and 8% of the total recurrent budgets. There is considerable similarity between the regional patterns. The proportion of spending on direct productive services ranges between 53 and 60% in all the regions, and the proportion spent on other categories does not vary too greatly.

It is tempting to conclude from this similarity that the differences shown in regional capital allocations for the period were muted in the day to day operations of the agricultural ministries. This is not necessarily so. The recurrent budgets reflect the administrative structures within the ministries; these have evolved from a common origin and are quite naturally similar. But within these similar administrative frameworks resources may be deployed in quite different ways. This is especially true of the staff allocations of the Field Services Divisions, where deployment of personnel appears to reflect the patterns of spending in the capital budget. Perhaps the greatest hidden cost of the large government directed investments was their absorption of personnel who would otherwise have been engaged in extension activities. Unfortunately the lack of a functional distribution of recurrent expenditure precludes any attempt to appraise the overall cost of the different direct investment programs.

4.3 *The Strategy of Agricultural Development in the 1962-68 Plan*

From this cursory review of budgetary allocations and the observation of the various project components of the development plan, it is possible to piece together the general approach to agricultural development which appears to have been pursued from the beginning of the plan period to the outbreak of civil war in 1967. This strategy is perhaps best set out in the plan document's original statement that the "highest priority has been given to agriculture, industry and training of high and intermediate level manpower."

The linking of these three items together leaves the question of priority somewhat unresolved, but the general import of the statement is contained in the recognition that both the agricultural and industrial sectors could only absorb limited quantities of capital (effectively) within a given time period. (The importance attached to manpower training appears to have been related to an attempt to increase the absorptive capacities of these sectors.) The "priority" thus claimed for agriculture is somewhat modified, and the analysis may be reduced to the following propositions:

(1) If the targets with respect to growth were to be achieved, the plan had to represent a marginal shift of government effort toward directly productive types of investments in the agricultural and industrial sectors.

(2) The capacity of these sectors to absorb investment effectively was limited; and this constituted the effective limitation on the rate of growth.

(3) The causes of limited absorptive capacity were to be traced, *inter alia*, to shortages of knowledge and trained manpower; hence the emphasis on increased training of intermediate and higher level skilled personnel.

At no point is priority claimed for the agricultural sector because its slow development appeared to be interfering with the potential for growth in other sectors, and at no point is the growth of the agricultural sector seen as making a contribution to anything but the generalized growth of the economy.

If this analysis was basically correct, then the major problem in agricultural investment policy lay in identifying potentially successful forms of directly productive investment. More research and manpower training were called for as a matter of course, but the most difficult problems were those of choosing the type of directly productive investments these activities will be used to support. Stated in terms of the classification presented above, these problems resolved to the careful choice of types of directly productive activities and forms of organization, i.e. the allocation of activities between government directed projects, extension efforts, processing and marketing investments, and the use of credit. Since the major "priority" in agriculture appeared to be that of raising productive capacity, and since the major experience of the ministries in the past had been with extension types of investment efforts, one would have expected the investment mix selected to focus its main productive efforts on extension types of investments together with the required complementary investments in marketing and processing facilities. There would have been experimentation—at the pilot project level—with directed investments to explore new forms of organization and amass information for future projects. In all cases, one would have expected initial investment levels to be low, building up in areas which proved effective as the plan ran its course.

The budgetary allocations examined here seem to indicate that the governments lost sight of these goals. The bulk of directly productive investment during the first 5 years of the Plan went into large, unwieldy government directed projects; and instead of being started slowly on a pilot basis these were expanded rapidly on the basis of the most superficial initial analysis. The beneficiaries of these investments were the relatively few farmers hired or served by them, and their capital costs totally precluded their emulation. Many of them rested on the same specialized exports about which concern was expressed at the beginning of the plan period. The allocations of the former Northern Region constitute the only exception to this investment pattern; it concentrated its main effort at directly productive investment in the direction of extension activities; spreading its effort over a wide variety of different projects. The progress that these have made is rather hard to assess at the present time, but a few of them, notably the farm extension and fertilizer distribution program, appear to be at least potentially successful. The variety of efforts backed by reasonably good record keeping laid some basis for selecting future investments and afforded a degree of learning from the investments undertaken. It is interesting to note that the total value of capital allocations expected in the North was vastly scaled down from that of the original plan, and that the rate of spending of even the reduced allocation was lower than that in the Southern regions, which in 1967 were still planning to spend roughly the amounts originally allocated.

What can account for the emphasis put upon the directed form of investment? In the early stages of plan formulation this was probably the result of enthusiasm for the "transformation" approach to agricultural development and a misreading of the nature of the priority given to agriculture. It is much more difficult to explain why considerable flows of resources continued to be directed to this form in spite of its increasingly evident lack of performance. The reasons which can be adduced to explain this are impressionistic and quite unsettling. They appear to lie more in the realm of administrative inflexibility than of outside political pressure, and one gets the strong impression that there was neither the information gathering capacity to carry on continuous appraisal of investments nor the flexibility in organization and decision-making to respond to changing conditions in the field. The structure of the recurrent budgets easily masked heavy drains on resources into individual projects, and, in spite of a plethora of record keeping, there was little in the way of on-going functional project analysis.

Thus the effective constraint to absorption of investment in the agricultural sector appears to have lain not so much in shortages of capital, knowledge, or manpower as in the mechanisms available for coordinating these factors. The dichotomy between the accounting forms for recurrent and capital expenditures reflected a more serious dichotomy between the demands of significant government effort in agriculture and the organization of existing institutions to channel resources through government into the sector.

In what sense did agriculture receive the priority claimed for it in the Development Plan? A larger proportion of resources than previously was channeled into the sector, and the range of government activities in the sector was somewhat expanded. But in the sense of removing barriers to effective absorption of investment by the agricultural sector, the intended priority of the Plan did not—at the beginning of 1967—appear to have been effectively achieved.

NOTES

1. The "priority" given to agriculture in the plan document's discussion of goals may not be immediately evident in the proportion of capital resources devoted to agricultural improvement (13.6 per cent) but it is perhaps more evident in the extent to which agricultural problems and allocations are discussed in the plan document. A quick count indicates that about 25 per cent of the document is devoted to these topics, most of this in the rather lengthy Regional project lists. See *National Development Plan, 1962-68* (Lagos: Federal Ministry of Economic Development, 1963).

2. This distinction parallels one drawn in formal planning theory by Tinbergen between "quantitative" and "qualitative" policy—the former representing values given to certain (instrument) parameters within a given economic structure, and the latter involving changes in the qualitative aspects of that structure. See Jan Tinbergen, *On The Theory of Economic Policy* (Amsterdam: North-Holland Publishing Co., 1963). The inclusion of price policy and taxation in "institutional" policy illustrates a divergence between Tinbergen's definition and the one being used here. He would appear to include these two items in

"quantitative" policy, though he does not elaborate on his original distinction. They are included in the "institutional" category here because they do not relate to the direct allocation of resources by government in the agricultural sector. Taxation is most certainly relevant to budgeting—but as part of the generalized problem of obtaining revenues. Its specific impact on the agricultural sector is most likely to be found in the form of affecting incentives, altering the distribution of income, and the like; in this role it affects allocational decisions but does not constitute a direct form of allocation. Furthermore, tax policies are not automatically considered in determining the agricultural budget.

3. This bifurcation is dramatically evident in two of the most popular recent studies on agriculture and economic development. See John W. Mellor, *The Economics of Agricultural Development* (Ithaca, New York: Cornell University Press, 1966); and Herman M. Southworth and Bruce F. Johnston (eds.), *Agricultural Development and Economic Growth* (Ithaca, New York: Cornell University Press, 1967). In both cases discussions related to institutional policy receive considerable attention, but are not mentioned at all in the chapters on "agricultural planning." In spite of this deficiency both books provide excellent introductions to the problems of institutional and allocative policy.

4. Peter B. Clark, "Economic Planning for a Country in Transition: Nigeria," in *Planning and Economic Development*, edited by Everett E. Hagen (Homewood, Illinois: Richard D. Irwin, Inc., 1964); and W. F. Stolper, *Planning Without Facts: Lessons in Resource Allocation from Nigeria's Development* (Cambridge, Massachusetts: Harvard University Press, 1966).

5. The single exception to the lack of discussion of institutional policy in agriculture is United Nations, F.A.O., *Agricultural Development in Nigeria 1965-1980* (Rome: F.A.O., 1966), which has a section of 100 pages on "Organizational and Institutional Aspects" (pp. 281-380) dealing with the agricultural institutions of government, land tenure problems, marketing problems, education, and statistics. This comes the closest to a consideration of institutional policy, but it is quite largely descriptive and some of the items relate to allocational overheads more than institutional policy in the sense used here.

6. The number of studies undertaken reflects the interest of Nigerian research agencies such as N.I.S.E.R., E.D.I. and R.E.R.U, and of donor agencies such as U.S.A.I.D. and the Ford Foundation, which have financed a number of these studies. Among the studies currently existent are the MacFarlane and Oworen study of oil palm plantations, *Investment in Oil Palm Plantations in Nigeria* (Enugu: Economic Development Institute, 1965); Nanjundiah's study of rubber plantations, *A Study of the Development of ENDC Rubber Estates* (Enugu: Eastern Nigeria Development Corporation, 1965) (mimeographed); Kolp's appraisal of potential cocoa and rubber investments in the Mid-

west, *Smallholder Cocoa Project: Midwestern Nigeria* (Benin: Project Appraisal Unit, Ministry of Finance and Economic Development, 1966) (mimeographed); Olatunbosun's examination of School-leaver farm settlements, *Nigerian Farm Settlements and School Leavers' Farms: Profitability, Resource Use, and Social-Psychological Considerations,* Consortium for the Study of Nigerian Rural Development, CSNRD-9 (December, 1967); and Roider's thorough examination of the Western Farm Settlements, *Nigerian Farm Settlement Schemes* (Berlin: Institut fur Auslandische Landwirtschaft an der Technischen Universitat Berlin, 1963) (mimeographed). The F.A.O. survey of agricultural development, United Nations F.A.O., *op. cit.,* included a number of benefit-cost analyses of investments in specific crops. The author has been engaged in collating the various project studies. See Jerome C. Wells, "Appraising an Agricultural Project in Northern Nigeria: A Problem in Investment Evaluation," *Nigerian Journal of Economic and Social Studies,* V, 1 (March, 1963), pp. 127-40; Jerome C. Wells, "An Appraisal of Agricultural Investments in the 1962-68 Nigerian Development Program," unpublished Ph.D. dissertation, Ann Arbor, University of Michigan, 1964; and Jerome C. Wells, "The Israeli Moshav in Nigeria: An Estimate of Returns," *Journal of Farm Economics,* XLVIII, 2 (May, 1966), pp. 279-94.

7. The plan document includes a discussion of the budgetary implications of recurrent resource requirements, *National Development Plan, 1962-68 op. cit.,* and a series of consistency tests of national income components prepared in conjunction with the plan document. W. F. Stolper, *Prospects for the Nigerian Economy: Principles and Procedures Adopted in Projecting National Accounts* (Lagos: Nigerian National Press, 1962), Supplementary paper to 1962-68 Development Plan, stresses the impact of the program on recurrent resource requirements. The implications of the plan on recurrent budgets are discussed in more detail in Stolper's review of the Nigerian planning process, "The Main Features of the 1962-68 National Plan," *Nigerian Journal of Economic and Social Studies,* IV, 2 (July, 1962), chapters 3 and 4, and pp. 204-18.

8. Professor Nixon's recasting of the budgetary allocations along functional lines, "An Analysis of Nigerian Government Expenditure Patterns, 1950-62," (chapter 6) deserves comment not only for the magnitude of the effort involved and the relative speed with which it was carried out, but also with respect to his stated reasons for undertaking the project. He claimed that such a breakdown was essential to infer changes in the political priorities resulting from self-government and independence. P. N. C. Okigbo, *Nigerian Public Finance* (Evanston: Northwestern University Press, 1965), uses the first functional breakdown of government expenditures known to the author, but his series is rather cursory and he gives it remarkably little emphasis in his discussion of public finance in Nigeria.

9. Stolper, *op. cit., Prospects for the Nigerian Economy.*

10. L. M. Hansen, "Comprehensive Economic Planning in Nigeria" (chapter 11).

11. Stolper, *op. cit.,* "The Main Features of the 1962-68 National Plan," and Stolper, *op. cit., Planning Without Facts.*

12. United Nations F.A.O., *op. cit.*

13. The Western Region section of the plan document, *National Development Plan, 1962-68, op. cit.,* pp. 334-36, does contain a cursory discussion of manpower requirements and a list of students in various technical fields (including agriculture) expected to become available during the plan period; the extent to which this indicates a consideration of manpower requirements of Western Regional agricultural projects cannot be determined. Stolper's discussion of manpower planning, *op. cit., Planning Without Facts,* is related to problems of educational expansion, but he consistently argues that the manpower limitations in government, together with other constraints, ideally would have dictated a smaller plan than finally determined. See Stolper, *op. cit., Planning Without Facts,* pp. 50-51, 264-66.

14. Stolper, *op. cit., Planning Without Facts,* chapter 2.

15. Peter B. Clark, *op. cit.*

16. In a number of particular cases, fairly strong differences of opinion on the value of particular projects arose between ministries of agriculture and ministries of economic development—the farm settlement programs of the Eastern and Western Regions provide two immediate examples. The issues arose after the inception of the military regime, and appear to have been dealt with by the senior civil servants. In the West the issue was temporarily resolved in favor of the Ministry of Agriculture and in the East a special study group was appointed to appraise the settlement program.

17. The program of the former Northern Region's Ministry of Agriculture provides an excellent example of this evolution. In early 1962 a number of major projects listed in the Plan document had been subject only to the most cursory projections of costs and returns, and problems of implementing their initial stages were absorbing the great proportion of Ministry efforts. By 1966, however, the Ministry had created an Economic Planning Unit which was engaged on two major tasks: a systematic review of major projects and an analysis of the recurrent resource requirements of the various programs of the Ministry.

18. The criteria used for project analysis in Nigerian agriculture stem from the discussions of investment criteria and development planning of the 1950s. The major references to this literature are the review articles by Hollis B. Chenery, "Development Policies and Programs," *Economic Bulletin for Latin America,* III (March, 1958), pp. 51-77, and Siro Lombardini, "Quantitative Analysis in the Determination of the Efficiency of Investment in Underdeveloped Areas," translated by

E. Henderson, *International Economic Papers*, No. 9 (London: MacMillan Co., 1959). A discussion of the form and application of such criteria in the Nigerian context is provided by the author, Jerome C. Wells, "Investment Criteria and the Nigerian Development Plan," *Nigerian Journal of Economic and Social Studies*, VI, 3 (November, 1964), pp. 277-304. Problems of project evaluation in government expenditure and use of the benefit-cost form of analysis are discussed widely, the major references being Prest and Turvey, "Cost Benefit Analysis: A Survey," *Economic Journal*, LXXV (December, 1965), pp. 683-785; Peter O. Steiner, "The Role of Alternative Cost in Project Design and Selection," *Quarterly Journal of Economics*, LXXIX, 3 (August, 1965), pp. 415-30; and Roland N. McKean, *Efficiency in Government Through Operations Analysis* (New York: John Wiley and Sons, 1958). Problems of project evaluation in Nigerian agriculture will be discussed in a forthcoming book on agricultural policy in Nigeria by the author.

19. This framework will be used in Section 4 to trace capital expenditure to 1967. For a more extensive discussion see Wells, *op. cit.*, "Nigerian Government Spending on Agricultural Development: 1962/3-1966/7."

20. The author has argued elsewhere, Jerome C. Wells, "Government Investment in Nigerian Agriculture: Some Unsettled Issues," *Nigerian Journal of Economic and Social Studies*, VIII, 1 (March, 1966), pp. 37-48, that this can be done indirectly and in an informal fashion by examining the case with which promising directly productive investments are proposed; this link between infrastructural investments in education and research and investments directly aimed at raising production should at least be considered, even if it cannot be precisely formulated.

21. Nixon, *op. cit.*

22. The level of aid to Nigerian agricultural development cannot be ascertained without a study of allocations by donors and a careful review of the Nigerian budgets as well, for some of the aid allocations are taken through the budgets as sources of funds, and others—often those involving personnel assistance—are omitted. The magnitude of the aid flows involved is not small: USAID alone by 1965 had obligated £17 million to Nigerian agricultural development, and by the end of fiscal 1965 (July), over £6 million had been spent. How much of this is omitted in the budgetary allocations remains a matter of conjecture.

23. The categories omitted include university expenditures on departments of agriculture and related activities; in recent years in the North this includes the costs of the major research station. The orders of magnitude involved in this category are not small; total university capital expenditure came to about £5.1 million in the first five years of the Plan, and recurrent allocations to agricultural departments and the like are estimated at £2-3 million per year. See Wells, *op. cit.*,

"Nigerian Government Spending on Agricultural Development: 1962/3-1966/7."

24. For a more extensive analysis of the recurrent budgetary allocations, see Wells, *op. cit.*, "Nigerian Government Spending on Agricultural Development: 1962/3-1966/7. The application of the analytical framework involved considerable reworking of the budgetary categories and the author is grateful to Olu Awoyelu and Segun Famoriyo of the Nigerian Institute of Social and Economic Research for their aid in this process.

25. This figure overstates the amount of resources going to agriculture in the Plan itself. The Federal component of expenditure includes a grant of £10 million to the Regions for agricultural development, but this has not resulted in any increase in regional programs, it has merely served as a means of financing those listed in the plan. In the analysis here another £1.17 million is removed from the Federal allocation because it deals with geologic survey and mineral exploration.

26. "Estimated expenditure" refers to the actual allocations of 1962/3-1964/5 and the approved or revised estimates of expenditure for the remaining two fiscal years. These should be reasonably good indicators of actual government expenditure except that the approved estimates tend to overestimate the amount which is actually spent. Thus the figures shown here should be treated as the maximum likely expenditure during the period under review.

27. Several conventions used in the classification need to be noted. Schemes for farmer training are placed in category 4 unless they exclusively serve a government directed project; and the processing and marketing allocations in category 2 exclude both major processing projects (considered as part of industry) and processing facilities included in government directed plantations. The seventh category records miscellaneous activities and the acquisiton of equipment which cannot be attributed to specific categories.

28. This is because the larger processing investments are either recorded under "industry" or linked to government directed facilities.

29. The Western Region's settlements, in spite of their stated goal of aiding in diversification of Western Region agriculture, rest almost entirely on the fortunes of cocoa and egg prices. See Jerome C. Wells, *op. cit.*, "The Israeli Moshav in Nigeria: An Estimate of Returns."

14. New Sources of Growth in a Stagnant Smallholder Economy in Nigeria: The Oil Palm Rehabilitation Scheme

MALCOLM J. PURVIS

I. Oil Palm and Nigerian Economic Growth

Oil palm products are the oldest established "legitimate" exports of Nigerian agriculture.[1] Unlike all the other principal Nigerian exports which were negligible or nonexistent before 1900 (cocoa, rubber, groundnuts, and cotton), palm kernel and palm oil have been exported from Nigeria for several centuries. The major expansion of oil palm exports, however, did not take place until the 1840's in response to the decline in the slave trade and to the growing demand in Europe for vegetable oils—especially for the manufacture of stearic candles.[2] By 1900, palm oil exports had reached 45,508 tons. Although exports continued to grow steadily for the first part of the twentieth century, they reached a peak in the 1930's and have declined somewhat since then. (See Table 1, Chapter 1). This pattern of growth and expansion is consistent with a "vent for surplus" explanation of export growth as illustrated in the first three chapters of this volume. The oil palm industry is a classic example of development through international trade of an established smallholder commodity with minimal innovation in the cultivation and harvesting of the product.[3] Innovations in the Nigerian oil palm industry have been almost exclusively in processing and marketing—the introduction of screw presses and pioneer oil mills, replacements of wooden casks by steel drums for assembling and storing, and the use of bulk oil palm plants for preparation for export.[4] Although these innovations resulted in remarkable improvements in quality there has been no sustained expansion in production in the last thirty years. Most of the improvement in quality has been even more recent, taking place in the early 1950's after institutional changes had been made in the marketing system and appropriate price signals put into effect to communicate world market requirements to smallholders.[5] Since this time there has been a period of stagnation in the oil palm economy of Nigeria. Exports have declined somewhat in the last decade (although seasonal fluctuations are large which obscures any definite trend up or down[6]). Coupled with this stagnation has been a general downward drift in producer prices (especially in "real" terms),[7] principally because the Marketing Boards have taken a larger share of the export price.[8]

Thus, for whatever reason, the oil palm economy has in the last thirty years shown no appreciable growth in exports. The only changes in recent years have been improvements in the quality of the output (relative shifts in grades of oil).[9] Compared to the rates of growth of Nigeria's other major export crops, growth rate of palm produce exports has been very poor. Production of cocoa, rubber, timber, groundnuts and cotton has been growing at rates of between 6 and 9 per cent per annum 1956/58-1962/64.[10]

The present oil palm economy of Nigeria can be described as a system of collection.[11] The palm bush of Southern Nigeria is a high canopy of varying density which yields an economic product without cultivation.[12] The ripe bunches only need to be harvested. The sole production decisions are whether to utilize the palm for palm fruits (to obtain palm oil and kernel), or to tap the palm for palm wine, or cut the fronds for goat feed or housing construction. In addition, a long-run production decision is made when a new tree is permitted to grow or an old palm is cut down. As a result the palm groves of Nigeria are an expression of an established but slowly changing ecological balance between man and his demands for various palm products and for other crops competing for land. Such an economy was initially capable of large and sustained production increase as a result of the opening up of foreign markets and growing population.[13] Little or no investment is required for the production of palm fruits and investment requirements, in the past, for processing equipment was also very modest.[14] However, once the land became densely and permanently settled, as in the palm belt of Eastern Nigeria, palm expansion lagged behind rates of growth of other export crops.[15]

II. Early Attempts at Modernizing Palm Groves

Numerous attempts have been made to introduce "modern" quasi-plantation methods of cultivation for smallholder oil palm in Southern Nigeria but until recently these have met with little success. The concept of growing palms of selective genetic material, in straight lines, to the exclusion of food crops, with laborious inter-row weeding and fertilizing was rejected by most smallholders. Thus attempts to distribute "agricultural" seedlings before the Second World War met with very limited response.[16] In the 1950's, a smallholder oil palm rehabilitation scheme was attempted but failed. The scheme was launched in 1953 in the Uyo area of old Calabar Province. The Eastern Region Production Development Board (the precursor of the E.N.D.C.) agreed to finance subsidies of £5 per acre (£3 for felling, clearing and planting and £2 for maintenance spread equally over 4 years) and a limit of 5 acres per participant was specified. In 1954-55, the scheme was extended to Abak Province and parts of Owerri Province. In the first year, 97 acres were planted and a maximum of 506 acres was reached in 1957. The scheme was abruptly halted in 1957 because of "delay by ERPDC in payment of 1956 subsidies and attendant suspicion and loss of confidence in the scheme by farmers."[17] It was later reported that, "Many of these former subsidized rehabilitated plots have fallen into varying states of neglect and some of them have suffered severely from fire damage."[18]

The results of the rehabilitation scheme of the early 1950's are summarized in a 1951 article in *West Africa* (italics added):

> But in practice the results of *giving* farmers selected oil palms to plant in small plots have been disappointing. It has not been possible to give the necessary instruction and supervision over wide areas. Equally, no farmer is likely to have enough land for a large plantation *when its advantages as a paying proposition are uncertain.* There are similar difficulties in the way of introducing improved strains of food crops, and methods of cultivation.[19]

Other equally unsuccessful attempts were made to organize smallholders in cooperative ventures to consolidate their land resources for planting oil palm. One such scheme at Asejire in Western Nigeria became something of a show place and was written about optimistically by such an experienced observer as K. D. S. Baldwin in India's *Economic Weekly*.[20] A visit by the author in 1968 found that the Asejire "plantation" had reverted to bush and the pioneer oil mill, which was an integral part of the project, was lying idle. Equally, more recent government schemes to plant and operate new oil palm estates[21] and farm settlements have been unsuccessful for a wide variety of different reasons.[22] The absence of any large scale (expatriate) development of estates in Nigeria, as a result of deliberate colonial policy, also resulted in the absence of any major new growth of output from modern estates and possible spread effects that this may have had on the smallholders.[23] Thus despite all the attempts to find ways of redeveloping the palm bush of Nigeria, the industry remained in a semi-wild, technologically underdeveloped state which had steadily been losing ground to the more technologically advanced palm economies of other parts of Africa and especially those of South East Asia.[24]

III. Rehabilitation and Hybrid Palms

Irregardless of the unfortunate past attempts to modernize the palm bush the Eastern Region developed an Oil Palm Grove Rehabilitation Scheme, (OPRS), to replant 60,000 acres with new hybrid palms during the 1962-68 Development Plan. The OPRS was the major agricultural scheme of the Eastern Nigerian Ministry of Agriculture during the 1962-68 Plan.[25] The progress of the OPRS scheme in the first five years of the Plan indicated that the 60,000 acre goal would have been surpassed if the Civil War had not errupted in 1967. By the end of the 1966 planting season, 45,951 acres had been replanted through the efforts of 4,315 participants. (Table 1.)

TABLE 1. *Eastern Nigeria: Oil Palm Rehabilitation Scheme, 1962-66*

| | Number of | Acreage | |
YEAR	Participants	Target[b]	Planted
1962	278	2,000	1,728
1963	565	5,000	3,724
1964	1,225	8,000	10,480
1965	1,592	14,000	13,630
1966	2,169	15,000	20,389
Total	4,315[a]	44,000	49,951

SOURCE: Information supplied by Eastern Region, Ministry of Agriculture.

[a] Total gives actual number of participants. Year to year figures do not discriminate between new and repeating participants.

[b] The target for 1967-68 was 16,000, giving 60,000 acres for the 1962-68 plan period.

Of the funds earmarked for the 1962-68 Development Plan in the Eastern Region, 40 per cent was allocated to agriculture (£30.4m), where "the main emphasis (was) on the rapid expansion of tree crops to lead to an early increase in cash farm income, Government revenue from purchase taxes and export duties and Marketing Board profits."[26] Correspondingly, 75 per cent of the capital outlay for agriculture in Eastern Nigeria was allocated to tree crop development. The OPRS accounted for only 8.4 per cent of the total proposed expenditure on tree crops (including rubber and cocoa as well as oil palm) while Farm Settlements and Eastern Nigeria Development Corporation (ENDC) estates accounted for an additional 77 per cent. In terms of acreage, however, the OPRS was by far the most significant scheme, and was also the most successful (Table 2). The acreage planted in five years under the scheme exceeded the combined acreage of the ENDC estates, Farm Settlements and private estates.

TABLE 2.   *Eastern Nigeria: Target Acreage and Actual Plantings Under Three Oil Palm Development Schemes*

SCHEME	Target Acreage 1962-68	Planted Acreage (as of March 1967)
Oil Palm Rehabilitation Scheme	60,000	49,951
Eastern Nigeria Development Corporation Estates	40,000	29,100[a]
Government Farm Settlements	16,320	5,353

SOURCE: Information supplied by Ministry of Agriculture and Eastern Nigeria Development Corporation.
  [a] Approximation.

The OPRS was a subsidy scheme; "incentive" payments were given to farmers during the first 5 years until the hybrid palms came into production. Participants were given a direct cash subsidy of £10 per acre (spread over 5 years) and also received fertilizer and ready-to-plant hybrid seedlings. The cash subsidy payments were contingent upon inspection of the rehabilitated groves, thus enabling the extension service to check on proper planting and maintenance operations. The only stipulation for farmer participation was that a minimum of five acres be planted at one time in not more than two adjacent plots. This facilitated supervision of the new hybrids. Participants were also required to cut down most of their old palms. No more than 20 old palms per acre could be left standing and in the fifth year of the program, these too, had to be cut down. Farmers were also permitted to intercrop (yams, cassava, etc.) until the leaf cover of the grove becomes so dense that intercropping was impossible.[27]

In addition to private and group farmer participation, the OPRS was being used, along with the other agricultural extension programs, by the Ministry of Rural Development in establishing cooperative "plantations." Approximately 4,000 acres of oil palm have been planted in these rural development farm projects. Oil palm plantings account for the major share of the total acreage developed by the Ministry of Rural Development.[28] While most of these farm projects are larger in size than the privately owned operations, they still averaged less than 100 acres.

The main innovation in the OPRS was the large scale availability of new highly productive planting material bred at the Nigerian Institute for Oil Palm Research (NIFOR), germinated and grown to field seedlings by the Ministry of Agriculture and distributed free of charge to participants.[29] These new oil palm plants were the highly productive *dura* x *pissifera* crosses which yield thin shelled (and hence give a high ratio of oil bearing tissue in the fruit) *tenera* hybrids. These hybrid seeds were produced at NIFOR as a result of breeding work done there and at the Institut de Recherches pour les Huiles et Oleagineux (in the Ivory Coast) and in Southeast Asia.[30]

These crosses have a current potential yield of up to 17,000 lbs. of bunches per acre and an oil content of 28 per cent (oil to bunch) which is an available[31] oil yield per acre of 5 times that of the semi-wild palm bush. However, these yields, although low compared with yields obtained in Malaysia, are only obtainable under the very best conditions of soil and management in Nigeria. More reasonable production estimates for smallholders are 6-8,000 lbs. of bunches with an oil content of 24 per cent or better. This still represents a 2-3 fold increase over yields of the palm bush (3-4,000 lbs. of bunches at 20-23 per cent oil content). A production breakthrough of this magnitude can be expected to have significant impact on smallholder producers and to stimulate significant new investment.[32] The availability of planting material with such a market superiority in yield performance (easily the equivalent of new "miracle" and "wonder" rices developed in Southeast Asia,)[33] was the *sine qua non* of the OPRS. Without this development in yield increasing technology the response of farmers would probably not have been any different than prior attempts to encourage the replanting of groves with "agricultural" seedlings.

This breakthrough in oil palm technology came from years of sustained biological and plant breeding research[34] supported by agronomic investigations under smallholder conditions. (See Chapter 1) As a result by the early 1960's not only were the new hybrids available in quantity but also there was accumulated experience in planting, fertilizing, spacing and intercropping which led to new and improved inputs and practices. Much of this research was centered at the NIFOR substation in the Eastern Region at Abak, and large numbers of extension workers received intensive and specialized training both at Abak and NIFOR headquarters at Benin. Finally NIFOR had put out a number of extension bulletins on the care of the new oil palm groves. In short, a successful extension program was under way.[35]

Based upon the initial success of the program and the enthusiasm shown by farmer-participants, the Eastern Region Government made plans to rehabilitate an additional 330,000 acres, and applied to the IBRD for a loan. This request was well received although no final decision was taken because of the political disturbances of 1966. The proposed scheme was essentially the same as the 1962-68 OPRS, with the exception that cash subsidy payments for the first five years would be increased from £10 to £13.5 per acre.[36] The Food and Agricultural

Organization has also endorsed an enlarged Oil Palm Rehabilitation Scheme and suggested that a total of 290,000 acres be rehabilitated and an additional 60,000 acres be planted by smallholders in Eastern Nigeria by 1973-74.[37]

Thus oil palm rehabilitation occupied a major role in the 1962-68 Plan. The acreage planted in the first five years under the OPRS was larger than the combined total acreage of the farm settlements, ENDC and private estates. The scheme and its proposed expansion in the Second Plan could have had a substantial effect on investment and growth of agricultural production for the entire region.

IV. New Investment and Resource Use by Smallholders

A survey of participants in the OPRS was undertaken in the first half of 1967 to evaluate the program and explore the opportunities for a major expansion of the scheme. The survey included interviews with 235 farmers, and field measurement of their new oil palm plots (to measure growth, establishment, intercropping and prior use of land).[38] The survey showed that the extension program which administered and controlled the OPRS, although one of the most successful in Nigeria, was still far from satisfactory. The high administration costs (estimated to be equal to the value of the cash subsidy and in kind goods distributed to the farmers)[39] the lack of timeliness in ordering and delivering seedlings and fertilizers, and lack of awareness by many farmers of proper timing of many farm operations all needed to be improved. The 1962-66 experience with the scheme showed that the hybrid seedlings on an average were about two years behind in their physical growth compared with the same seedlings planted on NIFOR experimental plots. The proper and rapid establishment and growth of palm seedlings is essential for high yields. Nevertheless, even with rather pessimistic yield and price assumptions the OPRS promised a (social) internal rate of return of 10 per cent[40] or a private return to land and management of £8 per acre[41] which compares very favorably with alternative agricultural investment opportunities in Eastern Nigeria.[42]

There was no doubt that participants were convinced of the economic value of the scheme. They could be characterized as energetic entrepreneurs actively seeking new ways of converting their resources into future income streams. Many of them were involved in planting other tree crops (cocoa and rubber), had taken part in the OPRS in more than one year, had planted acreages of oil palm substantially above the minimum 5 acres (average acreage per participant after 5 years of the scheme was 15.2 acres) and almost all intended to plant more new oil palms, even without the cash subsidy.[43] Needless to say, they were not "typical" Eastern Nigerian farmers. Most of them had had some commercial or urban experience (as petty traders, school teachers, processors, or laborers). The resources under their control, principally labor and land, were considerable. Almost without exception participants were hiring labor to assist in the planting and maintenance of the new palms and many had acquired new land by purchase or redemption from pledge. This acquisition of land by purchase, redemption or other means for planting a tree crop took place in a traditional land tenure system which historically has prevented such individual action, and demonstrates that traditional institutions can adapt to new economic incentives. Traditional institutional systems affecting inputs of land and labor were not constraints on the expansion or acceptance of the OPRS. However, a major problem facing any future expansion of the OPRS is the problem of creating new institutions for supplying the *new* productive resources. The important yield increasing technology is in the capital investment in real resources, e.g. seedlings, fertilizer and human knowledge.[44] In the last operational year of the scheme (1966) the Ministry of Agriculture was involved in germinating 5 million seeds (under controlled conditions of applied heat and humidity), planting up tray seedlings, supervising the operation of over a hundred field nurseries (run by the extension service, by Young Farmers Clubs, schools, prisons and by Rural Development projects) and in distributing nearly 2,000,000 seedlings and 3,400 tons of fertilizer to 2,169 participants. These activities placed considerable strain on the administrative and physical capacity of the Ministry of Agriculture. In each year of the plan the number of participants and the acreages planted was limited by the availability of seedlings and other supporting supplies, including extension agents, but not by lack of demand from smallholders to be included.[45] An equally important problem was the timeliness of delivery of the new inputs. Forty-four per cent of all participants were supplied one month or more late with seedlings and 64 per cent received fertilizer late.[46] Individual farmers had no direct control over these inputs and at least in the early years of such schemes, there was no service market or institution outside of government which could supply the real resources in which farmers were anxious to invest. Clearly any large scale expansion of oil palm rehabilitation would have required new institutions to handle the production and distribution of these new inputs during early states of development of demand for such inputs.[47] Levels of investment and rates of growth will also be constrained by the availability of these real investment resources.[48]

V. New Sources of Growth and Future Development

The OPRS is of particular significance to Nigerian agricultural development in that it was a considerable departure from historical patterns of output expansion. Although examples can be found in Nigeria of similar departures, such as use of fertilizer on groundnuts (in Northern Nigeria) since 1960 and spread of cocoa spraying, the OPRS involved substantial technological change which was land saving, required conscious investment in a hitherto "wild" crop and gave a new dynamic to a traditional and stagnant agricultural system.

However, the importance of the response of smallholders to a technological change in oil palm production in Eastern Nigeria is not only in their alacrity in adopting it but the long run effects of a change from a land and labor extensive system of output expansion to a land saving, innovating source of growth. Two features of this change from a classical "vent for surplus" type of growth to a "neo-classical" growth are particularly noteworthy—the effects of changing resource use and control on the rural economy and the high cost of "growth through investment" compared to growth via "vent for surplus."

If the OPRS is ever successful in achieving a massive replanting of palm bush, which seems technically feasible within the existing economic and social system, the change in the pattern of growth will also create far reaching changes in the social and economic systems. In particular it will create an unequal distribution of wealth and an unequal development of rural incomes. This has been well summarized by Kenneth Parsons as follows:

> . . . it has seemed to me that agriculture in West Africa is just about at the breakover point from customary tenure and credit institutions to legally sanctioned property arrangements . . . The question is whether economic institutions, basically of tenure, should be shaped in direction of an individualized economy . . . Such considerations come to a focus upon the questions of whether one of the specifications of agricultural development should include attempts to build a middle class in agriculture, or whether a country should follow policies which will likely lead to the emergence of a rural proletariat.[49]

Perhaps even more significant is that development of a middle class in Nigerian agriculture will lead to the development of a landless class. For, as scarce land becomes concentrated in the hands of successful farmers, they become increasingly the source of employment for landless peasants. It was evident that the energetic entrepreneurial farmers participating in the OPRS in the densely settled parts of Eastern Nigeria were the beginning of such a middle class. Such growth under changing conditions of resource combination (due to introduction of technology and the restriction of output growth from traditional sources) will as surely lead to "structural" problems in Nigerian agriculture as it has in other developed and less developed economies.[50]

The changing source of output growth in Eastern Nigeria's oil palm industry also demonstrates the high levels of investment needed to sustain rates of expansion comparable to the historical rates of growth from "surplus" factors of production. The effect of this new form of output expansion on exports is severely limited by the relatively high rate of growth of internal demand for palm oil. Even if both the original 60,000 acre OPRS scheme and a massive investment in a rehabilitation scheme, such as those under the FAO and IBRD schemes, of a further 150,000 acres are completed by 1976, Eastern Nigeria's exports will increase by only 20 per cent above the level of 1965.[51] Expansion of output along vent for surplus lines is (in the 'pure' case) costless but once surplus resources are no longer available there has to be an investment of resources with positive opportunity cost. The use of land, for example, formerly largely used for food farming, is no longer costless in terms of product foregone and its exclusive use for palm trees is only rendered profitable by investment in new productive technology.[52] Although growth by investment in *new* resources may yield sustained rates of growth of agricultural output equal or better to those obtained by past growth from expansion of *existing* resources, it demands a continuous input of productivity increasing technology.[53]

If, as seems likely, Nigeria's economy continues to grow through export expansion it cannot be assumed that this will be from "traditional" smallholder sources of output growth. Continued expansion of agricultural exports will increasingly be dependent on investment and technological improvement. The changing sources of growth in the oil palm industry is but an example of these developments.

NOTES

1. And the only indigenous export crop. The exact origin of the Oil Palm is debated but usually agreed to be on the West Coast of Africa. See W. D. Raymond, "The Palm Oil Industry," *Tropical Science*, III, 2 (1961), pp. 69-89.

2. "A production scattered over that country with a bountiful hand has been found . . . The African Oil Palm . . . but it did not assume that importance which it now claims until the introduction of new processes for manufacturing stearic candles from it . . . ." See B. Seeman, *Popular History of the Palms* (London, 1856). This "coincidence" of changing market demands and of technological change in the consuming countries is a neglected factor in explaining changing patterns of export

agriculture. The discovery of suitable technologies for vulcanization of rubber and for the manufacture of margarine from groundnuts were also important in opening up markets for these products (also see chapter 3 by Hogendorn in this volume).

3. Allan McPhee, *The Economic Revolution in British West Africa* (London: Aberdeen, Routledge and Sons, 1926).

4. A. N. Iwuchukwu, "Influence of Marketing Boards System and Preliminary Purification on Nigerian Palm Oil for Export" (paper presented at Tropical Products Institute Conference, London, May 3-6, 1965).

5. P. T. Bauer and B. S. Yamey, "Response to Price in an Underdeveloped Country: A Rejoinder," *Economic Journal*, LXX (December, 1960), pp. 855-56; and V. W. Hogg, "Response to Price in an Underdeveloped Economy," *Economic Journal*, LXX (December, 1960), pp. 852-55.

6. There is substantial evidence that weather is not only responsible for these fluctuations but also has been more unfavorable in the last five years than in the first five years of the period 1955-1966 contributing to the apparent decline in exports. See Malcolm J. Purvis, "Annual Yield Variation in Oil Palm: Marketing Board Purchases in Eastern Nigeria, 1955-56," *Journal of the Nigeria Institute for Oil Palm Research* (forthcoming).

7. G. K. Helleiner, *Peasant Agriculture, Government and Economic Growth in Nigeria* (Homewood, Illinois: Richard D. Irwin, Inc., 1966), pp. 58-67.

8. Glenn L. Johnson, "Removing Obstacles to the Use of Genetic Breakthroughs in Oil Palm Production: The Nigerian Case," *Agricultural Research Priorities for Economic Development in Africa—The Abidjan Conference*, Washington, D.C.: National Academy of Science, 1968.

9. C. W. S. Hartley and S. C. Nwanze, "Factors Responsible for the Production of Poor Quality Oils" (paper presented at Tropical Products Institute Conference, London, May 3-6, 1965).

10. W. Arthur Lewis, *Reflections on Nigeria's Economic Growth* (Development Centre Studies, OECD, Paris, 1967), p. 17. For these other products production is measured by exports but for palm products and cotton by marketing board purchases. Since domestic consumption of oil is currently approximately equal to marketing board purchases, palm oil expansion could not have been more than 2 per cent (half of an estimated maximum rate of growth of consumption of 4 per cent per annum, i.e., somewhat above the population growth rate).

11. Carl K. Eicher, "Reflections on Capital Intensive Moshav Farm Settlements in Southern Nigeria," in *Agricultural Cooperatives and Markets in Developing Countries*, edited by K. Anschel, E. Smith and R. Brannon (New York: Praeger, 1969).

12. For a description of the palm groves of Southern Nigeria and their ecological balance see A. C. Zeven, "Oil Palm Groves in Southern

Nigeria: Part I. Types of Groves in Existence," *Journal of the Nigerian Institute of Oil Palm Research*, IV (August, 1965), pp. 226-250; A. C. Zeven, "Oil Palm Groves in Southern Nigeria: Part II. Palm Groves as They Develop and Deteriorate and Their Rehabilitation," *Journal of the Nigerian Institute of Oil Palm Research*, IV (forthcoming); and A. C. Zeven, *The Semi-Wild Oil Palm and its Industry in Africa*, Agricultural Research Reports, 689 (Wageningen, 1967). Food crops are frequently cultivated beneath the oil palm canopy.

13. Oil palm is a principal ingredient in Southern Nigerian diets and the main source of fat, as well as source of oil for lamps and for soap making, by villagers.

14. It was estimated that 32 per cent of all palm oil in Eastern Nigeria in 1965 was still being produced by hand squeezing which involves no mechanical equipment. See S. Bahiri, "Proposal for Effective Introduction of Stork Hand Hydraulic Press," Institute of Administration (Enugu, 1965) (mimeographed).

15. For a graphical exposition of these growth rates since 1910 see Zeven, *op. cit.*, "Oil Palm Groves in Southern Nigeria: Part I. Types of Groves in Existence."

16. Sir Keith Hancock, *Survey of British Commonwealth Affairs*, II (London: Oxford University Press, 1940).

17. Olatunde Oloko, "A Study of Socio-Economic Factors Affecting Agricultural Productivity in Annang Province, Eastern Nigeria," N.I.S.E.R. (Ibadan, 1963) (mimeographed).

18. Eastern Nigeria, Ministry of Agriculture, *Annual Report 1957/58* (Enugu, 1959).

19. Oloko, *op. cit.*

20. K. D. S. Baldwin, "Group Farming in the Western Provinces of Nigeria," *The Economic Weekly* (Bombay, February 2, 1952).

21. Leken Are, "An Assessment of Some Plantation Problems in Western Nigeria," *Tropical Agriculture*, XLI (January, 1964), pp. 1-13.

22. Dupe Olatunbosun, *Nigerian Farm Settlements and School Leavers' Farms—Profitability, Resource Use and Social-Psychological Considerations*, Consortium for the Study of Nigerian Rural Development, CSNRD—9 (December, 1967); and Carl K. Eicher, *op. cit.*, "Reflections on Capital Intensive Moshav Farm Settlements in Southern Nigeria."

23. A. C. Zeven, *op. cit.*, "Oil Palm Groves in Southern Nigeria: Part II. Palm Groves as They Develop and Deteriorate and Their Rehabilitation"; Malcolm J. Purvis, "The Nigerian Palm Oil Industry: A Comment," *Food Research Institute Studies* Vol. VIII, no. 2 (1968), 191-198; and R. G. Saylor, *A Study of Obstacles to Investment in Oil Palm and Rubber Plantations*, Consortium for the Study of Nigerian Rural Development, CSNRD—15 (Michigan State University, May, 1968).

24. Peter Kilby, "The Nigerian Palm Oil Industry," *Food Research Institute Studies*, VII, 2 (1967), pp. 178-82; and C. W. S. Hartley, "The Decline of the Oil Palm Industry in Nigeria," Nigerian Institute for Oil Palm Research (June, 1963) (mimeographed).

25. For a detailed description of the OPRS and analysis of cost and returns see the author's report for the Consortium for the Study of Nigerian Rural Development, Malcolm J. Purvis, "Report on a Survey of the Oil Palm Rehabilitation Scheme in Eastern Nigeria, 1967," CSNRD— 10 (Michigan State University, June, 1968).

26. *National Development Plan, 1962-68* (Lagos: Federal Ministry of Economic Development, 1963), p. 211.

27. Experiments at NIFOR have shown that inter-cropping is not detrimental to the establishment of seedlings, provided adequate fertilizer is used, but may be beneficial since it ensures proper weeding (NIFOR experiment 507-3).

28. 133 of 220 farm projects were planting oil palm.

29. C. W. S. Hartley, *The Oil Palm* (London: Longmans, 1967).

30. C. W. S. Hartley, "Oil Palm Breeding and Selection in Nigeria," *Journal of the West African Institute of Oil Palm Research*, II, 6 (1957), pp. 108-115; C. W. S. Hartley, "Advances in Oil Palm Research in Nigeria in the Last Twenty-Five Years," *Empire Journal of Experimental Agriculture*, XXVI, 102 (April, 1958), pp. 136-51; M. Ollaganier and J. P. Gascon, "La Selection du Palmier a Huile a l'I.R.H.O" (paper presented at Tropical Products Institute Conference, London, May 3-6, 1965); and L. D. Sparnaaij, T. Mendenex and G. Blaak, "Breeding and Inheritance in the Oil Palm (Elaesis Guineensis, Jacq.) Part I. The Design of a Breeding Programme," *Journal of the West African Institute for Oil Palm Research* (1963).

31. Actual yield depends on the method of oil extraction used. Estates using modern machinery can obtain extraction rates 50 per cent higher than the methods normally used by smallholders. See William L. Miller, "An Economic Analysis of Oil Palm Fruit Processing in Eastern Nigeria" (unpublished Ph.D. dissertation, Michigan State University, 1965); and Malcolm J. Purvis, *op. cit.*, "The Nigerian Palm Oil Industry: A Comment."

32. David Fogg, "Economic and Social Factors Affecting the Development of Smallholder Agriculture in Eastern Nigeria," *Economic Development and Cultural Change*, XIII (April, 1965), pp. 278-292.

33. Sam-Chung Hsieh, "New Outlook for Asian Agriculture," *International Development Review*, X, 3 (September, 1968), p. 8.

34. Carl K. Eicher, "The Dynamics of Long-Term Agricultural Development in Nigeria," (see chapter 1).

35. The Diffusion Project surveys found that 81 per cent of 947 village leaders and progressive farmers knew about the OPRS, even though some of its sample villages were outside the oil palm areas. See

Diffusion of Innovations Project, "Phase I: Preliminary Report of Selected Descriptive Findings for Leaders and Progressive Farmers in 71 Eastern Nigerian Villages," Economic Development Institute (Enugu, April, 1967) (mimeographed); and Diffusion of Innovations Project, "Phase II: Preliminary Report of Selected Descriptive Findings for 1347 Rural Farmers and Innovators in 18 Eastern Nigerian Villages," Economic Development Institute (Enugu, April, 1967) (mimeographed).

36. Eastern Nigeria, Ministry of Agriculture, "Oil Palm Grove Rehabilitation Scheme: Smallholder Development Project" (Enugu, no date) (mimeographed).

37. United Nations F.A.O., *Agricultural Development in Nigeria, 1965-1980* (Rome: F.A.O., 1966), pp. 134-41.

38. Malcolm J. Purvis, *op. cit.*, "Report on a Survey of the Oil Palm Rehabilitation Scheme in Eastern Nigeria, 1967."

39. *Ibid.*, p. 48.

40. Lewis, *op. cit.*, p. 66.

41. Purvis, *op. cit.*, "Report on a Survey of the Oil Palm Rehabilitation Scheme in Eastern Nigeria, 1967," p. 68.

42. Including estate investment in oil palm and other tree crops.

43. 95 per cent of all respondents in survey thought they would make money from their new groves; 97 per cent intended to plant more oil palm and 91 per cent voiced intentions to plant even without the survey.

44. Glenn L. Johnson, "A Note on Nonconventional Inputs and Conventional Production Functions," in *Agriculture in Economic Development*, Edited by Carl Eicher and Lawrence Witt (New York: McGraw-Hill Book Co., 1964), pp. 120-24.

45. C. A. P. Takes, "Problems of Rural Development in Southern Nigeria," *Tidjschrift van het Koninklijk Nederlandsch Aardrijkskundig Genootschap*, LXXXI, 4 (1964), and N.I.S.E.R. Reprint Series, 9 (Ibadan), p. 14.

46. The experience in 1967 showed considerable improvement over that in 1963, particularly in respect to payment of subsidies as well as the scale of the planting schedules. See Carl K. Eicher and William L. Miller, "Observations on Smallholder Palm Production in Eastern Nigeria," Economic Development Institute (Enugu; December, 1964) (mimeographed).

47. Thus L. Witt has written, "Demand for such inputs needs to be created along with the distributing institutions, before we can expect a substantial improvement in the factor market institutions that distribute many of the non-farm inputs." See Lawrence Witt, "Factor Market Institutions in Agricultural Development," (paper for Seminar North Central Land Economics Research Committee, Chicago, Illinois,

November 2, 1967. Duplicated by Department of Agricultural Economics, Missouri Agricultural Experiment Station, Columbia, Missouri), p. 6. See also discussion by Glenn L. Johnson, "Factor Markets and Economic Development," in *Economic Development of Tropical Agriculture*, Edited by W. McPherson, (Gainesville: University of Florida, 1968), pp. 93-111.

48. This is another aspect of the "capital shortage illusion." See Sayre P. Schatz, "The Capital Shortage Illusion. Government Lending in Nigeria," *Oxford Economic Papers*, XVII (July, 1965), pp. 309-316 and N.I.S.E.R. Reprint Series, No. 13 (Ibadan). The rate of investment in oil palm rehabilitation is more likely to be restricted by supplies of real resources than supplies of investment funds.

49. Kenneth H. Parsons, "Discussion: Specification of the Agricultural Development Process," *Journal of Farm Economics*, XLIX, 5 (December, 1967), pp. 1183-87.

50. For example, Malay smallholder land ownership and economic wealth was severely challenged under rather similar conditions by Chinese and Indian rubber development and was only constrained by legislation reserving land for Malays and by the traditional Malay rice economy. This has had the effect of retaining considerable Malay land control but presumably at the expense of some economic growth.

51. Purvis, *op. cit.*, "Report on a Survey of the Oil Palm Rehabilitation Scheme in Eastern Nigeria, 1967," pp. 75-76.

52. However, this investment is very low in foreign exchange requirement and is principally a classical "wage fund." Eighty one per cent of the OPRS land was previously used totally or in part for food cropping. See *Ibid.*, p. 25.

53. Martin H. Billings, "The Economics of Commercial Egg Production in Eastern Nigeria," (Department of Agricultural Economics, Michigan State University, 1968) (manuscript).

15. Contractor Finance and Supplier Credit in Economic Growth*

A. A. AYIDA

The structure and composition of the foreign indebtedness of a developing economy is one of the most significant phenomena in its growth particularly in the long run. The pattern and distribution of the maturities of external debts determine the extent of the burden of servicing such debts over a period of time. The absolute level of such debts is important at any given time but it is the amortization schedule determined principally by maturities distribution, which really affects the future growth potential of an economy.

Foreign short-term indebtedness creates a number of problems[1] which could *a priori* retard rather than accelerate the development process in the recipient country in the long run. In isolating the problems of contractor finance, supplier credit and other short-term indebtedness for study in this paper, one is dealing with one of the potential sources of complete paralysis in the development of the Nigerian economy.

One of the fundamental assumptions in this paper is that foreign capital is channelled towards investment in growth-sensitive areas in the developing economy and such investment would not and could not take place from domestic resources at the particular time without postponing some equally important and high rating priority investment. Foreign capital in-flow thus supplements and is intended to be additional to the fullest utilization of domestic or national resources. This is the only rational basis for importing foreign capital with its foreign indebtedness or obligations by way of interest or dividend payments and repayment of principal. In practice, this may not always be the case. Domestic resources may not be fully utilized before foreign debt obligations are assumed. Most lenders nowadays insist on lending substantial capital only to countries with National Development Programmes and sometimes to projects within such Programmes. For the private investor, it is the pay-off or profitability of the project that

---

* From *The Nigerian Journal of Economic and Social Studies*, Vol. VII, No. 2, July 1965. Reprinted by permission of The Nigerian Economics Society.

matters. Many public agencies in a world of tied lending find it more convenient to channel their capital aid to projects implemented with machinery and equipment from their own manufacturers. Such loan assistance is export promotion credit as far as the lender is concerned. The test of rationality derived from the supplemental nature of foreign capital is intended for the wise borrower anxious to develop at a fast rate of growth and not the lender.

The other fundamental assumption is that foreign indebtedness involves some form of transfer of real resources in the long run. Before oversimplifying the so-called Transfer Problem,[2] it is essential to distinguish between the various forms of international flow of capital:

- (*i*) grants including technical assistance by way of personnel and equipment;
- (*ii*) loans and credits on public account;
- (*iii*) loans and credits on private account;
- (*iv*) commercial arrears (payments for external commercial transactions are withheld for as long as possible);
- (*v*) surplus food programmes;
- (*vi*) military expenditures.

The last three have been relatively negligible sources of external capital for Nigeria, Ghana and Liberia although commercial arrears appear to have assumed greater significance in Ghana's recent experience. Loans and credits on public and private accounts have been the major forms of capital inflow into the three countries.

The transfer problem in our context can be analysed in three stages. The first stage is for machinery and equipment plus services of foreign experts and technicians to be imported into the recipient country for the implementation of a capital development project. In the case of grants, surplus food programmes and military assistance, this is the first and final stage as far as the transfer problem is concerned. Where repayment of principal or interest and dividends are involved, the recipient country has to meet these out of its own savings or the proceeds of a new loan.

The second stage is for such savings to be translated into foreign exchange earnings through exports thus involving a retransfer of real resources from the borrower to the lender country. There are balance of payments implications here. Have exports increased or imports decreased sufficiently as a result of the foreign capital import to enable the domestic savings to be translated into foreign exchange disbursements without serious repercussions on the borrower's balance of payments? We will return to this important question in more specific form later.

The third stage is the net position of the borrower after the re-transfer of the real resources involving interest and dividend payments and amortization. The borrower's resultant position will be determined by the application of the borrowed funds, or the return on the investment and the structural and other changes induced by the capital import. These can be assessed at two levels:

    (*i*)   the viability or profitability of the project financed by the capital in-flow; and

    (*ii*) the external economies, income multiplier effects and other indirect benefits to the economy generated from the capital import.

On both counts, the longer the period of the loan or credit arrangement, the greater the benefit to the economy other things being equal. The cardinal point in assessing the resultant net position of the borrower is to judge his total benefits against the total cost of servicing the foreign capital imported. If economic growth is looked at as a continuing process, the question that arises is how much asset by way of productive capacity and/or increased productivity and income can the borrower create out of the borrowed capital before repayment? Put in this way, the significance of the terms and maturity of the credit assumes very great importance for the borrower.

Loans and credits can be divided into five categories by reference to their maturities:[3]

    (*a*) "Accommodation" credits lasting less than one year;

    (*b*) "Short-term" credits involving deferred payments over one year and less then ten years;

    (*c*) "Medium term" credits with maturities ranging from ten to fifteen years;

    (*d*) "Conventional" loans of fifteen to twenty-five years;

    (*e*) "Soft" loans with nominal interest charge of about ¾ of one per centum and repayment spread over thirty years and above.

Contractor finance, supplier credit and other deferred payments arrangements are usually "short-term" credits although a few of them spill over into the "medium term" range when there are special considerations. The cost of these forms of foreign indebtedness to the recipient economy is *ipso facto* very high.

This conclusion may not be obvious. But if the present value or cash equivalent of a given amount of loan or credit at a fixed rate of interest is determined for varying maturities as in Table 1, the shorter the period, the higher the cost to the recipient economy other things being equal. For a £5 million loan, it is as high as £3.9 million for

5 years and as low as £1.15 million for 30 years. On our assumption that use of domestic resources is maximised through the life of the loan, the longer period is more beneficial to the growth of the recipient economy. On such an assumption, it is misleading to assess the cost of foreign capital in terms of the total disbursements in column (iii) of Table 1 which is only £5.71 million for 5 years but £9.7 million for a 30-year period. The distinction is very important. Very often, borrowers assess their credit requirements by basing their calculations on total disbursements and then opt for the shorter period instead of using the present value concept which favours longer maturities. These considerations apply to any borrower be it a firm, a statutory corporation or a developing economy. In practice, however, it is sometimes difficult to realise the full resources utilisation assumption throughout the life of the loan. In such a case, there would be periods when the borrower might be accumulating idle resources while servicing its external debt. This could obviously be uneconomic and inefficient.

The cost of foreign indebtedness cannot be fully assessed without relating this to the benefits. The cost/benefit ratio as stated earlier can be derived for a given project in isolation or for the economy as a whole. The former can be easily quantified through complete project appraisal while the external economies and possible structural changes involved in the latter cannot be so easily determined outside the framework of a National Development Plan. Even within the context of such a framework, the basic question remains—whether or not debtor developing countries can rely on short-term credits as a source of capital formation and development capital expenditure.

The thesis of this paper is that such reliance must be restricted and circumscribed because from the debtor country's point of view, the cost/benefit ratio can only be less than unity under severely limited assumptions. This proposition is derived from the nature and *modus operandi* of contractor finance and supplier credit and the recent experiences in Nigeria, Ghana and Liberia. The financial and economic consequences of these credit arrangements are taken into account as well.

The following detail analysis of the nature, *modus operandi* and the economic consequences of short-term credits is limited to the public sector of the economy.[4] The private sector has been excluded because:

(*i*) given the traditional profit maximisation motive, private borrowing is determined by the viability criterion;

(*ii*) where the risk calculations go wrong, the borrower is called upon to meet the full consequences of his misjudgement by way of built-in sanctions such as bankruptcy and liquidation;

    (*iii*) both the borrower and the lender bear the risks involved in the investment financed from private credit unlike the public sector where the lender is absolved from "normal" risks;

    (*iv*) data on private credit transactions and foreign indebtedness are not available and discussions on such transactions in spite of their serious implications for the development of the Nigerian economy and balance of payments are not likely to be very fruitful in the context of this paper.

Short-term credits in the public sector analysed are: (*i*) Contractor Finance, (*ii*) Supplier Credit and (*iii*) Guaranteed Private Investment. The characteristics of each require special and separate treatment.

Contractor Finance

A public authority, Federal or Regional Government, Local authority or statutory corporation commissions a contractor to undertake a construction project. The contractor agrees to "pre-finance" the construction costs and the borrower pays the contractor over an agreed period of time. The terms of such deferred payments vary considerably and the credits bear interest usually higher than the prevailing market rates as such interest charges are sometimes "concealed" as finance charges or "flat" rates.[5] As a rule, the borrower pays 5-10% of the cost of the contract as down payment on signing the contract. This enables the contractor to mobilise his equipment. On commencement of the works, he pays another 10-15% to enable the contractor to meet his initial expenses. Thereafter, the so-called contractor-cum-lender finances the rest of the operations occasionally from his own resources, usually by discounting the promissory notes issued by the borrower. Any rational contractor would pass on the discount charges to the borrower. Other things being equal, such additional charges could be avoided by the borrower raising the funds direct. Other things are not always equal and firm inferences cannot be drawn here. The borrower's ability and knowledge of borrowing may be comparatively limited and he may have to incur other charges from trying to borrow on his own.

The cost/benefit relationship in a complicated transaction oversimplified here depends on the nature and productive capacity of the project, its place in the borrower's scale of priorities and what it can contribute to the structural development of the recipient economy. In Nigeria contractor finance is being increasingly used for infra-structure and (social overheads) civil engineering projects such as university buildings and office blocks and it is precisely for these projects that they are most unsuitable particularly where "soft" and conventional credit terms are available for such projects if fully prepared. The controversial question revolves around the use of contractor finance in place of domestic resources for say, defence capital expenditures to which the receipient country is reasonably committed. Here there is no clear-cut answer but the time sequence is very important. If we take a plan period of six years in which all domestic resources available to the public sector are fully committed, and credit arrangement of less than six years maturity or falling due during the Plan period will not make any additional financial resources available to the borrower.[6] The borrower's fixed debt service charges would have risen to reduce his future current income stream to the extent of the short-term credit. Such contractor finance offers cannot therefore be regarded as an additional source of development finance by the end of the sixth year. But such offers could ease the financial strain in any given year where the resources available that year are fully committed. If care is not taken to assess the full consequences, the financial position in a subsequent year could be worsened by the payments falling due under the contractor finance obligations unless there is a future "windfall" from other sources of development finance or the project financed generates enough resources to 'pay-off' the loan. This is precisely what would happen to contractor finance proposals involving riskless gold mining or the construction of a viable electric diesel power station but never roads, bridges and ports extensions which require much longer time to "pay-off." Financing the latter proposals under "short-term" or "medium term" credit proposals have in principle the same effect as financing them from domestic resources when the six-year plan period is taken as a whole.

Supplier Credit

A supplier credit operation is similar to contractor finance but the central figure is the machine "peddler" who sells an equipment and agrees to be reimbursed by the purchaser or borrower over a period of time. A supplier credit is really an export credit and very often the public authorities and banking institutions in the seller's country provide the funds or the guarantee cover for the seller. There are no difficulties at all in obtaining suppliers credits once the borrower has any form of creditworthiness and is prepared to purchase the right amount of capital equipment. The competition between industrialised countries to provide export credits to their manufacturers is so great that the maximum periods of supplier credits are laid down by the Berne Convention.[7] What is important from the point of view of developing countries is to assess the full implications of this type of credit for the growth of their economies.

Guaranteed Investments

The latest variant of the contractor finance supplier/credit theme is the guaranteed riskless investment under which the government of a recipient country gives two guarantees:

> firstly, to provide the necessary foreign exchange to enable suppliers credit to be made good when due and
> secondly, to meet all obligations falling due if the investment is not viable.

Such investment may be an industrial project sponsored by a company in which a foreign private investor provides about 5% to 10% of the equity capital and a public development agency or government in the recipient country provides the rest. The equipment required for the project is supplied by the foreign partner to the company under supplier credit arrangements. There are known cases where the foreign investor is the consultant who prepared the feasibility study for the project, the financial adviser and banker who finalised the credit arrangements, the manufacturer who supplied the equipment, the technical partner and managing agent who runs the factory under a managing agency agreement with fees or commissions. This economic "Mikado" then gets a government guarantee that if the project fails, the government would from its budgetary resources service the loan for the equipment! What a pity there are no Gilberts and Sullivans in developing countries like Nigeria, Ghana and Liberia. The whole arrangement does not make economic sense and any attempt to industrialise on a large scale this way might lead to a high cost economy particularly as the recipient country has to give all the protection required for the survival of the "guaranteed" plant.[8]

There is nothing in principle to prevent the recipient country from safeguarding its own interests in these arrangements. The foreign partner could assume greater risk capital in the enterprise by contributing 45% to 50% and above of the equity which should bear closer relationship to the value of the machinery and equipment imported under supplier credit instead of the common arrangement whereby a £3 million plant is imported by a company with paid-up capital of £250,000 in which the foreign partner subscribes less than 10%. The company could employ independent consultants to prepare and/or evaluate the feasibility studies. With adequate safeguards, the industrialisation process can be accelerated in this way particularly where there is a large domestic market as in Nigeria. This is a very important tool for bringing about structural changes in the method and pattern of production in developing countries. Besides, this appears to be the only way open for African countries to industrialise very quickly particularly as there are no 'soft' loans for industrial under-takings. The urge to export machinery and equipment out-weighs the traditional considerations of developing countries as the source of raw materials.

He would have taken no risk, lost nothing but gained everything at the expense of the Nigerian taxpayer. The basic question that arises is: Would the Nigerian Government not be justified in not honouring such guarantees unless the foreign partner meets part of the debt from his group's resources outside Nigeria where it is subsequently shown that the contractor-cum-consultant-cum-technical partner-cum-machine ped-dler-cum-lender acted in bad faith in preparing the project? This ques-tion is the more pertinent where there is subsequent evidence to prove 'collusion' with vested Nigerian interests whose actions cannot be said to be bona fide at the relevant time. Should Nigeria's international creditworthiness be called to question if she subsequently repudiates such guarantees unilaterally? These are real and not academic questions for Nigeria and some other developing countries in Nigeria's position.

"Turnkey" jobs mainly industrial enterprises where the foreign partner literally hands over the key of a completed factory to the borrower, are also a variation on the supplier credit theme. The borrower pays for the goods and services (or factory) supplied over an agreed period of time. This is the main 'Eastern bloc' approach to assistance to developing countries. Sometimes, the supplier agrees to receive in repayment agricultural export commodities over the agreed period with all the disadvantages inherent in quasi-barter trade. But from the point of view of opening new markets for commodities like cocoa, such an arrangement could be eminently satisfactory provided there are no resales or dumping of such commodities in the traditional markets. The other problem associated with this type of operation is the difficulty of evaluating the machinery and equipment built to standards and forms with which Western-trained local engineers and technicians are not familiar. At the initial stages at least, the servicing and maintenance costs would be relatively high. Inefficiencies might also arise from introducing new types of machinery against equipment accumulated from the former metropolitian country. But such diversifi-cation appears to be inevitable with political independence. The im-portant thing is for the recipient country to try to get value for the goods and services promised in a 'turnkey' supplier credit arrange-ment from any source.[9]

Disadvantages of Short-Term Credit

There might be some advantages in summarising at this stage the disadvantages inherent in contractor finance and other short-term credits *sui generis* as a source of capital formation and development expenditure:

  (*i*) the cost/benefit ratio is less than one unless the project has a very quick "pay-off." Thus, there is great disadvantage in financing infrastructure and basic growth-inducing projects in this way.

  (*ii*) there is usually a budgetary problem. The resources generated by the project and the gross savings may not be sufficient to service the short-term credit with its heavy amortization schedule. The borrower may thus be called upon to service the credit from current income from other sources. This reduces the volume of savings available for investment from those sources. In the case of governments,[10] budgetary surpluses which should be the main source of public investment, are used to service short-term credit obligations.

  (*iii*) most short-term credit obiligations are discharged in foreign currencies even when denominated in local currencies. The 'pre-financed' project does not normally generate sufficient foreign exchange resources by way of export expansion or import restriction by substitution, to service the credit. In transferring the domestic savings to foreign exchange disbursements, the balance of payments position of the recipient country will be adversely affected at least in the short-run.

  (*iv*) when given a Plan period of six years, short-term credit facilities maturing within the period do not provide an additional source of funds for financing the Plan; what is gained in the credit swing is lost in the rounds of reductions in current income or budgetary surpluses. The only exceptions are where the credit facilities are extended to project with quick 'pay-offs.' (Short-term credits contracted in one plan period could jeopardise the capacity of the borrower to finance future capital development in a subsequent plan period.)

  (*v*) maintenance of national plan priorities is oftener than not, incompatible with short-term credit proposals. In the case of Nigeria, some projects implemented by this method are not even in the National Development Plan 1962-68. Experience has shown that the momentum generated behind a contractor finance project soon develops into an avalanche sweeping overboard all rational considerations!

    (*vi*) "irrational considerations" often associated with con-
tractor finance proposals tend to lead to negotiated
tenders, 'rigged' pricing, sale of 'dud' equipment and
other inefficiencies.

These "malpractices" are however not inherent in the nature of contractor finance proposals neither are they exclusive to them. There is
no reason why short-term credits cannot be obtained on doubly competitive tender terms: competitive as to both the contract price for
the project and the credit facilities offered.

It is often said that many developing countries resort to contractor
finance proposals in order to bypass the cumbersome and time-consuming procedures and requirements of orthodox lenders. The German
Loan for the Second Lagos Bridge was negotiated over nearly four
years! Orthodox loan negotiations tend to overemphasize adequacy of
feasibility studies and so forth. But what happens with many contractor
finance proposals is that the whole process is turned upside in Marxist-
Hegelian fashion. The contractor finance agreement is initialled or concluded before the feasibility studies are undertaken and technical problems solved during the implementation or construction stage or sometimes after. In practice, the completion of contractor finance projects
may take just as long as those financed from orthodox or conventional
loans particularly where the recipient insists on adequate value added
for money owed.

The short-term credit experiences in Liberia, Ghana and Nigeria in
descending order of magnitude (historically) are illustrated in Tables
2 and 3. Table 2 shows the growth in Nigeria's total external public
debt which by 1963 stood at about 4% of the Gross Domestic Product.
It also shows the phenomenal growth in Ghana's external public debt
(supplier credit only) from £9.7 million in 1960 to £60.2 million
in 1963, an increase of about 520% in four years. By 1963, Ghana's
external public debt stood at 10% of the Gross Domestic Product. As
a proportion of total government revenue, the annual short-term debt
service charges for 1963 were for Nigeria 6.1%, Ghana 7.8%, Liberia
92.3%.

The more interesting comparison is the projection of the Public
Debt structure 1963-70 given in Table 4 showing the percentage of
short-term credits to total Foreign indebtedness. The Liberian proportions are based on the projections after her external debts had been
renegotiated with her creditors and rescheduled under the auspices of
the International Monetary Fund. From the peak of 86.6% in 1963,
the proportion falls to about 37% in 1970. The proportions in Nigeria
rise from about 19% in 1963 to a peak of about 55% in 1967. The
Ghanaian proportions remain constantly high at 96% to 96.8%. This

is because by definition, practically all Ghana's external public debt falls into the category of short-term credits with the notable exception of the £15 million (end 1964 estimate) loan for the Volta River Project excluded from the projections. These short-term credits appear to have been contracted as a matter of deliberate policy objective to alter the basic structure of the Ghanaian economy notwithstanding the investments in some prestige projects, and to provide a solid basis for the rapid growth of the Ghanaian economy.[11] Whatever the policy objectives, the inevitable consequences of large short-term credit operations for the borrower have now hit the Ghanaian economy and the visit of the International Monetary mission in May 1965 might lead to a rescheduling of Ghana's debt obligations similar to the experiences in Liberia, Brazil, Argentina and other developing countries which have contracted short-term obligations on a large scale.

The interesting question is whether or not Nigeria will follow the Liberia, Ghana, Brazil, and Argentina pattern and experiences with short-term credits and external payments liquidity crisis. Nigeria has the advantage over Ghana of relatively wider economic base with much greater and more diversified foreign exchange earning potential particularly with the growth of the Nigerian Oil Industry. What is relevant here however is the net foreign exchange earning of savings from oil after allowing for capital movements on account of profits, dividends and amortization payments and service charges. It is therefore misleading to regard the gross foreign exchange earnings estimated at £100 million per annum by 1967[12] as a guarantee that Nigeria will not experience an external liquidity crisis and balance of payments difficulties of the Ghanaian type. The Oil Revolution will materially affect the Nigerian situation but such relative advantages could be wiped out by the Nigerian authorities' excessive reliance on contractor finance and other short-term credits as the instrument for capital formation in the public sector particularly for infra-structure and Social Overheads and General Administration projects. The Federal and Regional Governments and their statutory corporations and agencies will through their respective policies determine the pattern of future development in these areas though the leadership clearly rests with the Federal Government which constitutionally retains exclusive legal powers for external borrowing, guarantees and foreign exchange control.

The major conclusion from the preceding analysis is that short-term credits create debt service obligations which increase rapidly over time. This affects adversely the debt servicing capacity of the borrower leading to an imbalance in the structure of its external indebtedness. Short-term credits have resulted in a similar imbalance in the composition of international indebtedness.[13] The rapid increases in debt service obligations might lead to a liquidity crisis both from the increasing demand on the budgetary resources of the borrower and the balance of external payments position for the economy as a whole. The creditworthiness of the recipient country would thus be impaired as the debt service obligations assume too high proportion of current export earnings (whatever its theoretical limitations most lenders still regard the conventional 10% limit as a starting point for measuring debt servicing capacity and creditworthiness[14]). The consequences of short-term credits on the creditworthiness of the recipient could be quite grave where the assumed service charges have not been properly projected and integrated into one schedule of payments falling due.

There is nothing inherently bad or good about contractor finance and other short-term obligations. The abuses of this method should be clearly distinguished from short-term credits as a supplementary or marginal source of capital formation and development capital expenditure limited to high priority projects and not the projects chosen at random by the contractor or machine "peddler" and his friends. Excessive reliance on this method may, however, impair the debt servicing capacity and creditworthiness of the borrower particularly where they are used for starting numerous infrastructure and other projects all of which cannot be completed and supported by total domestic resources available to the borrower. In such circumstances, short-term credits would retard the long-term growth of the recipient economy due partly to the disorganisation, lack of foreign exchange resources, loss of foreign confidence and inadequate capital inflow which follows the temporary inability to service such credits. In the final analysis, short-term credits remain the major instrument for developing countries to industrialise and alter the structure of their economies for growth purposes and their cost/benefit ratios cannot be appraised in isolation from the other major growth determinants in the recipient economy.

TABLE 1. *Amount of Loan £5m. at 5% per Annum using Archers Table.*

(i)	(ii)	(iii)	(iv)
Maturity (years)	Annual Payment of Principal & Interest (Equated Annuity) (£)	Total Disbursement (£m.)	Present Value (£m.)
5	£1,142,587	5.71	3.9
10	641,471	6.41	3.05
15	477,776	7.17	2.4
20	398,362	7.97	1.9
30	323,534	9.7	1.15

TABLE 2.   *Growth in External Public Debt.*

YEAR	£ million
1935	9.9
1946	10.2
1951	14.4
1952	21.2
1958	17.1
1960	16.7
1962	42.9
1963	46.2

GHANA
(SUPPLIER CREDIT ONLY)

1960	9.7
1961	25.4
1962	37.9
1963	60.2

TABLE 3.   *Debt service of selected West African Countries as percentage of gross Domestic Product and total government revenue for the year 1963/64.*

Country	Gross Domestic Product 1963 (£m.)	Total Govt. Revenue 1963 (£m.)	Debt Service Charge 1963 (£m.)	Debt Service Charge as % of GDP	Debt Service Charges as % of Govt. Revenue
Nigeria	1,072.3	183.3	11.2	4%	6.1%
Ghana	586	145.0	11.3	10 %	7.8%
Liberia	27.5	13.0	12	43.6%	92.3%

Sources: 1. National Governments' Budgets.
2. Outlines and selected indicators of African Development plans ECA 1965.

TABLE 4. *Structure of Public Debt Projections 1963-70.*

	1963			1964			1965			1966		
	Nigeria	Liberia	Ghana[1]	Nigeria	Liberia	Ghana	Nigeria	Liberia	Ghana	Nigeria	Liberia	Ghana
Total Debt Service Charges (£m.)	11.2	12.0	11.3	6.9	6.5	24.2	9.5	6.9	23.3	18.1	6.2	22.5
Short-Term Credits	1.7	10.3	11.1	2.9	4.7	23.9	4.8	5.1	22.8	6.1	4.5	22.1
% of Short-Term Credit to Total Indebtedness	15.2	86.6	98.2	42.0	72.3	98.8	50.5	86.4	97.9	33.7	72.6	98.2

	1967			1968			1969			1970		
	Nigeria	Liberia	Ghana	Nigeria	Liberia	Ghana	Nigeria	Liberia	Ghana	Nigeria	Liberia	Ghana
Total Debt Service Charges (£m.)	12.5	4.9	22.4	13.0	3.9	19.5	13.0	3.1	15.6	12.1	2.4	12.4
Short-Term Credits	6.9	3.2	22.	7.1	1.9	19.1	6.1	1.6	15.1	4.2	0.9	11.9
% of Short-Term Credit to Total Indebtedness	55.2	65.3	98.2	54.6	48.7	97.9	46.9	51.6	96.8	34.7	37.5	96

[1] Ghana's figures exclude the Volta River Project Loans estimated at £15 million at the end of 1964.

Sources: Various official publications including:
Nigerian National Development Plan Progress Report 1964 published by the Federal Ministry of Economic Development, Lagos.

The Ghana Budget 1965 published by the Ghana Planning Commission, Accra.

NOTES

1. The author led a group discussion on "Problems of Short-Term Lending" which could have been called "Problems of Short-Term Borrowing" at the Dag Hammarskjoeld Foundation Seminar on "International Finance and National Development" at the end of which he became convinced that the problems required more systematic treatment for a few borrowers with varying experiences like Nigeria, Ghana and Liberia. The summary proceedings of the Seminar have been published in an Essay by Professor Sune Carlson and Dr. O. Olakanpo in "International Finance and Development Planning in West Africa" (Institute of Business Studies, University of Uppsala, 1964).

2. See controversial discussions on Reparation Problems including effect of transfer on debtor's terms of trade: J. M. Keynes, *The Treatise on Money*, and his earlier contributions in the Economic Journal, March, June, September, 1929 on The German Transfer Problem, The Reparations Problems and Views on the Transfer Problem. Also, Bertil Ohlin, *Transfer Difficulties, Real and Imagined*.

3. A distinction is sometimes made between "hard" and "soft" loans when referring to short-dated loans with high interest rates and long-dated loans with relatively low interest rates respectively.

4. Contractor finance arrangements have been a major source of substantial fixed investment in high income residential buildings particularly in the low density residential areas in the Federal territory of Lagos. The social and economic effects of these arrangements including the implications for distribution of income and power, national allocation of scarce resources and balance of external payments warrant a separate study based on intensive research.

5. A "flat" rate of 5 per cent per annum of £100 loan repayable by equal annuities in 5 years means that £5 interest is payable annually even in the last year of the loan when only £20 is outstanding unlike the conventional interest rate payable on reducing balance basis. One of the formulae for converting "flat" rate of interest to normal interest payable on reducing balance is given by the rate of interest multiplied by the years of the loan multiplied by 24 divided by the number of installments plus i, e.g. 6 per cent flat for four years payable at 48 monthly installments is thus equivalent to 11.755 per cent normal interest by the reducing balance method.

6. It is theoretically possible to envisage a situation where additional development finance is provided within a plan period through a sort of revolving credit from many short-term credit facilities and refinancing operations. But each credit is not only tied to purchases for a project but entails additional debt servicing obligations. The additional development capital is thus transient.

7. The Berne Convention (Union Assureurs des Credits Internationaux) was established in 1934 by organisations directly and indirectly involved in the provision of credit insurance covers for exports. The Union is based on a number of written statutes including, *inter alia,*

  (a) Members undertake to place at the disposal of the Union all their policy forms and essential documents regarding their methods; and

  (b) they agree on their honour not to conceal any fact nor to put forward any item of information likely to mislead other members.

These provide the basis for regular consultations and exchange of information with a view to reaching common understandings on credit insurance practice and technique. One such understanding is that five years' post-delivery credit should be the maximum period for which supplier credit insurance can be extended. Although official institutions can on their government's instruction extend cover beyond this period to say, ten years and credits can be extended without cover or at a penal rate beyond five years, this understanding has been a major restraint on supplier credit competition.

8. cf. the presentation at page 20 *et seq.* of *Nigeria National Development Plan Progress Report 1964* published by the Federal Ministry of Economic Development, Lagos:

"This method of financing industrial development has severe limitations:

  (i) the foreign investor has no substantial stake in the success of the enterprise he is to manage thereby violating the fundamental canon of sound private investment that the investor should bear the full risks and consequences of his judgment or miscalculation and entrepreneurship;

  (ii) the foreign investor or group of investors usually undertakes the feasibility study of the project, provides the technical management of the new company, acts as consultants to the company, purchases the machines and equipment from sources within the group on the advice of members of the group, provides the suppliers' credit to be guaranteed by the Nigerian Government thereby creating a vicious circle which with the best intentions cannot produce satisfactory results;

  (iii) the industries established under high protective tariff walls, will tend to become high cost, if not inefficient, units giving the vicious circle in (ii);

  (iv) an unduly high proportion of Nigerian resources would be devoted to promoting such high cost industries to the detriment of the future growth of the Nigerian economy;

  (v) where the project fails, the foreign investor can fall back on the Nigerian Government guarantee and take the next available plane back to his country before looking for his next victim, another developing country anxious to industrialise very quickly.

9. Many developing countries have suffered irreparable damages in the hands of private "turnkey" companies formed with a nominal capital of £100 to undertake a £5 million project particularly when the Agreements allow for the importation of second-hand capital equipment. Nigeria has had very limited experience in this field so far.

10. Liberia contracted short-term credits so indiscriminately that in 1963, public debt service charges were almost equal to estimated total government revenue for the year. Liberia had to renegotiate and reschedule her obligations to her creditors. The new Mid-West Region appears to be following the Liberian example and the Federation of Nigeria might be fortunate to learn at first hand the serious limitations involved from the relatively small-scale operations in its smallest region.

11. The *London Financial Times* of April 20, 1965 in a commentary entitled "Ghana's Day of Reckoning," assessed the Ghanaian experience in the development process of the African continent as:
"It is a measure of Ghana's lead over the other newly independent countries of Africa that she has got to the point where her ability to finance new economic development is impaired by the servicing of the debt on existing development. Argentina and Brazil have been facing a similar problem and their Western creditors have had little alternative but to argue on a funding operation to postpone debt repayments."

12. cf. the apparent overstatement in "Nigeria's Oil Revolution," a leader in *West Africa* No. 2497, of April 10, 1965:
"Oil is now Nigeria's main foreign exchange earner. Even a conservative estimate puts the amount of its earnings at £100 million by 1967," and quoting with approval from the Rededication Budget Speech 1965 by the Federal Minister of Finance, "By 1967, Nigeria's balance of payments will be 'transformed almost overnight.'" In addition the Nigerian Oil Refinery will save foreign exchange costs of £15-20 million a year. If one adds the remarkable growth in industry and the consequent saving and sometimes earning of foreign exchange, one can see that Nigeria is in sight of escape from that persistent problem of the world's poorer countries, a balance of payments deficit." There are no published data on the projected net foreign exchange position of the Nigerian Oil Industry by 1967/68.

13. See D. Avramovic and R. Gulhati, *Debt Servicing Problems of Low Income Countries 1956-58*, p. 11 and chapter 4.

14. Debt service ratios should really be regarded as a range of about 10 per cent-30 per cent as countries whose external debt service charges exceed 30 per cent of their current export earnings inevitably suffer from liquidity crisis. See "Economic Growth and External Debt—An Analytic Framework" presented to the U.N. Conference on Trade and Development 1964 by IBRD staff as E/CONF 46/84 and *Economic Growth and External Debt*, chapter 4 by D. Avramovic and Associate by Johns Hopkins Press.

16. *Nigerian Entrepreneurship in Industry*

JOHN R. HARRIS

The participation of Nigerian entrepreneurs in the economic development of their country has been striking in comparison with the experience of most other African countries. Internal trade, importing, road transport, non-financial services, building and construction, commercial agriculture, and industry have been areas of active growing entrepreneurial effort by Nigerians in recent years. It is true that the vast majority of large scale enterprises have been in the hands of expatriates or government agencies, yet the many small and medium scale Nigerian firms have played an important part in the structural transformation of the economy.

All of the field work on which this paper is based was carried out during 1965; hence, no indication can be given of the possible repercussions of the military coups of January and July 1966 and the ensuing civil war.[1] Detailed interviews were conducted with some 250 wholly Nigerian private firms and 19 joint ventures in which Nigerian private interests were dominant.[2] On the basis of (1) a high proportion of Nigerian owned firms; (2) dispersal of the industry in more than one geographical region; and (3) a range of firm sizes; sawmilling, furniture, printing, rubber processing, and garment making were the industries selected for intensive study. Baking and shoe manufacture also met these criteria but were excluded outside of Lagos since they had recently been the subject of comprehensive industry studies.[3] Several other industries comprised of only a very few firms such as beverages, lime making, bone crushing, pipeline welding, gramophone record pressing, brick making, sign making, metal working, electrical equipment, transport equipment, perfume blending, and tanning were also included. We are confident that this sample included more than 80 per cent of the Nigerian owned firms with over 20 employees and about 25 per cent of those with more than 10 but less than 20 employees in each of these industries selected for study.[4] The individual who was primarily responsible for the founding of the firm or, in a few cases, the present principal owner (in the cases of inherited or purchased firms) was interviewed.

Tables 1 through 3 show the distribution of the 269 firms according to various characteristics. These tables are self explanatory and will be useful for reference throughout the rest of this paper.

TABLE 1. *Distribution of Firms by Industry.*

Industry	Number of Firms
Sawmilling	65
Furniture	34
Rubber Processing	10
Printing	48
Garment Making	30
Baking	38
Other Industries	44
Total	269

TABLE 2. *Distribution of Firms by Number of Employees.*

Number of Employees	Number of Firms
Less than 20	123
21- 30	46
31- 50	38
51-100	37
101-500	22
Total	266*

* This information was not available for 3 of the firms.

TABLE 3. *Distribution of Firms by Geographical Region.*

Geographical Region	Number of Firms
Greater Lagos*	168
Western Region	35
Mid-West Region	16
Eastern Region	39
Northern Region	11
Total	269

* This includes the areas of Mushin and Ikeja which were formally included in the Western Region in 1965. All other regions denote the political organization of Nigeria in 1965.

Space does not permit a detailed exposition of the theoretical framework underlying the rest of this paper. It will have to suffice to say that I think in terms of a modified supply and demand analysis in which potential opportunities provide the demand for entrepreneurial services while various social, psychological, and political factors along with education, training, experience, and access to conventional factors of production affect the supply (or responsiveness) of entrepreneurial services. The latter factors listed under supply explicitly affect the demand side as well. This framework allows one to examine the many aspects of entrepreneurship without resorting to a "single factor" psychological, social, political, or economic approach to the problem. All such factors are important and we can try to identify their interactions.[5]

I. ENTREPRENEURIAL MOBILITY

First let us examine the geographical, occupational and social mobility of Nigerian entrepreneurs. If entrepreneurship were found only in some few minority groups within the society, one would expect considerable geographical mobility; potential entrepreneurs would move from their homeland in search of opportunities. Table 4 shows a cross classification between the region in which the business is located and the entrepreneurs' region of birth.

TABLE 4. *Cross-Classification of Entrepreneur's Region of Birth and Region in which Business is Located.*

REGION OF BIRTH	Greater Lagos	Western	Mid-West	Eastern	Northern	TOTAL
Greater Lagos	34	0	0	0	0	34
Western	92	35	0	1	2	130
Mid-West	12	0	16	0	0	28
Eastern	22	0	0	38	2	62
Northern	3	0	0	0	7	10
TOTAL	163*	35	16	39	11	264

* Region of birth could not be ascertained for 5 of the entrepreneurs in Lagos.

Aside from movement into Lagos, the Federal Capital and largest commercial center, the lack of geographical mobility is indeed quite striking. Interregional mobility is practically nil. Only five of the entrepreneurs in the various regions were operating businesses outside of their region of birth. Further analysis has shown that inter-provincial mobility within the regions is surprisingly limited—only natives of Ijebu province in the Western Region and natives of Onitsha and Owerri provinces in the Eastern Region have migrated in any appreciable proportion. Within the Western Region only Ibadan, the commercial center and capital, draws a significant proportion of migrants as is the case with Port Harcourt, the principal industrial center of the Eastern Region. Some 77 per cent (126) of the Lagos industrialists were born in Lagos or the immediately adjacent provinces of the Western Region, Ijebu and Abeokuta.

There are several possible reasons for this lack of mobility. If entrepreneurial resources are widespread, it is to be expected that opportunities will be exploited by entrepreneurs already living in the area since they are in the best position to become aware of the possibilities. Hostility of residents to "outsiders" may also be a deterrent to the migration of potential entrepreneurs, yet geographical mobility in other entrepreneural activities such as trade and transport has been much more important than in industry.[6] This is explicable both in terms of greater security for a fixed investment in one's home area, and of the dependence of industrialists on personal contacts in the procuring of materials and marketing of goods in a country in which many markets are still relatively rudimentary. These constraints tend to be less binding in Lagos, with its system of land registration and the important role of the Federal Government as a major purchaser of goods.

Another indication of potential entrepreneurial responsiveness is the willingness of individuals to move from one occupation to another. Table 5 reveals considerable intergenerational and individual occupation mo-

TABLE 5. *Occupational Background of Entrepreneurs, Their Fathers, and Grandfathers.*

OCCUPATION	Grandfather's Occupation	%	Father's Occupation	%	Own First Occupation	%	Own Previous Occupation	%
Subsistence Farmer	92	44.0	66	25.1	7	2.6	0	0
Cash-Crop Farmer	39	18.7	51	19.4	3	1.1	1	0.4
Small Scale Trader	9	4.3	11	4.2	16	6.0	10	3.7
Large Scale Trader	24	11.5	46	17.5	3	1.1	37	13.9
Employed Artisan	1	0.5	10	3.8	74	27.8	31	11.6
Self-employed Artisan, Contractor or Transporter	12	5.7	44	17.0	46	18.5	116	45.5
Clerical	0	0	4	1.5	59	22.2	19	7.1
Teacher	0	0	2	0.8	32	12.0	6	2.2
Gov't. Svc.	2	1.0	14	5.4	17	6.4	30	11.5
Professional	4	1.9	5	1.9	6	2.3	10	3.7
Traditional High Rank	26	12.4	9	3.4	0	0	1	0.4
TOTAL	209	100.	262*	100.	263*	100.	261*	100.

* Totals of less than 269 result from non-responses.

bility. Coming from a group of grandfathers who were preponderantly farmers or chiefs, and fathers who were farmers, craftsmen, or traders, these men started their economic lives as craftsmen, clerks, small-scale traders, teachers, and government servants, and were primarily self-employed as craftsmen, contractors, transporters, and large-scale traders immediately prior to founding their industrial enterprises. It is particularly significant to note the movement of these individuals from "modern" occupations such as clerical work and teaching into self-employment. When compared with the general occupational structure of Nigeria it becomes clear that agriculture (with approximately 78 per cent of the labor force in 1952)[7] has been less "productive" of industrial entre-preneurship in Nigeria than have been trade and craft activities.

Closely related to occupational mobility, but not the same, is status mobility. A rough index of status was constructed based on occupation, income, and positions of leadership within society.[8] Table 6 gives a cross classification of the entrepreneur's status with that of his father.

TABLE 6. *Cross-Classification of Entrepreneur's Status and That of His Father.*

STATUS OF ENTREPRENEUR	STATUS OF FATHER					
	Highest	Upper	Middle	Lower	Lowest	Total
Highest	13	9	8	6	0	36
Upper	8	12	6	21	2	49
Middle	3	7	36	35	11	92
Lower	1	5	17	26	24	73
Lowest	0	0	0	1	3	4
TOTAL	25	33	67	89	40	254*

* It was impossible to obtain rankings for father's status in 15 cases.

There is a significant positive relationship between the father's and the entrepreneur's status (Goodman-Krushkal's Gamma has a value of .493 which is significant at the $p < .001$ level), indicating that entrepreneurs with high status ranking tended to come from fathers with relatively high status.[9] Nevertheless, entrepreneurial activity has been an avenue of up-ward status mobility for many entrepreneurs. An examination of Table 6 shows that 122 observations lie above the principal diagonal, indicating that the entrepreneur is now of a higher status than his father, while only 42 observations lie below the diagonal. It is quite clear that entrepreneurial activity is a means of moving one or two "notches up the ladder" which is consistent with mobility patterns observed in western countries. Furthermore, this scale tends to underestimate the degree of upward mobility because many of the individuals now of lower status than their father are young men whose businesses are still expanding—hence it is to be expected that their wealth and leadership position will increase as they get older.

In summary, Nigerian entrepreneurs in industry have been geographically immobile but highly mobile in terms of occupation and status. Given the explanations preferred for the lack of geographical mobility, the evidence is not consistent with the existence of a "traditional society" of the sort described by Hagen[10] for Nigeria as a whole.

II. CULTURAL AND ETHNIC VARIATIONS

A great deal of interest has been aroused in recent years by theories which relate entrepreneurial response and performance to psychological or social variables.[11] Space precludes detailed examination of these theories here, but the important point to be drawn from them is that entrepreneurial response should vary systematically among ethnic or cultural groups according to their social structure and child rearing patterns.

On the basis of recent work by LeVine[12] and examination of ethnological studies of groups not covered by this study, we would predict the following order of responsiveness (ranged from high to low) of the major ethnic groups of Nigeria: Ibo, Ibibio, Yoruba, Edo, and Hausa.[13] Let us examine these theories in terms of our sample.

In Table 7 the relative proportions of entrepreneurs from each ethnic group are compared with the distribution of ethnic groups within the entire Nigerian population. The table indicates that the Edo, Yoruba,

TABLE 7. *Distribution of Entrepreneurs by Ethnic Grouping Compared with That of the Nigerian Population.*

ETHNIC GROUP	(1) Per Cent of Entrepreneurs	(2) Per Cent of Nigerian Population (1952-53 Census)	(3) Index of Representation (1)/(2)
Ibo	21.6	17.9	1.2
Ibibio, Efik, and Ijaw	1.9	2.5	.8
Yoruba	63.5	16.6	3.8
Edo	9.3	1.5	6.2
Hausa-Fulani	2.6	18.2	.2
Other ethnic groups	1.1	43.3	.03
TOTAL	100.0	100.0	

and Ibo groups are over-represented in our sample, while Ibibio, Efik, and Ijaw, Hausa-Fulani, and other groups are under-represented. The order of representation is: Edo, Yoruba, Ibo, Ibibio, Efik, Ijaw, Hausa-Fulani, and other groups. Although this ranking is inconsistent with the prediction based on psychological and sociological theories, one must be very cautious in giving any weight to this "test." First of all, the census is out of date and of questionable reliability, though it is unlikely that errors in the census would change these findings. The sampling procedure, however, does not allow much confidence in these estimates. The investigation was restricted to a limited number of industries in major urban areas, therefore this is not a representative sample of *all* Nigerian industry. Even if it were, it would not provide a significant test of the hypothesis. Industry represents a very small portion of the economy, and geographical differences are confounded with ethnic groups (note that the Edo are concentrated entirely in rubber processing and sawmilling—the Mid-West being the principal area of high forest and rubber cultivation). Therefore, one cannot claim that participation in industry is an appropriate test for entrepreneurial responsiveness. Trade, transport, and services are all quantitatively more important outlets for entrepreneurial energy.

Rather than mere participation, qualitative differences between entrepreneurial performance of different ethnic groups might shed more light on the hypothesis under question. Table 8 presents a cross-classification between ethnic grouping and size of firm (measured by number of employees). Although there is clearly some tendency for the Ibibio, Edo, and Ibo entrepreneurs to have larger firms than the Yoruba or Hausa, the relationship is not statistically significant (after further grouping, a chi-square test was not significant at the .10 level).

One of the obvious difficulties that arises in evaluating Table 8 is whether or not size of firm is an appropriate measure of entrepreneurial performance. A measure of firm growth and/or profitability might be better. A rough index of success based on the rate of growth of assets and profitability was constructed which gives a reasonably accurate and useful ordering of the firms with regard to these variables.[14] (Sixteen of the firms could not be evaluated because they were too new or major reorganizations had recently been made.) Table 9 shows the distribution of entrepreneurs by success and ethnic group.

Table 9 reveals that Ibo and Ibibio entrepreneurs tend to be relatively more successful than Yorubas and Edos. Hausas perform about the same as the average of all groups, but the small number makes this difficult to interpret. Application of a chi-square test for association reveals that the relationship in Table 9 is even weaker than that in Table 8. Other measures of differential entrepreneurial performance include innovation,

Table 8. *Ethnic Group of Entrepreneur and Number of Employees in Firm.*

Ethnic Group	Less than 20		21-30		31-50		51-100		More than 100		Total	
	%	No.	%	No.	%	No.	%	No.	%	No.	%	No.
Ibo	39.7	23	13.8	8	13.8	8	20.7	12	12.1	7	100	58
Ibibio, Efik, and Ijaw	20.0	1	20.0	1	20.0	1	20.0	1	20.0	1	100	5
Yoruba	52.4	88	18.5	31	13.1	22	10.1	17	6.0	10	100	168
Edo	29.1	7	8.3	2	25.0	6	25.0	6	12.5	3	100	24
Hausa	14.3	1	57.1	4	14.3	1	0.0	0	14.3	1	100	7
Other	66.6	2	0.0	0	0.0	0	33.3	1	0.0	0	100	3
Column Total as % of Grand Total	46.1		17.4		14.3		14.0		8.3		100*	
TOTAL		122		46		38		37		22		265

* Percentage totals differ from 100.0 on account of rounding.

Table 9. *Ethnic Group of Entrepreneur and Success of the Firm Index of Success.*

Ethnic Group	Very Successful		Successful		Average		Marginal		Unsuccessful		Total	
	%	No.	%	No.	%	No.	%	No.	%	No.	%	No.
Ibo	22.6	12	41.5	22	24.5	13	5.7	3	5.7	3	100	53
Ibibio, Efik, and Ijaw	20.0	1	60.0	3	0.0	0	20.0	1	0.0	0	100	5
Yoruba	14.1	23	35.0	57	25.8	42	20.2	33	4.9	8	100	163
Edo	14.3	3	33.3	7	9.5	2	38.1	8	4.8	1	100	21
Hausa	20.0	1	60.0	3	0.0	0	20.0	1	0.0	0	100	5
Other		0		0		2		1		0		3
TOTAL	16.0	40	36.8	92	23.6	59	18.8	47	4.8	12	100	250

306

changes made within the firm since founding, and plans for future expansion. On each of these measures Ibibio, Ibos and Hausas ranked higher than the other groups. The most highly significant relationship is that for innovation as shown in Table 10. While only 18 per cent of all entrepreneurs had innovated, 71 per cent of Hausas, 60 per cent of Ibibios, and 29 per cent of Ibos had done so.

TABLE 10. *Ethnic Group of Entrepreneur and Degree of Innovation.*

ETHNIC GROUP	Innovated		Did Not Innovate		TOTAL	
	%	No.	%	No.	%	No.
Ibo	29.3	17	70.7	41	100	58
Ibibio, Efik, and Ijaw	60.0	3	40.0	2	100	5
Yoruba	12.1	20	87.9	145	100	165
Edo	8.3	2	91.7	22	100	24
Hausa	71.4	5	28.6	2	100	7
Other	33.3	1	66.7	2	100	3
TOTAL	18.3	48	81.7	214	100	262

Chi-square = 29.968, 5 d.f., p < .001.

However, both size of firm and the index of success may well be correlated with the particular industry and access to credit, both of which may be importantly influenced by the economic structure of the particular region. Given the relative geographical immobility of these entrepreneurs, a better test of the hypothesis that entrepreneurial performance differs among ethnic groups would be an examination of the ethnic distribution of entrepreneurs by size of firm and success in Lagos only. Tables 11 and 12 show these data.

Both tables show a tendency for a greater proportion of Ibos to have large and successful businesses than is the case for Yorubas, but the relationship is even less strong than it was for the entire sample. Further tests were performed in which the particular industry was controlled and in which both region and particular industry were controlled. In each case, the relationship was in the same direction: Ibos and Ibibios higher than Yorubas and Edos, with Hausas occupying an intermediate position. However, the effect of controlling for additional variables was always to further weaken the relationship.

In summary, on the basis of social structure and psychological testing we were led to predict the following ordering of entrepreneurial performance by ethnic grouping: Ibo, Ibibio, Yoruba, Edo, and Hausa. Our data do not contradict this prediction but neither do they lend strong

TABLE 11. *Ethnic Group of Entrepreneur and Number of Employees in Firm (Lagos Only).*

| | Number of Employees | | | | | | | | | | | |
| | Less than 20 | | 21-30 | | 31-50 | | 51-100 | | More than 100 | | TOTAL | |
	%	No.	%	No.	%	No.	%	No.	%	No.	%	No.
Ibo	60.8	14	8.7	2	8.7	2	17.4	4	4.3	1	100	23
Yoruba	58.8	74	15.6	20	11.7	15	9.4	12	5.5	7	100	128
Bini	37.5	3	25.0	2	25.0	2	12.5	1	0.0	0	100	8
All others*	60.0	3	20.0	1	0.0	0	20.0	1	0.0	0	100	5*
TOTAL	57.3	94	15.2	25	11.6	19	11.0	18	4.9	8	100	164

* "All others" consists of 2 Ibibio-Efik and 3 "others."

TABLE 12. *Ethnic Group of Entrepreneur and Success of the Firm (Lagos Only).*

| ETHNIC GROUP | Index of Success | | | | | | | | | | | |
| | Very Successful | | Successful | | Average | | Marginal | | Unsuccessful | | TOTAL | |
	%	No.	%	No.	%	No.	%	No.	%	No.	%	No.
Ibo	23.8	5	28.6	6	33.3	7	14.3	3	0.0	0	100	21
Yoruba	16.0	20	36.0	45	23.2	29	20.0	25	4.8	6	100	125
Bini	12.5	1	25.0	2	25.0	2	37.5	3	0.0	0	100	8
All others*	20.0	1	40.0	2	20.0	1	20.0	1	0.0	0	100	5
TOTAL	17.0	27	34.6	55	24.5	39	20.1	32	3.8	6	100	159*

* Five Lagos entrepreneurs could not be rated on the success scale because of recent changes in the firm.

support to it. An alternative hypothesis that the differences in economic structure of the regions, exposure to western education, and "modern" occupational experience are responsible for the observed ethnic differences cannot be rejected.

III. EDUCATION, OCCUPATIONAL EXPERIENCE, AND TECHNICAL INFORMATION

Perception of opportunities, gaining command over resources, and managing the ongoing enterprise are primary functions of entrepreneurship. Regardless of the individual's willingness to undertake entrepreneurial activities, these desires will not be realized if the necessary capacity to carry them out is lacking. Education, occupational experience, and access to technical information should each play a crucial role.

Table 13 shows the distribution of this sample of entrepreneurs by level of formal education.

TABLE 13. *Education of Entrepreneurs.*

HIGHEST LEVEL OF FORMAL EDUCATION	*No. of responses*	%
None	34	12.7
Less than 6 years	36	13.5
6 years	93	34.7
Some secondary schooling	64	23.9
Secondary school certificate	22	8.2
Some post-secondary schooling	7	2.6
University degree	5	1.9
Post-graduate training	7	2.6
TOTAL	268	100.1

It must first be remarked that the level of schooling of entrepreneurs in our sample is high by Nigerian standards. According to the 1952-53 Census, only 5.8 per cent of the population over 7 years of age had completed more than four years of schooling. This percentage ranged from 0.9 per cent in the Northern Region to 10.6 per cent in the Eastern Region and 33.7 per cent in Lagos, the Federal capital. Although there has been great expansion of education since 1952[15] the census figures give a reasonable picture of educational levels of these entrepreneurs' cohorts since all were over 7 years of age in 1952. By contrast, 73.8 per cent of this sample had 6 or more years of formal schooling.

Education is seen to be positively but weakly correlated with size of firm (Gamma = .161), strongly correlated with innovation (Gamma = .454), and with plans for expansion (Gamma = .342). However, the relationship between formal education and size of firm is insignificant for the Lagos sample (Gamma = .07)—there is no ready explanation.

With respect to the index of success, there is a nearly significant positive correlation (Gamma = .154). Controlling for industry, education and success are positively correlated in sawmilling, furniture, printing, and garment making; essentially uncorrelated in baking and other industries; and *negatively* correlated in rubber processing.

The relationship between formal education and entrepreneurial performance is much weaker than had been expected. There are at least three possible explanations. First, those entrepreneurs with less formal education are more likely to have had longer periods of apprenticeship and on-job training than those with more education. Secondly, there may well be a compensatory mechanism at work. Two of the most successful entrepreneurs had left government service because their limited educations precluded promotion to higher posts and they felt determined to show that they could succeed in spite of this handicap. One of the entrepreneurs with no formal education taught himself to read after he had started his own tailoring business and later travelled to England to take a course in cutting—he is perhaps the best record keeper of the whole group! Finally, size of the firm may not be the appropriate test of the effect of education. Kilby found a similar lack of relationship between formal education and success in the Nigerian baking industry.[16] He attributed this to the fact that more educated entrepreneurs are likely to undertake several businesses. If this is the case total employees in all enterprises controlled by the entrepreneur is the relevant variable. The correlation between this variable and education is considerably higher (Gamma = .402).

Other recent studies of entrepreneurship have identified two types of industrial entrepreneurs—the trader-entrepreneur and the craftsman-entrepreneur.[17] Generally speaking, the craftsman-entrepreneur has emerged earlier in the process of industrialization, but has remained primarily a traditional artisan. The larger and more rapidly expanding enterprises have been founded by former traders. This is usually explained in terms of the traders' greater familiarity with the market and his general commercial and managerial experience.[18] Table 14 classifies the entrepreneurs by number of employees and previous occupation prior to founding the industrial enterprise.

It can be seen that these entrepreneurs came from a wide variety of backgrounds. The self-employed category demands some explanation—it includes both craftsmen who were working on their own (these dominate

TABLE 14. *Classification of Entrepreneurs by Number of Employees and Previous Occupation.*

Previous Occupation	Number of Employees											Total	
	Less than 20		21-30		31-50		51-100		More than 100				
	%	No.	%	No.	%	No.	%	No.	%	No.		%	No.
Farmer			100.0	1									100	1
Trader	36.2	17	25.5	12	12.8	6	8.5	4	17.0	8		100	47
Employed Craftsman	48.6	17	17.1	6	22.9	8	8.6	3	2.9	1		100	35
Clerical, Teaching and Professional	40.0	16	17.5	7	17.5	7	15.0	6	10.0	4		100	40
Self-Employed	56.0	56	15.0	15	9.0	9	18.0	18	2.0	2		100	100
Government	42.0	13	16.1	5	16.1	5	12.9	4	12.9	4		100	31
TOTAL	46.8	119	18.1	46	13.8	35	13.8	35	7.5	19		100	254

in the smaller firms) as well as contractors and transporters. Although a greater proportion of former traders are found in the largest size firms, individuals coming from governmental and professional backgrounds also tend to have larger than average firms.

According to permormance on the index of success, traders have done better than average, but there is no strong relationship between previous occupation and success. In a country such as Nigeria, highly skilled workers and supervisors are difficult to find; the man with experience in the shop tends to have an advantage. By and large, the former traders had considerable difficulties in the management of production, quality control, and equipment maintenance. The technical experience of the former craftsmen, and their tendency to concentrate on a single business, has compensated for their relative lack of commercial acumen. The importance of specific occupational experience differs between industries. Timber contractors have founded the largest sawmills; traders in rubber have gone into rubber processing; former craftsmen have predominated in furniture and printing; the miscellaneous industries (which have tended to be more innovative) have drawn entrepreneurs from government, professions, clerical work and trade.

Access to technical information has been rather haphazard. The most important source is one's own training and experience, followed by suppliers and repairmen, observing other firms, hiring experienced Nigerians, hiring expatriates, and making trips abroad. New ideas, when shown to be profitable, spread quickly through informal channels of communication.

Levels of technical competence in Nigeria are very low. Technical training has lagged far behind literary training in the schools and most apprenticeships are served under traditional craftsmen operating with hand methods and producing a low quality product. Only recently has engineering training been offered in the Nigerian universities and the need for sub-professional technicians is still largely unmet.[19] Industries into which Nigerian entrepreneurs have entered are relatively simple technologically. Indeed, the lack of technical training and experience effectively bars the entry of Nigerians into lines which require more advanced technical skills. Although some Nigerian entrepreneurs have overcome this problem to some extent by the hiring of expatriate personnel, this has not been uniformly successful.

Education, occupational experience, and access to technical information are each important in enabling an individual to perceive that a potentially profitable opportunity exists. Whether or not the perceived opportunity is actually exploited depends on the motivation of the individual and his ability to marshal the necessary resources.

IV. PROFITABILITY, ACCESS TO CAPITAL, AND
MANAGEMENT

Standard economic reasoning assumes that the principal motivation to entrepreneurial behavior is the quest for profit. Other writing has stressed drives for power, recognition, and immortality through founding a dynasty as motivating factors. In either case pecuniary gain becomes important since it is instrumental for achieving any of the latter goals.

The vast majority of these Nigerian entrepreneurs stated pecuniary reasons for undertaking entrepreneurial activity. In some cases industry exerted a pull by offering higher potential earnings than they had previously achieved. In other cases there were "push" effects, particularly in periods of depressed trading profits.

Indeed, these entrepreneurs have been quite successful by Nigerian standards of earnings. Half were earning more than £50 per month from the industrial enterprise and two-thirds of them earned more than this from all of their combined businesses. Keeping in mind that average wages paid by these entrepreneurs is under £7 per month and only 31 of them paid *any* employee over £40 per month, it is clear that they have done well by themselves.

Total personal assets of these entrepreneurs ranged from £1000 to over £1,000,000 with the median being near £15,000. One cannot help but be impressed with the general drive for wealth in Nigeria; wealth and status being virtually synonymous at least in the Southern regions.[20]

Much has been made in the literature of "traders mentality" deterring investment in industry because of an irrational desire for high liquidity. Although there may be some truth in the statement, it appears that the two principal deterrents to industrial undertakings are the greater technical and managerial requirements and slightly lower average profits than in trade or transport. After making allowances for implicit payments to owned factors, the return to investment in industry ranges from substantial losses up to 50 per cent per annum. The median return in the sample is between 8 and 12 per cent.[21] This is slightly higher than the average net return to investment in urban rental dwelling units which is between 5 and 10 per cent. It was impossible to obtain reliable data for returns in trade and transport although industrialists who were also engaged in these activities suggested that returns from industry are slightly lower on average but fluctuate less. It is significant to note that real estate was usually explained to be a secure investment which would provide an "annuity" if the individual were to become sick and unable to manage his other undertakings. Thus it would appear that Nigerians do respond to prospective profits subject to discounting for risk.[22] One does not have to resort to irrationality to explain the observed behavior.

Furthermore, it was evident that profits were substantially higher in newly introduced industries. Profitable ventures rapidly attract emulation, forcing returns down by competitive pressures. This pattern has been particularly noticeable in tire retreading, rubber processing, sawmilling, and offset printing. The most successful entrepreneurs attributed much of their success to an ability to keep "one jump ahead" of their competitors in finding new products or processes.

Out of the 269 entrepreneurs in this sample, only 48 could be considered as having innovated even under a very loose definition of innovation. Four opened up a new market for a good, two introduced the use of a new material, twelve introduced new production processes, twenty-five introduced new products, and five pioneered new business methods. All of the innovations represented adaptation of products or processes to Nigeria which were already in use in industrialized countries. Examples are: introduction of tire retreading; starting the manufacture of rubber and plastic foam; being the first to start processing a raw material which was being exported; or being the first to manufacture gramophone records in the country.

The relative lack of innovation does not mean that these businesses have been stagnant. Only 43 firms reported having made no changes since establishment and the majority of those were less than two years old. One hundred six of the firms had made major changes such as installing new and improved machinery or introducing new product lines, while another one hundred fifteen had expanded the scale of operations. This kind of rapid response to changing opportunities is also an important characteristic of Nigerian traders. Katzin has remarked, "Whatever the final judgment may be of Africans as innovating entrepreneurs, there can be no doubt of their proficiency as imitating entrepreneurs. . . . The search for new ways of earning a profit is unremitting."[23] The returns to innovation are sometimes high but usually short lived; the demonstration that a line of activity can be profitable considerably reduces the subjective risk to potential imitators.

Gaining access to capital is a major hurdle in starting any business. Table 15 shows that initial assets in these firms ranged from below £1000 (several started with less than £50) to upwards of £100,000. The median value is less than £1000. While not inconsiderable by Nigerian standards, the initial capital requirements in these industries are still quite modest. The median value of present assets of these firms is close to £10,000. It is obvious that the majority of the firms have experienced substantial growth of assets since founding.

Self-finance is of overwhelming importance in Nigerian industry.

Strengthening this argument is the observation that 76 per cent of the respondents indicated that their own savings was the single most important source of initial capital; 61 per cent of those respondents who had expanded their businesses relied on reinvested profits as the single most important source of funds for the expansion.[24]

Credit, however, has been more available than is usually believed to be the case. Loans from banks, government, and suppliers (in the form of hire-purchase agreements) have played a part in the financing of 76 per cent of these Nigerian industries. Table 16 shows the length of term for which loans have been made.

TABLE 15. *Assets of Nigerian Industrial Firms.*

VALUE OF ASSETS £	INITIAL ASSETS (No. of Firms)	%	PRESENT ASSETS (No. of Firms)	%
Less than 1,000	154	58.3	19	7.2
1,000-5,000	53	20.0	86	32.4
5,001-10,000	23	8.7	50	18.9
10,001-20,000	16	6.1	41	15.5
20,001-50,000	17	6.4	45	17.0
50,001-100,000	0	0.0	12	4.5
More than 100,000	1	0.4	12	4.5
TOTAL	264*	100.0	265*	100.0

* Totals less than 269 are caused by non-responses.

TABLE 16. *Type of Loans Received by Entrepreneurs.*

Term of Loan	Number of Loans	%
No loan	62	23.9
Overdraft	28	10.8
1-5 years	120	46.4
Over 5 years	49	18.9
TOTAL	259	100.0

Although a shortage of capital is frequently asserted to be a major impediment to the development of indigenous industry, and the respondents claimed inability to raise capital as their most serious problem, I am loath to accept this proposition. If capital is the principal bottleneck it will have two main effects. First, if economies of scale are important, firms without access to sufficient capital will be of less than optimal size. These firms would be less profitable than those which are able to start

TABLE 17. *Success of Firms by Amount of Initial Assets.*

	Initial Assets (£)											
	Less than 1,000		1,000-5,000		5,001-10,000		10,001-20,000		More than 20,000		TOTAL	
EVALUATION	No.	%	No.	%	No.	%	No.	%	No.	%	No.	%
Very successful	24	15.7	8	16.3	3	15.0	1	7.7	4	26.7	40	16.0
Successful	55	35.9	18	36.7	6	30.0	7	53.8	5	33.3	91	36.4
Average	38	24.8	11	22.4	6	30.0	3	23.1	2	13.3	60	24.0
Marginal	32	20.9	6	12.2	4	20.0	2	15.4	3	20.0	47	18.8
Unsuccessful	4	2.6	6	12.2	1	5.0	0	0.0	1	6.7	12	4.8
TOTAL	153	100.0	49	100.0	20	100.0	13	100.0	15	100.0	250	100.0

out on a larger scale. With profits providing the major source of capital for further expansion, the smaller firms would then tend to also have lower rates of growth. Table 17 shows that firms starting out on a small scale did just about as well in terms of profitability and growth as those firms starting out with greater assets. This implies that economies of scale are unimportant in the industries *contained in this sample*.

Secondly, if there are no economies of scale, or if all firms are of optimal size, capital shortage would be reflected by a high rate of return to existing capital and we would expect to observe intensive utilization of this stock. Table 18 indicates that the existing capital stock is worked at revatively low intensity. Our measure of utilization is per cent of effective 3 shift operation and while it is an inadequate and unsatisfactory measure, the conclusion is inescapable that considerably more output could be produced without increasing investment in additional fixed equipment. This reflects both a lack of cooperating factors and the rapid response of potential entrepreneurs to profitable opportunities.

TABLE 18.   *Per cent of Capacity (based on 3 shift operation) Utilized.*

% Capacity Utilized	No. of Firms	%
Less than 5	8	3.1
6-10	7	2.7
11-25	103	39.6
26-50	98	37.7
51-75	21	8.1
More than 75	23	8.8
TOTAL	260	100.0

These two findings (lack of relation between initial assets and success, and the existence of considerable excess capacity) give some substance, although certainly not conclusive proof, to the assertion that capital shortage is not a principal barrier to development of industry *of the type represented in this sample*. It has been possible to start with relatively limited capital and expand through reinvestment; this has been the pattern of growth of most of the successful firms in this study.[25]

Perceiving an opportunity and gaining command over the resources to establish a firm are not the sole functions of entrepreneurship. Management of the ongoing concern is an equally important entrepreneurial function and it is this skill which appears to be most lacking in Nigeria.

Generally, the level of efficiency within the firms was very low. Substantial increases in output could be achieved without additional investment. This has previously been shown by the author in a paper on the

Nigerian sawmilling industry, and by Kilby in two studies of Nigerian industry.[26] Closer supervision, better organization, improved layout, and quality control are desperately needed on the production side. The low levels of capacity utilization shown in Table 18 are largely a result of management deficiencies.

Most of the firms were one-man operations. When the business expands beyond the point that the owner can personally control everything serious problems are encountered. Admittedly, it is difficult to find capable subordinates and managers in Nigeria, but little has been done by these entrepreneurs to train and develop such personnel. Many have now sent sons overseas for training in engineering, accounting, or business management which suggests that the problem will ease over time. In the meantime some have hired expatriate managers but the experience has been largely unhappy. Recruitment of capable and trustworthy expatriates is difficult and the ability to delegate authority to such personnel while still keeping adequate control is generally lacking. This inability to delegate authority successfully is attributable primarily to a lack of experience in large scale organizations.

A factor that has been frequently claimed to be a serious impediment to the development of successful Nigerian management is the widespread dispersal of effort over several businesses.[27] It has not been uncommon to find entrepreneurs trying to juggle three or four firms with inadequate management control over any one of them. This may represent an attempt to pool risk through diversification, or it may be that limited markets prevent the further expansion of any one of the businesses. One hundred thirty three of our entrepreneurs had interests in additional businesses, but most of them were in related fields. For instance, sawmillers engaged in timber contracting; rubber processors were involved in the rubber trade; furniture makers were also building contractors; and garment manufacturers were large wholesalers of garments. Only 52 of these entrepreneurs indicated that less than 50% of their working time was devoted to the industrial enterprise. Dispersal of effort may be common, but it does not seem to be a major problem for the entrepreneurs in this sample. Industry is a full time operation for the majority, and it is a part of a rationally integrated business for most of the others.

The principal obstacle now facing these firms is finding sufficient markets at present levels of capacity and costs. Each of the major industries in this study has expanded considerably since 1955, and productive capacity has been increasing more rapidly than demand for the products at existing prices. Profits have been made even at relatively low operating levels, although they seem to have been declining. It remains puzzling that in these industries, each having several firms, prices are relatively inflexible while entry is free. The result is that profits are driven down to "normal" through new entrants and expansion of existing firms giving rise to excess capacity at constant product prices. Kilby has documented similar behavior in the baking industry with overcapacity giving rise to occasional price wars and withdrawal of capacity.[28]

It may well be that the competitiveness of these industries gives rise to such rapid response to price changes by competitors that each entrepreneur believes the demand curve facing him to be downward sloping. The situation is rather like the standard kinked demand curve analysis of oligopoly. It is unlikely that the action of one sawmiller in Lagos to reduce price would not be known by his 29 competitors by the next day and they would be forced to match his price or lose a large part of their business. Therefore, it may be quite rational for each sawmiller to view his demand as one thirtieth of market demand and the failure to cut price arises from profit maximization. When asked about price cuts entrepreneurs reply in terms of not wanting to "spoil the market" for everyone.

The point is that response is extremely rapid to industrial opportunities characterized by low levels of technology and insignificant economies of scale. For the most part these firms produce low price-low quality goods. There is potential for rapid expansion of low price-high quality goods although much of the expansion would be at the expense of existing producers. In fact the vast majority of these entrepreneurs are potentially vulnerable to competition from efficient competitors since their present operations are quite inefficient.

Technical and managerial personnel appear to be the primary bottlenecks to increasing the efficiency of existing firms although considerable improvement may be expected in the near future. Problems of machinery procurement and maintenance have declined in importance as sales and servicing facilities have improved greatly in recent years.[29] Nevertheless, 103 out of the 269 firms in this sample have well developed plans for further expansion within the next eighteen months. It remains to be seen if markets will support such expansion.

V. POLICY IMPLICATIONS

The principal findings and policy implications are as follows:

(1) Observed ethnic differences in entrepreneurial response and performance were generally consistent with the predictions of both psychological and sociological theories of entrepreneurship, but had little explanatory power. The alternative hypothesis that observed differences arise from variations in the structure of economic opportunities, occupational experience, and educational levels in each of the regions cannot be rejected.

(2) Education and previous occupational experience in trade, craft, or clerical work make some contribution to entrepreneurial success. The importance of these variables would appear to lie with their conditioning the individual's ability to perceive opportunities and to manage the on-going firm.

(3) Nigerians have responded quite promptly to profitable opportunities in industry which they have the capability to exploit. At the present time sufficient markets and the shortage of personnel with technical and managerial skills appear to be the principal obstacles to further expansion of this sector.

(4) Availability of capital has not been a serious obstacle to the expansion of industries which are technologically simple and have a fairly low investment threshold.

(5) Standards of management in Nigerian owned industries are very low. This stems primarily from a lack of experience in large scale organizations. Improvement can be expected as individuals gain technical and managerial training and experience.

It appears that in Nigeria *ability* to respond, rather than *willingness,* is the primary deterrent to the expansion of effective entrepreneurship. If this is the case, the development strategy called for is one of increasing opportunities for potential entrepreneurs, while at the same time upgrading their capacity to exploit more demanding opportunities.

Government can play a strategic role in making the perception of opportunities easier. Pilot plants, market studies, foreign aid assistance, and dissemination of technical information can each play a part. Even more important, as public and expatriate corporations undertake strategic investment programs which lead to fundamental structural changes in the economy, additional ancillary projects will be opened up for private entrepreneurs. This is in fact Hirschman's unbalanced growth proposal.[30] His point is that as imbalances develop, the investment priorities become more obvious, hence more easily perceived, and decision making becomes easier. A clear example of this process is seen around the oil industry in Port Harcourt. Nigerian owned firms making furniture, printing, clearing drilling sites, welding pipelines, and supplying specialized heavy transport equipment have all sprung up since 1960 to meet the demands of the expanding oil industry. The response has been prompt.

It has been demonstrated that Nigerians can be expected to exploit additional opportunities in industries characterized by simple technology and low investment threshholds. In the longer run, technical training, improved capital markets, and the gaining of managerial experience should considerably increase the ability of Nigerians to respond to opportunities that are now beyond their competence to exploit. These measures are likely to be far more effective than the unsuccessful credit arrangements to date.

NOTES

1. I am deeply indebted to many persons for their advice and assistance in this research. First of all, Professor Harold F. Williamson, Sr. who was my thesis advisor. Useful comments and suggestions were also received from George Dalton, Lester B. Lave, Edwin Dean, Jerome Wells, Robert Clower, Sayre P. Schatz, Peter Kilby, Everett E. Hagen, E. W. Nafziger, T. David Williams, and H. M. A. Onitiri. Mrs. Mary P. Rowe collaborated in the field research and has made useful suggestions.

   I wish also to acknowledge the generous financial support of the SSRC/ACLS Foreign Area Fellowship Program, the Nigerian Institute of Social and Economic Research, Northwestern University Council for Intersocietal Research, and the M.I.T. Department of Economics. Computing Facilities have been made available at the University of Lagos, Northwestern University, and M.I.T.

   Of course, none of the above individuals or organizations are responsible for remaining errors.

2. Mrs. Mary P. Rowe conducted all of the interviews in Lagos; all other interviews were conducted personally by the author.

3. Peter Kilby, *African Enterprise: The Nigerian Bread Industry* (Stanford University: The Hoover Institution, 1965); and Wayne E. Nafziger, "Nigerian Entrepreneurship: A Study of Indigenous Businessmen in the Footwear Industry" (unpublished Ph.D. dissertation, University of Illinois, 1967).

4. Detail concerning the sample selection and interview procedure can be found in J. R. Harris, "Industrial Entrepreneurship in Nigeria" (unpublished Ph.D. dissertation, Northwestern University, 1967), chapter 1.

5. I have expanded the theoretical framework in detail in *Ibid*, chapter 2.

6. Ibos were particularly important in trade and transport in the North. One need only note the concern, widely voiced in the press, over the disruption of the Northern economy caused by the mass exodus of Ibos following the communal bloodshed in May and October of 1966. Also Yoruba and Hausa traders have long played an important role in trade throughout West Africa. See Michael Crowder, *The Story of Nigeria* (London: Faber, 1962); James S. Coleman, *Nigeria: Background to Nationalism* (Los Angeles: University of California Press, 1960); and P. T. Bauer, *West African Trade* (Cambridge: Cambridge University Press, 1954).

7. Federation of Nigeria, *Annual Abstract of Statistics 1964* (Lagos: Federal Office of Statistics, 1965), section 2.

8. Harris, *op. cit.*, chapter 9.

9. As shown by H. L. Costner in "Criteria for Measures of Association," *American Sociological Review*, XXX, 3 (June, 1965), pp. 341-53,

Gamma can be interpreted as the proportional reduction in error of estimation made possible by the ordinal relationship. Linton Freeman, *Elementary Applied Statistics: For Students in the Behavioral Sciences* (New York: John Wiley and Sons, 1965) contains a discussion of Gamma in Chapter 8 and a table of significance for Gamma is reproduced in Appendix B.

On breaking Table 6 down by Lagos and non-Lagos, it becomes apparent that the status ranking of both entrepreneurs and their fathers is much lower for Lagos. This may reflect the different structure of Lagos society, dominated as it is by the national elite of politics, the civil service, and professions, or it could also reflect interviewer bias in the construction of the scale (crude and subjective as it is). Nevertheless, the conclusions hold: for non-Lagos respondents, Gamma has a value of .506 with 53 cases above the diagonal and 8 below; for Lagos respondents Gamma has a value of .425 with 70 cases above the diagonal and 34 below. A further explanation of the difference between the two scales is the smaller average size of the Lagos firms (median employment in Lagos firms was 15; in non-Lagos firms it was 25).

10. E. E. Hagen, *On the Theory of Social Change* (Homewood: The Dorsey Press, Inc., 1962), chapter 4.

11. The most important statements of psychological theories are *Ibid.* and D. McClelland, *The Achieving Society* (Princeton: Van Nostrand, 1961). A sociological interpretation of the same phenomena is given by J. Kunkel, "Values and Behavior in Economic Development," *Economic Development and Cultural Change*, XIII (April, 1965), pp. 257-77.

12. Robert A. Levine, *Dreams and Deeds* (Chicago: University of Chicago Press, 1966).

13. Harris, *op. cit.*

14. *Ibid.*, chapter 9.

15. F. Harbison, "From Ashby to Reconstruction: Manpower and Education in Nigeria," see chapter 20 in this volume.

16. Kilby, *op. cit., African Enterprise: The Nigerian Bread Industry.* It is interesting to compare these findings with Harbison's discussion of the need for a reorientation of education in Nigeria to meet the needs of small-scale industry and agriculture. See Harbison, *op. cit.*

17. J. J. Carroll, *The Filipino Manufacturing Entrepreneur: Agent and Product of Change* (Ithaca: Cornell University Press, 1965); A. Alexander, *Greek Industrialists* (Athens: Center of Planning and Economic Growth, 1964); and G. Papanek, "The Development of Entrepreneurship," *American Economic Review*, LII (May, 1962), pp. 46-58.

18. Charles Wilson, "The Entrepreneur in the Industrial Revolution in Britain," *Explorations in Entrepreneurial History*, VII (February,

1955), pp. 129-45. Charles Wilson argues that although entrepreneurs came from all classes and areas of Britain, the common factor was "a sense of market opportunity combined with the capacity needed to exploit it," p. 141.

19. Harbison, *op. cit.*

20. Levine, *op. cit.*; and H. Smyth and M. Smyth, *The New Nigerian Elite* (Stanford: Stanford University Press, 1960).

21. This is consistent with the findings for shoe manufacturing by Nafziger. Nafziger, *op. cit.*

22. For an excellent discussion of the risk of investment in underdeveloped countries, see Henry Aubrey, "Industrial Investment Decisions: A Comparative Analysis," *Journal of Economic History*, XV (December, 1955), pp. 335-51.

23. Margaret Katzin, "The Role of the Small Entrepreneur," in *Economic Transition in Africa*, edited by M. J. Herskovits and M. Harwitz (Evanston: Northwestern University Press, 1964).

24. "Although extended families were a frequent source of capital, they were not of great quantative significance. It appeared that extended families were a positive element for entrepreneurship, particularly among Ibos. In addition to providing capital, families sometimes provided trustworthy key personnel for the firms. Prestige accorded "successful sons" seemed to be an important source of motivation. Almost all of the successful entrepreneurs had found ways of limiting consumption demands by relatives and refused to hire relatives who did not perform well on the job." See Harris, *op. cit.*, chapter 9 for a discussion of the effects of extended family on entrepreneurs.

25. S. Schatz, *Development Bank Lending in Nigeria: The Federal Loans Board* (Ibadan: Oxford University Press, 1964), chapter 6; and S. Schatz, "The Capital Shortage Illusion," *Oxford Economic Papers*, XVII, 2 (July, 1965), pp. 309-16. Schatz concluded that capital shortage is more apparent than real under existing institutional arrangements.

26. J. R. Harris and M. P. Rowe, "Entrepreneurial Patterns in the Nigerian Sawmilling Industry," *Nigerian Journal of Economic and Social Studies*, VIII, 1 (March, 1966), pp. 67-96; and Peter Kilby, "Organization and Productivity in Backward Economies," *Quarterly Journal of Economics*, LXXVI (May, 1962), pp. 273-91.

27. Schatz, *op. cit.*, *Development Bank Lending in Nigeria: The Federal Loans Board*; and Kilby, *op. cit.*, *African Enterprise: The Nigerian Bread Industry*.

28. Kilby, *op. cit.*, *African Enterprise: The Nigerian Bread Industry*, chapter 6.

29. S. Schatz, "Economic Environment and Private Enterprise in West Africa," *The Economic Bulletin of Ghana*, VII (December, 1963), pp. 42-56. Schatz argues that entrepreneurs in developing areas face

greater problems than businessmen in industrialized countries. He particularly stresses problems of ordering, maintaining, and replacing machinery. He also argues that skilled labour such as machinists presents a critical bottleneck.

30. A. O. Hirschman, *The Strategy of Economic Development* (New Haven, Yale University Press, 1958).

PART FOUR: *Problems and Prospects for the Nigerian Economy in the 1970's*

Nigeria in the 1970's faces a number of major problems, including reconstruction, planning and financing of the new states, uneven economic development between the Northern and Southern states and a population which is anticipated to increase from around 65 million in 1970 to 90 or 100 million by 1985. To cope with such a population explosion, Nigeria must provide education and other social services and employment.

The five chapters in Part Four focus on problems and prospects for the Nigerian economy with special emphasis on planning for the new states, the petroleum boom, educational and agricultural policies and a West African common market.

Since Wolfgang Stolper—author of *Planning Without Facts*—played such an important role in preparing Nigeria's 1962-68 Plan, his reflections on Nigeria's planning problems in the 1970's are especially interesting. Stolper argues that a major problem facing the Nigerian economy is one of formulating and pursuing policies which will make the economy more productive and flexible within the context of Nigeria as *one national market* which is closely integrated into the world economy. He contends that "unless Nigeria succeeds in developing effective policies rather than administrative controls, overall policy rather than central command, local initiative rather than bureaucratic orders, it is difficult to foresee both growth and the gradual healing of the wounds and reestablishment of confidence and effective peace."

Petroleum looms importantly in the future of Nigeria's economic development as the "growing points" of the economy have gradually expanded from export crops to include modern manufacturing in the early 'sixties, and then petroleum in the mid-sixties. Scott Pearson of Stanford University reports on Nigeria's petroleum industry in Chapter 18 and attempts to assess the implications that the production and export of crude oil might have on medium-term planning in the early 1970's. Pearson uses Hirschman's framework and analyzes the possible impact of petroleum on the Nigerian economy through forward and backward linkages. One of the obvious impacts of petroleum on the Nigerian economy is foreign exchange earnings. Pearson rightly points out that "In analyzing the balance-of-payments impact of a large extractive export industry such as petroleum, export values have relatively little meaning," because what really matters is the petroleum balance-of-payments entry which is *net* of all oil industry foreign exchange needs. Pearson computes the net petroleum balance of payments impact and notes that petroleum can supply from one-third (low projection) to almost one-half (high projection) of the foreign exchange availability by 1973. He thus concludes that petroleum has the potential of significantly easing Nigeria's balance-of-payments problems in the 1970's.

Another key point in the analysis of the petroleum industry is the projected impact of petroleum on government revenue. Pearson suggests that government revenues from petroleum may yield from £120 million to £200 million by 1973, or from one-third to one-half of all government revenue. His estimates of projected government revenue from petroleum have a central bearing on agricultural policy and marketing board policies in the 1970's.

Nigeria's agricultural sector employs about two-thirds of the population and generates about half of the GDP in 1970. Moreover, in light of Nigeria's projected population boom there is little reason to expect that the relative percent of population will decline by more than a few percentage points in the 1970's. For these reasons the central question posed by policy makers is "How can Nigeria's agriculture be modernized?" The answer to this question is unlikely to be found in academic discussions of capital-output ratios, shadow pricing, and whether Nigeria is a land or labor surplus economy and whether shifting cultivation, climate, etc., are constraints on Nigeria's agricultural development.

The key question of *how* to modernize Nigerian agriculture can only be resolved on a state by state, province by province and commodity by commodity analysis. In Chapter 19 Eicher and Johnson report on such a detailed analysis of how to promote Nigerian agricultural development over the 1969-1985 period. One of the central messages of this analysis is the key role of incentives in Nigerian agricultural development in the 1970's. In fact, Eicher and Johnson argue that agricultural development in the 1970's can be substantially expanded if the domestic terms of trade are turned in favor of agriculture by substantially reducing or eliminating taxes on export and import substitution crops and using petroleum as a substitute for export agriculture as an important source of government revenue. In addition, they contend that effective demand is a major constraint on Nigerian agricultural development and that a consideration of a lack of effective demand (purchasing power) must receive important attention by planners in the 1970's. Finally, Eicher and Johnson argue that an export-led strategy of Nigerian agricultural development along the lines of Myint's vent-for-surplus model should be immediately *supplemented* by a major investment in biological research to generate economically superior varieties of plants and animals to feed Nigeria's burgeoning population. Although it will likely take five to seven years to develop this new technology for food crops, it is important to greatly expand research now to provide the lead time involved in keeping ahead of the population explosion in the late 1970's and early 1980's.

The 1960's, as Frederick Harbison points out in Chapter 20, was a period of substantial achievement in high level manpower training in Nigeria. In fact, Harbison concludes that Nigeria's five universities have done a remarkable job in meeting the high level manpower needs but in 1967, "In relative terms, Nigeria was over-investing in university education." Harbison notes that the non-agricultural sector is an important *but* limited source of employment for the expanding labor force in the 1970's. He suggests that a rural transformation is needed in order to solve Nigeria's major problems of unemployment and underemployment. Harbison challenges manpower planners to redirect their attention from industrial-urban labor requirements to a careful appraisal of the intermediate and high level manpower required to support a rural transformation.

Although Nigeria has a large internal market there are obvious economic, political, scientific, and educational benefits to be gained through a closer affiliation between Nigeria and other West African countries. For example, there are a few commodities, such as nitrogenous fertilizer and iron and steel, that require a larger market than presently available in Nigeria. Likewise, there are obvious scientific benefits to be gained through close cooperation among countries in West Africa. Since a substantial amount of biological research to support agricultural development is "location-specific" in nature, there are obvious benefits to be gained from exchanging biological research within West Africa. For example, the oil palm research in Ivory Coast, the rubber research in Liberia and the cocoa research in Ghana can be of immense benefit to Nigeria and vice versa.

Since Nigeria has about two-thirds of West Africa's one hundred million population, Nigeria has an important potential role to play in West African economic integration. For this reason and the above reasons, this volume concludes with an article which is considered to be the best analysis to date of West African economic integration—Director H. M. A. Onitiri's "Towards a West-African Economic Community."

17. Economic Growth and Political Instability

in Nigeria: On Growing Together Again

WOLFGANG F. STOLPER

Few subjects can be shrouded in as much uncertainty as economic growth and political instability. Prophecy is not a necessary part of an economist's qualifications. The future remains unknown and unknowable. Nevertheless, two points can be asserted unequivocally. Nigeria, like most African countries, will not easily achieve political stability in the foreseeable future. And Nigeria, unlike many other African countries, has a very substantial potential for growth.

It would be tempting to analyze briefly the background of the civil war and go on to likely future political developments and their effects on growth. It seems, however, preferable to discuss first the economic requirements for growth, and to consider next the political organization needed to achieve it.

I. ECONOMIC PRECONDITIONS: CONCENTRATION
ON PRODUCTIVITY

The Limited Role of Targets

Before developments were interrupted by military coups, counter-coups, secession, and civil war, Nigeria grew at a satisfactory rate. The Plan had suggested a growth rate of 4% p.a. *or more*. In fact Nigeria seems to have grown by more than 5%, a substantial achievement by African standards. No analysis has been made as to whether that rate was maintainable, whether excessive import substitution might have to be paid for very soon by a lower growth rate, or whether there was an excessive amount of spending in directions with a dubious long-term payoff. Certainly, the *Progress Report 1964* suggested some misdirection of expenditures, and the responsible civil servants never tired in their watchfulness.

In any case, the real problems and achievements of growth rarely come out in aggregative statistics. Overall targets are at best rough estimates to allow a consistent framework for detailed policy making.

Criticisms of the Nigerian Plan which stressed that it (implicitly) assumed wrong capital-output ratios, or was too conservative in its aims, or missed targets are essentially beside the point. Growth requires planning; it does not require a Plan. What happens does not depend on what one assumes, but on what one does. Planning is a continuous and continuing activity, involving the continuous making of economic policy. Like all policy, it is made at a particular time, with limitations of time and space; it is made in a given situation which one can try to influence but which no man can choose.

The starting point for all policies, economic and otherwise, is a given ethnic, political, cultural and economic situation, to name the most important complexes of characteristics of the framework within which development must proceed. We can argue to what extent each hampers or stimulates growth, but it is foolish to be unaware that growth must always proceed within such a framework.

The Limited Effectiveness of Policy Instruments

The distinction between planning and the Plan implies a criticism of much developmental theory. Economic policy implies action. The instruments of action will vary, depending on the particular economy. The theory of economic policy, as developed by Tinbergen, and as somewhat unthinkingly applied by all too many people, essentially assumes a productive and flexible economy. Even in such an economy, it is not always easy to define the interrelationships among instruments necessary to achieve particular targets. Thus, in the United States it is difficult, by means of fiscal and monetary policy alone, to achieve simultaneously an acceptable stability of prices and an acceptable level of unemployment. We have here two targets—prices to increase not more than x% per year, unemployment not to exceed y%—and two instruments—fiscal policy and monetary policy; yet it is troublesome to achieve price stability and full employment simultaneously once unemployment falls somewhere between 3½ and 4%.

The point is not trivial. Much more is involved than counting targets and instruments. It is, of course, not a criticism of Tinbergen. He and others have pointed out not merely that one ought to have at least as many instruments as targets, but that not all instruments are suitable for all targets, and that all instruments will have more than one effect. We must add—which is also hardly news to Tinbergen—that the effectiveness of any instrument depends very much on the precise nature of the economy to which it is applied, and on the particular situation in which it is applied. Obviously, if unemployment in the United States were, say, 10% it would be quite easy to achieve both price stability and fuller employment by the two means usually recommended for the purpose.

Obviously, too, there is nothing eternally fixed about a floor of 3½—4% unemployment before the instruments lose their power. Gradually, by other means, the floor can be lowered, as it has in the past, and, as one is told *ad nauseam,* other policies become easier if at the same time fiscal and monetary measures of the more old-fashioned kind are pursued.

The point, however, remains: The efficiency of any policy instruments depends upon and is severely limited by the nature of the economy, particularly by its flexibility, its adaptability, its productivity. The more flexible and the more productive it is, the more it is possible to do, the more policy instruments (which in a less productive economy exist only in a shadowy way) become real and powerful.[1]

The major policy aim in any economy must therefore be to make it more productive and flexible. Other policy aims must necessarily remain subordinate, however desirable they may be for many reasons. The nature of the economy will not permit their achievement to any desirable degree. If they are nevertheless made central in the political scheme of things, the failure to achieve them will have serious political results. And if short term palliative measures are used (such as free spending and the quick rundown of foreign exchange reserves) which are inherently short-lived, the long term price may be very high indeed.

One must even go a step further. In low-productivity economies that have a large amount of subsistence production and that are also under-developed in many other respects, other policy aims cannot even be precisely defined. There is no precise way to define full employment or unemployment.[2] Of course, there are unemployed school leavers; of course there are idle periods during the farming cycle in the country. But there is no sense to deal with these perfectly real problems or with these social phenomena as if they were the problems and phenomena of Germany or the United States in 1931.

Making an economy more flexible and productive requires the mobilization and economically effective allocation of as many resources as possible. This hardly controversial statement becomes immediately politically explosive when, as is the case in Nigeria (but also elsewhere), productivity is initially low, the country is big, and there is a multitude of ethnic, sectional, tribal, class, group, and any other kind of interests.

Growth requires that not too many decisions are made in an un-economic, not to say anti-economic, manner. "Uneconomic" may mean simply a waste of resources, when factories are built whose output has no market; when costs are too high; when budgetary resources are spent on schools and hospitals that cannot be staffed.[3] Corruption may aggravate the problems, but basically the pressures for uneconomic spending come from the combinations of scarce resources and a plural society, from the desire to do something for everyone; from the real or supposed need to distribute "progress" more or less evenly over the whole area of the country; from the desire to have the State direct investments and spending into one's own area, that is from the existence of legitimate political pressures.

Much of the misallocation would disappear if locational decisions could be made on economic grounds alone, if people benefitting from schools or hospitals had to pay for them a little more than they do, if government were not given direct control over many of these matters, if there were more market rather than administrative decisions, if there were more decentralization. All of these would reduce the pressure on the cohesiveness of society and the economy. All of them would reduce friction, would reduce corruption, would increase growth.

And all of them are controversial—at least among politicians, intellectuals, and planners. I shall come back to many of them. Let me continue for the moment with the conditions of growth. The first is, as pointed out, the priority of attention to productivity. The second is the *political* necessity to make decisions in an *economic* way. This is required in order to generate resources rather than to use them up, and to minimize frictions in a plural society.

Creating a National Market

This should be done both in a nation-wide and a world-wide context. There is much talk about creation of national markets, of regional integration, of import substitution. All of them mean something. Yet, take import substitution: An uneconomic import substitution is a wage cutting device that necessarily reduces growth and may bring it to a complete halt. Uneconomic import substitution is a contradiction in terms; it is no import substitution at all.[4]

There is a similar ambivalence in talk about Nigeria being a big market of over 50 million people and a GNP of over £1 billion. But what does that mean? The market for the Nkalagu or Abeokuta cement plants is quite different from that of the Sokoto cement plant. A car assembly plant in Lagos has quite a different sales potential from one located in Port Harcourt, or in Kaduna, because transport cost of materials coming in and of final goods going out are different, hence the economics of production and sales differ, and so do profitability and productivity. Someone always must pay for the cost of transport.

To make sense of terms like national markets or regional integration requires more than to add GNP's and people. Space itself has to be allowed for. But that means first of all transport costs, which are the price we pay to overcome distance. It means secondly (and that is usually discussed first) a movement of goods "interfered with" only by transport cost; and it means thirdly that factors, particularly labor, can be spatially rearranged.

Thus creation of a regional market implies in the first instance not merely free trade in goods, but a particular economic location of production. Gradually as the market increases, production will be dispersed.[5] As roads are built and transport costs fall—i.e. as the economic size of the market increases with the conquest of its physical size—not only will the market for the existing production increase, but more production will become economic further away from the initial centers of production.

Locational Considerations

A short digression into location theory should suggest how this process works, and what the policy implications are.

A common market requires common monetary and fiscal policies and wage policies which allow for regional price, wage, and interest differentials. Before the normal process of dispersal of production can start there will be concentration of production in the most economic location, where the existence of raw materials and/or soil and/or an existing market and/or a supply of other factors of production suggests potential success. Economies of concentration will continue to favor some few locations until the preemption of space and of other local factors combine to raise wages and rents, which, in turn, will induce newcomers to look elsewhere. Thus the process of dispersal implies wage (or more generally income) differentials leading to increased import demand from lower by higher income areas, and thus providing both the inducement for additional production to take place elsewhere and the market for products.

Uniformity of actual wage and interest rates will increase the concentration in a few favored spots beyond what is economically necessary.[6] The concentration will be further enhanced by policies favoring urban areas, e.g., by providing subsidized public services. The differentials are, on the other hand, increased by policies subsidizing outlying production centers. Thus one finds counteracting policies of subsidization and of wage policies which, on balance, threaten to be net consumers of real resources without benefit to anyone.

Factor Mobility

Regional or national integration requires therefore subtle policies including much more than common industrial markets. The free movement of goods is almost a definitional characteristic of a common market. It must ideally be accompanied by a reasonably free movement of people. This last point is both theoretically and politically the most sticky one.

Theoretically: the pure theory of international trade assumes immobility of factors and shows (a) that allocation according to free trade will improve income *within* each country, and (b) that trade is at least a partial substitute for factor movements. It points out that interference with free trade may improve the situation of one country but at the expense of another. But if you are serious about building a national market, favoring one area at the expense of another is permissible only as the result of a deliberate policy decision of the richer part to help the poorer part of the country. On principle, the welfare of all people within the country counts the same. There can be transfer payments but there must not be any beggar-your-neighbor policies.

But, more importantly and still theoretically, we deal now not with international trade theory, but with location theory. Location theory explicitly introduces the extent of the earth while international trade theory, by ignoring transport cost within a country, implies that a country is a point-like island. Location theory assumes that everything except land is mobile at a price, and that the changing utilization of land substitutes for its physical immobility. As a result some mobility of labor may become economically desirable all around. Moreover, because of transport cost, factor prices will not tend towards equality and such factor price equalization imposed from above directly or indirectly by, e.g., an imposed equalization of goods prices will do considerable harm. Within an economy, the function of factor prices is very similar to that of an exchange rate between countries.

Politically, the movement of strangers is everywhere bound to create great difficulties. The difficulties are compounded by numbers and cultural differences. It is easy to absorb a few strangers, explosive when many are dumped upon you. They become particularly aggravating when the immigrants have some superior knowledge or abilities. The typical colonial situation has its counterpart in the alleged past Ibo domination of much Northern economic life, and of alleged Northern domination of much Southern political life. The fact that it may have benefitted Northern economic development or that it may have held the country together, even when true, cuts about as much ice as a similar argument would to justify colonialism.

Yet a judicious free movement of people with the right and security to engage in economic activities is a boon to development, and within a country is of the essence. When it becomes difficult or impossible, and to the extent to which it is limited by the political and cultural restraints of plural societies, the free movement of goods and the location of production for predominantly economic reasons become all the more important, both if growth is to reach acceptable proportions and if the separate markets are to become fused into a national or regional market. The location of economic activities for economic reasons then requires all the more local initiative and policy decisions.

Not only goods and factor movements, but also movements of labor and capital can substitute for each other: land, of course, is by definition immobile. Capital movements involve essentially investment funds that are scarce. It is a legitimate political and economic consideration to distribute scarce investment funds where they will stimulate growth most effectively, subject to the economic and political restraints of the economy. If labor cannot move why not create the production center near the labor by shipping the required funds to labor?

The point has been already discussed. The subsidization[7] of particular areas can reduce political tensions which the immigration of labor might have brought about. But this is bought—legitimately—at the expense of growth. This fact sets obvious limits to how much can be done without being economically self-defeating.

But the process of subsidization is also apt to become politically self-defeating. If only a few people are involved, not much will be needed to keep them happy where they are. But if everybody is to be kept happy where he is, the state becomes just a redistribution device for common funds. I find it difficult to imagine that such a situation could last politically, or why the richer groups of the country should consent to subsidize the poorer ones continuously, and why such a situation, built upon a community of dislike and distrust, mitigated by buying freedom from each others' company by subsidies should have any nation building effect at all!

II. POLITICAL PRECONDITIONS: POLICY, LOCAL INITIATIVE, AND THE LIMITS OF THE POWERS OF THE STATE

The preceding section has concentrated on a crucial element of the conditions of economic growth: the economic allocation of resources, more specifically, the priority to be given to the creation of a productive, flexible economic base, which alone can sustain the more widely dispersed attention to health and education and other not directly productive government services. The present section intends to consider the political organization suitable for the purpose. I shall in particular try to sketch somewhat more precisely the role of government, the desirable extent of decentralization, the function of policy.

Limitations on Government

Government must operate under several limitations. There is first the recalcitrant nature of the economy. There is secondly the fact that we deal with plural societies. There is thirdly the lack of sufficient numbers of well-trained people, capable of running things. The three aspects are closely interwoven.

The underdeveloped economies are not only low productivity economies. They are also economies in which the knowledge of what could possibly be done is scarce: soil surveys, mineral surveys, potential crops, potential uses of fertilizer, are all less well-known than would be desirable. They are also economies in which it is exceedingly difficult to shift resources quickly to alternative uses. Farmers may shift quickly between alternative crops known to them, but once technically trained for certain performances it is not easy to shift, say, extension workers to new activities without either additional training, or substantial investments, nor can farmers or business men do the same.

This inflexibility and low productivity of the economy limits what can be done at any moment of time, and it forces attention to economics. There just are not enough resources to pursue very many non-economic aims, however worthy; and wasteful behavior quickly cuts into important alternative (economic and non-economic) uses with economic and political penalties quickly arising. The less attention is paid to the productivity of those activities which are essentially economic in nature, the less resources are generated for those activities in which political choices are both legitimate and unavoidable.

The plural society means a great variety of aims of society which are bound to conflict with each other, and whose conflict becomes quickly obvious because resources do not exist to satisfy too many of them simultaneously. The implication is that aims must be restricted, targets limited.

The lack of administrative capacity, and the existence of what Gunnar Myrdal has recently called the "soft state" means that aims have to be achieved by indirection, that policies have to predominate rather than direct controls, and that the government must limit itself or break down.

Implications of Pluralism

All societies are plural. There is never any reason to believe that everybody's interests will coincide with everybody else's, or that everybody will always subordinate himself to the needs of society. Every society must have some sense of belonging together. In Nigeria, pluralism has the obvious form of tribal, language and religious divisions. But, of course, there are also conflicts between farmers and the beneficiaries of the taxes collected from farmers; between recipients of farm settlements payments and taxpayers; between importers and domestic producers; between government civil servants with fixed incomes and positions of power and the public.

Most planning models begin with the specification of targets. Yet there are not only economic reasons why this may be possible only in a limited way; there are also serious political problems involved. There exists a substantial body of literature dealing with the problem of how by some process of "voting" targets are set politically. There is a grave danger on the side of political scientists and/or politicians to neglect the objective limitations which economic possibilities place upon their political aims. But economists are just as vulnerable in neglecting the political limitations on what can be assumed. It is stupid of politicians to set impossible aims and expect economists to tell them how to achieve the impossible in the best possible manner. It is no more sensible for the economist to expect to be given clearcut political aims to the fulfillment of which he is to address himself. Nor is it sensible to say that this or that is "really" political in nature, or that the economist could do this or that if only the political will were not lacking.

Not that there is not a considerable amount of truth in all of these positions. Nevertheless they bespeak both an ignorance of mutual problems and a refusal to deal with them on the grounds that they are "really" someone else's business.

If a strong consensus exists in a society that something is to be achieved the voting problem does not arise. Any system of voting, or any process of decision-making, would give the same result. All Nigerian political parties, all tribal groups, all groups of ruling people wanted independence in 1960 or at least had persuaded themselves that they wanted it.[8] Their motivations may have been different and mutually inconsistent. They may not have seen problems ahead; they may have seen them but have underestimated their complexity and seriousness; they may each have been confident of their ability to hold their own and even to run the show. The point is that at the time there was a consensus on what was wanted then.

Independence is a dramatic event. Most economic decisions are humdrum and most decisions build up day after day. Pressures become unbearable gradually, not suddenly. In such cases voting procedures are not easily agreed upon and, even when agreed upon, decisions are neither easily arrived at nor enforceable when arrived at. Democratic processes can break down when no decisions can be arrived at, or when large segments of the population feel that decisions will always go against them, or have been arrived at in a manner felt to have been unfair.

When societies are very heterogeneous and particularly when various groups are of roughly equal strength the only way out may be—and I believe is—to avoid putting the society to the test of having to come to too many decisions in the first place. A dictatorship does not change the problem either, whether it is the dictatorship of the proletariat, or of one tribal group over others. Even dictatorships must not attempt the impossible, and they break down when they do not command an efficient civil service and a ruthless police.

Economically, this means that one should *not* try to specify too clearly a social welfare function—with implications on economic policy to be discussed further on. In fact such aims as that GNP should grow at a certain rate are, when all is said, really very unspecific. One can, of course, make long lists of *desiderata,* a kind of child's letter to Santa Claus. But this hardly constitutes a serious instruction to planners and policy makers. Moreover, if such lists were actually taken seriously, bitter fights would quickly arise about who should get what, and what should be done when. This, in turn, would exacerbate all differences and would make it impossible to arrive at any targets at all.

Thus it was relatively easy in Nigeria to come to an agreement on the Niger dam, or the oil refinery. But a steel mill was kept from becoming real not only by the dubious economics of such an enterprise—for which one should be grateful—but also by serious fights about who should get that supposed plum. The compromise of several mills that was in the offing merely multiplied the extent of the nonsense. There are other instances such as a car assembly plant which might have made economic sense, but which politico-ethnic rivalries kept from becoming reality. Our Nigerian friends could multiply examples, and every country can provide much too much of the same.

One would think that the manifest impossibility of defining a meaningful (because specific) social welfare function, both economically and politically, would force itself upon the observers. Take the time horizon required for such a formulation: history has no beginning and no end. Everything has a root, and there always is another day. Therefore, any plan period must be completely arbitrary. Time horizons do, of course, exist but it is questionable how much such favored devices as perspective plans of twenty years, flights of fancies into an even longer future, more detailed three-to-six year plans, sector plans and the rest really contribute. They are useful, occasionally even necessary, exercises, but one should not take them more seriously than they deserve and should not waste scarce talent on them beyond the limited usefulness they have.

All of this argues both economically and politically for limiting one's vision as to what is possible in the reasonably foreseeable future, to concentrate upon raising productivity as the major need to gain more freedom of action, and to remove pressure both from resources and particularly from people, by *not* forcing them into agreements they cannot feel or keep. It is much better to solve one thing at a time, and since one cannot help doing that anyway, it is much better to try to get a consensus on one thing at a time and limit it to the most important issues at that time.

There must be a political sense of direction, and decisions must be made in a manner that allows different groups a sense of participation as well as a sense of benefitting from being members of the political community. It would be good if it were generally understood that decisions involving economics and productivity directly were to be made on economic grounds. It would be good if it were understood that only in this manner can the productive base be built that allows a more even distribution of those government activities which are not merely or not primarily economic, and that allows a certain distribution of benefits on other than economic grounds.

Nevertheless, a little vagueness about the social welfare function helps. There are enough problems that must be solved without asking for solutions of problems whose solution can be postponed and which, with luck, may never arise. I have been accused of being scientifically obscurantist for holding this view, as well as politically dishonest. I emphatically reject both charges. There is nothing obscurantist in rejecting an impossible assumption, merely because it has been a convenient one to make for certain planning models, particularly if alternative solutions can be given. And there is nothing dishonest about insisting that people should not be forced to make unnecessary choices if making the choices might mean either suppression or, at worst and by no means unrealistically, the blowing up of society.

The impossibility to specify a welfare function, and the inherent divisiveness of a plural society argue strongly for limitations on what the government should be asked to do, and the methods government should employ to do them. The arguments are reinforced by the inherent weaknesses of governmental administrations.

Limited Role of Government

Everyone knows that nothing ever gets done unless someone decides that it should be done; that someone really wants it done; and that someone keeps pushing, keeps at it, sees it through. Nowhere are decisions made once and for all. There always have to be whole chains of command, of people who keep pushing, keep doing, keep seeing to it that things really become real, keep things going. In the literature, a nice distinction is occasionally made between planning and execution. If this means that the people with ideas who can direct and develop policies are different in training and temperament from those who carry out the direction, there is sense in the distinction, as there is sense to any division of labor. But if thereby is meant that whether a plan can be realized is not the business of the policy maker, then the distinction is, of course, nonsensical.

In all countries it is difficult to get many competent chains of command. In a very real sense one never has enough. In the first place, no problem is solved forever, and every problem that is solved generates hydra-fashion seven new ones. There is always more to do than one can, and the more people there are to do things—provided of course the economy itself gets developed—the more things need doing. Everyone knows that top policymakers are among the more easily come-by people, mainly because relatively few of them are needed. This is also why they are more easily imported than executors at lower levels. If one wants to get things done, therefore, the choice is either to build up a tremendous chain of bureaucracy or to use as many indirect means as possible, to use incentives rather than direct controls, to avoid administrative decisions as far as possible, to make as many decisions automatic as possible, to reduce the element of administrative discretion, and increase policy direction.

This prescription seems old-fashioned, and it seems to contradict an earlier analysis: that aggregative economics does not get very far in underdeveloped countries and attention has to be directed to specific bottlenecks, to productivity. But there is no such contradiction. All simple formulations are, of course, suspect, but earlier a distinction between general and specific policies was made. The issue now is, whether you tell someone to do something, or whether you induce him to do it; it is whether he can do what he pleases unless it is forbidden; or whether everything is forbidden that is not specifically allowed, or worse, that he is not specifically enjoined to do. Or to put it into the most unfavorable terms: whether you can get people to think of things to do themselves or whether you have to tell them everything.

There are many areas of economic policy where these problems arise. Take pioneer certificates. Who should get them? Who gives licenses? Does an applicant have a right to a license? Within what period has he a right to expect an answer? Is he required to use it within a specified period of time? Suppose another producer of a competing good does not want special pioneer treatment. Should the pioneer be protected from him? Does this mean more licensing? The amount of arbitrariness involved and the strain on the civil service at different levels varies considerably depending on the answers to each of the questions raised, and a host of others that could be raised. All of this assumes that some sort of pioneer-type policy is to be pursued in the first place.

Or take wages policy. Should there be a minimum wage legislation? How is it to be enforced? Who should be covered? What kind of controls should be instituted? Or, what should be the procedures to get land in an industrial estate? At what rents? Should there be some price control? How enforced? How are tariff schedules set up? How much discretion does the customs officer have? How are import licenses administered? Who can get them? All of these represent obvious problems in any country. They tax the administrative apparatus even in the most advanced countries. They induce some arbitrariness everywhere. You cannot help getting some arbitrariness in any formulized process. This is why it does not make sense to enlarge the areas of arbitrariness unnessarily.[9]

Each of the direct command measures requires additional paper work, additional administrative procedures. The strain and delays become quickly serious. At best there is a cumbersomeness introduced into economic decision making and execution that is bound to raise real cost and slow down growth. At worst the arbitrarinesses lead to a most unhealthy relation between government and people, and a complete stifling of all development. We are not unfamiliar with this in the United States. There are Ombudsmen in Scandinavian countries to protect the citizen from his servants. It is a tossup whether the situation is worse when an efficient bureaucracy imposes an arbitrary and inefficient policy, or whether an inefficient bureaucracy tries to cope with problems that in themselves may be sensible to deal with but which could be dealt with more easily in a different way.

Now imagine that you do not have the chains of command needed. Corruption becomes almost inevitable. To get things done, they have to be "expedited." Someone gets paid off. It is beside the point that, at least initially, the corruption may not be counterproductive. It is beside the point that up to a point corruption introduces into the picture the price mechanism that direct regulation has been trying to eliminate. Very quickly "productive" corruption turns into a counterproductive one. One need only refer to the enormous growth of supplier's credits, not all of which are corrupt or uneconomic or indefensible, but a very large proportion of which are bound to be.

When there are important tribal and other differences, the power inherent in arbitrary decision making introduces a further divisive element. It is no use blaming politicians. They are no better or no worse than other people. You cannot operate with a system which inherently asks for perversion. When you have many capable civil servants at all levels, enough to have competition among those who want to get in and alternative employments for those who want to get out, you get reasonable salary scales in relation to the rest of the economy and the same kind of people (except perhaps for differences in temperament), the same kind of efficiency. It then makes sense to complain about corruption, with the ones who are being caught misbehaving being replaced by others. When these conditions are not met, the only way to fight corruption is to reduce the administrative decisions that have to be made by an overstrained civil service.

One thinks of corruption much too much as the big payoff for the big fellow. This does lead, of course, to misallocation of resources on a large scale. But there is the corruption at all levels: the customs officer who waits for his baksheesh before he lets you through; the policeman who is willing to quash a parking ticket for a few cents; the junior civil servant who will juggle the pile of papers to bring yours near the top of the pile; the public works fellow who will assign road crews to a road of interest to you; the import license which can be bought. The list can be extended almost *ad libitum*. All of them raise cost perceptibly and influence the allocation of resources adversely.

All of this must lead to a gradual, and eventually accelerating dissolution of society. You trust only your kinsmen and give them preference. You get out of society and the economy what you can. You are a leader to enrich yourself and you may, of course, deceive yourself for a while that, being the leader, you deserve to get what you can, even if you do not get it by a legal process. In plural societies, this sort of behavior, induced by overloading the state with activities which it cannot possibly execute, necessarily prevents the emergence of social cohesiveness beyond the clan or tribe and destroys what cohesiveness there is. It cannot possibly lead to the emergence of a strong nation or a capable state.

There seems to me considerable confusion on these points. It is now agreed that "the people" ought to have some say. There is talk of local initiative and execution, sometimes of a "strong" leadership that imposes its will. My point is that the government has very important functions beyond the maintenance of law and order, that it can "run" a country and economy by policies, but that it will not succeed by trying to enforce matters directly in the absence of a strong capable civil service (not to mention secret police!). The result is the paradox that on the one hand governments lack the imagination to see the power of indirection and instead envisage their function as legislating all over the map in great detail, in ordering people around, in using administrative control. On the other hand, there is no real way in which they can impose obligations on their people and command the voluntary compliance with unenforceable policies. Social discipline and cohesion fall victim of a free-for-all to get or buy (or inherit or marry) favors. Enforcement of laws becomes increasingly impossible—much as the United States to this day suffers the consequences of prohibition.

Myrdal, in analyzing the conditions of Southeast Asia has referred to this situation as "the soft state." It is a situation in which "national governments require extraordinarily little of their citizens. There are few obligations either to do things in the interest of the community or to avoid actions opposed to that interest. Even those obligations that do exist are enforced inadequately if at all."[10] Again this is to some extent due to the destruction of old relationships as, with colonial penetration new and essentially alien, hence imperfectly understood social relations are introduced. But, it is essential to realize that the imposition of administrative controls in all circumstances weakens the voluntary social structure whenever it does not rest upon a consensus and when it is not necessary and not felt to be necessary to achieve social ends. And when it cannot be enforced, it destroys social cohesion.

It all adds up to one conclusion: the coercive functions of the government have to be sharply restricted if a "strong state" is to be built up at all. This restriction of the functions and the change in their nature does thus not imply a reduction in the importance of the government. Quite the contrary. For, as Myrdal has also pointed out,

> In Western countries it was during the liberal interlude between Mercantilism (with its many vestiges of feudalism) and the modern welfare state that the strong state came into being. During that interlude state activity was reduced to a minimum. When in a later epoch the state again intervened in the economy on a large scale, it had a legal, political and administrative system whose quality only needed to be protected and preserved. The Southeast Asian countries, on the other hand, have to improve law and law enforcement and stamp out corruption in an epoch of their history when the activities of the state are proliferating—and when preference is given to discretionary controls, in my opinion even more than is necessary.[11]

This is just as much true in Nigeria as in Southeast Asia. The corruption is not inherent in the societies except insofar as all societies are potentially, and more or less, corrupt. Neither is it, on the other hand, true that we unjustifiably apply Western concepts and ideals to traditional societies, as it is sometimes asserted; certainly not in Nigeria. Nigerians, or Ghanaians, or everyone else has felt the corruption to be just that. It has not been an inherent part of traditional society felt to be good or at least acceptable. It is a consequence of the methods of government used. The methods of economic development must be adapted to realities. The realities are economies with low productivity and plural societies. It is *not* true that the state "must" do all sorts of things, and it is even less true that it "must" do them by discretionary methods and adminisrative coercion. It is understandable that countries do not like the state of affairs in which they must live. We are all in the business of changing that state of affairs as fast as possible. Changing requires coming to terms with realities, doing one thing at a time, restricting activities to what can be achieved.

It is essential to realize that the future will require governments to restrict their activities; to use policy rather than administrative discretion; to use indirection; to make it therefore easier for local initiative to emerge. All factors come together to argue limitations on the power of the state and decentralization.

III. MINIMUM CONDITIONS IN NIGERIA

What does this mean for the future of Nigeria? With the civil war at the time of writing still unresolved, and talks between the warring brothers only beginning, the future constitutional arrangements must still be uncertain. The one feature that seems fairly certain is that there will be a greater degree of decentralization than in the past.

It may be useful to sketch briefly some of the relevant developments of the past that help to explain the present impasse. I can claim no perfect foresight: when I left Nigeria in 1962 I expected and predicted many troubles but not the catastrophe that actually happened. What happened when the Prime Minister was assassinated was, however, a break in history of much greater significance than independence, and of almost as much significance as the creation of Nigeria itself. For the assassination meant not merely the murder of one man, but the abandonment of constitutional and legal processes that had been maintained after a fashion for a hundred years. A hundred years of growing together were cut; a hundred years of gradually losing suspicions of each other, of tolerating each other even if not always liking each other, of some peaceful coexistence, were broken. With the fratricide of the Ibos in the North and the fighting, the gulf has become almost unbridgeable. No matter how the war will be solved, it is not easily imaginable that the free movement of persons that had existed before will be reestablished soon.

Everyone knows that Nigeria has three major ethnic groups, many significant less important groups and subgroups, and hundreds of smaller tribal and language groups. The federalization of Nigeria with which independence was started has been attacked as inherently unstable. Perhaps so. Yet it is easy to point to mistakes all around that were not necessary, and a little more patience on all sides would have made living together feasible. If the West had not given an opportunity to the North, if the East had not joined the North and jumped at the West when the latter was down, if the Northerners had not pressed in on the South, used their elbows a little more subtly, if a Federal election had not been stolen, if the President had not advocated a strong presidential constitution obviously and rather naively with himself as the strong President, if Catholic Ibo majors had not killed the Moslem Premier in the North who was also a religious leader; if, as the last straw, an Ibo general had not proclaimed a unitary state, if the massacre of Ibos in the North could have been avoided by Federal troops . . . one could go on with "ifs," none of which were in the nature of a deterministic necessity. The Ni-

gerian case is a tragedy, yet not quite a Greek tragedy, in which heroes
are inevitably doomed by jealous gods and an ineluctable fate. Of all
Nigerians the Prime Minister understood best the value of and necessity
for time and patience, and with some luck it might have been better
understood all around that he was slowly building up a power base in the
South that would make him independent of the North, that his policies
served his country well.[12]

Whatever might have been will never be known. It is certain that it
took many events, each of them logical yet unnecessary, to rip apart the
strong ties that had already formed among Nigerians as Nigerians, rather
than as members of specific ethnic groups or religions. It is equally certain
that for the foreseeable future there will remain distrust and fear, and
that the secessionist tendencies that have been started will not easily disappear. Thus I believe that the creation of nine states in the area originally controlled by Federal forces will become a reality, and that three
more may become a reality in the original Biafran territory. If the
country is to hold together the new states will have to become a reality.
But who will control the Center? And will it be possible to contain
further secessionist tendencies?

Political scientists no doubt will prefer a many-body problem to the
old three-body problem. On the face of it, none of the proposed twelve
new states will be strong enough to impose their will in the manner of the
old North. I would not bet on it however. It may be so. But it is also
possible that all kinds of coalitions among states may arise. It may be
that civil servants will run each government, or perhaps military men.
But they all will of necessity become politicians. Distrusts will not die
immediately just because the old kind of politician is not around any-
more.

In other words, stability of the twelve-state arrangement will depend
upon the free consensus of each individual state to respect the other
eleven, not to interfere, not to expand the powers and actions beyond
mutually agreed limits. Otherwise twelve power centers may arise, in the
manner of the Chinese war lords, with no particular power except to
promote a general instability.

Assuming that this will not happen, what does the Center need to keep
the country effectively together and to prevent the states from becoming
a centrifugal force? Problems arise always around money, the army and
the police. Police clearly must be more local than ever, not necessarily in
the constitutional sense of being state rather than federal, but in the
sense that the local constable is a local boy, from the same tribal group,
etc. This is easy to do for the police. It is a much more difficult requirement for the army to fulfill, but there, too, one would think it wise for a
while to station mainly troops of local origin in a particular area. What-

ever the final constitutional arrangement, the states cannot control the army if any degree of stability is desired, and the Federal Center has to be exceedingly discrete in its use of troops.

Only one more political statement before I turn to economics. There must be some way in which national consciousness can find expression. This has been the function of political parties and of politicians, however corrupt they may have been. The present military regime has recognized that basic fact by incorporating within itself civilians of known political appeal. How is this problem going to be solved in the future? A civil service cannot forever perform that function by itself. A military cannot either unless it does not care for more than to keep itself in power—again the Chinese war lords come to mind, or some of the more old-fashioned Latin American dictators—or unless it becomes itself political.

Thus the future looks unstable. If it is possible to be optimistic to a point, it is because of the past evidence of the tremendous pragmatism of Nigerians. But the country can be held together and its government can become again a decision making and executing agency only by carefully restricting itself to matters it can do, to matters where there is a reasonable consensus, and by using persuasion and policy rather than coercion and direction.

Persuasion and policy are also indicated because twelve states imply a tremendous strain on manpower and fiscal resources. A preview of what is involved is given by the experience in Ibadan when the Midwest State was created. The exodus of many first class civil servants left the Western Region service weakened without creating a top-notch Midwestern one. Twelve states require twelve services. None of them can possibly be very powerful or effective for the time being. This puts the Federal service into a potentially very powerful position. The state governments will necessarily have to restrict their activities. This may be all to the good provided that good policies bring about local initiatives. But if administrative direction is not abandoned for policy, the weak civil services necessarily will hamper local initiative much more than in the past.

Twelve governments will cost a lot of money—and money is resources, not something you can print. They will want capitals and courthouses; housing and ministries, etc. At the same time their fiscal resources will at best be no stronger than in the past and are likely to be much weaker. If they have groundnuts or cocoa to tax, they are likely to continue to do so, even though it may mean killing the goose that lays the golden egg. But no matter what, government consumption is bound to rise. Savings by the public sector are bound to decline unless again severe restrictions are placed upon the functions of the government.

The Federal Government, sitting in the major port of exports and imports, will be in a central position with a crucial role. No hint is known to me—though it may exist within the government—of the proposed tax base of the Federal Government; of any decisions on the problem of contributing to the revenues of the states; whether there is to be a distributable pool, etc. Though some states with good export products may be reasonably affluent, on the whole the Federal Government is likely to be even stronger financially vis-à-vis the states than was the case in the past vis-à-vis the Regions.

If so, the Federal Government will contribute to savings relatively even more[13] than in the past, and it will, through the manner in which it spends its funds outside of the Federal District, be able to exert considerable leverage. This not only puts pressure upon the constitutional solution of who controls the Federal Government, but it raises the whole gamut of principles according to which money should be spent.

It seems too much to hope that there will be a substantial freedom of movement of people. But it will be essential to insist on a freedom of movement of goods and an *economic* distribution of those investments that increase productive capacity directly. It is essential to make a distinction between investments that raise productive capacity directly, and those whose justification must be social rather than economic. There is much to be said for aiding everyone with schooling, certainly when the trained people can leave to wherever the jobs are, probably also when this is not the case. The same is arguable for health. But while a state that wants to attract private investments by subsidies from its own resources ought not be prevented from doing so, neither should the Federal Government aid it in this effort. Highly subsidized industries are not worth having in the first place, but the Federal Government, if it has available investable resources, must insist on an economic use without political interferences that in the end must hurt everyone.

This means largely that the principles that were supposed to be followed in the first national Plan will be more rigorously enforced. In the past, each Region prepared its Plan and was expected to finance all of its current and half its capital cost, the rest coming from abroad. There was some provision for a transfer of funds for education and perhaps for agriculture—the latter was never too clearly specified even later on. The Federal Government had, of course, large investments in the Regions through Statutory Corporations or the Investment Bank. But in principle (if not in reality) such investments were to be made primarily on *economic grounds*. It could easily be provided that a certain percentage of Federal investment funds could be set aside for regional or state use. But one has to be clear that such Federal-state transfers will produce beneficial short or medium term effects only if they themselves are used economically; and I believe this to be true also in the long run. The weakness of the state governments should make it easier than in the past for the Federal Government to insist on purely economic criteria for investments. This means that substantial differences in local investment expenditures must be expected, and that some investment transfers may occur. But what will happen will then depend very much on who controls the Federal Government.

The constitutional arrangements of the past have been criticized on the grounds that they gave too much autonomy to the Regions. But there is some misunderstanding in this matter. In effect, Regions had every incentive to coordinate plans and policies with other Regions and with the Federal Government. Given the politics of the situation, a considerable autonomy was inevitable. This will continue to be the case in the future. At the same time, limitations on inter-governmental transfers reduced political friction and put considerable pressure on the Regions to mobilize their own resources and to allocate them as well as they could. Only in this manner would they produce recurrent surplusses for investments; only in this manner would they get hold of foreign funds on the basis of the 50:50 ground rules.

With twelve states the pressures for local mobilization and economic allocation could be made to work much more strongly, and federal policy could become more dominant. This undoubtedly has escaped neither the states nor the Civil Service at the Center. It will no doubt lead to considerable infighting when the future constitutional arrangements are being worked out as how precisely the Federal Government is constituted, elected, and run.

To run a country, as distinct from a Confederation of Sovereign States, there must be a common tariff and a common administration of money, banking, and currency as well as of foreign exchange. And there must be Federal control of external and probably of internal borrowing. Again this is not too different from the past, but its importance will become even greater.

Central Bank policy had begun to be effective through centralization of foreign assets, the influence on Marketing Board prices, and financing of imports and exports. Control over local banks will become more effective. Problems will arise with foreign and domestic borrowing. It is difficult to conceive that individual states would be allowed to borrow abroad on their own as long as the balance of payments and the foreign debt burden are likely to remain a problem, or for that matter that they would in the foreseeable future find any takers for their issues. An exception might be politically motivated lending to support a favorite local government and possibly the attempt by a foreign government to make trouble.[14]

But it is conceivable that domestic borrowing within a state could be left to the individual states, if they felt that they could in this manner increase their available resources. One could imagine the emergence of

(Central) Bank eligible and (Central) Bank ineligible papers. Not that state borrowing is likely to be very important. I just want to stress that in this area there is some leeway for local autonomy, where there can be virtually none for borrowing abroad.

Neither can there be any leeway on tariff and exchange control policy. This must be a prerogative of the Center. But import licensing is an open invitation for shenanigans and arbitrariness and corruption. Despite the good press which such methods occasionally have in the literature, and despite the fact the civil war will leave Nigeria denuded of foreign reserves and will make such controls inevitable for a while (i.e. until petroleum revenues become substantial and reconstruction has been finished), I feel strongly that policy must be directed to get rid of them as fast as possible, and to make them in the meantime as automatic as possible. There is no question in my mind that even under the best of circumstances their economic efficiency has been greatly exaggerated. When political tensions and administrative difficulties are added they can be defended only as emergency measures and not at all as means of development policy.

The real power of the Center will consist precisely in its control of the exchange rate, the issue of money, the rules under which action must take place. It will also have influence by wage policies including governmental salary structures, tax policies and the enforcement of free internal movement at least of goods, and after a cooling-off period increasingly also of people. It will be in a strong position to enforce more or less rational policies in the states by its control over central policies. It will not be able, and hence should not try, to ensure an equal development everywhere. Such a goal is self-defeating. It will be able to mitigate only the grossest inequalities. It must control the movement of goods also physically, i.e. the road and rail system, and aviation. But it will be handicapped more than in the past by a limitation on its resources, and so will the states. With decentralization the policy importance of the Center will increase. The diminution of the available resources will work in the same direction.

IV. A COMMENT ON THE UNIVERSALITY OF THE PROBLEMS

I should like to conclude with two final comments. First, though I would not deny that my own personal inclinations run in the direction of decentralization of execution and use of policy rather than of commands to influence the course of events, this is nevertheless a logically defensible conclusion rather than one that is based merely on hidden or—in my case—openly acknowledged value judgments. And it should be noted that it is not identical with the outmoded antithesis of a socialist versus a capitalist economy, nor with that of a one-party versus a two-party or multi-party system, as developments in Yugoslavia, Poland, Czechoslovakia, and even Russia suggest. Reforms and "Liebermanism" have made neither Yugoslavia nor Russia capitalist. The real issue has been how decisions are being made, how they are to be executed.

Similarly, with one-party states. Again the problem is not the formal arrangements, but how decisions are to be arrived at within a group—and I might add—what happens to the people who lose in the process. The "liberal" people want a freer discussion and a live-and-let-live attitude, so that the losers do not necessarily lose their jobs or lives. The problem is how to get efficiency and participation.

Not unnaturally I believe that our non-Communist solutions are better. This belief does not rest on the assumption that we make less mistakes, but because in the institutions of bankruptcy and of new elections we have orderly processes of getting rid of our mistakes.

The second point is to remember that Nigeria is still at war, and that the resolution of the conflict, and the nature of the situation when reconstruction and renewed growth can begin are totally unknowable at the time of writing. It is therefore idle to try to be more specific.

Having stated this, I believe however that the general direction in which Nigeria should go follows inevitably from the economics and politics of low-productivity economies and plural society realities. Whether what I suggest will work I do not know. But unless Nigeria succeeds in developing effective policies rather than administrative controls, overall policy rather than central command, local initiative rather than bureaucratic orders, it is difficult to foresee both growth and the gradual healing of the wounds and reestablishment of confidence and effective peace. Moreover, the arguments sketched are relevant beyond the borders of Nigeria. There must be strong leadership, particularly in a democracy, particularly in a diffuse situation. But a wise leadership will show patience and reluctance to use force, or to transgress beyond carefully set limits.

NOTES

1. It is easy to set up a central bank. All one has to do is to copy the laws of other countries suitably modified to allow for local flavor. It is, however, difficult to specify precisely what the central bank can do. It is easy to print money. But whether printing money—literally or in a more sophisticated form of credit—will achieve desirable ends depends on a great deal more than the existence of unemployment.

2. Myrdal has most recently pointed this out in the Asian context, but many observers have stressed this before. G. Myrdal, *Asian Drama*, III (Pantheon, New York, 1968), pp. 2041-2062, devotes a whole Appendix 6 to this problem. One should not discuss this problem as mainly semantic. In medicine, even if many symptoms of two diseases are the same, it would be foolish to call them the same disease if the treatment required would be as different as the treatment of Asian or Nigerian "unemployment" and that of the American Great Depression.

3. Money can be wasted on schools even if they can be staffed, if the graduates cannot be employed for lack of complementary resources. The gains from social overhead investments become real only as they facilitate directly productive investments—or, of course, as they are felt to be ends in themselves. But to the extent to which they are ends in themselves they are better treated as consumption rather than as investment expenditures.

4. Harry G. Johnson, "Tariffs and Economic Development," *The Journal of Development Studies*, I, 1 (October, 1964), has made this point. I have made it in my *Planning Without Facts*. The truth is that import substitution has at times been a cause of balance of payments troubles, rather than a cure. See most recently Harry G. Johnson, *Economic Policies Towards Less Developed Countries* (Brookings and Praeger, 1967), which deals with the necessary economic policies *by* as well as *towards* less developed countries.

5. See the discussion in A. Losch, *The Economics of Location* (Yale University Press, 1954).

6. As late as the 'thirties interlocal wage and interest differentials of several hundred percent were quite normal in the United States. It has taken the substantial postwar growth and very substantial improvements in labor and capital markets to reduce these interregional differences to what are still substantial proportions.

7. If no subsidization is involved, capital should (and would) move anyway, and an economic problem would arise only if it were prevented from moving by political reasons.

8. This is not too unfair a description of the Northern agreement to the Southern pressures for independence.

9. To avoid a misunderstanding: obviously in an emergency, in a war, in a sudden, unforeseen and unforeseeable balance of payments crisis you have to do all sorts of things, just as you have to wear crutches when you break your leg. Only do not pretend that the crutch is better than the healthy leg! Thus balance of payments crises brought on by a war or a catastrophic fall in export prices are one thing; balance of payments crises brought about by faulty resource allocation are something else again.

10. Gunnar Myrdal, *Asian Drama*, II, p. 896.

11. Gunnar Myrdal, "The 'Soft State' in Underdeveloped Countries," Address, February 17, 1968, Conference, School of Law at UCLA, p. 22 (mimeographed).

12. I am aware that this is the view of one man, a view that I have strongly held for a long time. I never had any patience with the attacks on the Prime Minister that he was not "dynamic;" like his Roman predecessor, he served his country well by hesitating. I have always thought that he was the greatest of Nigerian statesmen, and not the Sardauna or any of the Regional premiers. I always thought that he towered above such "leaders" as Nkrumah or Sekou Toure, and I see no reason to modify this opinion. Nkrumah had a much easier task which he thoroughly botched. As *The Economist* remarked, "President Nkrumah's profoundest mark on the region was his wanton destruction of all significant links between Nigeria, Ghana, Sierra Leone, and Gambia," *The Economist* (May 11, 1968), p. 37. Nigerian troubles would be easier if Balewa had succeeded; Ghana's troubles would have remained more manageable if only Nkrumah had failed.

13. But probably absolutely less, unless oil revenues become federal and very large—which is quite possible.

14. In the past, a Regional Government could conceivably have forced the hand of the Federal Government by interesting a foreign government in the financing of a project within its own area and then presenting the Federal Government with a *fait accompli*, in which the Federal Government had no choice but to permit the loan, regardless of its overall impact, e.g., on the balance of payments or of other effects of interest to the country as a whole. No such case seems to have actually occurred. The smaller size and reduced economic power of the twelve states makes it less likely that such a situation will arise in the future. The Federal Government could make it clear that only federally approved foreign loans were eligible for preferential tax and exchange treatment. But it might just as well be banned altogether in the interest of a harmonious political as well as economic development of the country. But will all new states agree to such a ban?

18. *Nigerian Petroleum: Implications for Medium-Term Planning*

SCOTT R. PEARSON

The principal concern here is to examine possible implications that the production and export of crude oil in Nigeria might have, especially over the five years ending in 1973.[1] This medium-term projective analysis presupposes a reasonably quick end to the internal military strife; it is assumed that normal petroleum exploration and production activity will be resumed in mid-1969. If the civil war is prolonged in duration so as to vitiate this assumption, the entire sets of projections must be shifted into the future accordingly.

I. THE EXPLORATION/PRODUCTION COMPANIES IN NIGERIA

The search for oil in Nigeria began in 1908 when a German company, Nigerian Bitumen Corporation, drilled fourteen wells in what is today Lagos State before ceasing operations with the outbreak of World War I.[2] Interest in the possibility of discovering oil in Nigeria revived in 1937 with the establishment of Shell-D'Arcy Exploration Parties, a consortium owned equally by Royal Dutch Shell and British Petroleum which later became the Shell-BP Petroleum Development Company of Nigeria, Limited. In November, 1938, this company received an Oil Exploration License (OEL) covering all of Nigeria; by 1957 Shell-BP had reduced its acreage to 40,000 square miles of Oil Prospecting Licenses (OPL's). Shell-BP converted nearly 15,000 square miles of its OPL acreage into Oil Mining Leases (OML's) in 1960 and 1962 and returned the residual to the Nigerian Government. (Under Nigerian law Shell-BP had to give up at least half of its OPL acreage upon conversion of its concession into OML's.)

Between 1938 and 1941 Shell-BP undertook preliminary geological reconnaissance; after a five-year interruption caused by World War II, it intensified and followed up this activity with geophysical surveys in the 1946-51 period. In 1951 Shell-BP drilled its first wildcat well; it

352

came up dry. During the next four years the company concentrated its efforts in the Cretaceous areas rimming the Niger Delta without discovering any oil producing wells. After shifting focus to the Tertiary area of the Delta itself, Shell-BP made Nigeria's first commercial discovery in 1956 at Oloibiri in what is now Rivers State. This touched off a period of extensive exploration activity in the Tertiary which is still continuing.[3]

Even before Shell-BP started exporting oil from Port Harcourt in 1958, other companies began to show interest in Nigeria. Mobil carried out reconnaissance work in the northwestern corner of the country in the mid-1950's and then shifted to the coastal area in what is now Lagos between 1958 and 1961, drilling four dry holes before abandoning the area. Following Shell-BP's release of acreage, Tenneco, Gulf, Agip, Safrap, and later Phillips obtained onshore OPL's. Additional onshore OEL's were later granted to Esso, Safrap, and Great Basins. Furthermore, in 1960 Nigeria divided its offshore continental shelf into twelve blocks of about 1,000 square miles each. Ten of these blocks were taken up in 1961—four by Shell-BP, two by Gulf, two by Mobil, and two by Amoseas. The latter made Nigeria's initial offshore oil strike in 1963. Of the remaining two offshore blocks, Gulf took one in 1964 and Union obtained the other in 1967. Half of each of the original ten offshore concessions will have to be relinquished in November, 1968, unless the Nigerian Government grants extensions.

The resulting pattern of concessions is summarized in Table One which also contains detailed information about each of the companies currently active in Nigeria. For further reference the map in Figure One indicates the locations and outputs of each of Nigeria's major producing oil fields during April, 1967, one of the last months of normal production prior to the outbreak of the civil war. Unlike Shell-BP and Safrap which were forced to discontinue production, Gulf alone has been virtually unaffected by the war while developing its offshore production areas in the Midwestern State. Table Two summarizes the historical production and export performance of Nigerian oil; here the very rapid rates of growth of petroleum output and export from the early 1960's to the 1967 stoppage are apparent. To place Nigerian oil production and exports in perspective, 1966 output amounted to 1.2% of the world total while 1966 exports were 2.3% of total world crude petroleum trade.

TABLE 1. *Petroleum Exploration/Production Companies Holding Nigerian Concessions, April, 1968*

Name of Company	Country of Incorporation	Ownership	Concessions (OPL's and OML's) (square miles)			Location of Concessions
			Onshore	Offshore	Total	
American Overseas Petroleum Company	U.S.A.	Caltex, i.e. Standard of California & Texaco (U.S.-private)	—	1,931	1,931	Rivers State
Mobil Exploration Nigeria Limited	U.S.A.	Mobil (U.S.-private)	—	2,025	2,025	South Eastern State
Nigeria Agip Oil Company Limited	Nigeria	E.N.I.-50% (Italian-government); Phillips-50% (U.S.-private)	2,031	—	2,031	East Central State; Mid-Western State; Rivers State
Nigeria Gulf Oil Company Limited	U.S.A.	Gulf (U.S.-private)	3,965	2,890	6,855	East Central State (onshore); Lagos State (offshore); Mid-Western State (offshore and onshore); Rivers State (onshore); South Eastern State (onshore); Western State (offshore)
Phillips Petroleum Company	U.S.A.	Phillips (U.S.-private)	1,401	—	1,401	Mid-Western State; Western State
Safrap (Nigeria) Limited	Nigeria	Société Anonyme Francaise de Recherches et d'Exploitation de Pétrole (SAFREP)-50% Regie Autonome des Pétroles (RAP)-40%; Société de Gestion des Participations de la RAP (SOGERAP)-10% (French-government and private)	9,336	—	9,336	Benue-Plateau State; East Central State; Kwara State; Mid-Western State; Rivers State

354

Company	Country	Ownership				Location
The Shell-BP Petroleum Development Company of Nigeria Limited	Nigeria	Shell-50% (Dutch-British-private); British Petroleum-50% (British-government and private)	14,992	3,906	18,898	East Central State (onshore); Kwara State (onshore); Mid-Western State (offshore and onshore); Rivers State (offshore and onshore); South Eastern State (offshore and onshore); Western State (onshore)
Tenneco Oil Company of Nigeria Limited	U.S.A.	Tenneco-50%; Sinclair-25%; Sunray-25%; (U.S.-private)	1,380	—	1,380	Mid-Western State; Rivers State
Union Oil Company of Nigeria	U.S.A.	Union Oil of California (U.S.-private)	—	1,000	1,000	Lagos State

SOURCES:

Annual Report of the Petroleum Division of the Federal Ministry of Mines and Power, 1965-66 (Lagos, Nigeria: Federal Ministry of Information, 1967), p. 9; updated and supplemented by unpublished individual company information.

NOTES:

a—Esso Exploration Incorporated which formerly held two OEL's in what is now East Central State, South-Eastern State, and Benue-Plateau State no longer operates in Nigeria.

b—Great Basins Oil Company (of Los Angeles) has held an OEL in what is now Benue-Plateau State, Kwara State, and North-Western State and is negotiating to convert portions of this into OPL's.

c—Delta Oil (Nigeria) LTD., a Nigerian company incorporated by Godfrey Amachree, has applied for an OPL in the Mid-Western State.

355

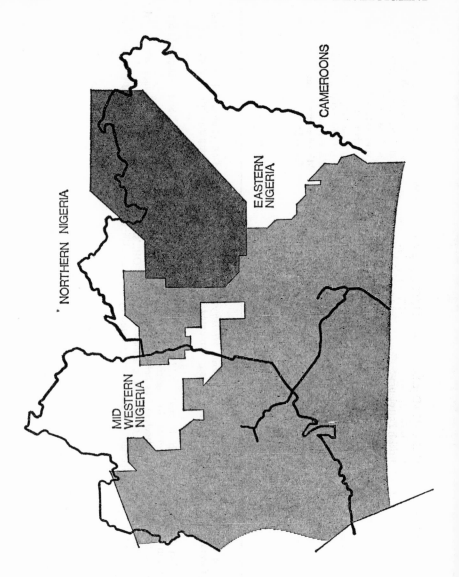

TABLE 2. *Petroleum Production and Exports (1958-67) (Volume = thousands of barrels per day; Value = millions of £ Nigerian).*

	1958		1959		1960		1961		1962	
	Volume	Value	Volume	Value	Volume	Value	Volume	Value	Volume	Value
Production	5	1	11	3	17	4	46	11	68	17
Exports	5	1	11	3	17	4	46	11	68	17
Local Sales	—	—	—	—	—	—	—	—	—	—

	1963		1964		1965		1966		1967	
	Volume	Value	Volume	Value	Volume	Value	Volume	Value	Volume	Value
Production	76	20	120	32	270	69	415	100	317	77
Exports	76	20	120	32	266	68	383	92	300	72
Local Sales	—	—	—	—	4	1	32	8	17	5

SOURCES: *Annual Report of the Petroleum Division of the Federal Ministry of Mines and Power, 1965-66* (Lagos, Nigeria: Federal Ministry of Information, 1967), p. 11; unpublished individual company data.

357

II. RECENT IMPACT OF PETROLEUM PRODUCTION
ON THE NIGERIAN ECONOMY

To investigate the possibility of petroleum export-led growth in
Nigeria and therefore the extent of the economic gains that might
be associated with Nigerian oil, it will be necessary to examine
Nigeria's institutional framework, the technological properties of the
oil industry's production function and the responsiveness of domestic
factor-owners.[4] The institutional framework, within which the export industry operates includes the industrial organization of and the legal codes
applying to the export industry, as well as the workings of those portions of the rest of the economy with which the export industry is
likely to interact most significantly. This framework together with
the export industry's production function set the bounds for the transmission process to the rest of the domestic economy. What effects the
export industry might have is initially a function of the response by
the factor owners in the economy. Within these overall limits the
growth process initiated by the export industry is communicated to
the remainder of the economy directly through the attraction or creation of factors of production and indirectly through linkage effects.

Because the Nigerian petroleum industry is foreign-owned, international institutional aspects are brought into play. For Nigeria the most
important result on this score is that the large, vertically-integrated international oil companies have chosen to take most of their profits
in the producing stage of operations, thereby establishing artificially
high crude transfer prices and thus the possibility of unusually large
rents for host country governments. Domestically, the operation of
each petroleum production company in Nigeria is constrained and
heavily influenced by its dealings with three institutions—its head office,
the remainder of the industry in Nigeria, and the Nigerian Government.
In all three cases the most important issue at stake is the industry's
financial arrangements with the Nigerian Government, the importance
of which is twofold. The level at which oil production is taxed has a
direct bearing, first, on the economic and psychological rationale behind head office decisions regarding production levels for Nigeria, and
second, on the actual amounts of revenues that the Government receives as a result of oil production. Both of these factors are instrumental in determining the scope of oil's impact on the remainder of
the Nigerian economy.

Within this institutional framework, the potential transmission of
petroleum export growth is further constrained by the oil industry
production function. In Nigeria this function is capital intensive, has

significant indivisibilities, and requires advanced technological skills. Its material input requirements for the most part involve technologically advanced methods of production and/or have sufficiently high value/transport ratios so that much the largest portion of materials must be imported at least initially. And its labor requirements result in the need for relatively large amounts of skilled human inputs with virtually no seasonality or normal cause for labor turnover. Though there is some room for substitution, petroleum production technology is such that non-economic goals would have to take precedence before this picture could be changed much. In short, the Nigerian petroleum production function is conducive to large economic rents in the form of payments to Government, moderate but significant levels of wages and salaries, small usage of local materials and concomitantly large imports of materials as well as services.

One mechanism through which the Nigerian oil industry transmits growth to the rest of the Nigerian economy is by attracting or creating factors of production. Petroleum industry payments to the Nigerian Governments, which were £27 million in 1967 or about 17 per cent of total tax revenues, lead to potential domestic public savings. Petroleum export earnings and net private foreign capital inflows provide foreign exchange in amounts significantly in excess of oil industry current account requirements; in 1966, the last full year of normal operation, the Nigerian oil industry contributed nearly one-sixth (net of leakages) of the total amount of foreign exchange available for use by the non-oil sectors of the Nigerian economy. Finally, through its initial importation of management and skilled labor followed by the gradual training of indigenous replacements and future local entrepreneurs, the Nigerian oil industry has brought about a fairly significant upgrading of a very limited spectrum of Nigeria's human resources; for example, in 1966, 550 of the 2,900 Nigerians employed directly by the oil exploration/production companies occupied high level positions. If, however, the Nigerian economy reaches a point at which further growth is constrained by a lack of skilled manpower, it is highly doubtful that the petroleum industry will be able to do much about breaking this bottleneck. Petroleum's much more important role in providing factors for Nigerian development lies in its contribution of foreign exchange and its supplying of domestic savings through payments to the Nigerian Government.

A second vehicle for the transmission of export-sector growth is the existence of linkage effects, externalities—economies or diseconomies—contributed by the export sector to the rest of the domestic economy.[5] These effects can be conveniently divided into two major categories—those that operate through the market and those that do not. Market linkages, the first category, include two separate but related externalities, investment (including backward and forward) linkages and final demand linkages.[6] The non-market externalities consist of two sub-categories, technological linkages and socio-political linkages. All four ultimate linkage effects are related to a fifth category termed fiscal linkages.

The nature of the petroleum industry and the state of Nigerian technology imply a very low input of Nigerian local materials and only a slightly greater use of Nigerian services and thus a limited opportunity for backward linkages; as evidence of this, in 1965 only 2 per cent of the £72 million of oil industry expenditures ultimately went for the purchase of local Nigerian materials, while about 10 per cent was local wages and salaries and probably 1 per cent amounted to local profits and interest. Forward linkages are more important; in a normal year Nigeria's refinery produces about £14 million worth of petroleum products with an annual net foreign exchange saving of about £13 million while Nigerian utilities and industries use more than £1 million of natural gas for energy purposes.[7] Final demand linkages, which derive from the expenditure of income that is generated by the export industry, have moderate but not unimportant impacts. Wages and salaries paid locally by the oil industry have recently amounted to about £7.5 million per annum and residual payments (profits, interest, depreciation, etc.) controlled by Nigerians have run at about one-tenth of this level.

Technological linkages are caused by the entrance of non-priced factors in non-oil industry production functions. In Nigeria the petroleum industry's construction of roads and other social overhead capital and its training of labor deserve greater attention than casual observers generally give to them. Socio-political externalities pervade nearly all aspects of economic activity. On the broadest scope operation of the export industry may bring about social and political reorganizations usually as a result of attempts to gain greater control over the benefits associated with the export proceeds. These struggles might result from conflicts between industry-owners and the Government or within the Government itself. At a more micro level, non-market side effects of the export industry lead to positive or adverse social, political, or organizational impacts on further economic behavior. These involve the cross-current impacts of the ability to make or not to make various decisions as well as the need to adopt, circumvent, or adapt domestic factors or materials.[8] Finally, fiscal linkages arise when the Nigerian Governments use the revenues collected from the oil industry either in undertaking recurrent or capital expenditures or in reducing the tax bite on other sectors of the economy. They have been limited to date by the relatively low amounts paid by the industry to the Government, but are likely to be the most important type of external effect associated with oil in the near future.

III. ALTERNATIVE PROJECTED IMPACTS OF PETROLEUM ON THE NIGERIAN ECONOMY [PROJECTED PETROLEUM PRODUCTION AND EXPORTS]

Any crystal-ball gazing at the impacts of oil in Nigeria must begin with projects of petroleum production and exports; all of the other economic variables to be discussed depend ultimately on output levels. Conditions are currently too uncertain in Nigeria to allow a direct causal analysis moving from factors affecting future levels of Nigerian crude output to production projections. A complicated mix of factors enters into oil company head office decisions about production levels in any given producing area. Among the most important of these are international demand for petroleum products, the political and economic outlook in the producing country under examination, production costs and the return on capital within the company's vertically integrated framework, financial arrangements with the host country government and expectations regarding their stability, and special features pertaining to crude production in the area.

Since international demand for petroleum products should continue to be very buoyant, attention centers on head office determination of relative acceleration in various producing areas. On the whole the international oil industry is relatively optimistic about prospects in Nigeria, the civil war and the recent changes in financial arrangements with Government notwithstanding.[9] These negative factors seem to be more than compensated for by Nigeria's special advantages (location, crude quality, etc.).[10] Therefore the industry is planning a rapid reentry into those parts of Nigeria in which productive activity has been precluded by the civil war as soon as conditions allow.

Table Three sets out two alternate projections for production, exports, and local sales of Nigerian crude. The following broad assumptions underlie the projections: first, that the current financial arrangements of the petroleum companies with the Nigerian Government remain unchanged throughout the period under consideration; and second, that the internal conflict in Nigeria is resolved so that the petroleum companies may resume production in the Eastern States by mid-1969.[11] The Low Projection assumes that the petroleum industry is somewhat

TABLE 3. *Petroleum Production and Exports (1968-73)* (*Volume = thousands of barrels per day; Value = millions of £ Nigerian*).

A. Low Projection

	1968		1969		1970		1971		1972		1973	
	Volume	*Value*	*Volume*	*Value*	*Volume*	*Value*	*Volume*	*Value*	*Volume*	*Value*	*Volume*	*Value*
Production	100	25	315	79	533	134	736	185	939	236	1,142	287
Exports	100	25	300	75	500	125	700	175	900	225	1,100	275
Local Sales	—	—	15	4	33	9	36	10	39	11	42	12

B. High Projection

	1968		1969		1970		1971		1972		1973	
	Volume	*Value*	*Volume*	*Value*	*Volume*	*Value*	*Volume*	*Value*	*Volume*	*Value*	*Volume*	*Value*
Production	100	25	515	129	1,133	284	1,436	360	1,639	411	1,842	462
Exports	100	25	500	125	1,100	275	1,400	350	1,600	400	1,800	450
Local Sales	—	—	15	4	33	9	36	10	39	11	42	12

SOURCE: Author's estimates.

slow in returning to normal activity following the end of hostilities and that it is relatively conservative in expanding in Nigeria. Alternatively, the High Projection assumes that the industry expands very rapidly as soon as it is able to resume normal operations throughout Nigeria. Petroleum exploration/production companies make production plans for at least as far as five years ahead; the precise annual levels of output under both projections are aggregations of individual company plans. Though company head offices change plans periodically, the general orders of magnitude are reasonable.[12] When most of the Nigerian oil industry was forced to shut down in July, 1967, production was about 600,000 barrels per day. The Low Projection nearly works out to a doubling of this level by 1973 while the High Projection foresees a tripling of the 1967 level in the same time span.

Projected Other Local Payments

Other local payments (i.e. other than payments to the Nigerian Government) comprise three categories of interest—local goods and services, local wages and salaries, and harbor dues and port charges. Payments in the first two instances include all payments in Nigerian currency to expatriates and expatriate-owned firms as well as to their Nigerian counterparts, while harbor dues go entirely to the Nigerian Ports Authority. Table Four summarizes recent movements in these categories and in addition attaches Low and High Projections that might be associated with the two production forecasts.

The very gently rising levels foreseen for local goods and services and for local wages and salaries (in spite of rapidly expanding production levels) reflect the unusually low costs of production (or high valuation of output) that is part of the curious institutional framework of the international oil industry. The wages and salaries shown in Table Four apply only to the exploration/production companies; naturally a certain portion of the payments to local suppliers and contractors will be used to make local wage or salary payments. By 1973 the entire crude oil industry in Nigeria might employ about 23,000 Nigerians and 2,100 expatriates and pay on the order of £10 million in wages and salaries on the basis of the High Projection and perhaps a fifth less than these levels under the Low Projection. Finally, harbor dues and port charges can be estimated directly from export projections; unless the presently very high rates are lowered so as to be put more in line with international standards, the amounts involved should become highly significant and might best be considered conceptually as increments to the totals for payments to Government, treated below.

TABLE 4. *Other Local Payments (1963-73)*

(millions of £ Nigerian)

A. Historical

	1963	1964	1965	1966	1967
Local Goods and Services	7	10	19	28	22
Local Wages and Salaries	1	1	3	3	2
Harbour Dues and Port Charges	2	2	2	3	3
Total Other Local Payments[a]	10	14	23	33	27

B. Low Projection

	1968	1969	1970	1971	1972	1973
Local Goods and Services	19	23	25	26	27	28
Local Wages and Salaries	2	2	3	3	3	3
Harbor Dues and Port Charges	1	3	5	7	9	11
Total Other Local Payments	22	28	33	36	39	42

C. High Projection

	1968	1969	1970	1971	1972	1973
Local Goods and Services	24	28	30	31	32	33
Local Wages and Salaries	2	3	3	3	4	4
Harbor Dues and Port Charges	1	5	11	14	16	18
Total Other Local Payments	27	36	44	48	52	55

SOURCES:
Unpublished individual company data; author's estimates.

NOTES:
a—may not equal sum of components due to rounding errors.

Projected Payments To The Nigerian Government

One of the most significant impacts that the Nigerian oil industry is likely to have on the Nigerian economy is the contribution to domestic public savings via large and increasing payments to Government. Petroleum company payments to the Nigerian Governments include Royalties, Rentals, Petroleum Profits Taxes, Custom and Stamp Duties, Premia, and other minor taxes. To date the totals have been dominated by Royalties and Rentals both of which are in large part automatically redistributed mainly to the states of origin. For example, the breakdown of the £27 million paid in 1967 is as follows (in million of £ Nigerian): Royalties—14.9; Rentals—5.2; Petroleum Profits Taxes —5.5; Customs Duty—0.7, and Stamp Duty and other—0.7. In the near future, however, Petroleum Profits Taxes which have been held down due to the companies' use of accumulated depreciation allowances will become much the largest item in total Government revenues from oil. Under existing legislation this tax is wholly retained by the Federal

TABLE 5. *The Impact of Petroleum Revenues on Total Government Revenues (1963-73)*

(*millions of £ Nigerian*)

A. Historical

	1963	1964	1965	1966	1967
Petroleum Revenues	5	12	13	19	27
Non-Petroleum Revenues	142	161	177	180	136
Total Revenues	147	173	190	199	163
Petroleum Revenues as a Percentage of Total Revenues	3%	7%	7%	9%	17%

B. Low Projection

	1968	1969	1970	1971	1972	1973
Petroleum Revenues	14	30	45	65	90	120
Non-Petroleum Revenues	140	150	165	180	190	200
Total Revenues	154	180	210	245	280	320
Petroleum Revenues as a Percentage of Total Revenues	9%	17%	21%	27%	32%	38%

C. High Projection

	1968	1969	1970	1971	1972	1973
Petroleum Revenues	14	40	100	145	170	200
Non-Petroleum Revenues	140	150	165	180	190	200
Total Revenues	154	190	265	325	360	400
Petroleum Revenues as a Percentage of Total Revenues	9%	21%	38%	45%	47%	50%

SOURCES:
Unpublished individual company data; author's estimates.

Government. Barring changes in the current laws, a shift of fiscal power to the Federal Government on a growing scale is inevitable.

Table Five contains historical and projected oil company payments to Government as well as comparisons of petroleum and non-petroleum revenues. No great faith is attached to the non-petroleum revenues projection; it is relatively conservative and assumes that pre-war levels are regained by 1971. Using the Low Projection, 1973 total revenues are 160 per cent of the 1966 peak with oil revenues moving from a tenth to two-fifths of the rising total. Alternatively, on the basis of the High Projection during this same period, total revenues double while oil revenues increase to one-half of the 1973 total.

Government revenues reaching these magnitudes will almost certainly provide rising amounts of domestic public savings. Placing numerical estimates on this statement requires guesses about future behavior of Government current expenditures. Current spending grew at the very

fast pace of 9 per cent per year between 1959 and 1966, attaining a
level of nearly £190 million in the latter year. If this high growth
rate is maintained through 1973 (perhaps reflecting increased administrative expenses of the twelve-state system, rehabilitation and reconstruction expenditures, greater spending on military and ex-military
personnel, etc.), then the Nigerian Governments could dissipate all of
the Low Projection total revenues during the entire period under consideration as well as High Projection total revenues through 1970
(thereafter a surplus growing to over £50 million develops by 1973).
But spending on this order would surely cause the non-petroleum
revenues to grow much more rapidly than is allowed for in Table
Five, since the major item in this category consists of customs and
excise payments. And hopefully the Nigerian governments will be able
to exercise somewhat more prudence in their spending policies. Overall,
therefore, the inability to make very firm guesses about future Government spending activity precludes any conclusion that claims more than
that petroleum revenues should offer a tremendous potential for large
and increasing domestic public savings.

Projected Petroleum Industry Contributions to the Nigerian
Balance-of-Payments

Petroleum is almost sure to have its most immediate impact on the
supply of foreign exchange available for use by the non-oil sectors of
the Nigerian economy. In analyzing the balance-of-payments impact of
a large extractive export industry such as petroleum, export values have
relatively little meaning. In the context of Nigerian oil what really
matters are the amounts of foreign exchange that the oil industry
brings into the country to exchange for domestic currency in order to
make payments to the Government or to purchase local goods and
services. In Table Six historical and projected Balance-of-payments
Impacts are thus found by subtracting the oil industry's Proceeds from
Local Sales (mostly crude sales to the Nigerian refinery) from the
sum of its Payments to Government and Other Local Payments. As
can be seen from the Table, foreign exchange earnings from petroleum
in 1973 are three times their 1967 level using the Low Projection
and more than five times this level on the basis of the High Projection.[18]

The oil industry foreign exchange contributions are of real interest
only in the context of overall Nigerian foreign exchange availability
and use. In Table Seven the recent Nigerian foreign exchange situation
is reviewed and a plausible picture is portrayed for the medium-term
future using both Low and High Projections. Underlying the entry
entitled Non-petroleum (Exports + Net Capital Flows), which is
identical for both projections, is a forecast of all non-oil balance-of-

TABLE 6.   *Petroleum Industry Balance-of-Payments Impact (1963-73)*

(millions of £ Nigerian)

A. Historical

	1963	1964	1965	1966	1967	
Payments to Government	5	12	13	19	27	
Other Local Payments	10	14	23	33	27	
Proceeds from Local Sales	1	1	1	9	8	
Balance-of-payments Impact[a]	14	25	36	43	47	

B. Low Projection

	1968	1969	1970	1971	1972	1973
Payments to Government	14	30	45	65	90	120
Other Local Payments	22	28	33	36	39	42
Proceeds from Local Sales	1	6	12	13	14	15
Balance-of-payments Impact	35	52	66	88	115	147

C. High Projection

	1968	1969	1970	1971	1972	1973
Payments to Government	14	40	100	145	170	200
Other Local Payments	27	36	44	48	52	55
Proceeds from Local Sales	1	6	12	13	14	15
Balance-of-payments Impact	40	70	132	180	208	240

SOURCES:
Unpublished individual company data; author's estimates.

NOTE:
a—may not equal sum of components due to rounding errors.

payments entries with the exceptions of imports of goods and services and transfer payments. The most important assumption attached to this forecast is that non-oil exports will grow at a rate of 3¾ per cent per annum after 1969 (between 1968 and 1969 non-oil exports are projected to undergo a once-for-all quantum recovery from depressed civil war levels).

Foreign exchange generated by the Nigerian oil industry is measured by the Petroleum Balance-of-payments Impact entry which is net of all oil industry foreign exchange needs. At the same time, the non-oil sectors generate amounts of foreign exchange of their own as indicated in Table Six by the line Non-petroleum (Exports + Net Capital Flows). Summing these two items gives the total amount of foreign exchange that is available for the Nigerian non-oil economy to purchase non-petroleum imports of goods and services, to pay net transfers abroad, or to build up foreign exchange reserves. The importance of the petroleum sector's contribution of foreign exchange can therefore be gauged by comparing the oil balance-of-payments impact with

Table 7. *Petroleum Industry Contribution to Nigerian Foreign Exchange Availability and Use (1963-73).*
(millions of £ Nigerian)

A. Historical

	1963	1964	1965	1966	1967
Foreign Exchange Availability					
Petroleum Balance-of-payments Impact	14	25	36	43	47
Non-petroleum (Exports + Net Capital Flows + Errors and Omissions)	170	220	255	209	174
Total^a	185	245	291	252	221
Foreign Exchange Use					
Non-petroleum Imports of Goods and Services	227	262	282	263	252
Net Transfer Paid Abroad	3	*	−3	−2	*
Net Increase in Foreign Exchange Reserves	−45	−17	12	−9	−31
Total	185	245	291	252	221
Petroleum Balance-of-payments Impact as a Percentage of Foreign Exchange Availability or Use	8%	10%	12%	17%	21%

B. Low Projection

	1968	1969	1970	1971	1972	1973
Foreign Exchange Availability						
Petroleum Balance-of-payments Impact	35	52	66	88	115	147
Non-petroleum (Exports + Net Capital Flows)	195	230	250	265	275	285
Total	230	282	316	353	390	432
Foreign Exchange Use (Non-petroleum Imports of Goods and Services, Net Transfer Paid Abroad, Net Increase in Foreign Exchange Reserves)	230	282	316	353	390	432
Petroleum Balance-of-payments Impact as a Percentage of Foreign Exchange Availability or Use	15%	18%	21%	25%	29%	34%

C. High Projection

	1968	1969	1970	1971	1972	1973
Foreign Exchange Availability						
Petroleum Balance-of-payments Impact	40	70	132	180	208	240
Non-petroleum (Exports + Net Capital Flows)	195	230	250	265	275	285
Total	235	300	382	445	483	525
Foreign Exchange Use (Non-petroleum Imports of Goods and Services, Net Transfer Paid Abroad, Net Increase in Foreign Exchange Reserves)	235	300	382	445	483	525
Petroleum Balance-of-payments Impact as a Percentage of Foreign Exchange Availability or Use	17%	23%	35%	40%	43%	46%

SOURCES: Table A-2, "The Impacts . . . ," pp. A-8—A-11; author's estimates.

NOTES:

*—between +£0.5 million and −£0.5 million.
a—may not equal sum of components due to rounding errors.

369

the total foreign exchange availability or use during any given year. Under the Low Projection, foreign exchange availability, propelled by oil contribution increases, regains its 1965 peak by 1970 and then rises by 1973 to 50 per cent above the 1965 figure. The growth of foreign exchange availability using the High Protection is more spectacular; the 1965 peak level is attained by 1969 while the 1973 figure is 80 per cent again as large as that of 1965.

Projected Linkage Effects

Speculation about future linkage effects is a very fragile undertaking. Linkages for the most part are specific to individual cases and thus defy wide generalization, especially as concerns the future. Some possible opportunities for the emergence of important externalities associated with the production of crude oil in Nigeria, however, can be sketched broadly.

The potential for important backward linkages developing vis-à-vis the Nigerian petroleum industry is not very promising. For reasons already alluded to the exploration/production companies' purchases of local goods and services are not likely to expand very much. There is room for Nigerian entrepreneurs to participate more widely in servicing and supplying activities and many of the goods that the petroleum industry now imports could and presumably will be produced in Nigeria; but not too much of this is expected to happen in the period under treatment here. There is much less chance that Nigerian factors will be able to substitute for the highly technical imported services of the oil industry. Until Nigerian industrialization and technical expertise expand considerably, backward linkages associated with the petroleum sector are likely to be very limited.

There is probably more hope for the establishment of important forward-linked industries than for backward-linked. Nigeria's refinery is expected to grow in step with domestic demand; talk of additional refineries is heard periodically but unless inroads could somehow be made on the export market, new refineries in Nigeria would be more politically than economically based. In addition, Nigerian utilities and industries have barely begun to tap the extremely wide potential for natural gas-based energy. Along with expanded use of natural gas for energy purposes, there are two potential forward-linked industries which might well be established in Nigeria that use natural gas as a raw material in their production processes—a plastics and caustic soda complex and a nitrogenous fertilizer plant.

Much of what has been said about backward linkages applies equally well to final demand linkages. The amounts of factor payments (in Nigerian currency) that will remain in the country to have an impact are severely restricted by the petroleum industry production function.

As previously mentioned, locally paid wages and salaries associated with the petroleum exploration/production industry and its suppliers and contractors might grow to £ 10 million by 1973. Domestically expended residual payments (profits, interest, depreciation, etc.) are limited by the high degree of expatriate ownership in the industry (including suppliers and contractors). In light of all this, final demand linkages will be limited, though not wholly insignificant.

Non-market linkages are even more difficult to speculate about than are the market linkages just treated. Two technological linkages—labor and management training, and construction and maintenance of roads—should continue to have real but marginal impacts, yet in neither case is there latitude for much expansion of activity. Future socio-political linkages of the Nigerian oil industry determine the extent of political costs resulting from petroleum production, while the evolution of fiscal linkages directly involves subsequent government policy decisions. Both of these topics are treated in the ensuing discussion.

Projected Petroleum Industry Value-Added

Much of the projected information that has been developed can be pulled together to indicate the direct contribution of the Nigerian petroleum exploration/production industry to Nigerian gross product, using either domestic or national income accounting concepts. In Table Eight petroleum value-added and its contribution to Nigerian GDP is given annually as a percentage of the total. From the depressed 1968 base, total GDP grows at annual rates of nearly 8 per cent (Low Projection) and 10 per cent (High Projection), principally on the basis of increments in oil value-added.

In general, national rather than domestic accounting concepts are more relevant in dealing with foreign-owned export sectors.[14] Compound rates of growth of GNP based on the same underlying projected data (6 per cent for the Low Projection and 8 per cent for the High Projection) are lower than those of GDP (8 per cent and 10 per cent respectively) for the period 1968-73. Leaving out the unusual years, 1968 and 1969, the GNP growth rates for 1970-73 are about 6 per cent for both Low and High Projections, as compared with 7½ per cent for both GDP projections.[15] In the final analysis, no matter how one measures it, the direct contribution of the petroleum industry to Nigerian value-added should be substantial.

IV. POLICY IMPLICATIONS

The major policy issues that the production of petroleum in Nigeria generates for the Nigerian Government fall into two groups—questions dealing with the accrual and with the use of oil-related revenues. The

TABLE 8. *The Contribution of Petroleum Value-Added to Nigerian Gross Domestic Product (1963-73)*[a]

(*millions of £ Nigerian*)

A. Historical

	1963	1964	1965	1966	1967
Petroleum Value-added	9	11	37	53	45
Non-Petroleum Value-added	1,199	1,209	1,262	1,292	1,320
Gross Domestic Product (factor cost)	1,208	1,220	1,299	1,345	1,365
Petroleum Value-added as a percentage of GDP	1%	1%	3%	4%	3%

B. Low Projection

	1968	1969	1970	1971	1972	1973
Petroleum Value-added	(7)	41	94	144	194	244
Non-Petroleum Value-added	1,361	1,432	1,489	1,563	1,640	1,722
Gross Domestic Product (factor cost)	1,354	1,473	1,583	1,707	1,834	1,966
Petroleum Value-added as a percentage of GDP	(1%)	3%	6%	8%	11%	12%

C. High Projection

	1968	1969	1970	1971	1972	1973
Petroleum Value-added	(14)	92	234	309	359	409
Non-Petroleum Value-added	1,361	1,432	1,489	1,563	1,640	1,722
Gross Domestic Product (factor cost)	1,347	1,524	1,723	1,872	1,999	2,131
Petroleum Value-added as a percentage of GDP	(1%)	6%	14%	17%	18%	19%

SOURCES: Unpublished individual company data; Table A-1, "The Impacts . . . ," pp. A-1—A-7; author's estimates.

NOTES:

( ) indicates a negative figure.

a—all figures pertain to domestic production national income accounting concepts.

first set of issues mainly concerns how the Government can maximize its income from petroleum; this necessarily involves the evolution of the oil industry's financial arrangements with the Government. If, as seems likely, the international petroleum cost-price structure retains its current shape, Nigeria could certainly do much worse than to continue doing business with the international oil corporations. Tax increases in early 1967 made the oil company fiscal arrangements in Nigeria approximately equal to those existing in other major oil-producing underdeveloped countries. In changing tax terms the Nigerian Government traded off its medium-term prospect of extremely rapid rates of growth of oil output (i.e. significantly faster than those still anticipated) to gain a large percentage increase in the per barrel tax rate.

Whether this change was economically correct is a moot point. But it is quite clear that further significant increases in the tax rate on petroleum production could very likely have serious detrimental effects on future levels of output and therefore payments to government and other positive economic impacts. If Nigerian policy-makers feel that petroleum industry participation is needed to help "pay for the war" (the exact meaning of this often-heard phrase is not clear), then they should seek advance payments, not rate increases. The issue is not that the international oil industry could not stand to pay incremental taxes; the industry would merely shift plans for expansion away from Nigeria to other sources of supply. It is essential that the goose laying the golden eggs for Nigeria should not be strangled in its infancy.

Given that Nigerian Government policy evolves in a way that promotes future oil production, a second set of policy questions arises. Naturally a fully detailed treatment of the use of oil-related revenues is a complete, separate topic of investigation in itself; however, a few speculative comments can be made. Though the physical limitations of Nigerian petroleum reserves have not yet been determined, there is every possibility that the scope of future Nigerian oil production may be fairly limited. If this should be so, then oil-related revenues, somewhat like foreign aid, could be expected to decrease over time. In this light it becomes especially important for Nigerian policy-makers to make good use of the petroleum bonanza while it lasts, for oil may not be a panacea that lubricates the machinery of economic development indefinitely.

While petroleum should not be viewed as an everlasting panacea for future Nigerian economic development, benefits associated with the production of crude oil are likely to facilitate the difficult structural changes that Nigeria will have to undertake in her quest for modernization. For this to occur on a massive scale it is essential that the Nigerian Government, as an integral intermediary in the process of transmitting oil export growth to other Nigerian sectors, make prudent social overhead and directly productive investments and sensible economic policy decisions. Only in this way can the potentially large fiscal linkages be achieved. And successful fiscal linkages are the principal vehicle through which the economic benefits of Nigerian petroleum can be attained in magnitude sufficient to more than compensate for any oil-associated political costs.

NOTES

1. In large degree this essay is an abbreviated version of certain parts of my thesis, "The Impacts of Petroleum Production on the Nigerian Economy," (unpublished Ph.D. dissertation, Department of Economics, Harvard University, 1968), completed in July, 1968. For invaluable assistance with this larger work I am indebted to Professors Albert O. Hirschman, Walter P. Falcon, and Wilson E. Schmidt.

2. Information in this section is drawn from the following sources: *The Shell-BP Story* (Port Harcourt: Shell-BP Petroleum Development Company of Nigeria, Limited, 1965); R. K. Dickie, "Development of Crude Oil Production in Nigeria, and the Federal Government's Control Measures," paper presented to The Institute of Petroleum, London, January, 1966; and E. J. Frankel and E. A. Cordry, "The Niger Delta Oil Province—Recent Developments Onshore and Offshore," paper presented to the Seventh World Petroleum Congress, Mexico City, April, 1967.

3. Interest and activity have recently shifted back to the Cretaceous area as well. In 1967 Safrap made two commercial discoveries in the Cretaceous, an oil well in the Anambra River basin and a gas well further east at Ibandiagu. Both are on the East Central State side of the border with Kwara State.

4. This analytical framework is elaborated in greater detail in my "The Impacts . . . ," pp. 4-11.

5. The concept of linkages, as first developed by Albert O. Hirschman in his *The Strategy of Economic Development* (New Haven: Yale University Press, 1958), p. 100, is broadened in the ensuing discussion.

6. Melville H. Watkins coins the term, final demand linkages, in "A Staple Theory of Economic Growth," *The Canadian Journal of Economics and Political Science*, XXIX (May, 1963), p. 146.

7. The refinery went on stream in October, 1965, and operated until the outbreak of the civil war in July, 1967. At the end of this period the 31,000 barrels per day rate at which the refinery was processing crude was just sufficient to meet domestic Nigerian demand for the most important petroleum products produced by the refinery.

8. See Albert O. Hirschman, *Development Projects Observed* (Washington, D.C.: The Brookings Institution, 1957), pp. 86-153.

9. In late 1966 and early 1967 the Nigerian Government altered the existing financial arrangements with the international petroleum companies by reducing the rates at which depreciation allowances accrue and increasing petroleum profits tax rates. For a complete discussion of the evolution and economic meaning of the oil industry's financial arrangements with the Nigerian Government see Appendix C in my "The Impacts . . . ," pp. C-1 — C-16.

10. Location advantages include both international shipping charges and security of supply route factors; in this regard Nigeria is favorably located with respect to her main markets in Western Europe and her secondary markets in South and North America. Quality advantages associated with Nigerian crude derive from its relatively low sulfur content, a property that becomes increasingly important as anti-air pollution legislation is passed in consuming countries.

11. The projections were made before the Nigerian Government instituted the "Companies Decree 1968" and do not take into consideration any changes in petroleum company production plans that might follow the implementation of this decree.

12. The High Projection may even be on the conservative side. *The Economist*, for example, foresees Nigerian petroleum output at 2.5 million barrels per day in 1975. See "What Happens Next Time?", *The Economist* (June 10, 1967), p. 1134.

13. Allowing for leakages reduces the contribution of Other Local Payments to the oil balance-of-payments impact by as much as one-fourth. But this lowers the total petroleum balance-of-payments impact in any single year by only 5-15 per cent (excluding 1968).

14. Gross Domestic Product exceeds Gross National Product by the amount of net factor payments made abroad; these payments are often very large where foreign export industries are involved. GDP accounting thus gives an inflated view of the amounts of goods and services actually available to indigenous factor owners.

15. The explanation for the equivalent growth rates within each accounting approach lies in the High and Low production assumptions. From 1970 to 1973, growth of oil output is assumed to be about equal under both projections, though the High Projection is made from a significantly larger base.

19. Policy for Nigerian Agricultural Development in the 1970's[1]

CARL K. EICHER AND GLENN L. JOHNSON

In previous chapters numerous references have been made to the important point that export agriculture has been the mainspring of Nigerian economic development from 1900 to early 1960's. In the early 1960's, however, modern manufacturing started to grow at a rapid rate followed by a boom in petroleum exports in 1964. However, even though manufacturing was growing at 15 per cent per annum in the mid-1960's, W. A. Lewis noted that "It is unlikely that Nigerian income benefits by as much as 30 per cent of the value added in large-scale manufacturing because most of the other 70 per cent of value added goes abroad" in the form of factor payments.[2] In addition, the modern manufacturing sector is still of modest size (6 per cent of GDP)—and even if it grows at a rapid rate in the 1970's—it will be unable to provide employment for the increasing members of the labor force arising from Nigeria's population boom. In the 1970's Nigeria has three leading sectors—export agriculture, petroleum, and manufacturing—instead of export agriculture which dominated the economy for the past half century. The central policy question for the 1970's is how can Nigeria develop an effective strategy of development which harnesses these three leading sectors and achieves both growth of the economy and development for the rank and file Nigerian.

In Nigeria and in most African nations there is a growing consensus that agricultural development is one of the most important problems that must be tackled in the 1970's. However, there is little agreement on *how* to increase agricultural output in Nigeria. We can gain a perspective on how to promote agricultural development in Nigeria by focusing on a four year interdisciplinary study of strategies for Nigerian rural development for the 1969-1985 period. This study was carried out by the Consortium for the Study of Nigerian Rural Development (CSNRD) in cooperation with a number of Nigerian universities and institutions.[3]

The CSNRD study had a strong, problem-solving orientation directed toward answering practical questions about strategies and policies for promoting Nigerian rural development and spelling out the implications

376

of these strategies and policies for external lenders, including the World Bank and AID.

THE CSNRD APPROACH TO STUDYING NIGERIAN RURAL DEVELOPMENT

The Consortium for the Study of Nigerian Rural Development team analyzed the theoretical tool kit of development economists and decided that growth stage models, dual sector models, input-output models, and the project approach that was emphasized by external lenders such as the World Bank and AID were of limited use in answering practical questions of *how* to promote Nigerian rural development in the 1970's. Consequently, the team undertook a three-pronged research study. First, the economic history of agricultural development was carefully reviewed. Then studies of the major Nigerian agricultural export and import substitution industries—cocoa, oil palm, rubber, groundnuts and cotton—were analyzed and supplemented when necessary with field studies in order to determine the expected payoffs on investments on a crop-by-crop basis over the 1970-85 period. Lesser but still significant attention was directed to analyzing the performance and prospects for nutritionally superior foods and staple foods. Food import trends were also carefully analyzed. Population data were scrutinized. This research process was essentially a building-block exercise to determine how Nigeria's widely varying agriculture in organized, the bottlenecks to expansion of agriculture on a commodity by commodity basis, and the expected payoffs or profits under present and new technology, modified pricing policies, etc.

The second emphasis of the study was directed at an analysis of how economic policies—trade, marketing boards, taxation, etc.—affected the production incentives of farming units and the performance of individual projects such as tree crop, groundnut and cotton schemes. The third emphasis of the study was directed at an analysis of institutions that supported rural development, credit, extension and agricultural research.

After these phases of our research were completed, CSNRD researchers developed three alternative sets of policies and programs to describe and quantify future consequences of alternative agricultural development policies over the 1970-85 period. These three alternative sets of policies and programs were described as three CSNRD policies: CSNRD I is a continuation of present agricultural and general economic policies and institutional support for agriculture; CSNRD II represents more favorable (than present) agricultural and general economic policies and institutional support for agriculture; CSNRD III represents less favorable (than present) agricultural and general economic policies and institutional support for agriculture.

The study then focused on CSNRD II policies for agricultural development and developed detailed production campaigns for the major export and import substitution crops over the 1970-85 period. Detailed physical, manpower and financial requirements for implementing the recommended production campaigns were also developed. Projections were then made of the likely aggregate farm incomes, foreign exchange earnings, and government revenues from the production campaigns for export and import substitution crops and the research and development programs for nutritionally superior and staple foods over the 1970-85 period.

We now turn to an analysis of the performance of the Nigerian agricultural economy since Independence in order to identify problems and bottlenecks to expanded agricultural development as a background for developing strategies for promoting Nigerian agricultural development over the 1970-85 period.

PROBLEMS AND PERFORMANCE OF NIGERIA'S AGRICULTURE: 1960 TO 1969

Nigeria is a land of an estimated five or six million small farms; these small farms have been the engine of growth of the Nigerian economy for generations. (See Chapter 1.) The CSNRD analysis focused on the 1960-69 period in order to appraise the performance of the Nigerian economy since Independence in 1960. The CSNRD analysis did not evaluate the performance of the agricultural sector since 1960 by comparing the government's intended capital recurrent outlays on agriculture during the First Plan with its actual expenditures. This approach is essentially a tedious exercise that is of little value in explaining the determinants of agricultural development or in providing an operational tool for preparing agricultural plans for the future. Also this approach may be misleading if inappropriate investment priorities and inappropriate types of agricultural projects—such as farm settlements and government plantations—received a large share of government capital and recurrent outlays during the time period being analyzed. Therefore, CSNRD researchers evaluated the performance of the agricultural sector during the First Plan by examining (a) rates of return on investment in government projects such as farm settlements and government plantations, (b) the performance of smallholders, private plantations, etc., (c) the magnitude and changing composition of food imports, food prices and agricultural exports, and (d) the performance of agricultural institutions such as agricultural extension, research, credit, sub-university and university level agricultural education, etc.

Export Crop Boom Led by Smallholders

The volume of export crops expanded from 1960 to 1967 at an annual compound growth rate of 4-6 per cent.

The second aspect of export crop production concerns the performance of various types of farm organizations producing these crops. Early land legislation in Nigeria virtually reserved agricultural production for Nigerian farmers until the early 1950's when regions were permitted to develop government plantations and encourage foreign private investors in agricultural production schemes. However, as Olatunbosun[4] and Saylor[5] have pointed out, plantation schemes were insignificant and, Nigerian small farmers were still the mainspring of agricultural development on the eve of Independence. Since Independence increasing attention has been devoted by the Regional governments in Southern Nigeria to government-sponsored land settlements and government-owned plantations. However, several studies have shown that government-sponsored farm settlement schemes and plantations were yielding low internal rates of return on investment while the school leaver and smallholder tree crop schemes were yielding favorable—10-20 per cent—internal rates of return on investments.[6] The general finding that the expansion of export and import substitution crops by smallholders was more profitable than government plantations and farm settlements leads to the conclusion that agricultural policy in the 1970's should phase out government plantations and government-sponsored farm settlement schemes as rapidly as possible and focus on assisting small farmers.

Effective Demand: A Major Constraint

Staple food output has expanded more or less automatically in line with population growth since Independence. Food imports were only about ten per cent of the total value of all imports over the entire 1954-67 period as shown in Table 1. Three-fourths of the food imports in 1966 and 1967 were a processed form of four nutritionally "superior" foods—(1) fish, (2) wheat and flour (3) milk and cream, and (4) sugar—as shown in Table 2. Domestic food prices fluctuated mildly during this period, and food prices increased only modestly from 1960 until the first military coup in 1966.

One of the significant findings of the CSNRD study was the identification of the lack of effective per capita demand (purchasing power) as a major constraint on the expansion of staple and nutritionally superior foods.[7] Although nutritionally superior food industries—poultry, pork, cattle—had spurts of rapid growth in the early 1960's, the low levels of per capita income restricted their expansion and prevented these foods from appreciably influencing the overall value of GNP contributed by the agricultural sector.

TABLE 1. *Total Nigerian Imports and Food Imports by Value as Percentage of Total Imports—1954-67.*

Year	Total imports £	Food and live animal imports £	Food imports as percent of total imports %
1954	114,069,000	12,031,000	10.54
1955	136,116,832	12,953,259	9.51
1956	152,713,477	16,044,900	10.50
1957	152,457,877	18,328,433	12.02
1958	166,450,983	18,164,543	10.91
1959	178,405,339	20,846,335	11.68
1960	215,890,804	23,911,334	11.07
1961	222,013,067	22,723,578	10.23
1962	203,217,500	23,492,838	11.56
1963	207,556,248	21,902,263	10.55
1964	253,879,677	20,620,281	8.12
1965	275,148,985	23,037,514	8.37
1966	256,371,945	25,784,308	10.05
1967	222,800,000[1]	21,279,526[1]	9.52

SOURCE: *Annual Abstract of Statistics*, 1950-54, and *Nigeria Trade Summaries*, 1960-66.

[1] Provisional data from the Federal Office of Statistics, Lagos.

TABLE 2. *Major Food Imports of Nigeria—1966, 1967*

Food Imports	Value 1966 £	Value 1967[1] £	Percent of All Food Imports 1966 %	Percent of All Food Imports 1967[1] %
All fish	7,467,066	4,900,208	28.96	23.02
Wheat	5,718,236	4,576,564	22.18	21.51
Milk and cream	4,025,707	3,606,113	15.61	16.95
Sugar	2,519,790	2,792,677	9.77	13.12
Other (including cattle)	6,053,509	5,403,964	23.48	25.40
TOTAL	25,784,308	21,279,526	100.00	100.00

SOURCE: *Nigeria Trade Summary*, 1966.

[1] Provisional data from the Federal Office of Statistics, Lagos.

Southern Nigeria's experience in developing a commercial egg industry to satisfy the protein needs of the poor illustrates the danger of overinvesting in nutritionally superior foods with limited markets (inadequate effective demand). The commercial egg industry in the Western and Eastern Regions of Nigeria (a) grew rapidly in the early 1960's, (b) moved through an import substitution phase and replaced imports with locally produced eggs, and (c) reduced the price of eggs to consumers from $1 (U.S. equivalent) a dozen in 1960 to 50¢ a dozen in 1965 and 1966. The expansion in egg production created an egg "marketing problem;" however, the problem was not a marketing problem in the usual sense of inefficiency but simply the reflection of a lack of effective demand. The average wage earner still did not earn enough to buy eggs even though the price had been cut in half. This experience suggests that planners were wise in promoting poultry as an import substitution industry in the early 1960's, but they overinvested in egg production given the limited market for eggs. However, planners were unwise in thinking that the protein problem of the poor could be solved by eggs and poultry. The majority of the poor lacked the effective demand or purchasing power to satisfy their protein needs from such a relatively expensive source of protein. As we shall point out later the effective demand constraint has major implications for agricultural planning in the 1970's.

Rural-Urban Income Differentials

Rural versus urban real incomes is an issue which has an important bearing on rural to urban migration, school leavers, and incentives for investment in agriculture. Here the focus is on an analysis of the dual forces which influence the rural-urban real wage or income differential in Nigeria: (a) government wage policy which adjusts money wages for government workers every few years and (b) government taxes on export and import substitution crops—marketing board taxes, export duties and producer purchase taxes—which depress real incomes received by farmers producing these crops.

In Nigeria and many other African nations the government is the largest employer in the industrial-urban sector and government minimum wage legislation more or less determines the wage scale for wage employment in the entire economy.[8] In Nigeria, government wages are set after a commission of inquiry has investigated into wages and conditions of employment every few years. Government wages were adjusted in 1954-55, 1959 and 1964 and the minimum wage for general labor was increased from 4s8d in 1954-55 to 5s10d in 1959 to 7s8d in 1964. This increase of 67 per cent in money wages in ten years was almost matched by the same rise in real wages in light of the small changes in the price level.[9] Government wage determination has been dominated by political and institutional forces while supply and demand considerations were given secondary consideration. Rural to urban migration has been stimulated by this rapid increase in money wage in the urban sector.

The other aspect of the rural-urban real wage (income) differential is the profitability of farming. Since marketing board taxes and other taxes skim off from one quarter to one third of the potential producer prices of most export and import substitution crops, we shall examine the operation of Nigeria's marketing boards in some detail. Marketing boards were an important institutional innovation in the 1940's in an agriculturally dominated economy where: (1) inflationary pressures generated by the shortage of consumer goods during and immediately following World War II had to be checked, (2) the export trade was controlled by a few large foreign firms who could easily exert their monopolistic and political influences on Nigerian society, (3) foreign firms were restricted from establishing easy to tax plantations, (4) administrative skills were lacking to inaugurate a land tax, income tax, etc., and (5) most importantly, an alternative major source of government revenue such as petroleum, minerals, was not available.

Nigeria's marketing boards have pursued a negative tax policy over the past 20 years and have turned the domestic terms of trade against agricultural export crops and import substitution crops such as cotton. Although some of the marketing board "surpluses" were transferred back to agriculture as input subsidies—e.g., fertilizer, pesticides, etc.—the net effect has been a substantial transfer to the non-agricultural sector.[10] Marketing boards have performed an important fiscal role (source of government tax revenue). After acknowledging that marketing boards have helped finance non-agricultural development, two questions follow: (1) What was the impact of the marketing board taxes on the rate of growth of export and import substitution crops and (2) What can be said about the efficiency of the government's use of these marketing board taxes? On the first question, with the exception of palm oil, the volume of Nigeria's agricultural exports has grown at an annual compound rate of 4-6 per cent during the past 10-15 years in spite of high marketing board taxes. Specifically, cotton production grew at an annual compound growth rate of 9.5 per cent from 1949-50 to 1964-65.[11] The volume of groundnut exports (including groundnut oil equivalents) grew at a 5.2 per cent annual compound growth rate between 1956-58 to 1964-66. The volume of cocoa exports has grown at a compound average growth rate of 7 per cent over the 1956-58 to 1965-67 period. On the other hand, rubber exports, which have *not* been so taxed have grown at a 6.25 per cent annual compound growth rate between 1956-58 and 1964-66. The impressive growth rates of cotton, groundnuts, and cocoa in spite of marketing board taxes no doubt led Helleiner to his optimistic statement in 1964 that "It can therefore unambiguously be stated that Nigerian development has been aided through the device of channelling a portion of its export earnings via the marketing boards from the producer to other (governmental) decision-makers."[12]

As to the second question, marketing board surpluses have been used to finance regional political parties as Charles Nixon. (See Chapter 8.) Also, marketing board surpluses have sponsored many-dubious projects as elaborated in the Coker Commission Report[13] and in the Northern Region's 1967 White Papers on the Northern Nigerian marketing boards and Development Corporation.[14] These papers dramatically point out the shortcomings of marketing board-financed government industrial schemes. Also, the pricing policy of the marketings boards has contributed to the massive rural to urban migration, has restricted the rise in rural land values by government's taxing away the rent and has held down the growth of effective demand among farm people.

In light of the government's inefficient use of marketing board surpluses we conclude that, on balance, the record of marketing boards through 1969 is less impressive than Helleiner reported in 1964. However, even though rates of growth of Nigeria's export crops may have been higher in the absence of marketing board taxes, and even though marketing board surpluses helped finance political parties, "white elephant" industrial schemes and government hotels, no practical alternative was available for breaking the foreign exchange constraint and financing structural change of the economy until the quantum jump in petroleum exports began in 1964. The projected petroleum boom has good prospects of breaking the foreign exchange constraint, and, as a result, policy makers can now realistically consider shifting from a negative to a positive price policy for export and import substitution crops in the 1970's. (See Chapter 18.)

Population boom

Nigeria's official population figures are still open to question. However, CSNRD used the official 1963 census figure of 55.6 million as a benchmark and projected that the population would grow to about 100 million by 1985. We assumed that the population growth rate would increase gradually from 2.4 per annum in 1969-70 to 2.9 per cent by 1985 (Table 3). Even if our 100 million population figure for 1985 is somewhat high, Nigeria will likely have a population of 90 million by 1985. A rate of growth of population that will result in 90-100 million people by 1985 has major implications for agricultural and educational policies for the 1970's.

The population explosion carried with it a new problem of great difficulty—the employment problem. Harbison has concluded that Ni-

TABLE 3.   *Projections of Population in Nigeria.*[1]

Year	Population
	Million
1963	55.6
1966	60.8
1970	67.0
1975	75.9
1980	86.6
1985	99.6

SOURCE: AID data book, 1963, 1966.

[1] Growth rates of population are assumed as follows:
  1963-66—2.3 percent per year.
  1967-70—2.4 percent per year.
  1971-73—2.5 percent per year.
  1974-76—2.6 percent per year.
  1977-80—2.7 percent per year.
  1981-84—2.8 percent per year.
  1985   —2.9 percent per year.

geria's nonagricultural sector can increase employment by no more than three percent per year and, as a result, agriculture should in his judgment, be viewed as the "self-employment sector" for the next 10-15 years. (See Chapter 20.) Thus, Nigeria—like many other less developed countries in their early stage of industrialization—will experience an *absolute* increase in population in agriculture even though the relative percentage of population in agriculture will decline by a few percentage points in the 1970's. The likely one million annual absolute population increase in Nigeria's agricultural sector in the 1970's requires imaginative agricultural policies to employ people in agriculture. The growth in petroleum provides a means of breaking the foreign exchange constraint and reducing the tax burden on exports from agriculture. However, petroleum will generate relatively little employment; for example, in Venezuela, petroleum provides employmnt for only one per cent of the labor force.

Summary of the Performance of Nigeria's Agriculture in the 1960's

The discussion of the performance of the agricultural sector since Independence points out that the government has wisely pursued an open market food policy that has supplied the present per capita effective demand with a diet adequate in calories but inadequate in protein—particularly in Southern Nigeria. In short, food production has kept up with the growth in effective demand for food. However, protein needs were not met in Southern Nigeria prior to the Civil War; the protein problem was not a production or supply problem. The main bottleneck to expanded protein intake in Southern Nigeria was a combination of a lack of effective demand and nutritional education.

The volume of agricultural exports has grown at 4-5 per cent per annum in spite of a negative tax policy on export and import substitution crops. However, the negative tax policies have (a) aided the migration to urban areas, (b) held down rural land values by taxing away the rent, (c) diverted potential foreign investors in agricultural production to other African countries such as Liberia and the Cameroons, (d) held back the introduction of new agricultural technology such as hybrid palms[15] and perhaps most importantly, (e) restricted the expansion of the effective demand of rural people—who comprise 75 per cent of Nigeria's population. This last point is frequently overlooked by many economists who favor policies to promote growth in per capita income as the *central goal* of planning and promote the goal of more equitable distribution of income only secondarily. However, as we shall later elaborate the recommended agricultural policies for the 1970's assign a high priority to the expansion of production by smallholders through more favorable commodity prices because (a) smallholder export crop production is profitable (b) it is an effective way of translating increases in production into increases in effective demand for the bulk of Nigeria's population—rural people—and (c) it is a vital component of progressive industrial development by import substitution.

STRATEGIES AND POLICIES FOR NIGERIAN RURAL DEVELOPMENT IN THE 1970's[16]

We pointed out earlier that CSNRD research was designed to search for opportunities for fostering Nigerian rural development in the 1970's. CSNRD personnel were convinced that the "prime movers" of the Nigerian economy in the 1970's will be: (1) export crop expansion, (2) petroleum and (3) selective industrialization.

Two strategies are recommended for fostering Nigerian rural development over the 1970-85 period. The first concentrates on immediate expansion of export[17] and import substitution crops and distributing the resulting increases in income to a large number of rural people. Increased farm incomes will expand the effective demand of the bulk of the population, absorb employment in agriculture and provide the savings for financing an increase in production by small farmers.

The second strategy is designed to provide lead time to feed the projected 90-100 million people in Nigeria by 1985. This strategy involves greatly expanded support for biological research in order to develop economically superior varieties of plants and animals which will reduce the cost of producing staple foods and feed grains that are essential for reducing the cost of producing such nutritionally superior foods as poultry. Success in developing high-yielding dwarf sorghum and millet varieties in the Northern States will release land and labor for expanding cotton and groundnut production and make available food and feed grains for the southern states as they increase their specialization in tree crops. The two strategies are spelled out in operational terms in Table 4.

Three major policies are essential in order to implement these two strategies:

(1) The first involves providing farmers with more favorable incentives by raising the prices of export and import substitution crops through reduced taxes.

(2) The second involves giving direct, short-run, public support to farmers producing commodities with high economic payoffs. Provincial and state production campaigns are recommended for each of the major export and import substitution crops.

(3) The third involves the provision of infrastructure support, including research, extension credit and other supporting services for both strategies.

Improved Incentives

We shall now comment on each of these three policies. The first—improving producer incentives—is a key policy that involves a substantial improvement in the domestic terms of trade for agriculture by substituting petroleum revenues for taxes on export agriculture. Improving the profitability of farming will do far more to make farming attractive to young people than teaching agriculture in the primary schools. A policy of improving incentives for export crop expansion, of course, supports industrialization, as exports earn the foreign exchange that pays for capital imports needed by industrialization, generates effective demand for rural people who can then purchase consumer goods produced by the industrial sector, and provides the raw materials—cotton, kenaf, sugar— for progressive import substitution industries.

Production Campaigns

Concentration of public support on production campaigns for crops with high payoffs requires close coordination between state and national agencies and considerable local and state initiative in the pragmatic design and implementation of campaigns on a state-by-state basis. Smallholders should be assigned the central role in expanding export and import substitution crops. Primary attention should be given to cocoa, oil palm, groundnuts, and cotton; minor attention should be given to rubber

TABLE 4. *Type of Government Investment Activity Recommended to Facilitate Expansion of Nigerian Agriculture, by Commodity Groups, 1970-1985*

	Strategy I. (Expand Production)		Strategy II. (Research and Development)
	Export and Import Substitution Commodities (e.g, cocoa, oil palm, groundnuts, sugar, cotton, kenaf)	Superior Foods (e.g., rice, poultry, high lysine maize)	Staple Foods (e.g., sorghum, millett, yam, wheat, cassava)
Type of Government Investment Activity Required	1. Organize and direct major commodity campaigns for cocoa, oil palm, groundnuts, and cotton.	1. Organize and promote restricted production campaigns	1. Major government investment in research on plant breeding to develop new "models" of crops to lower production costs by the 1975-1980 period
	2. Invest in production of seedlings and in distribution of inputs—fertilizer, seeds, etc.	2. Expanded adaptive research on production and processing problems	2. Long term research on soil fertility, animal production, and animal diseases
	3. Improve quality of technical assistance and expand credit to smallholders	3. Invest in human nutrition campaigns for both urban and rural people	3. Expand field research of fertilizer, animal powered mechanization, farm level processing, etc.
	4. Expand transport, feeder roads, port storage, etc.	4. Invest in joint public-private research to search for new markets in West Africa, Africa, and other nations for Nigerian agricultural products such as rice, livestock, etc.	
	5. Improve competence of research staff at CRIN, NIFOR, etc.		
	6. Expand research on rubber and initiate research on new crops—citrus, tea, etc.		

production provided the new crumb rubber processing technology, which is proceeding so well in Malaysia and Liberia, can be adapted to the smallholder type of farm organization in Nigeria. Production campaigns should emphasize developing a package of inputs, such as hybrid oil palm seedlings and fertilizer, and extension assistance for oil palm farmers and fertilizer for groundnut farmers. Major attention in production campaigns should be given to smallholders producing export and import substitution crops while minor attention should go to production campaigns for nutritionally superior foods such as poultry, eggs, etc.

Supporting Services for Agriculture

Government infrastructure support should be implemented for the production campaigns, including extension, inputs such as fertilizer, seedlings, credit and research. This policy involves the concentration of research, extension, credit and supporting services in geographical areas and commodity groups where there are profitable investment opportunities rather than scattering supporting services on an equitable basis—district by district, and province by province. For example, we recommend that Nigeria not follow the FAO recommendation of providing one extension agent per x number of farmers. Frequently, a comparison is made between the United States, which has one extension agent per 300-400 farmers, and an LDC, which may have one extension agent per 2,000 to 5,000 farmers. Instead of invoking the U. S. experience, one extension agent for 40 to 100 progressive farmers is included in the CSNRD recommended production campaigns and then the number of farmers served by the agent is expanded as more experience is gained and as real resources—fertilizer, seedlings, etc.—can be provided at the farm level.

PLANNING IN THE NEW STATES IN 1970's

On April 1, 1968 Nigeria's four regions were converted into twelve states. Planning for the new states is a major task which requires fresh thinking on how the states can be given considerable initiative in developing agricultural policies and programs, and projects which are *relevant* to local conditions. However, there is a danger that the new states will develop "inward looking" policies and concentrate on developing state self-sufficiency objectives for the major food crops. For this reason, strong and imaginative leadership is also required by the Federal planners in order that planning supports the development of one national market —rather than 12 state markets—and on the basis of one national market which is closer integrated into the world economic system (See Chapter 17).

The two recommended CSNRD strategies for rural development in the 1970's—expand export and import substitution crops and accelerate research and pilot production campaigns for nutritionally superior foods and staple foods—can be executed by Nigeria's planners and able civil servants. However, planners should shift their attention from viewing agriculture as a source of public revenue—through taxes and export crops—to viewing agriculture as a potential dynamic source of growth which can increase effective demand for the bulk of Nigeria's population—rural people—generate foreign exchange earnings, and serve as a "self-employment" sector until population control programs—if implemented in the early 1970's—become effective in the mid or late 1980's.

If Nigerian planners shift their attention to viewing agriculture as a potential dynamic source of growth of the overall economy, then they should concentrate on designing effective policies for guiding the decision of millions of small farmers in Nigeria. Since Nigeria does not have the human resources for detailed supervision of government land settlement and plantation schemes, the expansion of commodity output can most efficiently take place by small farmers in the 1970's. For this reason we recommend that Nigeria concentrate on formulating policies to assist Nigeria's millions of farmers in expanding agricultural output rather than on focusing attention on government production schemes in agriculture.

Nigeria is fortunate to have the technological base for greatly expanded production of export and import substitution crops in the 1970's. However, agricultural production is highly location specific and requires detailed physical data on a crop by crop and state by state basis.[18] For this reason, agricultural planning units should be built into state governments in order that the states can move into detailed physical planning on a crop by crop basis. Physical planning is required in order that financial planning is firmly supported by physical data and in order that investments in directly productive activities can be reconciled with investments in human resources and infrastructure components such as credit, agricultural research, extension and university and middle level manpower training.

A final note on the interdependence between agricultural policy and general development policy is in order in light of the agricultural policy focus of this chapter. We have made a strong case for moving beyond statements about the need for a rural transformation in Nigeria and have urged that the agricultural sector be disaggregated in order to determine strategies and priorities for rural development on a sub-sector and on a commodity by commodity basis. We have attempted to show *how* to arrive at strategies for rural development in Nigeria over the short run— next 10-15 years. We have also shown how agricultural strategies are closely linked with the main growing points of the economy in the

'seventies—export and import-substitution crops, petroleum, and industrialization. Since effective demand is a major short-run constraint on
the expansion of staple and nutritionally superior foods, we have suggested that a smallholder export led strategy of development can assist
in achieving growth of the economy as well as development for the rank
and file Nigerians who are and will be mainly rural people in the 1970's
and 1980's. *However, an export led strategy of development cannot be a
substitute for a long-run transformation of the structure of the economy.*
Obviously, an export led—vent for surplus—strategy needs to be supplemented with vigorous research on staple foods and nutritionally superior
foods in light of the population explosion. Also, an export led strategy
needs to be carefully articulated with policies which will channel public
revenues from petroleum into capital rather than recurrent expenditures
and into reduced taxes on agriculture in the short-run until alternative
methods can be devised to tax agriculture without substantially destroy-
ing producer incentives. Also, industrial policies must be articulated with
agricultural policies in order to promote long-run structural change of the
economy. For the above reasons, the policies for agricultural development should be examined in light of their ability to change the center of
gravity of the economy from a primarily agrarian to an industrial society
over time rather than viewing our recommended policies for agriculture
as policies of agrarian fundamentalism—that is an expansion of agricultural output for the benefit of the agricultural sector.

NOTES

1. This chapter draws heavily on the findings of a four year research
   study which is reported in the following publications; Glenn L. John-
   son, O. J. Scoville, George Dike and Carl Eicher, *Strategies and
   Recommendations for Nigerian Rural Development, 1969-1985,* East
   Lansing, Michigan: Consortium for the Study of Nigerian Rural
   Development, Michigan State University, 1969. Also the chapter
   draws on a paper based on the CSNRD study by Carl K. Eicher,
   "Reflections on West Africa's Rural Development Problems of the
   1970's." Symposium on Africa in the 1980's, Adlai Stevenson Institute,
   Chicago, April 1968 which is reprinted, in part, by permission of the
   Adlai Stevenson Institute.

2. W. A. Lewis, *Reflections on Nigeria's Economic Growth,* Paris: OECD
   Development Center, 1967, p. 26.

3. The CSNRD study was financed by AID and carried out by a number
   of American Universities and governmental agencies in cooperation
   with a number of Nigerian institutions. The American universities
   and institutions participating in the CSNRD study include Michigan

State University, Kansas State University, University of Wisconsin, Colorado State University, U. S. Department of Agriculture, U. S. Department of Interior and the Research Triangle Institute of North Carolina. As the study evolved cooperative links were established between CSNRD researchers and Nigerian institutions such as the Federal Ministry of Economic Development, Federal Ministry of Agriculture and Natural Resources, National Universities Commission, Federal Department of Agriculture, NISER, EDI, etc. O. J. Scoville of Kansas State University served in Lagos, Nigeria as Field Project Leader for the Consortium for the Study of Nigerian Rural Development. Professor Scoville is mainly responsible for developing cooperative working links with the appropriate Nigerian government officials and university scholars.

4. Dupe Olatunbosun, "Nigerian Farm Settlements and School Leavers' Farms—Profitability, Resource Use and Social Psychological Considerations," East Lansing: Consortium for the Study of Nigerian Rural Development, Michigan State University, 1967.

5. R. Gerald Saylor, "A Study of Obstacles to Investment in Oil Palm and Rubber Plantation," East Lansing: Consortium for the Study of Nigerian Rural Development, August, 1968.

6. See David MacFarlane and Martin Oworen, *Investment in Oil Palm Plantations in Nigeria*, Enugu: Economic Development Institute, University of Nigeria, 1965; Jerome Wells, "Issues in Agricultural Policy During the 1962-68 Development Plan," (See Chapter 13), and Carl K. Eicher "Reflections on Capital-Intensive Moshav Farm Settlements in Southern Nigeria," in *Agricultural Cooperatives and Markets in Developing Areas*, Edited by E. Smith, K. Anschel and R. Brannon (New York: Praeger, 1969).

7. Carl K. Eicher, "Effective Demand and Agricultural Planning," *Ceres—The FAO Review*, Vol. 3, No. 3, 1969 and Glenn L. Johnson, "Food Supply, Agricultural and Economic Development," East Lansing: Consortium for the Study of Nigerian Rural Development, Working paper No. 8, September 1968.

8. Charles R. Frank, Jr., "Urban Unemployment and Economic Growth in Africa," *Oxford Economic Papers*, Vol. 20, No. 2 (July 1968), pp. 250-274.

9. *Ibid.*, p. 264.

10. Gerald Helleiner, "The Fiscal Role of the Marketing Board in Nigerian Economic Development, 1947-61," (See Chapter 7).

11. Food and Agriculture Organization of the United Nations, *Agricultural Development in Nigeria, 1965-1980*, Rome: 1966, p. 505.

12. Helleiner, *op. cit.*

13. Federal Ministry of Information, *Report of the Coker Commission of Inquiry Into the Affairs of Certain Statutory Corporations in Western Nigeria*, Lagos: 1962.

14. Government of Northern Nigeria, *A White Paper on the Military Government's Policy for the Reorganization of the Northern Nigeria Development Corporation*, Kaduna: Government Printer, 1966 and *A White Paper on the Northern Nigeria Military Government's Policy for the Comprehensive Review of Past Operations of the Northern Nigeria Marketing Board*, Kaduna: Government Printer, 1967.

15. Glenn L. Johnson, "Removing Obstacles to the Use of Genetic Breakthroughs in Oil Palm Production: The Nigerian Case," *Agricultural Research Priorities for Economic Development in Africa—The Abidjan Conference*, Washington, D. C.: National Academy of Science, 1968.

16. This section draws heavily on the research of CSNRD economists who studied public and private direct investment opportunities in Nigerian agriculture and reported their research in the following publication: C. K. Laurent, H. C. Kriesel, Dupe Olatunbosun, M. Purvis and R. G. Saylor, *Agricultural Investment Strategy in Nigeria* East Lansing: Consortium for the Study of Nigerian Rural Development, January 1969.

17. Advocates of industrial fundamentalism sometimes advance the case for giving priority to industry on account of the low income elasticity of demand for primary (agricultural) products. However, in spite of the gloomy forecasts for world trade of primary products, these global parameters do not offer much guidance to an individual LDC. In spite of the arguments that international trade cannot provide an engine of growth for LDC's, during the 1955-63 period, the value of total exports from Africa increased by 42 per cent while those from Latin America and Asia increased by 22 and 10 per cent respectively. The implication of this analysis is that each LDC must assess the demand conditions for and the profitability of its particular export products rather than assuming exports from agriculture are doomed. As an example of the type of demand analysis on a crop by crop basis, see Robert Gray, "Projections of Demand for Nigeria's Export Crops, 1969-1985," Ph.D. dissertation in progress, Department of Agricultural Economics, Michigan State University, 1969.

18. See George L. Brinkman, "Reconciling Proposed Investments in Agricultural Education, Infrastructure and Production in Nigeria, 1969-1985," unpublished Ph.D. dissertation, Department of Agricultural Economics, Michigan State University, 1969.

20. From Ashby to Reconstruction: Manpower and Education in Nigeria

FREDERICK H. HARBISON

INTRODUCTION

The Ashby Commission Report of 1960 opened an era of education and manpower development in modern Nigeria.[1] Issued at the time of Nigerian independence, it immediately won wide acclaim and acceptance throughout the new nation. The nine members of the Commission[2] proclaimed boldly that their recommendations were "massive, unconventional, and expensive." They argued with great conviction that it would be a disservice to the nation if they were to come forth only with "modest, cautious proposals likely to fall within the budget," for such proposals, they thought, would be totally inadequate to maintain even the current rate of economic growth in the country. In a summary of their recommendations, the Commission members declared:

> We propose a rate of investment in education which far outstrips the probable growth of Nigeria's economy by 1970. . . . We propose almost to double the number of primary school pupils, almost to quadruple the number of students in secondary schools, and to multiply by more than five the present number of university students in Nigerian institutions.[3]

The Nigerian officials were bolder than the Commission. In a White Paper issued in 1961,[4] the Federal Government accepted the Commission's report in principle as a minimum basis for building education in Nigeria for the next ten years. It then went further and raised many of the Ashby targets, particularly those for primary education in the North and for university and secondary school enrollments for the country as a whole. Thus, as it emerged as an independent nation, Nigeria had an announced strategy for development of education even before it had a plan for national economic development. And this strategy, most observers believed, was well designed to meet the problems which then appeared to have the top priority.

THE RECORD OF ACHIEVEMENT AFTER INDEPENDENCE

By 1967, just before the outbreak of the tragic civil war, it was apparent that Nigeria had already made impressive progress in building its educational system. Enrollment in Nigerian universities was over 8,000 students and would probably have reached 12,500 by 1970 if the war had not taken place. The Ashby Report proposed only 7,500 by 1970, a target which was increased to 10,000 by the White Paper. There were five operating universities, a sixth in process of development (Port Harcourt), and still another contemplated (in Benin), in contrast to the Ashby Report recommendation that four would be sufficient. The intake into secondary grammar schools had already climbed from 12,000 in 1958 to over 37,000 in 1965, and it was growing by nearly 20 percent each year. The Ashby Report had suggested a secondary school intake target of 30,000 by 1970, which the White Paper increased to 45,000 for the same year. Clearly, secondary grammar school enrollments were exceeding the boldest hopes and expectations of the Commission and the Government. The same trend was apparent in sixth form enrollments.

Even more remarkable, however, was the tremendous increase in expenditures for education. When the Ashby Commission started its work, Nigeria was probably devoting a little more than 1½ percent of GDP to education; by 1966 it was spending over 3 percent. Indeed, the annual compound growth rate of recurrent expenditure on education was averaging about 15 percent, as compared with a GDP annual growth rate of about 4 percent.[5]

Few, if any, African countries can match Nigeria's post-independence record of achievement in educational development. By the end of 1966 Nigeria had built an extensive network of institutions and mechanisms for human resource development. In accordance with the Ashby recommendations, a National Manpower Board had been set up as part of the development planning machinery and a National Universities Commission had been established. Nigeria had been successful in getting large amounts of external aid and technical assistance for secondary and higher education. The rapidly growing universities were of high quality. Government, as a result of strong pressures from the people, was giving the highest priority to development of secondary and higher education. The response to the Ashby Commission recommendations was indeed massive, unconventional, and spectacular. The effort was much greater than could have been anticipated in 1960.

The questions now are these: Were the tremendous resources devoted to education properly allocated, considering the goals at the time of independence? In what respect are the issues faced today different from those in 1960? What are the high priority goals for building a program of development and utilization of human resources for the next decade?

In some areas, Nigeria failed to follow the guidelines or to achieve the targets set forth in the Ashby Report. In the North, it became obvious that it would be impossible to meet the Ashby target of 25 percent of the primary age group in school by 1970; the White Paper had suggested a 50 percent goal. It was clear that teacher education was far below the target range. From 1960 to 1965, for example, enrollment in teacher training institutions for secondary and post-secondary levels had expanded at an annual compound rate of only 2 percent, in comparison with annual growth rates in pupil enrollments of nearly 20 percent for secondary grammar schools, 40 percent for sixth forms, and 24 percent for Nigerian universities. The consequence was a lowering of quality of secondary education in many areas and a lingering dependence on expatriate teachers. Moreover, aggregate enrollments in primary education did not increase at all from 1960 to 1965.[6]

Even more serious was the shortfall in intermediate technical training. The Ashby Report called for an *annual flow* of 2,500 students into post-secondary technical colleges by 1970. The White Paper raised this target to an *output* of 5,000 technicians from such institutes. In 1965 the annual intake into the technical colleges was less than 500 and the output was less than 450.[7] The National Manpower Board repeatedly warned that rapid development of technical institutes was the most critical problem of manpower development in Nigeria. Writing in 1967, the country's leading manpower economist, Professor T. M. Yesufu, stated that Nigeria needed at least thirty more full-fledged secondary technical institutes and ten more colleges of technology, and to achieve this he argued that university expansion should be proportionately curtailed.[8] The shortfalls in training of agricultural assistants, veterinary assistants, nurses, and medical technicians were equally disappointing.

It was clear by 1967 that, in relative terms, Nigeria was overinvesting in university education and in that kind of secondary education which was geared to preparation for university entry. It was underinvesting in sub-professional technical training, and it was failing to produce an adequate supply of qualified teachers at all levels. But this distortion in allocating resources was probably attributable more to student demand, political pressure, and an antiquated colonial wage and salary structure than to failure to recognize problems or to poor planning. Both the Ashby Report and the White Paper had charted a better balanced program of development.

Even more disturbing, however, were the shortcomings of resource allocation within the very areas of over-achievement of targets. By 1967 it was clear that Nigerian universities had too many students in law, liberal arts, and social studies. Graduates in these areas were finding it difficult to get senior level positions; many were forced to accept intermediate-type jobs for which a university education is by no means necessary; some were already entering the ranks of the unemployed. On the other hand, too few graduates were being produced in agronomy, veterinary medicine, some branches of engineering, and the natural and physical sciences. As Professor Yesufu observed:

> A careful analysis of manpower data has indicated that not less than 60 percent of Nigeria's manpower must receive at least a basic training in science and technology. The present position is almost the reverse with 60 percent of Nigerian students in institutions of higher learning enrolled in the liberal arts or the social studies.[9]

Here, the major problem was probably the inability of the secondary schools to prepare students for entry into the science and technology faculties in higher education, principally because of teacher shortages in mathematics and science in the secondary schools.

The extremely high cost of university education in Nigeria was especially serious. In terms of cost-per-student, Nigeria's universities were among the most expensive in the world. Student-faculty ratios averaged about six-to-one; salaries were very high because of large-scale employment of expatriates. Because of small enrollments in each of a wide range of faculties, economies of scale were not possible, and the costs of providing on-campus housing for students and staff were staggering. The Ashby concept of the new University of Lagos as a non-residential city university was rejected. And finally, the universities were beginning to press for post-graduate education, a costly venture which would make it more difficult to lower expenditures per student.

Another serious problem was the orientation of secondary education toward preparation for further education at the university level. This single-purpose preoccupation of secondary grammar schools in effect overlooked the needs of the majority of students who terminated their formal education at that level. Most of the curriculum was highly academic and tended to deflect the interest of students from higher sub-professional training and intermediate-level employment. Thus, those who failed to gain access to universities quite rightly had a sense of failure. The sixth form which was geared exclusively to university entry reinforced the single-axis orientation of secondary education. And the available places in the small number of secondary technical schools were crowded with those who failed to gain entry into grammar schools. The university was casting its shadow over secondary education which in turn was dictating the curriculum of the primary schools. The single-purpose educational system at the primary and secondary levels, oriented to university entry which only a few could achieve, was in many respects operating as a vast mechanism to make failures out of the majority of students.

These and other shortcomings of education development, however, should not be overemphasized. On balance, Nigeria was making solid progress by 1967. Government officials and educators were aware of the serious distorting of secondary education. At least the idea of multi-purpose comprehensive secondary schools was taking hold, particularly in the Western Region. Some demonstration comprehensive schools were in operation. More attention was being given to reform and expansion of technical training. The universities were under pressure to gear their program more closely to the needs of the nation, and, in the face of growing financial stringency at home and the prospect of curtailed aid from abroad, they were at least considering the necessity for "trimming their sails." The period of euphoria over independence had passed, and a new era of hardheaded planning was approaching. There was growing recognition, on the part of educators, planners, and politicians alike, that the country simply could not afford to devote an ever larger proportion of its resources to education and that, as a consequence, the resources being spent on it would have to be allocated more carefully in accordance with the development needs of the country. One could be reasonably optimistic, therefore, that many of the problems mentioned above were on the way to solution. No other African country was making more progress in high-level manpower development; no other country was more committed to investment in education.

At the time of the outbreak of the civil war, however, the critical issues and central concerns in the development and utilization of human resources were quite different from those at the time of independence. In the Ashby Commission days, the building of secondary and higher education institutions was the top priority concern. Now, having made substantial progress in high-level manpower development for government and industry, the focus of attention had shifted to underemployment, mounting unemployment in the cities, and the explosive frustration of school-leavers unable to find a place in the still relatively small modern sectors of the country. The need for a rural transformation in order to sustain any kind of industrial revolution was becoming clear. The dilemma of reorganization and reconstruction of a nation split by regional and tribal controversy which was casting its ominous shadow over every aspect of Nigerian life was recognized. Such baffling new problems now commanded the focus of attention in 1967.

THE NEW PERSPECTIVE OF THE MIDDLE SIXTIES

The problem of what to do with surplus manpower—unemployed and underutilized manpower in both urban and rural areas—is presently and potentially much more serious and more difficult to solve than the problem of high-level skill development. Hard facts and reliable statistics are not easy to find in Nigeria. A labor force survey is yet to be completed; population estimates are open to question; and the term "employment" is subject to a variety of interpretations. It is possible, therefore, to set forth only rough and tentative orders of magnitude. However, these do provide a basis for identification of the country's major manpower problems.[10]

Let us assume that Nigeria's present population is somewhere in the neighborhood of fifty million people. Reasoning (by Arthur Lewis' "rule of thumb") that about 33 to 38 percent of the population may be considered as in the labor force, about 17 to 19 million persons are either occupied in or trying to become engaged in productive activity of some kind.

About 85 percent of the labor force is in rural areas and about 15 percent in urban areas.[11] Roughly, then, there may be about 2.5 to 2.8 million people in the urban labor force and about 14.8 to 16.5 million in the rural labor force. To simplify the analysis, let us choose a figure of 2.6 million in the urban and 15.4 million in the rural, making a total labor force of 18 million.

Now a look at the so-called modern sector. In Nigeria, this sector includes the more productive enterprises, the government establishment, and government-supported services, such as education and health. For lack of any better criterion, this sector may be deemed to include most of those activities enumerated in various government establishment surveys, since such surveys are limited to the more visible and highly productive enterprises and government. On the basis of such surveys, there are probably between 700,000-900,000 persons employed in this modern sector, of which at least 600,000-750,000 are employed in the urban areas and the remainder in rural areas, agriculture, and related activities.

It is probable that less than 5 percent of Nigeria's labor force is employed in the modern sector. It is logical to expect, both from empirical calculations and inter-country comparisons, that the net average annual increase in the modern sector labor force will not exceed 3 percent. In this high wage, high productivity sector, the output-to-employment ratio is certainly not lower than three-to-one; the average increase in output (including government and modern enterprise) will certainly not exceed 9 percent; and there are indications that it may be far below this level. Indeed, in East African countries, such as Kenya, Tanzania, and Zambia, total wage earnings employment in the modern sector has actually *decreased* in the past six to eight years despite substantial growth in output.

It is obvious, therefore, that between now and 1980, the modern sector will barely hold its own in absorbing increments in the total labor force. On the assumption that Nigeria's total labor force, as a consequence of the estimated rate of increase in population, will grow at a rate of between 2½ and 3 percent per year, the proportion of the labor force employed in the modern sector in 1980 may be only slightly greater, if at all, than at present.

At the other end of the continuum from the modern sector is the subsistence or traditional sector. In rural areas, this consists mainly of farmers who have little contact with the money economy. In the cities it comprises persons underemployed in petty trade and casual labor, beggars and unemployed job seekers. Although there have been no attempts at precise measurement, probably over two-thirds of Nigeria's labor force is to be found in this very low productivity sector, mostly in the rural areas.

The remaining 25 to 30 percent of the labor force might be in a "middle band" or intermediate sector. In the rural areas this sector would include persons in small-scale and part-time commercial agriculture or animal husbandry. In both the rural and urban areas it includes those engaged in small-scale service, industrial, construction, and transport enterprises—traders, artisans and craftsmen, and small-scale miners. This intermediate sector is part of the monetary economy, but is distinguished from the modern sector by its far lower level of productivity.

The distinctions between these three sectors may be represented by a gradient rather than a series of cliffs. The modern sector, however, is more sharply defined. In this sector, the growth of output is relatively rapid, wages and salaries are many times higher than in the other sectors, and characteristically the rich are getting richer. In contrast, because of the pressures of the increase in the labor force and the relatively low levels of productivity, earnings levels in the other sectors may be declining rather than rising. Thus, the disparities between the rich and the poor in Nigeria are widening. Modernization is benefitting a fortunate minority and by-passing the masses.

INVESTMENT IN EDUCATION

The resources devoted to education in Nigeria are tremendous. They appear even larger when one considers that Nigeria's system of formal education is oriented almost exclusively to the modern sector which, as noted above, provides employment opportunities for only 5 percent of the labor force. For example, the combined annual output of Nigeria's formal education establishment is over 600,000 school-leavers. Most of this output is from primary schools, with a high proportion of drop-outs. Yet, the aspiration of the vast majority of school-leavers is to gain entry into the modern sector. The values, subject matter, and examination criteria at all levels of Nigerian education assume that school-leavers want to become government civil servants, teachers, and employees of relatively modern industrial and commercial establishments. But at present there are new employment opportunities each year for only about 40,000 persons in the modern sector. In coming years new employment opportunities in this sector may increase as much as 3 percent annually, but there will be a corresponding increase in the number of job-seeking school-leavers.

Except in a few categories, Nigeria's education and training system certainly is capable of meeting most of the country's future needs for *high-level* manpower in the modern sector. If anything, the universities are expanding too rapidly in relation to other parts of the educational structure. The problem, therefore, is not underinvestment in production of high-level professional and administrative manpower for the modern sector; on the contrary, one can argue that too great a proportion of the country's resources are committed to modern sector development at the cost of neglecting the needs of the economy's less productive sectors in which the vast majority of Nigerians must somehow earn a living.

It is apparent, therefore, that Nigeria must give higher priority in the future to expansion of output and employment in the intermediate and traditional sectors both in the urban and the rural areas. At best, the cities may be able to continue to absorb productively about 15 percent of the labor force, i.e. 5 percent in the modern and 10 percent in the other sectors. The urban areas can "accommodate" more manpower than this, but at the cost of a deterioration of already low productivity levels, an increase in the already high level of urban unemployment, and a probable increase in the numbers of beggars and petty thieves swarming in the city streets. It follows then that the rural areas will have to absorb well over four-fifths of the country's labor force for at least the next decade and a half.

THE NEED FOR A RURAL TRANSFORMATION

Nigeria's successful growth will depend primarily, though not exclusively, on improved levels of productivity and earnings in its rural sector. As stated earlier, a rural transformation is perhaps a necessary condition for effective industrial development. What then are the constituent components of such a transformation?

An increase in the quantity and quality of agricultural and livestock production constitutes the core of any rural transformation. Production for export and particularly expansion of production of food for local consumption must be encouraged. The development strategy includes programs to increase the efficiency of the modern sector as well as the upgrading of farmers from the subsistence to the intermediate sector and also from the intermediate to the modern sector.

A rural transformation, however, involves much more than agricultural development as such. It requires extensive village development as well, including extension of health and education services, expansion of village trading and commerce, the creation of local industries for processing of agricultural products, the improvement of housing, water supplies, sanitation, roads, and other public services. A rural transformation also calls for a massive program of rural public works, including construction of access roads, irrigation ditches, and communications systems. Manpower cannot be retained in rural areas unless the standards of living and productivity in rural communities are raised substantially.

Thus, a rural transformation will require large-scale investment of human and financial resources in *both* agriculture and rural community development. And if Nigeria is to press for such a transformation, it must give priority to this investment over additional expenditures on buildings, services, and other amenities in the cities. However, a sizable part of the necessary resources may be generated in the rural areas themselves, for experience has shown that rural inhabitants are willing to devote both labor and tax monies for projects from which they can clearly derive tangible benefits. However, it is unrealistic to treat agriculture as a major source of revenue for investment in industrial and urban development and, at the same time, expect more private investment of time and resources in agriculture. On the contrary, as W. Arthur Lewis has suggested, some of the profits generated in the industrial sector should be siphoned off to help finance rural development.

Characteristically, rural development activities require large amounts of labor. Of all economic activities, agriculture is probably the most labor-intensive. The construction of roads, terraces, ditches, and dwellings in rural areas require relatively large inputs of human effort. In planning these activities it is important to minimize the use of capital-intensive, labor-saving technology. Insofar as possible, the objective must be to *expand the output* of all individuals without displacing any of them. (Agricultural output surely can be increased through use of fertilizers, pesticides, and more intensive land cultivation and weed control instead of by mechanization.)

It is clear that the raising of output in the low productivity sectors in both urban and rural areas will require some basic changes in Nigeria's strategy of development. Rather than favoring spectacular increases in productivity through capital-intensive projects, much greater emphasis will need to be given to a wide range of modest increases in productivity in labor-intensive activities which allow participation of greater numbers of people. Indeed, it should be possible to achieve just as large a national income through effective implementation of such a policy as by concentrating on increasing output and incomes in the relatively small modern sector.

The investment needed to carry forward a rural transformation will be very great, but the limiting factor is more likely to be human rather than financial resources. It is most important, therefore, to consider the problems of developing the human agents needed to lead, manage, and direct this transformation.

It may be relatively easy to estimate the numbers of persons required for agricultural extension and to determine the means for training them. In a rough way, this was done in the 1965 FAO Report. The organization and staffing of research centers should offer no serious problem either. Today, a great deal is known about the nature of the institutions and techniques needed to train personnel for these activities.

When it comes to training community development workers, small-scale entrepreneurs, village leaders, and even rural school teachers, however, the requirements and needed programs are much less clear. Present knowledge about the processes of rural village development is sketchy. Even less is known about the forces which generate incentives for self-improvement in rural areas. And lastly, very few persons with much education and initiative are willing to commit themselves to service in the bush. In this respect, for example, the experience of countries such as India with village development is not encouraging. In any case, the art or science of rural development is probably the most underdeveloped and backward area of knowledge in the entire field of growth economics.

Let us elaborate this point by citing a few examples. In several African countries, proposals have been made to establish "Village Poly-technics" to develop among adults and children alike some of the essential but simple skills needed in rural areas, such as carpentry, latrine construction, canal digging, personal hygiene, use of fertilizers, seed selection, weed control, and many others. The idea is basically sound, and expensive equipment would not be required. But can the organizing talent be found to initiate these institutions? What kinds of people should be selected as instructors, and how would they be trained?

A more imaginative idea, recently proposed by President Nyerere of Tanzania, is to turn rural schools into "economic and social communities." According to Nyerere, each school should have a companion farm to provide much of the food eaten by the students and teachers. In this way, students would learn to cooperate in building self-reliant communities and at the same time making a contribution to the national income.[12] The selection, training, and proper motivation of the "teacher-farmer," however, is likely to be a very difficult task. Probably Nigeria's present teacher training institutions would be less than enthusiastic about this idea. And even if induced to accept it, who would train the teachers to operate a successful farm in addition to teaching reading, writing, and arithmetic?

Most planners agree that it is important to encourage the development of small industrial enterprises, cooperatives, repair shops, commercial establishments, and cottage industries in the rural villages. But this requires a good deal of competent technical assistance. What will be required to select, train, employ, and motivate the human agents to provide this kind of assistance? How many activists would be required, and in how many different areas would they need specialized knowledge or training?

Finally, many economists argue that a good deal of capital formation can result from mobilizing the efforts of the underemployed to build houses, community centers, local access roads, and other public works. In this way output can be increased by employing, for very little pay, under-utilized human energies. Here the critical factor is to find and develop the organizing talent to energize and direct such an effort.

More examples could be given to demonstrate the problems to be overcome in developing the human resources required to press forward a rural transformation. They would all show the importance of developing *innovators* and *organization builders*. But innovators and organization builders are perhaps the scarcest of resources in all sectors of a newly developing country. It is much easier to develop talent to organize a large industrial enterprise than it is to select, train, and motivate leadership for rural development projects. In most modernizing societies, it is becoming clear that the really perplexing problems of organization and human resource development lie in the traditional and intermediate rather than in the modern sectors of the economy.

Most manpower surveys, including those made in Nigeria, have ignored the problems of the low productivity sectors. They have focused on high-level manpower requirements of the modern sector. In this respect they have tended to give a distorted picture of the fundamental dimensions of the problems of human resource development and utilization. It is not possible, at this time, to estimate precisely the numbers of persons with strategic skills needed to achieve a rural transformation, although one could suggest some rough orders of magnitude.

Probably for every person required in agricultural extension activities another two or three trained persons would be needed to provide the other necessary and related productive services. These would include new educational instructors, organizers and supervisors of rural public works programs, small enterprise experts, community development workers, credit supervisors and marketing specialists, public health agents, and many others. The task of developing such personnel is larger and much more complicated than that of generating skilled manpower for the modern sector. For, as stressed above, in the modern sector the techniques are already known; expatriate personnel can be imported to fill temporary shortages of high-level skills; and a tremendous investment has already been made in education and training. In the rural areas, on the contrary, effective techniques of manpower development are yet to be discovered; expatriates cannot be easily recruited or utilized; and very few investments of human and financial resources have yet been made.

Finally, there remains the question of the role of rural schools in promoting a rural transformation. They can and do make a contribution by turning out some literate children who may remain in the area, but they also tend to drain the more talented and ambitious young people from the countryside to the cities. It is questionable, therefore, whether rural primary education, as presently organized, is a positive or a negative force in building Nigeria's rural economy.

The content and method of education in the rural primary schools, as in other schools in the country, is academically oriented. The emphasis is on preparation for higher levels of formal schooling. The school environment is quite different from that of the rural community. Parents send their children to school not to make them better farmers, but rather to provide for them an escape from traditional society. An educated child, therefore, has aspirations to move to "greener pastures"; he is no longer willing to accept a "life-sentence" to traditional agriculture. Under these circumstances, it is foolish to think that a solution can be found by "vocationalizing" the curriculum—teaching farming handicrafts, etc. At the same time, it is rather unrealistic also to assume that the spread of primary education will necessarily increase literacy in the rural areas. It may simply be an instrument for siphoning off the best talent to the urban areas.

The case for the spread of primary education as a *prerequisite* for improvements in traditional rural economies is very weak. There is no clear evidence to indicate that persons need to be literate in order to improve agricultural methods and to participate in community development activities. Certainly, such improvements will not come simply from literacy by itself. And it is useless to make people literate if there is little for them to read.

It is now generally recognized that, for a rural transformation, other productive services must be developed simultaneously with the spread of education. Unless conditions in the rural areas are improving and unless there are attractive job opportunities for local people in the rural areas, investment in formal education will bring disappointingly low returns. Thus, it is important to decide first to make massive investments of human and financial resources for improvements in agriculture, in rural public works, and in community development activities of all kinds. In this way, leadership opportunities will be created for local inhabitants; the prospects for a better life will be brightened; and the hold of rural communities on its more ambitious and talented manpower will be strengthened.

If this reasoning is correct, then these policy decisions follow: Insofar as possible, the new jobs in agricultural extension and Village Poly-technics, as well as organization of community activities and public works, should be reserved for local people. Initially, literacy should be a by-product of fundamental training of local inhabitants to organize and lead such "productive services." Thus, priority should be given to build-ing these productive services rather than to expansion of formal primary education. As the rural communities become transformed, greater re-sources then can be generated for formal education and more opportuni-ties will be provided for those able to obtain it. In short, the cart should not be put before the horse. In economies with limited resources, every penny spent on education may be money taken away from other vitally needed productive services. If these productive services can lead to higher productivity and earnings, the resources available for education will soon be increased, and the ultimate goal of universal primary educa-tion will be more easily and speedily attained.

THE PROBLEM OF NATIONWIDE UTILIZATION OF SKILLS

Even before the civil war crisis, regionalism was rapidly becoming a barrier to the efficient use of skilled manpower. The former Eastern Region was overpopulated in comparison with other areas of the country, but even more important it led the rest of the country in education and high-level manpower development. According to a 1963-64 National Register of Students, persons from the Eastern Region accounted for more than half of all those registered in the senior category.[13] And their lead was especially marked in key areas such as agriculture, veterinary service, sciences, business administration, education, and medicine. Pro-fessor Yesufu had prophesied, just prior to the Army take-over of gov-ernment in January 1966:

> It behooves all the Regions . . . to relax their regionalist em-
> ployment policies. Otherwise, because of the fundamental im-
> portance of human resources for economic and social devel-
> opment, one of two things is likely to happen, either of which
> has grave political and economic consequences for the country
> as a whole. In the first place, the disparity in economic de-
> velopment between Regions may widen still further than it is
> at present, to the relative advantage of Eastern Region be-
> cause of its superiority in the availability of trained manpower.

This may have the effect of accentuating Regional jealousies and worsening political dissension throughout the Federation. In the second place, the population pressure in the Eastern Region (and then in the Western Region) may become so great, manifesting itself in mass unemployment, that any continued failure of the Governments to liberalise their employment policies and permit a freer mobility of labour and settlement between the Regions would cause dissension. This dissension could be intra-Regional to start with, but it would sooner or later develop into a national issue; or it could, with political adroitness in the Region concerned, lead to a canalization of disaffection in that Region against the Federal and other Regional governments.[14]

The prospect of modern Nigeria, with twelve separate states, greatly complicates this problem. Two of Nigeria's universities—Ibadan and Ife—are in the Western state with a third, Lagos, on its very border. In 1968 these three accounted for over 80 percent of all enrollments in Nigeria. In what was formerly the Northern Region and now comprises six states, there is a single university—Ahmadu Bello—with an enrollment of only about 1,000 students. The University of Nigeria, one of the two largest universities and the one probably most directly geared to meeting high-level manpower needs of the country, was closed down after occupation of Nsukka and Enugu by the Federal troops.

The capacities of the twelve states to produce educated manpower differ tremendously. Complete new state governments are being set up in areas where higher education institutions were nonexistent and where only a handful of the local residents had completed or had access to secondary education. Obviously, unless there can be free flows of manpower from one area to another, some states will have an oversupply of talent under conditions of inadequate employment opportunities while others with severe skill shortages will be forced to import expatriate manpower for which Nigerian talent should be substituted.

Professor Yesufu and others have advocated a declaration (or even a law) stating that every Nigerian should have the right to work in any state of the Federation and that no expatriate should be employed except upon proof that no qualified Nigerian is available. Others have proposed that the system of higher education, and particularly the universities, must be nationalized, each providing access on the basis of merit to all qualified Nigerian students. But in a country ridden with tribal and sectional cleavages these measures are more easily prescribed than taken. There is wide agreement, nevertheless, that the problems of countrywide access to higher educational institutions for students and the creation of a nation-wide, nondiscriminatory market for talent lie far beyond the original Ashby Commission recommendations on university organization and administration.

THE MANPOWER PROBLEMS IN RECONSTRUCTION

The question of postwar reconstruction is of overriding concern. The price of the civil war in human and material resources is as yet unknown, but one may assume that at the least it will set back the nation's economic, social, and political development by many years. A discussion of the problems of political reconstruction lie beyond the scope of this paper. In the economic and social areas the most important single factor is likely to be the development and effective utilization of human resources.

During the war, large numbers of unemployed youth were recruited into the armed forces. This has temporarily stemmed the rise of unemployment among school-leavers, but with demobilization the unemployment crisis will be of paramount importance. Professor Yesufu estimates that, when the needs of displaced civilians and released soldiers are taken into consideration, perhaps two million persons will need new jobs and other kinds of resettlement.

A strong case is being made in some Nigerian quarters that there should be no haste in demobilizing members of the armed forces when the war ends. They argue that the forces should be deployed for reconstruction purposes and that the military should undertake a vast training program designed to prepare young soldiers for productive employment, particularly in the rural areas. It is argued that the rebuilding of roads, bridges, buildings, and public services can be carried out more quickly and at less cost by this means. Wages can be kept low, discipline can be maintained more easily, and administration may be simplified. Nevertheless, the use of the military primarily as a civilian employment and training instrumentality is a rather revolutionary idea. At best, such a program would have to be used as a transitional step to a more permanent system of employment generation and manpower development.

CONCLUSION

At the time of Nigerian independence, the Ashby Commissioners did a remarkable job in identifying problems, prescribing solutions, and dramatizing the importance of investment in education. Their report was perhaps the first attempt to build a logical and coherent strategy for the development of education in Africa. The response of the nation was spectacular and, on balance, the outcome was constructive. It is obvious, however, that the manpower perspective, the orientation of the education system, the organization and role of the universities, and the priorities in economic, social, and political development are fundamentally changed from those of 1960. The Ashby Report and the White Paper, important and constructive as they were for the first half-decade after independence, no longer provide an adequate program or relevant targets for educational development in the future. They were designed to solve quite different problems from those faced today. Reconstruction, rural transformation, the building of an employment-oriented growth strategy, the development of a multi-purpose educational system with broader orientation than preparation for university entry, the greater use of the military and the employing institutions as manpower training institutions, and the expansion of productive educative services for agriculture and small-scale industry now seem to command the greatest attention. The function, organization, and scale of post-secondary and higher education, which was the focus of the Ashby investigation, is under re-examination along with the other elements of a strategy for development and utilization of human resources.

The problems ahead are indeed formidable. The obstacles in the path of progress seem almost insurmountable. Yet, it may be well to remember an old and wise saying: "Hope is every bit as logical as despair."

NOTES

1. *Investment in Education*, the report of the Commission on Post-School Certificate and Higher Education in Nigeria (Federal Ministry of Education, Lagos, 1960), Chapter 10 in this volume.

2. The Commission consisted of three members from the United Kingdom, three from the United States, and three from Nigeria representing the country's three regions.

3. *Investment in Education, op. cit.*, p. 35.

4. *Federation of Nigeria, Educational Development, 1961-67*, Sessional Paper #3 of 1961 (Lagos: Federal Government Printer).

5. Education and World Affairs, *Nigerian Human Resource Development and Utilization* (New York: Education and World Affairs, 1967), chapter 9.

6. *Ibid.*, chapter 4.

7. *Ibid.*

8. T. M. Yesufu, "Labour in the Nigerian Economy," lectures delivered for the Nigerian Broadcasting Corporation (October, 1967) (mimeographed).

9. *Ibid.*

10. Most of the factual basis for this and the following section was developed by the staff of the Committee on Education and Human Resource Development of Education and World Affairs. The full analysis is set forth in *Nigerian Human Resource Development and Utilization, op. cit.*

11. i.e., in cities having population of 20,000 or over.

12. President Nyerere says, "this is not a suggestion that a school farm or workshop should be attached to every school for training purposes. It is a suggestion that every school should also be a farm; that the school community should consist of people who are both teachers and farmers, and pupils and farmers." From pamphlet entitled "Education for Self-Reliance," 1967.

13. See Yesufu, *op. cit.*, p. 16.

14. *Ibid.*, p. 17.

21. Towards a West African Economic Community*

H. M. A. ONITIRI

Everywhere—in Europe, in Asia, in Central and Latin America, and in Africa—some form of economic integration is either in existence or being seriously proposed. This widespread enthusiasm for economic integration derives from a complex of motives and sentiments. In particular, political and psychological considerations have always been mixed up with what is primarily an economic arrangement.

Among territories which are close neighbours or which are subject to a common political allegiance, some degree of economic co-operation is naturally to be expected. Thus, in West Africa, a certain amount of economic co-operation was achieved among the various political units during the era of colonial rule. In this respect, the countries of French West Africa advanced much farther than those of British West Africa. This was partly because the French West African territories, unlike the countries of British West Africa, had the advantage of geographical contiguity; but a more important explanation is that the French Empire, of which French West Africa was a part, was more closely knit economically than the British Empire to which the countries of British West Africa belonged.[1]

On the whole, however, economic co-operation among West African countries under colonial rule amounted to very little; and in particular, economic intercourse between the countries of French West Africa on the one hand, and those of British West Africa on the other, was hardly significant. Furthermore, the first years of independence witnessed the weakening rather than the strengthening of the economic ties which had been achieved among these countries before independence. Although in more recent years sporadic efforts have been made, especially by the countries of the French Community, to build on the foundation of past economic co-operation, the results so far have not been im-

* From *The Nigerian Journal of Economic and Social Studies*, Vol. 5, No. 1, (March 1963), pp. 27-54. Reprinted by permission of the Nigerian Economic Society.

pressive. In spite of this, the proposals for economic integration in West Africa which are now being put forward, go beyond anything which was achieved in the pre-independence period. Current proposals, in fact, centre on the possibilities of bringing the countries of this area together in a customs union, a common market, a free trade area, or an economic community. The purpose of this paper is to examine the economic basis for these proposals and to draw attention to the problems which are likely to be encountered in moving towards the objective of economic integration in West Africa.

II

There are considerable doubts among economists about the value of economic integration in under-developed areas and some writers have suggested that the enthusiasm for integration in these areas is to be explained largely by political considerations. While it is inevitable that a major economic arrangement such as a customs union or a common market, should have political implications, it will still be argued that the basis of the current interest in economic integration in West Africa is largely economic. West African leaders are unanimous in their belief that integration will promote economic growth and stability in their various countries and thus contribute to solving some of the pressing economic problems with which they are faced. In their minds, these problems are associated with the unbalanced structure of the West African economy and its dependence on a narrow range of commodity exports.

The enthusiasm for economic integration in West Africa can be interpreted, then, as a reaction against some of the economic consequences of the long period of political dependence of these countries on the advanced industrial nations of Europe. The present economic structure of West African countries and the existing pattern of their trade, are only partly the results of economic forces; they have been shaped in part by the political system from which these countries have just emerged. However, now that many of these countries are politically independent, political considerations (especially the reluctance to surrender any part of their newly-won sovereignty) constitute an obstacle rather than a spur to economic integration. While the enthusiasm for integration cannot be divorced entirely from politics, it is the economic considerations which appear to be paramount. In following this line of reasoning, it may help the discussion if from the onset we bear in mind the basic characteristics of West African economies to which we shall need to make frequent references.

Because they have been subject to similar political influences, West

African economies exhibit more similarities than differences. The similarities, which are already familiar, can be summarised as follows:

(1) The national income per head of population is everywhere much below the level in the advanced countries of Western Europe.

(2) Production for domestic use and for exports consists mainly of primary commodities (food and raw materials).

(3) The major part of manufactured commodities consumed at home is imported from abroad.

(4) The direction of trade of each country shows a strong concentration in favour of one of the major industrial countries—France in the case of the countries of the French Community, and Britain in the case of the British Commonwealth countries.

(5) The trade of each West African country with other West African countries and, indeed, with other African countries as a whole, is a negligible part of total trade.

(6) Each country depends predominantly on import and export duties for its public revenues.

(7) Each country derives a substantial part of its national income from foreign trade, and West African territories are therefore peculiarly susceptible to economic fluctuations originating abroad.

Within these broad similarities, however, certain important differences can be noted:

(1) The size of the market as measured by population and national income varies significantly between countries (Table 1).

(2) The mineral resources show important variations. (Table 2).

(3) Economic and commercial policies differ from country to country—the differences being especially noticeable between the countries of the British Commonwealth on the one hand and those of the French Community on the other.

The case for economic integration in West Africa has to be argued with particular reference to the characteristics thus outlined. Bearing these characteristics in mind, we may now examine the relevance to West African conditions of the theoretical framework within which the problems of economic integration have frequently been considered.

TABLE 1. *Population and Gross Domestic Product of West African Countries*

	Population (millions)	Gross Domestic Product (U.S. $ million)
Former French West Africa	22.4(1959-60)	2,523(1956)
Dahomey	1.9(1960)	
Guinea	3.0(1960)	
Ivory Coast	3.2(1960)	
Mali	4.1(1960)	
Mauritania	0.7(1959)	
Niger	2.9(1960)	
Senegal	3.0(1960)	
Upper Volta	3.6(1960)	
Former French Equatorial Africa	5.0(1959-60)	514(1956)
Central African Republic	1.2(1960)	
Chad	2.6(1960)	299(1956)
Congo Brazzaville	0.8(1959)	191(1956)
Gabon	0.4(1960)	120(1956)
Ghana	6.7(1960)	1,433(1959-60)
Gambia	0.3(1959)	16-20(1957)
Liberia	1.3(1956)	
Nigeria	35.1(1960)	2,628(1957)
Sierra Leone	2.4(1959)	

SOURCE: G. K. Helleiner, "Nigeria and the African Common Market" in *The Nigerian Journal of Economic and Social Studies*, Vol. 4, No. 3, November 1962.

III

The theoretical analysis has been pursued largely with reference to a customs union (which involves the complete freedom of trade between the countries forming the union and their adoption of a common external tariff.) Professor J. Viner, who initiated the discussion on this problem considered the economic consequences of a customs union in terms of its trade-creating and trade-diverting effects.[2]

The formation of a customs union between two countries, A and B, will, according to Professor Viner, cause an expansion of trade between them. This expansion may come about in two ways. The increase in A's imports from B may be either at the expense of domestic production in A (trade creation) or at the expense of A's trade with a third country, C, outside the customs union (trade diversion). Professor Viner's conclusion is that whereas trade creation is a good thing

TABLE 2. *Output of Principal Minerals in West Africa Average 1955-57 (Thousands of Tons)*

	Bauxite	Iron Ore	Gold	Manganese	Tin Concentrate	Diamonds Gems	Diamonds Industrial	Phosphate Rock	Colombium
Angola						464.6	318		
Cameroons									1.2
French Equatorial Africa								4.9	
French West Africa	437.1					49.6	81		
Ghana	149.0		21.9	292		129.3	207		
Liberia		1,302				203	2,372		
Nigeria					9,123				2,615.6
Sierra Leone		817				213	397		4.1

SOURCE: *United Nations, Economic Survey of Africa Since 1950*, pp. 33-34.

because it causes A and B to buy their imports from areas with lower costs of production, trade diversion is bad because it causes demand to be diverted from areas of lower costs to those of higher costs. Whereas trade creation increases the volume of world trade, trade diversion merely reallocates the existing volume of trade, uneconomically, in favour of countries participating in the customs union.

As Professor J. E. Meade later pointed out, however, a customs union is likely to be both trade-creating and trade-diverting and, in assessing the economic effects of the union, it would be necessary to weigh the economic benefits which would result from trade creation against the economic losses which would result from trade diversion.[3] Furthermore, whereas Professor Viner had pursued the argument in terms of constant total world output, constant total world consumption and constant costs of production of the relevant commodities, Professor Meade recognised (1) that the formation of a customs union, by lowering prices of imports in the participating countries, may increase consumption in these countries and thus expand the volume of trade between them; (2) that the changes in output resulting from the formation of a customs union may raise or lower mosts of production, and thus reduce or increase the economic benefits to be derived from the union. The main conclusion of Professor Meade is that an economic union will be more likely to raise economic welfare the greater is the extent that (a) it causes a primary expansion in trade between the participating countries, (b) the primary expansion in trade results from trade creation rather than trade diversion, and (c) it causes economies of large-scale production to be realized.

The major part of Professor Meade's discussion of this subjject is concerned with explaining the conditions under which an economic union will lead to a small or a large expansion in the trade between the participating countries and the extent to which this expansion will arise from trade creation rather than trade diversion. It is evident from Professor Meade's analysis that, in general, the expansion of trade between countries participating in a customs union will be greater (i) the higher are the obstacles to trade between them which are removed, (ii) the greater are the elasticities of demand in the member countries for the products which are now cheaper as a result of the removal of important duties, (iii) the greater is the extent to which each country is the principal supplier to the other of the products which it exports to the other, and the principal market for the products which it imports from the other, and (iv) the greater is the extent to which the economies of member countries are actually competitive but potentially complementary. The extent to which the primary expansion of trade between the participating countries will arise from trade creation rather than trade diversion will also be greater, the more the conditions outlined above are fulfilled, and the greater is the proportion of world's production, consumption and trade, which is accounted for by these countries.

Whether or not a customs union will cause economies of large-scale production to be realized will, of course, depend on the nature of the industries involved, the state of technology, the size of the market, and so on. No definite answer can be given to this question until a careful study has been made of each situation. This aspect of a customs union has been given greater attention by later writers.[4] While some are optimistic about the possibility of economies of scale being realized, others are of the opinion that these economies may not be as important as is generally supposed.

In the Economic Journal for December 1960, Dr. R. G. Lipsey[5] gave a succinct summary of the theory of customs union up to that time, and he himself laid down two general conditions for determining the welfare effects of a customs union. These conditions are contained in the following paragraph of the article:

> "This argument gives rise to two general conclusions, one of them appealing immediately to common sense, one of them slightly surprising. The first is that, given a country's volume of international trade, a customs union is more likely to raise welfare the higher is the proportion of trade with the country's union partner and the lower the proportion with the outside world. The second is that a customs union is more likely to raise welfare the lower is the total volume of foreign trade, for the lower is foreign trade, the lower must be purchases from the outside world relative to purchases of domestic commodities. This means that the sort of countries who ought to form customs unions are those doing a high proportion of their total expenditure on domestic trade. Countries which are likely to lose from a customs union, on the other hand, are those countries in which a low proportion of total trade is domestic, especially if the customs union does not include a high proportion of their foreign trade."[6]

These various generalisations—by Viner, Meade and Lipsey—have been frequently quoted by subsequent writers on the subject, and some have examined these generalisations with particular reference to the problems of economic integration in under-developed areas.[7] Because under-developed countries have often failed to satisfy the various criteria which have been enunciated, the conclusions as to the benefits of economic integration among these countries have usually been pessimistic.[8] Indeed, it is readily seen that, in the light of the basic characteristics of West African economies which we have outlined, a straightforward application of these criteria to West African conditions would lead us to the same pessimistic conclusions. There are, however, two reasons why these conclusions should not be regarded as of general validity. In the first place, it should always be borne in mind that in the conditions of under-developed areas, we are confronted with a situation vastly different from that of the developed countries on which the theory of economic integration has largely focussed. The under-developed areas are involved in a huge effort to alter the structure of their economy and to integrate their foreign trade more closely with it than before. Arguments based on the existing economic structure and the existing pattern of trade of these countries are out of touch with the most important problems with which they are faced. In the second place, in assessing the welfare effects of a customs union, it is necessary to make clear at every stage of the argument in whose welfare we are really interested. The case for economic integration may be pursued at four different levels of generalisation. Firstly, we may be interested in economic efficiency and welfare in the world as a whole; secondly, we may wish to confine our attention to the area of the customs union; thirdly, we may be interested in what happens to a particular member country of the customs union; and lastly, we may go a stage further down the scale and investigate how the union affects particular economic groups or particular regions within a member country of the integrated area.

From the contributions of Viner and Meade it is evident that these authors are concerned with the effect of a customs union on the world as a whole, while it seems from Dr. Lipsey's generalisations that he is concerned only with the group of countries forming the customs union. If we were considering the effect of a customs union among countries which together account for a large proportion of world trade, it will be necessary to consider the interest of the world as well as the interest of the countries forming the union. But if attention centres on the effect of a customs union in an area, such as West Africa, which accounts for only a small proportion of world trade, the argument may usefully be pursued mainly in terms of the interests of the countries forming the customs union.[9]

Even if we confine the discussion of economic integration in West Africa to its effects on the participating countries, it will still be found that little help can be drawn from Dr. Lipsey's general conclusions. The reason is that the critical factors on which these conclusions are based are some of the very factors which the West African countries are desirous of changing through economic integration. Also, once we ignore the effect of the union on the outside world, it becomes irrelevant to pursue the argument in terms of trade creation and trade diversion. What we need to do is to examine the customs union from the inside and endeavour to assess whether or not it will on balance lead to economic gains for the union countries as a whole.

At this stage, we may usefully recall a central feature of customs union which Professor Viner pointed out in his original analysis, namely that the union combines some elements of freer trade with some element of greater protection. As Professor Johnson has later put it "while it (i.e. the customs union) provides freedom of trade between the participating countries, it also provides more protection for producers inside the customs union area against competition from outside the area, since the protected market available to these producers is enlarged by the creation of a protected position in the markets of other countries partner to the union in addition to their protected position in their domestic market."[10]

In the light of this statement, we may examine the arguments for a customs union in West Africa in terms of its "free trade" effects and its "protective" effects. Although this will inevitably plunge us into the much discussed arguments for free trade and protection, it will be likely to throw more light on the subject than the traditional approach in terms of trade creation and trade diversion or the Lipsey formula in terms of the ratio of intra-union trade to the total trade of union members and the ratio of foreign to domestic trade.

Following the line of approach which we have suggested the most important questions which we have to answer are as follows:

   (1) Which of the arguments for free trade can be adduced in favour of the "free trade" aspects of a West African customs union? and

   (2) which of the arguments for protection can be used to justify the protective aspects of the union?

The case for free trade rests essentially on four pillars, namely:

   (*i*)   efficiency in distribution (i.e. maximisation of consumption from a given quantity of output),

   (*ii*) efficiency in production (i.e. maximisation of output from a given quantity of resources or minimisation of resources required for producing a given output),

   (*iii*) provision of a market for unusable domestic surplus (the vent for surplus argument) and

   (*iv*) the stimulation of economic growth (including the realisation of external economies).

The arguments for protection are numerous but we may concern ourselves with two of these arguments which are of immediate relevance to the purpose in hand. These are:

(i) the structural argument (i.e. temporary protection for the creation of infant industries and for the diversification of the national output) and

(ii) the terms of trade argument (i.e. the control of trade for the purpose of bringing about a redistribution of income between the trading countries).

Within the framework thus provided, it may be argued that the free trade aspect of a West African customs union can be beneficial only to the extent that it stimulates the economic growth of this area, and that the protective aspect of the union would have to be justified largely by the necessity of bringing about a structural change in the West African economy. Formulating the problems in this way seems to put the emphasis where I think it should lie—namely on the dynamic rather than on the static aspects of economic integration. If we view the situation from a static point of view and consider the advantages of economic integration in West Africa from the points of view of a better distribution of existing output, a more efficient allocation of resources being currently employed, and the immediate improvement of the terms of trade, we would be led to the conclusion that there is very little to be gained from the union. But if we regard economic integration, economic development and structural change as proceeding simultaneously, we are likely to reach a different conclusion. For example, an agreed policy on the future supplies of those commodities, such as cocoa, for which West Africa accounts for a large proportion of world output may enable the area to obtain higher prices for these products in the long run.[11]

Many writers on this subject are agreed that the gains of economic integration in the less developed countries must be sought for in the dynamic field of economic development, although some are still largely sceptical of the gains even in this sphere.[12] Unfortunately, empirical evidence does not, and cannot, offer any conclusive indication of the relationship between economic integration and economic development. Even if it is generally admitted that economic integration has contributed to the industrialisation and development of certain areas, it will be virtually impossible to isolate the contribution which can be attributed to this factor alone, quite apart from the problem of indicating whether development is the cause or the effect of integration. There is therefore considerable room for speculation and conjecture and because of this, more enlightenment can be gained through the investigation of particular cases than by broad generalisations. Bearing in mind these inevitable difficulties, we may proceed to examine the West African situation within the framework of the theoretical analysis.

IV

The inapplicability of the static argument to the West African situation is only too obvious. In the first place, there are no major obstacles to trade in local produce between West African countries at the moment. Customs control at the borders between them are directed mainly towards preventing the free movement across the borders of industrial goods not originating in West Africa. Duties on locally produced goods moving across the borders—mainly food—are either non-existent or are not rigidly enforced, so that they do not constitute great barriers to the free movement of these commodities across national frontiers.[13] In the second place, in production for home consumption and for export, the economies of West African states are, to a great extent, actually "competitive" and unless the economic structures of these countries alter substantially in the future they are not likely to become complementary. This is one of the crucial issues in the discussion. Any faith in the potential complementarity of West African economies and therefore in the possibility of fruitful integration of these economies must be based on the presumption that their structures are going to change substantially in future years.

In the West African countries at the present time, the major part of production for home consumption consists of local food crops and a glance at the crop map of West Africa shows the crop belts running horizontally from east to west, across many of these territories. The result of this is that each country is, to a large extent, self-sufficient in local food crops. The main directions of trade in these commodities are north to south (largely within each country) and vice versa, rather than east to west (or west to east). Trade in food crops between West African territories is therefore mainly directed towards relieving marginal shortages rather than supplying the bulk of local consumption. This situation is explained partly by the similarity of the physical conditions of production in the different countries and partly by the similarity of tastes.[14]

When we examine the case for economic integration in West Africa in the light of the dynamic theory, we must, of course, recognise that among the many policies which must be pursued by West African countries to realise the objectives of economic growth and stability, economic integration is only one and not necessarily the most important. There is no doubt at all that, even in the absence of integration, the process of industrialisation and development will continue in all areas, though the pace may differ from one country to another. What we must investigate is whether integration will accelerate the rate of growth by enabling each West African country to profit from the development of the other countries of this area.

The approach to the question thus posed must necessarily take full account of the known factor endowments of the various countries, the present stages of their development and industrialisation, and the plans and programmes which they have drawn up for the future. On these various issues, recent studies by the United Nations provide a considerable amount of information.[15] For the particular purpose in hand, the most important of these studies is, undoubtedly, that on *Industrial Growth in Africa* undertaken by the Economic Commission for Africa.[16] This study discusses these problems with particular reference to the possibilities of regional economic groupings. Indeed, it may be said that it carries the discussion of economic integration in Africa well beyond the stage of theoretical speculations and mere conjectures. The regional economic groupings which the study envisages as providing the basis for rapid industrialisation in Africa and the expansion of intra-African trade, are noted in the following paragraph:

> "There can and should be no rigid sub-regional groupings. What may be an appropriate grouping as an outlet for the product of one new industry may not be for another. Nevertheless, this report has assumed that there are certain natural broad groupings, even though the exact frontier may change from case to case and from time to time. One is North Africa, probably, including also the Sudan; another is West Africa to the Congo River; a third is East Africa including Somalia and Ethiopia and much of Central Africa. The Republic of South Africa may be regarded as a sub-region of its own. These sub-regions would seem to form the starting point for the detailed and intensive examination of industrialisation programmes in the light of the principles of international specialisation."[17]

Within the framework of these groupings, the study proceeds to examine the potentialities of economic integration in Africa with specific reference to four major industries: iron and steel, non-ferrous metals, engineering, chemicals and fertilisers, and textiles. Its conclusions as regards iron and steel, and textiles are particularly significant from the points of view of the potential gains of economic integration in West Africa and the problems which are likely to arise in moving towards this goal.

On the development of an iron and steel industry in West Africa, the study records the following observation:

"In West Africa, as has been shown, ample quantities of high grade iron ore are available. Suitable coking coal is not available, though it may well be that Nigerian coal could be adapted for this purpose. There would, however, be a strong case for locating a new iron and steel works on or near the sea coast."[18]

Leaving aside the possibility of exporting metal products to countries outside the African continent, it is evident that the establishment of such heavy industries as iron and steel can be feasible only within the framework of an economic integration of this area. A strong case is made in Nigeria's National Development Plan (1962-68)[19] for the erection of a steel mill to manufacture the cruder types of steel products, but the exact nature of the project has not yet been decided and precise calculations as to the profitability of the project are still to be made. However, considering the low grade of Nigerian ore, and also that in this industry, size is a most important determinant of cheapness, it is very likely that the project would have to be heavily protected from foreign competition. Once Nigeria starts to produce all her requirements of crude steel products in her own steel mill, based on her low grade ore, a substantial proportion of the West African market for steel products will be catered for, and the possibility of establishing another viable steel mill based on the high quality ores of Liberia and Sierra Leone, will be more remote than ever. But will Nigeria forgo her steel mills—one of the star projects of her National Development Plan and one which is expected to utilise about 13 per cent of the electric generating capacity of the Niger Dam? This is only one of the many difficult questions that would have to be decided by painstaking negotiations between the countries concerned. It will be readily agreed, however, that this kind of question cannot be resolved without a determined effort on the part of the various countries concerned to co-ordinate their separate development plans. It may be that a vertical disintegration of the one steel mill proposed for this area will be possible without substantial loss of efficiency, so that a group of countries may be involved in the intermediate stages of production or in the utilisation of crude steel for the manufacture of refined products.

The textile industry illustrates another kind of gain as well as another kind of problem. On the textile industry, the Report by the E.C.A. notes that "in terms of raw material supplies, in terms of markets, in terms of the gratifying increase in African production of textiles during 1948-1960, in terms of the fact that most branches of the textile industry can work with small units of capital investment, the textile potential of Africa is a proposition capable of large-scale realisation."

But it goes on to say that because of this combination of factors affecting the textile industry, "the textile industries will always be widely dispersed, over several hundred towns in a fairly but not entirely random distribution over the urban face of Africa."[20]

With the wide dispersal of raw materials and markets, the relatively small capital requirements, the semi-skilled nature of most of the labour demanded, and the possibility of small-scale operations, many of the countries of this area may want to have their own textile industries. Apart from processing raw materials for export and assembling the imports of machinery, appliances etc. for the domestic market, it is the simple consumer goods industries, such as textiles, which offer the best opportunity for development by all countries, however small. It is very likely therefore that the smaller countries especially will attempt to exploit this opportunity with as much tariff protection as is necessary, with consequent loss of efficiency. Here the gain of integration is not one of bringing into existence industries which otherwise will not be established, but one of keeping competition alive within the integrated area, in order to mitigate the consequences of the absence of competition from the outside world. When this has been said, however, it must be admitted that this kind of industry is also one which may have to be exempted from the full provisions of any economic grouping in order to maintain flexibility in the arrangement and so allow for the special circumstances of countries which are least favoured by integration. In terms of the terminology which has been widely employed in discussions of the Latin American Common Market, such industries would be referred to as "integration industries."[21]

The "concessions" which may be made to a backward country in the integrated area fall into two categories. Firstly, in order to maintain some industries in existence in the backward countries, these countries may be allowed to maintain some duties on imports from the other member countries even after these latter have entirely abolished duties on imports from one another. Secondly, in order to maintain a market for the exports of the backward countries, the other countries of the integrated area may continue to levy some duties on similar goods imported from one another. Although these concessions would detract from the requirements of full economic integration, they may in fact be the price that has to be paid in order to keep the more backward countries within the integrated area. If maintained for too long, however, these concessions are likely to defeat the ultimate objective of integration. The two concessions indicated are to be found among the recommendations of the Working Group on the Latin American Common Market.[22] They can be useful in dealing with regional problems in a customs union, provided that the system of common tariff chosen by the union is not such as to provide effective protection for all the budding industries within the integrated area. If this latter should be the case, the gains of integration would be largely reduced.[23]

The way in which the concessions indicated will work may be illustrated by a numerical example. Suppose that A, B and C are the three countries which propose to form a customs union and that D is a country outside the proposed union. Further, suppose that the cost of producing a particular commodity is £1 in D, £2 in A, £3 in B and £4 in C; and that there is perfect competition in each country so that these costs also represent the market prices in the respective countries. If before the formation of the customs union, the rate of import duty is 200% in A, 300% in B and 400% in C, the prices for the products of the various countries in the markets of A, B and C can be represented as in Table 3.* The figures in the diagonal of the price matrix show the costs of production in the various countries while the other entries show the prices ruling in A, B and C for each other's products and for the product of D. If A, B and C had no tariffs on imports, they would be all purchasing the commodity from D where the cost of production (and hence the price) is lowest. But with the various tariffs levied by A, B, and C being as indicated, none of these countries will import the commodity either from D or from each other. Each would meet its domestic demand entirely from domestic output, since in each country the domestic price of the domestic prod-

TABLE 3.   *Prices of Domestic and Foreign Goods Before the Formation of a Customs Union.*

	Price in A	Price in B	Price in C	Price in D
A's good (Rate of import duty in A=200%)	£2	£8	£10	£2
B's good (Rate of import duty in B=300%)	£9	£3	£15	£3
C's good (Rate of import duty in C=400%)	£12	£16	£4	£4
D's good (D is a net exporter—no duty is levied on imports)	£3	£4	£5	£1

* It is emphasised that in Tables 3 to 6, we are considering the prices of a single commodity produced simultaneously in all countries, imported by some and exported by others. The price ruling for the commodity in a particular country will, of course, depend on whether the country is an importer or an exporter and, if an importer, on the rate of import duty levied on imports.

l be less than the domestic price (including import duty) of the
ed product.

A, B, and C now form a full customs union, they will abolish
 on each other's products, and they will also impose a common
nal tariff on imports from D. If the common external tariff is
%, this will give adequate protection to the domestic industries in
three countries—but only with respect to competition from D's
ducts. As can be vertified in Table 4 (which shows the system of
ces on the formation of a full customs union), A will now be able
 undersell B and C within the customs union. This may not give
se to any difficulties if B and C also have industries in which they
an undersell A. But suppose that C is a backward country unable,
it least for the time being, to compete with A and B in any product.
In this case it will be necessary to invoke the kind of concessions
which we outlined before. For example, if C is allowed to maintain a
duty of 100% or more on imports from A and B, this will enable her
to protect her domestic industry from the competition of more efficient
industries in A and B.

TABLE 4. *Prices of Domestic and Foreign Goods After the Formation
of a Full Customs Union Between A, B and C, with a Common
External Tariff of 400% Against D*

	Price in A	Price in B	Price in C	Price in D
A's good	£2	£2	£2	£2
B's good	£3	£3	£3	£3
C's good	£4	£4	£4	£4
D's good	£5	£5	£5	£1

Another way in which A and B may provide help for C is, for B
(which we may assume to be a net importer of the product) to maintain a tariff of 100% or more on imports from A while completely
freeing imports from C. This will enable C's products to compete with
A's in B's market. Thus, while the first concession alone will provide
protection for C's good only within C's domestic market, the two concessions together will provide a market for C's good in the markets of
B and C.[24] This can be easily verified in Table 5.

If these concessions are granted to C, it will be advantageous to the
customs union if C is also allowed to fall out of line with the common
external tariff for the time being. The reason is that if the concessions
indicated are granted to C, the external tariffs maintained by A and

B will not have to be as high as 400%. Indeed, an external tariff of 300% will still enable A and B to protect their domestic industries; but C will have to be allowed to maintain an external tariff of 400% or more. This is evident in Table 6. Thus it can be said that if concessions on internal tariffs are found necessary, it is better that the backward country should also be allowed for the time being to fall out of line with the common external tariff. In this way, the average level of the external tariffs of the customs union will be lower than what it would be in the absence of these concessions.

It may, of course, be argued (as it has generally been done in considering the "infant industry" argument for tariff protection) that a subsidy is to be preferred to a tariff as a means of dealing with the problems of a backward country within a customs union, and this view cannot be disputed from the point of view of economic efficiency. But if a system of subsidies is to work well in the kind of situation with which we are faced, it may have to be combined with a fiscal arrange-

TABLE 5. *Prices of Domestic and Foreign Goods After the Formation of a Partial Customs Union Between A, B, and C, with a Common External Tariff of 400%. (C Maintains a Duty of 100% on Imports From A and B; B Maintains a Duty of 100% on Imports From A but not on Imports From C)*

	Price in A	Price in B	Price in C	Price in D
A's good	£2	£4	£4	£2
B's good	£3	£3	£6	£3
C's good	£4	£4	£4	£4
D's good	£5	£5	£5	£1

TABLE 6. *Prices of Domestic and Foreign Goods After the Formation of a Partial Customs Union Between A, B and C, With a Common External Tariff of 300%. (C Maintains a Duty of 100% on Imports From A and B; B Maintains a Duty of 100% on Imports From A But Not on Imports From C.)*

	Price in A	Price in B	Price in C	Price in D
A's good	£2	£4	£4	£2
B's good	£3	£3	£6	£3
C's good	£4	£4	£4	£4
D's good	£4	£4	£4	£1

ment within the customs union which is designed to transfer income from the richer members of the area to the poorer (or backward) members. If C is fully protected from the competition of D's exports, through a high external tariff, she may make her product competitive within the customs union by subsidies rather than by tariffs. If C is a net importer of the commodity from the other two countries, the granting of subsidy to C's industry would merely create a fiscal burden in C; but if C is desirous of exporting its products to A and B, the subsidization of exports by C rather than tariff concessions by A and B would be transferring income from the poor or backward country to the richer countries of the customs union. In other words, if there are member countries of the customs union whose industries, either because of poverty of natural resources or owing to the small size of the internal markets, cannot hope to compete on equal footing with those of the other areas, tariff concessions or subsidies will not provide the fundamental solution to this problem. It may, in fact, not be easy to find a fundamental solution. However, the problems involved will be considerably eased if the kind of union envisaged goes beyond a customs union and provides also for the free movement of factors of production between the countries participating in the union.

V

This leads us to a consideration of the form of economic integration which is best suited to West African conditions. The rationale of economic integration, it must always be borne in mind, is to bring economic relations between the participating countries closer to those which would exist between them if they had been merely different regions of the same country. The nearer an economic integration comes to achieving this objective, the greater are likely to be the benefits which it will confer on the participating countries.

In the terminology of economic integration, some concepts, such as "customs union" and "free trade area" have precise definitions, while others, such as "common market," "economic union" and "economic community" are still somewhat loosely employed. A fairly good summary of the terminology is given by Bella Balassa[25] in the following passage:

> "Economic integration, . . . can take several forms that represent varying degrees of integration. These are a free-trade area, a customs union, a common market, an economic union, and complete economic integration. In a free-trade area, tariffs (and quantitative restrictions) between the par-

ticipating countries are abolished, but each country retains its own tariffs against non-members. Establishing a customs union involves, besides the suppression of discrimination in the field of commodity movement within the union, the equalization of tariffs in trade with non-member countries. A higher form of economic integration is attained in a common market, where not only trade restrictions but also restrictions on factor movement are abolished. An economic union, as distinct from a common market, combines the suppression of restrictions on commodity and factor movements with some degree of harmonization of national economic policies, in order to remove discrimination that was due to disparities in these policies. Finally, total economic integration presupposes the unification of monetary, fiscal, social, and counter-cyclical policies and requires the setting-up of a supra-national authority whose decisions are binding for the member states."

The distinction made in this passage between an economic union and a common market is not to be regarded as a hard and fast one. A common market involves much more than the freeing of trade and factor movements; it involves as well the adoption of measures, such as the co-ordination of the social and economic policies of the participating countries, which would ensure that a single market truly prevails for goods as well as for factors of production. Again, it should be noted that what Ballassa describes as total economic integration may also be described as a full economic community such as the six European countries hope ultimately to achieve. (As an illustration of the imprecise usage of terms, it is interesting to note the frequent interchange of the expressions European Economic Community and European Common Market in the literature on European economic integration). Lastly, a common market or economic community may be confined to certain specific sectors of the various economies. An example which will readily come to mind is the European Coal and Steel Community, (E.C.S.C.) established in 1951 between the same six countries (Western Germany, France, Belgium, Italy, Netherlands and Luxembourg) which, in 1957, formed the European Economic Community. The European Coal and Steel Community illustrates the sectoral, as opposed to the total approach, to economic integration. This kind of approach has the advantage of enabling the countries concerned to experiment with a supranational institutional arrangement in a narrow field before they extend it to a large area of economic life.

When confronted with the problems of economic integration in West

Africa, one's immediate reaction would probably be that, in spite of the potential advantages of an Economic Community, West African countries do not appear ripe enough at the present time for this advanced form of economic integration. The strains and stresses, both political and economic, which are likely to arise within a West African Economic Community, it may be feared, will demand a greater feeling of co-operation among these countries than exists at the present time. However, a closer examination of the situation in the light of our theoretical analysis would at least suggest that the economic problems of a West African Economic Community will not be as formidable as may be supposed—certainly not as formidable as the problems which confronted the six countries of the European Economic Community. As has already been pointed out, the trade between West African countries is at present only a small proportion of their total trade and the immediate prospect of expanding this trade within the existing economic structure is not at all promising. Except as regards the few industries which are already established, the formation of a West African Economic Community is not likely to intensify competition between productive units in the various countries. However, if each country proceeds along its chosen path of development, without regard to what is going on elsewhere, the problems of a West African Economic Community will become increasingly more difficult. In the immediate period the major problems which are likely to arise from the formation of the Community may be listed as follows:

(i) The existence of different currencies in the various countries;

(ii) The pursuit of different economic and social policies in the various countries;

(iii) Possible changes in the terms of trade between the various countries and in the employment situation within each country;

(iv) The pursuit of different commercial policies by the various countries; and

(v) The opposition of organised labour in each country to the free immigration of labour from other territories.

With regard to the first problem, provided that the currencies of member countries are freely exchangeable, one for another, the existence of different currencies will not impede the development of trade between the countries of a West African Economic Community. Each member country will be required to ensure that its currencies are freely convertible to the currencies of other member countries. In other words, a country finding itself in foreign exchange difficulties will not be allowed to deal with such difficulties by imposing restrictions on payments by her residents to residents of other member countries of the Community. Since the existing trade between these countries is so small, balance of payments problems arising from the trade between them are not likely to be so serious as to require the imposition of restrictions on intra-Community payments. However, the Community cannot ignore the balance of payments problems of member countries with countries outside it; and it would be necessary for common rules to be established as to how these problems should be dealt with so as not to prevent the realisation of the basic objectives of the Community. Already, because of the pursuit of independent monetary policies through national central banks in the various West African countries, a black market now exists for many of these currencies. In meeting this kind of problem, there is much that West African countries can learn from European experience. While an institution similar to the European Payments Union will have little value as long as West African countries establishing are more dependent on the outside world than on each other, there is much that can be gained from some degree of consultation and co-operation between the central banks in West Africa.

The second problem indicated is bound up with the first. The stability of a country's currency depends to a large extent on the soundness of its domestic economic policies; it will therefore be necessary to establish certain elementary principles of sound economic policy which will be acceptable to all the countries of the Community.

In order to ensure that competition between productive units in the Community is as fair as possible, it will be necessary to co-ordinate domestic policies in relation to such matters as government aids to industries (in the form of income tax rebates, direct subsidies etc.) and government taxes on transportation (in the form of licenses or taxes on petroleum fuels).

The change in the terms of trade between member countries and in the fortunes of economic groups within each country, which may result from the formation of a West African Economic Community are not easy to predict. But, because the immediate expansion of trade between the countries of the Community will not be very large, these changes are likely to be such as can be easily dealt with by the creation of a joint social fund (for which foreign aid can be invited) which will be available to help member countries which may find the process of adjustment particularly difficult.

The creation of a joint social fund should also provide part of the answer to the opposition of organized labour in each country to the formation of the Community. But such opposition can best be met by ensuring adequate representation for labour on some of the institutions of the Community. In this regard, a Pan-African labour movement should be encouraged rather than discouraged, as such a movement will go a long way towards fostering a spirit of comradeship between the workers of the various countries.

The problem which is likely to present the greatest obstacle to the formation of a West African Economic Community is the pursuit of different commercial policies by the separate West African States—a problem which has now been made more intractable by the association of the former Belgian and French overseas territories with the European Economic Community. Under the terms of the new Convention of Association, the associated territories will benefit from the European Economic Community in three ways:

(i) they will be able to export their primary products to countries of the European Economic Community free of import duties, whereas exports to these territories from other West African countries will be subject to varying rates of import duties, or other levies;

(ii) they will participate in the managed marketing of agricultural products through long-term contracts, which is one of the features of the European Economic Community; and

(iii) they will obtain assistance from the European Development Fund which has been set up by the European Economic Community with the expressed objects of assisting economic and social investments in associated territories, and of stabilising primary commodity prices.

In consideration of these various advantages, the associated states themselves will grant the following concessions to the members of the European Economic Community:

(i) they will "suppress at the latest four years after the entering into force of the Convention all quantitative restrictions on imports from the six;"[26]

(ii) they will reduce import duties on imports from the six at the rate of 15% every year;

(iii) they will grant "right of establishment" (i.e. right to engage in and carry on non-wage earning activities, and also to set up and manage enterprises and, in particular, companies) to nationals of the six European Economic Community countries, similar to that which these countries are to grant to one another; and

(iv) they will not discriminate among the six[27] in their commercial policies.

The escape clauses are, however, to be noted. The most important are as follows:

(i) The associated states will be permitted "to impose, maintain or strengthen tariffs or quantitative restrictions if it is found necessary for economic development, industrialisation or fiscal reasons. They may also impose quantitative restriction if it is required by membership in regional organisations;"[28]

(ii) they will be permitted to form Customs unions or free trade areas with third countries if this is not "incompatible with the principles or provisions of the Convention."[29]

The second escape clause has a direct bearing on the subject of this paper. This clause contains a fundamental contradiction, since it would seem impossible for a country to belong simultaneously to two distinct preferential groups (in this case the European Economic Community and a West African Economic Community) without these groups being merged with each other. Unless the condition attached to this clause is deleted or very liberally interpreted, it is not likely that the Associated countries will be able to invoke this clause to justify their participation in a West African Economic Community.

Apart from the stringent trade and exchange controls of the immediate post-war years, which have now been considerably relaxed, commercial policy in the former British West African territories have been largely non-discriminatory. The notable exceptions have been with respect to the dollar area and Japan, but imports from these sources are now more or less freely encouraged.

None of the former British West African territories gives preferential tariff treatment to British goods and none of them now derives any significant benefit from the system of Imperial Preference. Unlike the countries of the French Community, therefore, the West African members of the British Commonwealth are not handicapped by any special commercial relationship with their former colonial masters.

But there are three other problems which are common to all the countries of West Africa, and which may present obstacles to the formation of a West African Economic Community. These are:

(i) the predominant reliance of all these countries on import duties for government revenue;

(ii) their increasing reliance on manipulating import duties both for encouraging the inflow of foreign capital for industrial development and for protecting the new domestic industries; and

(iii) the now noticeable tendency on the part of each country to conclude independent trade agreements with third countries.

These problems would make difficult, if not impossible, the adoption of a unified commercial policy towards third countries, which is one of the essential characteristics of an Economic Community. Unless the prospective members of a West African Economic Community are prepared to forgo a certain amount of freedom of action with regard to their commercial policies, the prospects of bringing such a Community into existence will not be very bright.

Are we then to lower our vision and confine our discussion to the level of a West African Free Trade Area? On the face of it, that would seem to be more realistic in the present circumstances. Such an Area will leave each country free to pursue its separate commercial policies and to conclude its separate individual commercial agreements with third countries. It must be remembered however, that it will not be an Area where trade will be completely free but one where only products of domestic origin can be traded without restrictions and where trade across national frontiers will be subject to as much regulation as it is at the moment, so that a car imported into Nigeria at a lower import duty than it would have been subject to in Ghana will not subsequently be sold at a profit in the latter country.

There would also be the problem of defining "products of domestic origin." Suppose that Nigeria and Ghana, both have identical industries which rely partly on imported materials. If these materials are imported into Nigeria at lower duties than they are subject to in Ghana, then the products of the Nigerian industry may be able to undersell the Ghanaian product in Ghana. In order to meet this kind of problem, both countries must co-ordinate their various measures for fostering domestic industries. Such a co-ordination will cover not only the rates of import duties chargeable on raw materials, but also government taxes on, and subsidies to, domestic industries.

It is seen, then, that whether the desire is for an Economic Community or a Free Trade Area, there are too many matters that would have to be settled beforehand by negotiation and agreement and there would have to be provisions for a permanent machinery not only to put the agreement into effect, but also to take decisions on possible differences of interpretation that may arise in the ordinary functioning of the Union.

Although it seems that a Free Trade Area will be easier to achieve than an Economic Community, there is no reason why attempt should not be made to set up an Economic Community with the aim of realising its full advantages over a long period of time. In the first few years attempts may be made to bring into operation those provisions of the Agreement dealing with the establishment of free trade in products of domestic origin. The immediate establishment (even though it does not mean the immediate realization) of a West African Economic Community will arouse a greater psychological and emotional interest than the establishment of a West African Free Trade Area.

This paper has done little more than draw attention to some of the major problems of economic integration in West Africa. More specific recommendations would have to be based on a more detailed study and on such fresh information as will come to light in the near future from the various researches that are now being pursued on the subject. As the very first step towards economic integration in West Africa, a *Council for West African Economic Co-operation* or similar body can be set up without delay. It will consist of representatives of all West African governments and will be served by a small secretariat headed by a Secretary who will be appointed by the agreement of the various governments. The Council will appoint a Study Commission which will serve as its research agency and which will have the assistance of the Secretariat. The Study Commission, which will be charged with most of the preparatory work, will submit recommendations to the Council on the problems and possibilities of both a Free Trade Area and an Economic Community in West Africa. The Council can later appoint a number of committees to deal with specific problems. For example there could be committees on:

(*i*)   commercial policy;
(*ii*) industrial development;
(*iii*) the expansion of agricultural output; and
(*iv*) immigration and travel.

It is possible that the discussions and debates which will be carried on within this institutional framework will serve to bridge the wide differences which now appear to stand in the way of economic integration of the West African countries.

It must be said in conclusion that the movement towards economic integration cannot but be bound up with political sentiments. From the various documents pertaining to the establishment of the E.E.C. it is clear beyond doubt that European economic integration is seen as only a stepping stone to ultimate political union. The very first sentence of the Rome Treaty asserts the determination of the signatory powers "to establish the foundations of an ever closer union among the European people." Having almost destroyed themselves in two major wars, the people of Europe have become united in a common aversion to war and a common feeling that their future destinies lie together. Similarly, the West African countries have been and are still united in a common aversion to colonial domination; but, with the emergence of most of these countries into political independence, this has not proved a strong enough sentimental basis on which to build a positive policy of economic co-operation. Seen in the context of the gigantic economic problems which face the West African countries, the present political wrangle between them is more than disappointing; it is childish. Unless the political relations between them improve, the progress towards economic integration in West Africa is bound to be slow.

APPENDIX

THE TRADE-CREATING AND TRADE-DIVERTING EFFECTS OF A CUSTOMS UNION

The trade-creating and trade-diverting effects of a Customs Union can be represented diagrammatically. If A, B, are two countries forming a customs union, and C, D, constitute the rest of the world, the trade relations between the four countries and the production of foreign-trade goods within each country can be represented as in fig. 1. Confining the analysis to the very short term, and assuming zero elasticity of supply of exportables and zero elasticity of demand for importables, in each country, the effects of the customs union can be represented as in figs. 2 to 4, where a plus means a decrease, a zero means no change and a question mark indicates that the situation is indeterminate.

It is evident from this formulation of the problem that the extent to which the customs union will give rise to trade creation in the short run will depend on how large are the domestic consumption of exportables and the domestic production of importables (i.e. aa, bb, cc, and dd). It is also evident from this formulation that a full assessment of the effects of the customs union on the world economy must take into account not only the trade created between A and B and the trade diverted away from C and D, but also the trade created between C and D in consequence of the fall in their exports to (and most likely in their imports from) A and B.★

★ This point is adequately emphasized by J. E. Meade in his *Theory of Customs Union.*

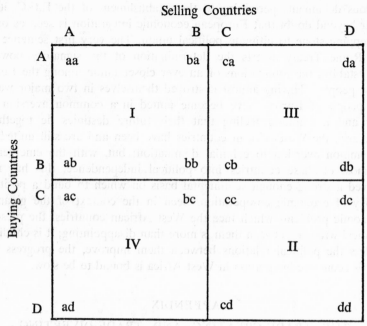

Fig. 1. Domestic and foreign trade in foreign-trade products

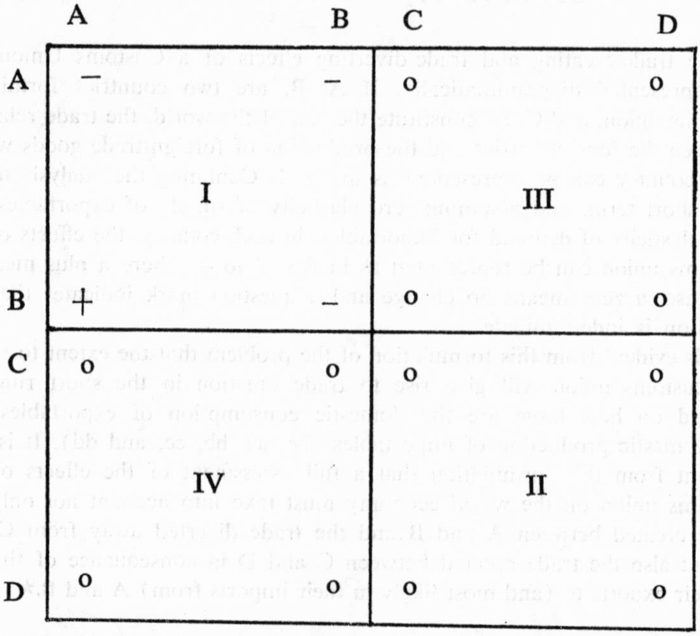

Fig. 2. A pure case of trade creation (i.e. there is a net increase in world trade)

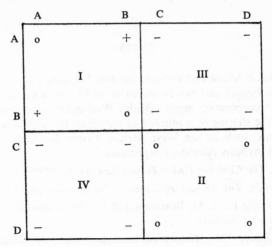

Fig. 3. A pure case of trade diversion (i.e. there is no net increase in world trade)

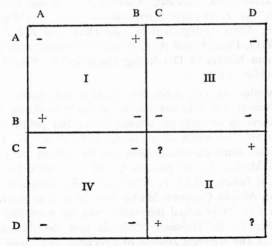

Fig. 4. A mixed case of trade creation and trade diversion

NOTES:
  I = The Customs Union.
  II = The Rest of the World.
  III = Imports into the Customs Union.
  IV = Exports of the Customs Union.
  ab = A's exports to B, ba = B's exports to A, and so on.
  aa = A's output of foreign-trade products sold at home.
These compromise two categories of products:
  (i) A's output of exportable products sold at home rather than exported; and
  (ii) A's consumption of importable products produced at home rather than imported.
Similarly for bb, cc, and dd.

Notes

1. French West Africa and French Equatorial Africa, each had a common currency, budget and tariffs. Apart from having a common currency, economic cooperation among British West African countries was confined to the sharing of a number of technical, research and commercial institutions, such as the West African Cocoa Research Institute and the West African Airways Corporation.

2. J. Viner, *The Customs Union Issue* (New York, 1950).

3. J. E. Meade, *The Theory of Customs Union* (Amsterdam, 1955).

4. See especially E. A. G. Robinson (ed.), *The Economic Consequences of the Size of Nations.*

5. R. G. Lipsey, "The Theory of Customs Union, A General Survey," *Economic Journal*, LXX (September, 1960), pp. 496-513.

6. *Ibid.*

7. See especially R. S. Bhambri, "Customs Unions and Underdeveloped Countries" in *Economica Internazionale*, XV, 2 (Maggio, 1962); Robert L. Allen, "Integration in Less Developed Areas" in *Kyklos*, XIV (1961), Fasc. 3; and A. J. Brown, "Economic Separatism versus A Common Market in Developing Countries" in *Yorkshire Bulletin*, XIII, 1 (May, 1961).

8. R. S. Bhambri, *op. cit.*, states that "there is little doubt that much of the enthusiasm for customs unions in underdeveloped countries is based ultimately on political considerations, but politicians have not been the only advocates of economic integration." G. K. Helleiner believes that some economic gains can be derived from an African Common Market, but he goes on to say: "It would be unfortunate, however, if failure quickly to achieve economic aims after the formation of an African Common Market were to lead to severe disillusion when, in fact, its principal motivation was not economic in the first place." See G. K. Helleiner, "Nigeria and the African Common Market" in *The Nigerian Journal of Economic and Social Studies*, IV, 3 (November, 1962).

9. A framework for examining the effect of a customs union on the world at large is suggested in the Appendix.

10. H. G. Johnson, *Money, Trade and Economic Growth* (London, 1962), chapter 3, page 47.

11. This objective can, of course, be achieved without the formation of a customs union.

12. See, for example, R. S. Bhambri and G. K. Helleiner, *op. cit.*

13. "In many English-speaking countries, the exemption (of local produce) is written in the tariff. In some French-speaking countries it operates

through tolerances." See E.C.A. Document on "Intra-African Trade in Local Produce," No. E/CN.14/STC/7 of 27th August, 1962, p. 2.

14. Even if production conditions are similar, differences of tastes may give rise to trade in local produce.

15. See for example the *Economic Survey of Africa since 1950*, the ECA's Economic Bulletins for Africa, and the Reports of the ECA's Standing Committees on Trade and on Industry and Natural Resources.

16. United Nations Economic Commission for Africa, *Industrial Growth in Africa—A Survey and Outlook*.

17. *Ibid.*, p. 231.

18. *Ibid.*

19. Federation of Nigeria, *National Development Plan 1962-68*.

20. *Industrial Growth in Africa, op. cit.*

21. *Industrial Growth in Africa, op. cit.*

22. United Nations, Department of Economic and Social Affairs, *The Latin American Common Market*.

23. It may, of course, be argued that even in this case integration may enable the countries to achieve greater economic stability.

24. The statement by R. S. Bhambri, *op. cit.*, p. 17 that the "special provisions suggested by the Working Group are either ineffective or unnecessary" applies strictly to a case in which there are only two countries in the common market.

25. Bella Balassa, *The Theory of Economic Integration* (London, 1962), p. 2.

26. See the ECA document "Information Paper on Recent Developments in Western European Economic Groupings," E/CN.14/207, 28 January 1963, p. 5.

27. Some observers insist that there is nothing in the new Association Convention which precludes the associated states from discriminating *against* the six countries of the EEC if this is necessitated by their participation in an African Common Market. This is a highly debatable point on which a valid opinion cannot be expressed until the full provisions of the Convention are made public.

28. ECA document No. E/CN.14/207, *op. cit.*, p. 5.

29. ECA document No. E/CN.14/207, *op. cit.*, p. 5.

Selected Bibliography
(1966-1969)

A. Bibliographies

Adetunje, Akinyatu. *A Bibliography on Development Planning in Nigeria, 1955-1968*. Ibadan: Nigerian Institute of Social and Economic Research, 1968.

Ike, Adebimpe O. *Economic Development of Nigeria 1950-1964: A Bibliography*. (Series I) Nsukka: University of Nigeria Library, 1966.

Lockwood, S. *Nigerian Official Publications: 1861-1965, A Guide*. Washington, D. C.: Library of Congress, 1966.

Nigerian Institute of Social and Economic Research, *Research for National Development*. Vol. II. Ibadan, Nigeria, April, 1967.

B. Books and Monographs

Abernathy, David. *The Political Dilemma of Popular Education—An African Case*. Stanford: Stanford University Press, 1969.

Aboyade, Ojetunji. *Foundations of an African Economy, A Study of Investment and Growth in Nigeria*. New York: Praeger, 1966.

Adedji, Adebayo. *Nigerian Federal Finance: Its Development, Problems and Prospects*. London: Hutchinson, 1969.

Bohannan, Paul and Bohannan, Laura. *Tiv Economy*. Evanston, Illinois: Northwestern University Press, 1968.

Brown, C. V. *Government and Banking in Western Nigeria—A Case Study in Economic Policy*. Ibadan: Oxford University Press, 1968.

Callaway, A. and Musone, A. *Financing of Education in Nigeria*. (African Research monographs, No. 15) Paris: UNESCO, International Institute for Educational Planning, 1968.

Gusten, R. *Studies in the Staple Food Economy of Western Nigeria*. New York: Humanities Press, 1968.

Helleiner, Gerald. *Peasant Agriculture, Government and Economic Growth in Nigeria*. Homewood, Illinois: Richard Irwin, 1966.

Hodder, B. W. and Ukwu, U. I. *Markets in West Africa*. Ibadan: University of Ibadan Press, 1969.

Hopkins, A. G. "Cocoa and Capitalism in Nigeria, 1880-1920." (forthcoming)

Johnson, Glenn; Scoville, O. J.; Dike, G. and Eicher, C. K. *Strategies and Recommendations for Nigerian Rural Development, 1969-1985*. East Lansing: Consortium for the Study of Nigerian Rural Development, Michigan State University, 1969.

Karmon, Yehuda. *A Geography of Settlement in Eastern Nigeria*. London: Oxford University Press, 1966.

Lewis, W. Arthur. *Reflections on Nigeria's Economic Growth.* (Development Centre Studies) Paris: O.E.C.D. 1967.

Lloyd, P. C., Mabogunje, A. L., and Awe, B., (eds.). *The City of Ibadan: A Symposium on Its Structure and Development.* New York: Cambridge University Press, 1968.

McFarlane, David and Oworen, Martin. *Investment in Oil Palm Plantations in Nigeria: A Financial and Economic Appraisal.* Enugu: Economic Development Institute, University of Nigeria, 1966.

Markets and Marketing in West Africa. Proceedings of a Seminar held at the Center of African Studies, April 20-30, 1966. Edinburgh, Center for African Studies, 1966.

Netting, R. *Hill Farmers of Nigeria: Cultural Ecology of the Kofyar of the Jos Plateau.* Seattle: University of Washington Press, 1969.

Ojo, G. J. Afolabi. *Yoruba Culture: A Geographical Analysis.* London: University of Ife Press and University of London Press 1966.

Oluwasanmi, H. A. *Agriculture and Nigerian Economic Development.* London: Oxford University Press, 1966.

Oluwasanmi, H. A., et. al. *Uboma: A Socio-Economic and Nutritional Survey of a Rural Community in Eastern Nigeria.* Cornwall: Geographical Publications Ltd., 1966.

Onyemelukwe, C. C. *Problems of Industrial Planning and Management in Nigeria.* London: Longmans, Green and Co., 1966.

Oyenuga, V. A. *Agriculture in Nigeria: An Introduction.* Rome: FAO, 1967.

Stolper, W. F. *Planning Without Facts: Lessons in Resource Allocation from Nigeria's Development.* Cambridge: Harvard University Press, 1966.

Suckow, Samuel. *Nigerian Law and Foreign Investment.* Paris: Mouton, 1966.

United Nations. Food and Agriculture Organization. *Agricultural Development in Nigeria, 1965-1980.* Rome: FAO, 1966.

Upton, Martin. *Agriculture in South-Western Nigeria.* (Development Studies No. 3) Reading: University of Reading, December, 1967.

C. *Official Government Documents*

1. *Federal Documents*

Expenditure Elasticities of Demand for Household Consumer Goods. Lagos: Federal Office of Statistics, February, 1966.

Guideposts for Second National Development Plan. Lagos: Ministry of Economic Development, June, 1966.

Industrial Survey of Nigeria, 1963. Lagos: Federal Office of Statistics, 1966.

Industrial Survey of Nigeria, 1964 and 1965. Lagos: Federal Office of Statistics, 1968.

Nigeria's Professional Manpower in Selected Occupations, 1966. (National Manpower Board, Manpower Study, No. 5) Lagos: Federal Ministry of Economic Development, 1967.

Report of the Interim Revenue Allocation Review Committee. Apapa: Nigerian National Press, 1969.

Rural Economic Survey of Nigeria, Farm Survey—1963/64. Lagos: Federal Office of Statistics, February 28, 1966.

Sectoral Manpower Survey, 1964: Manufacturing, Mining and Quarrying, Construction and Electricity Generation. (National Manpower Board, Manpower Study No. 4). Lagos: Federal Ministry of Economic Development, 1967.

2. *Regional and State Documents*

An Evaluation of the Cottonseed Crushing Potential in the Northern Provinces of Nigeria. Kaduna: Ministry of Trade and Industry, June, 1966.

A White Paper on the Military Government Policy for the Reorganization of the Northern Nigeria Development Corporation. Kaduna: Government Printer, 1966.

A White Paper on the Northern Nigeria Military Government's Policy for the Comprehensive Review of the Past Operations and Methods of the Northern Nigeria Marketing Board. Kaduna: Government Printer, 1967.

Consolidated Annual Report of the Progress of Cooperation in Northern Nigeria: 1958/59-1964/65. Kaduna: Government Printer, 1967.

Development Plan Statistics of Western Group of Provinces of Nigeria. Ibadan: Government Printer, 1966.

Directory of Industrial Establishments in Western Nigeria, 1966. Ibadan: Government Printer, 1967.

Eastern Nigeria Industrial Directory. (Eastern Nigeria Official Document No. 7 of 1966). Enugu: Government Printer, 1966.

Haynes, D. W. M. *The Development of Agricultural Implements in Northern Nigeria.* Samaru, Zaria: Institute for Agricultural Research, Ahmadu Bello University, 1966.

Midwestern Nigeria Industrial Directory, 1967. Benin City: Government Printer, 1967.

D. *Journal Articles and Book Chapters*

Aboyade, Ojetunji. "Relations Between Central and Local Institutions in the Development Process," *Nation by Design.* Edited by Arnold Rivkin, New York: Anchor Books, 1968, pp. 83-118.

Adamu, S. O. "Expenditure Elasticities of Demand for Household Consumer Goods," *The Nigerian Journal of Economic and Social Studies,* Vol. VII, No. 3 (November, 1966), pp. 481-490.

Adegboye, R. O. "An Analysis of Land Tenure Structure in Some Selected Areas of Nigeria," *Nigerian Journal of Economic and Social Studies,* Vol. VII, No. 2 (July, 1966), pp. 259-268.

—————. "The Need for Land Reform in Nigeria," *Nigerian Journal of Economic and Social Studies*, Vol. IX, No. 3 (November, 1967), pp. 339-350.

Aken'ova, M. E. and Anthonio, Q. B. O. "The Marketing of Ofada Rice in Ibadan City—A Pilot Survey," *Bulletin of Rural Economics and Sociology*, Vol. III, No. 2 (1968), pp. 267-234.

Aluko, S. A. "The Educated in Business: The Calabar Home Farm—A Case Study," *Nigerian Journal of Economic and Social Studies*, Vol. VIII, No. 2 (July, 1966), pp. 195-208.

Amachree, I. T. D. "Reference Group and Worker Satisfaction: Studies Among Some Nigerian Factory Workers," *Nigerian Journal of Economic and Social Studies*, Vol. X, No. 2 (July, 1968), pp. 229-238.

Anschel, Kurt, R. "Problems and Prospects of the Nigerian Rubber Industry," *Nigerian Journal of Economic and Social Studies*, Vol. IX, No. 2 (July, 1967), pp. 145-159.

Anthonio, Q. B. O. "Food Consumption and Income Relationships in Nigeria: Engle's Curve Functions," *Bulletin of Rural Economics and Sociology*, Vol. II, No. 1 (October, 1966), pp. 52-67.

—————. "The Stagnant Sector in Nigerian Economy," *Bulletin of Rural Economics and Sociology*, Vol. II, No. 3 (1967), pp. 211-228.

—————. "The Supply and Distribution of Yams in Ibadan Markets," *Nigerian Journal of Economic and Social Studies*, Vol. IX, No. 1 (March, 1967), pp. 33-49.

Asiodu, P. C. "Industrial Policy and Incentives in Nigeria," *Nigerian Journal of Economic and Social Studies*, Vol. IX, No. 2 (July, 1967), pp. 161-174.

Ayandele, E. A. "Observations on Some Social and Economic Aspects of Slavery in Pre-Colonial Northern Nigeria," *Nigerian Journal of Economic and Social Studies*, Vol. IX, No. 3 (November, 1967), pp. 329-338.

Ayorinde, Chief J. A. "Historical Notes on the Introduction of the Cocoa Industry in Western Nigeria," *Nigerian Agricultural Journal*, Vol. III, No. 1 (April, 1966), pp. 18-23.

Carney, David. "Observations on the Model and Implications of the 'Guideposts' for the Second Nigerian National Plan," *Nigerian Journal of Economic and Social Studies*, Vol. IX, No. 1 (March, 1967), pp. 3-10.

Clark, Peter. "Economic Planning for a Country in Transition: Nigeria," *Planning Economic Development*. Edited by E. Hagen. Homewood, Illinois: Richard Irwin, 1966. Ch. 9.

Daramola, R. D., et al. "Attitudes in Nigeria Toward Family Planning," *The Population of Tropical Africa*. Edited by J. C. Caldwell and C. Okonjo. London: Longmans, 1968, pp. 401-409.

Dean, E. R. "Factors Impeding the Implementation of Nigeria's Six-

Year Plan," *Nigerian Journal of Economic and Social Studies,* Vol. VIII, No. 1 (March, 1966), pp. 113-128.

Edozien, E. C. "Linkages, Direct Foreign Investment and Nigeria's Economic Development," *Nigerian Journal of Economic and Social Studies,* Vol. X, No. 2 (July, 1968), pp. 191-204.

Eicher, Carl K. "Reflections on Capital Intensive Farm Settlements in Southern Nigeria," *Agricultural Cooperatives and Markets in Developing Countries.* Edited by K. Anschel, E. Smith and R. Brannon. New York: Praeger, 1969.

Eke, Ifegwu I. U. "Population of Nigeria: 1952-1965," *Nigerian Journal of Economic and Social Studies,* Vol. VIII, No. 2 (July, 1966), pp. 289-310.

——————. "The Nigerian National Accounts—A Critical Appraisal," *Nigerian Journal of Economic and Social Studies,* Vol. VIII, No. 3 (November, 1966), pp. 333-360.

Essang, S. M. "The Middlemen in the Domestic Marketing of Palm Oil: Asset or Liability?" *Bulletin of Rural Economics and Sociology.* Vol. III, No. 1 (1968), pp. 38-68.

Ferguson, Donald S. *The Nigerian Beef Industry.* (International Agricultural Development Bulletin No. 9) Ithaca, New York: Cornell University, August, 1967.

Frank, Charles R. "Industrialization and Employment Generation in Nigeria," *Nigerian Journal of Economic and Social Studies,* Vol. IX, No. 3 (November, 1967), pp. 277-298.

——————. "Urban Unemployment and Economic Growth in Africa," *Oxford Economic Papers,* Vol. XX, No. 2 (July, 1968), pp. 250-274.

Gray, Clive S. "Planning Without Facts—A Review Article," *The Nigerian Journal of Economic and Social Studies,* Vol. X, No. 1 (March, 1968), pp. 3-31.

Grossmann, David. "The Effects of Migrant Tenant Farming in Nigeria's Eastern Region," *Food Production in Africa: Case Studies in Peasant Economies.* Edited by Peter McLaughlin, Johns Hopkins Press. (Forthcoming in 1969)

Gusten, R. "Can the Nigerian Economy Grow at 6% P.A. in the Near Future? A Pre-Planning Exercise," *Nigerian Journal of Economic and Social Studies,* Vol. IX (March, 1967), pp. 11-32.

Hakam, A. N. "The Motivation to Invest and the Locational Pattern of Foreign Private Industrial Investments in Nigeria," *Nigerian Journal of Economic and Social Studies,* Vol. VIII, No. 1 (March, 1966), pp. 49-66.

Harris, J. R. "Nigerian Enterprise in the Printing Industry," *Nigerian Journal of Economic and Social Studies,* Vol. X, No. 2 (July, 1968), pp. 215-228.

Harris, J. R. and Rowe, M. P. "Entrepreneurial Patterns in the Nigerian Sawmilling Industry," *Nigerian Journal of Economic and Social Studies,* Vol. VIII, No. 1 (March, 1966), pp. 67-96.

Hay, A. M. and Smith, R. H. T. "Preliminary Estimates of Nigeria's Interregional Trade and Associated Money Flows," *Nigerian Journal of Economic and Social Studies*, Vol. VIII, No. 1 (March, 1966), pp. 9-36.

Helleiner, Gerald. "Marketing Boards and Domestic Stabilization in Nigeria," *Review of Economics and Statistics*. Vol. XLVIII, No. 1 (February, 1966).

—————. "Typology in Development Theory: The Land Surplus Economy (Nigeria)," *Food Research Institute Studies*, Vol. VI, No. 2 (1966), pp. 181-194.

Hill, Polly. "Aspects of Socio-Economic Life in a Hausa Village in Northern Nigeria," *Rural Africana*, (Spring, 1969).

—————. "Notes on the History of the Northern Katsina Tobacco Trade," *Journal of the Historical Society of Nigeria* (Forthcoming)

—————. "The Myth of the Amorphous Peasantry: A Northern Nigerian Case Study," *Nigerian Journal of Economic and Social Studies*, Vol. X, No. 2 (July, 1968), pp. 239-260.

—————. "Why does Land Come into the Market: The Case of a Hausa Village," *Nigerian Journal of Economic and Social Studies*. (Forthcoming)

Hodder, B. W. "Some Comments on Markets and Market Periodicity," in *Proceedings of a Seminar on Markets and Marketing in West Africa*. Edinburgh: Centre for African Studies, University of Edinburgh, April, 1966.

Hogendorn, J. S. "Response to Price Change: A Nigerian Example," *Economica*, Vol. XXXIV, No. 135 (August, 1967), p. 289.

Ilori, C. O. "Towards a Policy of Marketing Improvement in Western Nigeria," *Bulletin of Rural Economics and Sociology*, Vol. II, No. 3 (1967), pp. 229-245.

Imoagene, Stephen O. "Psycho-Social Factors in Rural-Urban Migration," *Nigerian Journal of Economic and Social Studies*, Vol. IX, No. 3 (November, 1967), pp. 375-86.

Johnson, Glenn L. "Removing Obstacles to the Use of Genetic Breakthroughs in Oil Palm Production: The Nigerian Case," *Agricultural Research Priorities for Economic Development in Africa—The Abidjan Conference*. Washington, D. C.: National Academy of Sciences, 1968.

Johnson, Glenn L. "Food Supply, Agriculture and Economic Growth," paper presented at Second Western Hemisphere Nutrition Congress, San Juan, Puerto Rico, August, 1968.

Jones, William O. "The Structure of Staple Food Marketing in Nigeria as Revealed by Price Analysis," *Food Research Institute Studies in Agricultural Economics, Trade & Development*, Vol. VIII, No. 2 (1968), pp. 95-124.

Kilby, Peter. "The Nigerian Palm Oil Industry," *Food Research Institute Studies*, Vol. VII, No. 2 (1967), pp. 177-203.

_____. "Reply to the Nigerian Oil Palm Industry: A Comment," *Food Research Institute Studies in Agricultural Economics, Trade and Development,* Vol. VIII, No. 2 (1968), pp. 199-202.

Kriesel, Herbert C. "Some Considerations Bearing on International Transfer of Agricultural Technology with Particular Reference to Poultry in Nigeria," *Nigerian Journal of Economic and Social Studies,* Vol. VII, No. 2 (July, 1966), pp. 167-184.

Langley, Kathleen. "The External Resource Factor in Nigerian Economic Development," *Nigerian Journal of Economic and Social Studies,* Vol. X, No. 2 (July, 1968), pp. 153-182.

Laurent, Charles K. "The Use of Bullocks for Power on Farms in Northern Nigeria," *Bulletin of Rural Economics and Sociology,* Vol. III, No. 2 (1968), pp. 235-262.

Lee, B. J. S. "Cotton in Western Nigeria—History and Recent Developments," *The Empire Cotton Growing Review,* Vol. XLIII (April, 1966), pp. 85-97.

Liedholm, Carl. "Production Functions for Eastern Nigerian Industry," *Nigerian Journal of Economic and Social Studies,* Vol. VIII, No. 3 (November, 1966), pp. 427-440.

Luning, H. A. "Patterns of Choice Behavior on Peasant Farms in Northern Nigeria," *Netherlands Journal of Agricultural Science,* Vol. XV (1967), pp. 161-169.

Melamid, Alexander. "The Geography of the Nigerian Petroleum Industry," *Economic Geography,* Vol. XLIV, No. 1 (January, 1968), pp. 37-56.

Miracle, Marvin P. and Fetter, Bruce. "Backward-Sloping Labor Supply Functions and African Economic Behavior," in *Economic Development and Cultural Change,* 1969. (Forthcoming)

Netting, Robert McC. "Do-It-Yourself Economic Surveys: Field Methods for Data Collections," *Rural Africana,* (Spring, 1969).

_____. "Ecosystems in Process: A Comparative Study of Change in Two West African Societies," *Essays in Ecology.* (Forthcoming)

Okonjo, Chukka. "A Preliminary Medium Estimate of the 1962 Mid-Year Population of Nigeria," *The Population of Tropical Africa.* Edited by J. C. Caldwell and C. Okonjo. London: Longmans, 1968, pp. 78-96.

Olakanpo, O. "A Statistical Analysis of Some Determinants of Entrepreneurial Success: A Nigerian Case Study," *Nigerian Journal of Economic and Social Studies,* Vol. X, No. 2 (July, 1968), pp. 137-152.

Olayide, S. O. "Fodder Supply Problem in Northern States of Nigeria: A Simple Inventory Analysis of a Decision Problem Under Uncertainty," *Nigerian Journal of Economic and Social Studies,* Vol. X, No. 2 (July, 1967), pp. 204-214.

Onakomaiya, Samuel O. "The Spatial Structure of Internal Trade in Selected Foodstuffs in Nigeria," *Rural Africana,* (Spring, 1969).

Oni, Ola. "Development and Features of the Nigerian Financial System—A Marxist Approach," *Nigerian Journal of Economic and Social Studies*, Vol. VIII, No. 3 (November, 1966), pp. 383-402.

Onitiri, H. M. A. "Presidential Address—A Proposal for Nigerian Rural Development," *Nigerian Journal of Economic and Social Studies*, Vol. VIII, No. 1 (March, 1966), pp. 3-8.

Packard, Phillip. "A Note on Gross Domestic Investment and Fiscal Policy," *Nigerian Journal of Economic and Social Studies*, Vol. VIII, No. 2 (July, 1966), pp. 219-234.

_____. "The Need for Product Market Analysis: A Case Study of the Feasibility of Import Substitution in Nigeria," *Journal of Industrial Economics*, Vol. XVI, No. 1 (November, 1967), pp. 63-72.

Phillips, A. O. "Nigerian Industrial Tax Incentives: Import Duties Relief and the Approved User Scheme," *Nigerian Journal of Economic and Social Studies*, Vol. IX, No. 3 (November, 1967), pp. 315-328.

_____. "Nigeria's Experience with Income Tax Exemption— A Preliminary Assessment," *Nigerian Journal of Economic and Social Studies*, Vol. X, No. 1 (March, 1968), pp. 33-62.

Purvis, Malcolm J. "The Nigerian Oil Palm Industry: A Comment," *Food Research Institute Studies in Agricultural Economics, Trade and Development*, Vol. VIII, No. 2 (1968), pp. 199-202.

Schatzl, L. "Basic Data for Projecting Energy Production and Consumption in Nigeria," *Nigerian Journal of Economic and Social Studies*, Vol. VIII, No. 3 (November, 1966), pp. 403-426.

Shields, B. "Observations on Some Road Feasibility Studies in Nigeria," *Nigerian Journal of Economic and Social Studies*, Vol. VIII, No. 2 (July, 1966), pp. 185-194.

Siebel, H. D. "Some Aspects of Inter-Ethnic Relations in Nigeria," *Nigerian Journal of Economic and Social Studies*, Vol. IX, No. 2 (July, 1967), pp. 217-228.

Smith, Robert H. T. and Hay, Alan M. "A Theory of the Spatial Structure in Internal Trade in Underdeveloped Countries," *Geographical Analysis*. (Forthcoming)

Smock, David R. "Land Fragmentation and the Possibility of Consolidation in Eastern Nigeria," *Bulletin of Rural Economics and Sociology*, Vol. II, No. 3 (September, 1967), pp. 194-210.

Steele, W. M. "Agriculture Research in Kano," *Kano Studies*, Vol. III (June, 1967), pp. 35-37.

Taylor, Milton. "The Relationship Between Income Tax Administration and Income Tax Policy in Nigeria," *Nigerian Journal of Economic and Social Studies*, Vol. IX, No. 2 (July, 1967), pp. 203-216.

Teriba, O. "Development Strategy, Investment Decision and Expenditure Patterns of a Public Development Institution: The Case of

Western Nigeria Development Corporation, 1949-1962," *Nigerian Journal of Economic and Social Studies*, Vol. VIII, No. 2 (July, 1966), pp. 235-258.

_____. "Nigerian Revenue Allocation Experience 1952-1965: A Study in Inter-Governmental Fiscal and Financial Relations," *Nigerian Journal of Economic and Social Studies*, Vol. VIII, No. 3 (November, 1966), pp. 361-382.

_____. "The Growth of Public Expenditure in Western Nigeria," *Nigerian Journal of Economic and Social Studies*, Vol. IX, No. 2 (July, 1967), pp. 175-202.

Toluhi, Michael M.D. "The Role of Savings Banks in the Mobilization of Domestic Savings in Nigeria," *Nigerian Journal of Economic and Social Studies*, Vol. VIII, No. 2 (July, 1966), pp. 209-218.

Udo, R. K. "British Policy and the Development of Export Crops in Nigeria," *Nigerian Journal of Economic and Social Studies*, Vol. IX, No. 3 (November, 1967), pp. 299-314.

Ugoh, S. U. "The Nigerian Cement Industry," *Nigerian Journal of Economic and Social Studies*, Vol. VIII, No. 1 (March, 1966), pp. 97-112.

Upton, Martin. "Socio-Economic Survey of Some Farm Families in Nigeria," *Bulletin of Rural Economics and Sociology*, Vol. III, No. 1 (1968), pp. 7-37.

_____. "Tree Crops: A Long Term Investment," *Journal of Agricultural Economics*, Vol. XVII (March, 1966), pp. 82-90.

Vielrose, Egon. "Import and Export Substitution in Nigeria," *Nigerian Journal of Economic and Social Studies*, Vol. X, No. 2 (July, 1968), pp. 183-190.

Warren, W. M. "Urban Real Wages and the Nigerian Trade Union Movement," *Economic Development and Cultural Change*, Vol. XV, No. 1 (October, 1966), pp. 21-36.

Wells, Jerome C. "Government Investment in Nigerian Agriculture: Some Unsettled Issues," *Nigerian Journal of Economic and Social Studies*, Vol. VIII (March, 1966), pp. 37-48.

_____. "Nigerian Government Spending on Agricultural Development: (1962/63-1966/67)," *Nigerian Journal of Economic and Social Studies*, Vol. IX, No. 3 (November, 1967), pp. 245-276.

_____. "The Israeli Moshav in Nigeria," *Journal of Farm Economics*, Vol. XLVIII, No. 2 (May, 1966), pp. 279-294.

Welsch, Delane. "Rice Marketing in Eastern Nigeria," *Food Research Institute Studies*, Vol. VI, No. 3 (1966), pp. 329-352.

Whetham, Edith H. "Diminishing Returns and Agriculture in Northern Nigeria," *Journal of Agricultural Economics*, Vol. XVII, No. 2 (September, 1966), pp. 151-157.

Williams, S. K. Taiwo. "The Confluence of Extension Education, Agricultural Extension and Community Development," *Bulletin of Rural Economics and Sociology*, Vol. II, No. 3 (1967), pp. 184-193.

Zeven, A. C. "Oil Palm Groves in Southern Nigeria. Part II. Their Development, Deterioration and Rehabilitation," *Journal of the Nigerian Institute for Oil Palm Research*, Vol. IV, No. 16. (Forthcoming)

E. *Unpublished Ph.D. Dissertations*

Barry, David. "Nigerian Commercial Banking and Development." Northwestern University, 1968.

Berry, Sara Sweezy. "Cocoa in Western Nigeria, 1890-1940: A Study of Innovation in a Developing Economy." University of Michigan, 1967.

Bowles, Samuel S. "The Efficient Allocation of Resources in Education: A Planning Model with Application to Northern Nigeria." Harvard University, 1966.

Brinkman, George. "Reconciling Planned Public Investments in Agricultural Education, Infrastructure and Production in Nigeria, 1969-1985." Michigan State University, 1969.

Clark, P. B. "The Relationship Between Intertemporal Linear Programming Models and Micro-Investment Criteria with Reference to Development in Nigeria." Massachusetts Institute of Technology, 1968.

Davis, Edward Burl. "System Variables and Agricultural Innovativeness in Eastern Nigeria." Michigan State University, 1968.

Diejomaoh, Victor. "Financing Development Expenditures: Nigerian Experience Since 1950." Harvard University, 1968.

Edozien, E. C. "The Impact of Direct Foreign Investment on an Underdeveloped Economy: The Nigerian Case." University of Michigan, 1966.

Grossman, David. "Migratory Tenant Farming in Northern Iboland in Relation to Resource Use." Columbia University, 1968.

Harris, John. "Industrial Entrepreneurship in Nigeria." Northwestern University, 1967.

Hershfield, Allan. "Village Leaders and the Modernization of Agriculture: A Study of Leaders of Fifty-two Ibo Villages." Indiana University, 1967-68.

Hogendorn, Jan. "The Origins of the Groundnut Trade in Northern Nigeria." University of London, 1966.

Huth, William P. "Traditional Institutions and Land Tenure as Related to Agricultural Development Among the Ibo of Eastern Nigeria." University of Wisconsin, 1969.

Ilori, Christopher O. "Economic Study of Production and Distribution of Staple Foodcrops in Western Nigeria." Stanford University, 1968.

Keith, Robert. "Information and Modernization: A Study of Eastern Nigerian Farmers." Michigan State University, 1968.

Kellogg, Earl, "A Simulation Model of Nigerian Beef Marketing." Michigan State University, 1969.

Nafziger, E. Wayne. "Nigerian Entrepreneurship: A Study of Indigeneous Businessmen in the Footwear Industry." University of Illinois, 1967.

Olatunbosun, Dupe. "Nigerian Farm Settlements and School Leavers' Farms—Profitability, Resource Use and Social-Psychological Considerations." Michigan State University, 1967.

Sanders, Dean S. "Estimation of the Supply Elasticities of Nigerian Primary Export Commodities: An Evaluation of Marketing Board Policies." University of Michigan, 1968.

Spain, David Howard. "Achievement Orientation and Ethnicity in Bornu." Northwestern University, 1968.

Weeks, John. "Wage Behavior, Rural-Urban Income Trends, and Wage Policy in Nigeria." University of Michigan, 1968.

Williams, Saudiq Kolawole Taiwo. "Identification of Professional Training Needs of Agricultural Extension Agents in Western Nigeria as a Basis for Developing a College Training Curriculum." Cornell University, 1967.

F. *Conference on National Reconstruction in Nigeria*

A conference on reconstruction and development was held in Ibadan from 24–29 March, 1969. The conference was organized by the Federal Ministry of Economic Development and the Nigerian Institute of Social and Economic Research, Ibadan. A proceedings volume of the papers presented at the conference will be published. The names of the authors and the titles of the papers are as follows:

1. H. A. Oluwasanmi, "Agricultural and Rural Development"
2. NISER Staff, "An Economic and Social Survey, 1958-1968"
3. Adebayo Adedeji, "Federalism and Development Planning in Nigeria"
4. O. Aboyade, "The Development Process"
5. Ayo Ogunsheye, "Education and Manpower"
6. M. M. Diallo, "The Power and Energy Resources & Utilization of Nigeria"
7. Tillo E. Kuhn, "Transport & Communications Systems Planning for Reconstruction and Development"
8. A. Akene Ayida, "Development Objectives"
9. S. A. Aluko, "Prices, Wages & Costs"
10. Chief I. O. Dina, "Fiscal Measures"
11. Ukpabi Asika, "Rehabilitation and Resettlement"
12. P. O. Ahimie, "Health, Housing and Social Welfare"
13. P. C. Asiodu, "Planning for Further Industrial Development in Nigeria"
14. Peter O. Fasan, "Community Health and National Planning in Post-War Nigeria"

15. H. M. A. Onitiri, "Nigeria's External Trade Balance of Payments and Capital Movements, 1959-1968."
16. A. E. Ekukinam, "Main Trends in Banking and Monetary Policy to 1968: Projection of Possible Developments in the Next Decade in Terms of Development Policy, Strategy, and Institutional Arrangements"

The Contributors

A. AKENE AYIDA, Permanent Secretary to the Federal Ministry of Economic Development, Lagos, was trained at Oxford University and the London School of Economics. He joined the Federal Government of Nigeria in 1957 as Assistant Secretary, Federal Ministry of Education and thereafter served in various positions in the Finance Ministry before moving to his present position in the Economic Development Ministry in 1963. He has also served as Chairman of the National Manpower Board and as Secretary of the National Economic Council and has represented Nigeria at international meetings of the World Bank, the United Nations Commission for Africa, and the Commonwealth Ministers. He is the author of "Common Markets and Industrialization," "The Contribution of Politicians and Administrators to Nigeria's National Economic Planning," as well as several other articles on Nigerian economic development.

K. D. S. BALDWIN, Agricultural Economist, Food and Agricultural Organization, Rome, Italy, was trained at Oxford University. He has taught at University College of the Gold Coast and has served as General Manager of the National Development Corporation in Malawi. He is the author of *The Marketing of Cocoa in Western Nigeria* and a joint author (with R. Galletti and I. O. Dina) of *Nigerian Cocoa Farmers*.

SARA S. BERRY, Department of Economic and African Studies Program, Indiana University, was trained at Radcliffe College and the University of Michigan. She carried out field research among Yoruba cocoa farmers in Western Nigeria in 1966 and 1969, and has written articles on various aspects of economic development in West Africa.

LYLE M. HANSEN, Senior Economist, Eastern Africa Department, International Bank for Reconstruction and Development, was trained at the University of Chicago and Syracuse University, and has taught at Syracuse University, San Francisco State College and Williams College. He was a member of the Harvard Advisory Group to the Pakistan Planning Commission from 1957–59, participating in drafting the Pakistan Second Five-Year Plan, and economic adviser to the Ministry of Economic Affairs of the Federal Government of Nigeria from 1960–63.

FREDERICK H. HARBISON, Department of Economics and Wood-
row Wilson School of International and Public Affairs, Princeton University, was trained at Princeton University. In 1960, he prepared, at the
request of the Ashby Commission, the first survey of Nigeria's high-
level manpower requirements. He is the joint author (with J. Dunlop,
C. Kerr, and C. Meyers) of *Management in the Industrial World*, co-
author (with C. Meyers) of *Education, Manpower, and Economic
Growth* as well as the author of numerous articles in the fields of labor
economics, industrial relations, education, public administration and
economic development.

JOHN R. HARRIS, Department of Economics, Massachusetts Institute
of Technology, was trained at Northwestern University. He was an associate research fellow of the Nigerian Institute of Social and Economic
Research during 1965 and visiting research fellow, Institute for Development Studies, University College, Nairobi, 1968–69. He is the author of
"Migration, Unemployment and Development: A Two-Sector Analysis,"
and "Wages, Industrial Employment and Labour Productivity: The
Kenyan Experience," as well as several articles on entrepreneurship.

G. K. HELLEINER, Department of Political Economy, University of
Toronto, studied at Yale University where he subsequently joined the
staff of the Economic Growth Center. He conducted research at the
Nigerian Institute of Social and Economic Research in 1962–63 and
was at the same time a visiting lecturer at the University of Ibadan.
From 1966 to 1968 he was Director of the Economic Research Bureau,
University College, Dar es Salaam, Tanzania. He is author of *Peasant
Agriculture, Government, and Economic Growth in Nigeria*, and editor
of *Agricultural Planning in East Africa*.

JAN S. HOGENDORN, Department of Economics, Colby College,
Waterville, Maine, received his graduate training at the London School
of Economics, and has taught at Boston University. His main field of
research has been the development of agriculture in Northern Nigeria,
where he travelled in 1958 and was resident in Kano during 1965–66.
He is the author of several articles in the area of development economics.

GLENN L. JOHNSON, Department of Agricultural Economics, Michigan State University, and Director Consortium for the Study of Nigerian

Rural Development, was trained at Michigan State University and the University of Chicago. From 1963 to 1964, he served as the first Director of the University of Nigeria's Economic Development Institute at Enugu. He is the co-author of *Farm Management Analysis* as well as the author of numerous articles in professional journals.

CHARLES R. NIXON, Department of Political Science, University of California, Los Angeles, was trained at Oberlin College and Cornell University, and has taught at Smith College, Oberlin College, the University of Natal, and the University College of Rhodesia and Nyasaland. His African field experience includes work in: Durban, South Africa, 1954; Nigeria, 1959–60; and Federation of Rhodesia and Nyasaland 1960–61, and 1962–63. His work in Nigeria and in the Federation of Rhodesia and Nyasaland focused on the relation between political change and economic development policy. He is the author of articles on civil liberties, political activity in the U.S.A., and political conflict in Africa.

H. M. A. ONITIRI, Director, Nigerian Institute of Social and Economic Research, was trained at the London School of Economics, University of California, Berkeley, and Yale University. He taught in the Department of Economics, University of Ibadan, between 1958 and 1964 and became Director of the Nigerian Institute of Social and Economic Research in 1964. He has served on a number of United Nations Study Groups and is currently a member of the United Nations Expert Group on Land-locked Developing Countries. His major research interests are in the fields of international trade and economic development; he has contributed several articles on these subjects in various books and journals.

SCOTT R. PEARSON, Food Research Institute, Stanford University, was trained at the Johns Hopkins University and Harvard University. In 1961–63 he taught at the Sokoto Training College, Sokoto, Nigeria as a member of the first group of Peace Corps Volunteers in Nigeria. He carried out field reseach in Nigeria during 1965 and 1966 and in 1968 and 1969. He is the author of several articles concerning economic problems of Nigeria and Africa and of a forthcoming book on the economics of petroleum in Nigeria.

MALCOLM J. PURVIS, Department of Agricultural Economics, University of Minnesota, was trained at the University of London and at

Cornell University. His field experience includes research in Malaysia in 1964–65, in Eastern and Western Nigeria during 1966–68 as a staff economist for the Consortium for the Study of Nigerian Rural Development. He is currently engaged in agricultural planning work in Tunisia. He is the author of several articles on the technical and economic aspects of oil palm development.

WOLFGANG F. STOLPER, Director, Center for Research on Economic Development, University of Michigan, was trained at the Universities of Berlin, Bonn, and Zurich as well as at Harvard University. From 1960 to 1962, he worked in Nigeria as Head of the Economic Planning Unit, Federal Ministry of Economic Development, Lagos. He has also been the chief or a member of various World Bank, U.S.A.I.D. Economic Missions to Malta, Liberia, Tunisia, Togo, Dahomey and Turkey. He is the author of *The Structure of the East German Economy* and *Planning Without Facts*. In addition, he has written numerous articles in the fields of international economics and economic development.

JEROME C. WELLS, Department of Economics, University of Pittsburgh, was trained at Johns Hopkins University and the University of Michigan. He has served in the Economics Department at the University of Ibadan from 1961 to 1962 and at the Nigerian Institute of Social and Economic Research from 1965 to 1967. His research interests include investment studies of the farm settlements in Nigeria's Western State, irrigation and mechanical cultivation projects in Bornu Province, and a survey of the Nigerian government's agricultural investments during the first four years of the Plan. He has written several articles dealing with Nigeria's agriculture sector.